THE RARER ACTION

THE RARER ACTION

Essays in Honor of Francis Fergusson

Edited by
ALAN CHEUSE AND RICHARD KOFFLER

RUTGERS UNIVERSITY PRESS   *New Brunswick, New Jersey*

We gratefully acknowledge the following permissions:

From Atheneum, for the essay "Untuning the Othello Music," adapted from *Iago, Some Approaches to the Illusion of His Motivation*. Copyright © 1970 by Stanley Edgar Hyman. Reprinted by permission of Atheneum Publishers.

From The Clarendon Press, for the right to reproduce the frontispiece to *The Drama of the Orokolo* (Oxford, 1940).

From Penguin Books Ltd., for quotations of poems by Zbigniew Herbert in *Zbigniew Herbert: Selected Poems*, translated by Czeslaw Milosz and Peter Dale Scott, copyright 1970.

Yet with my nobler reason, 'gainst my fury
Do I take part. The rarer action is
In virtue than in vengeance.

The Tempest, Act V, Scene 1

Contents

CONTENTS

TRADITION AND TRANSLATION

THE HUMAN IMAGE

Editors' Foreword

We are presenting this collection of essays to honor Francis Fergusson upon his retirement from Rutgers. He has been more than teacher to us and to others far more numerous than our contributors. With them we share a common bond of respect and admiration and fondness for a man who has made the Aristotelian concept of action the living, human center of all his pursuits. Thus his retirement is an occasion for tribute from all whose lives he has affected: people in the working theater, here and abroad; graduates of Bennington, the New School of Social Research, Rutgers, and Princeton; the few who have attended the seminars at the Indiana School of Letters or the first Christian Gauss Seminars at Princeton; the many who have become acquainted with him only in his writings. That tribute, we felt, should take the form of a book distinct among its kind for not allowing one narrow preoccupation or theme to guide its conception. The professions of our contributors are diverse, as are their ages and interests; some are old friends of Mr. Fergusson's, others former students, still others have been colleagues over the years. Their choice of subjects was entirely their own. Their response made clear their recognition of Francis Fergusson as a rare and exemplary spirit, and they treated this occasion with the dignity to which, we hope, this volume attests.

We wish to acknowledge here the helpful advice of Miguel Algarin, Glauco Cambon, Warren Carrier, Joseph Frank, Peter Gruen, Francis Johns, John O. McCormick, and James J. Wilhelm. To Michelle Plummer, who typed part of the manuscript, and to Mary Rannells, who labored for us through a long, hard winter, our special thanks.

A. C., R. K.

ALLEN TATE

A Brief Tribute to an Old Friend

Although Francis Fergusson has retired from teaching, he has not retired. His critical intelligence was never more active and acute than it is today in his exploration of the Dantesque elements in Shakespeare. He has large erudition in three fields: Shakespeare, Dante, and the history of European drama. He is the historical critic as distinguished from the historical scholar whose procedure is to put everything he knows in everything that he writes; Fergusson uses only what is pertinent to the immediate critical problem. The elimination of scholarly rubbish has permitted him to develop a pellucid prose style.

Mr. Fergusson's virtues—the point to be made rather than the argument to be exhibited, and a perspicuous style—are not spectacular virtues; but they are indispensable in a critic whose work will last. His two books on Dante are expository masterpieces; I say expository, for in the process of setting forth the tropology of the *Purgatorio* and in his selective commentary on the entire *Commedia*, the subtlest critical discrimination is at work. I have no reason to believe that the professional Dantisti, here and abroad, have seen in Francis Fergusson their superior.

His *The Idea of a Theater* is a work comparable in range and depth with Auerbach's *Mimesis*. There is no other work by an American critic of which this can be said.

Perhaps I should change the opening sentence of this note of appreciation. Francis has not retired from teaching; he has merely left the classroom. For literary criticism is teaching, and his criticism is teaching at the highest level. I have had the honor of his friendship for exactly forty-two years. I wish I could look forward to forty-two more.

Sewanee, Tennessee

R. W. B. LEWIS

Glimpses of Francis Fergusson

I write this on a Tuscan hillside, surrounded by cypresses, villas and farmhouses, but quite bereft of the books I would need to consult if I were to attempt any close comment on Francis Fergusson's immense contribution to our literary understanding. That contribution is unique in its way; it has profoundly affected the way we perceive the structures—that is, the patterns of momentous development—of dramas and novels; and I should like to offer a general remark or two about it. Under the circumstances, however, I hope I'll be forgiven if I begin with a few personal reminiscences. They are intended primarily as a form of *hommage*.

For some time Francis Fergusson seemed to recede in front of me. I do not mean intellectually: in that regard, he was always quite out of sight. I mean almost literally. His essays—on *Oedipus the King*, on *Hamlet*, on Henry James—had struck me with something of the force of religious revelation, and I was eager to meet him and talk with him, to ask him to elaborate on some of his most stimulating but oddly elusive critical concepts, primarily of course the complex notion of "action." But I arrived at Bennington College in the fall of 1948 to discover that Fergusson, who had taught there for a dozen years, had just taken terminal leave to become a Fellow at the Institute for Advanced Study in Princeton. His shadow loomed with magisterial grandeur at Bennington. His presence was felt in the special orientation of literary studies, in the critical vocabulary on campus, even in the College's library resources (it was because of Fergusson that the little library surprisingly stocked Pico della Mirandola's *Oration on the Dignity of Man,* a text that was crucial for a course I wanted to give). I even came to grow impatient with the reports of his intellectual heroics and his powerful lingering authority and acquired quite a false impression of him as a gray eminence and canny dialectician whose rather dark influence none could dispel.

He was at Princeton University for a few years, organizing and presiding over the remarkably distinguished and successful series of Princeton Seminars in Literary Criticism. But by the time I in turn reached Princeton, in 1952, he had moved on to Rutgers, whose president created by fiat the position of University Professor chiefly to make possible an appointment for Fergusson. During his last year at Princeton, I happened to talk with Richard Blackmur, who was telling me about some large plans for a school of humanities at Princeton University. What was the purpose of such a school, I asked. Blackmur replied at once: "To keep Francis Fergusson around." The answer made perfect sense; but insofar as that was its excellent intention, the plan did not succeed.

It was thanks in good part to Fergusson that I too eventually moved over to Rutgers, where, in 1954, toiling hard, I at last caught up with him. I must admit I pressed a little in the early days of our friendship (or perhaps I should say my discipleship and his benevolent patronage). We invited him with his wife to dinner on a series of summer evenings, and my wife, working from dawn, served a variety of sumptuous lobster dishes, which, as it turned out much later, Fergusson detested. He was much too kind to say so, however, and it was not long before I realized that my image of a towering authoritarian was ludicrously wrong and that Fergusson was a man of remarkable simplicity of spirit, of warm affections and unquestioning loyalties, as well as extraordinary tenacity and clarity of mind—and in the most casual conversations, one of the greatest teachers I had ever known. (My own experience is that the great teachers I have encountered—Fergusson, F. O. Matthiessen, Mark van Doren, Newton Arvin, Stringfellow Barr—reveal their capacities even more in conversation than in the classroom.)

In the winter of 1958, I was in Paris for a week, holding discussions with Albert Camus. The latter was directing rehearsals for a revival of his play *Caligula,* and I received his permission to bring Francis Fergusson, who was also in town, along to the theater one afternoon. My wife and I had just come from Munich, where the pre-Lenten *Fasching* was in progress, and we brought and gave Fergusson one of the anticly designed black masks which gentlemen wear to the more exuberant of the *Fasching* gatherings. I can still see Fergusson striding across the Pont Royal, under a gray winter sky, his coattail flapping while he dangled the black mask from his hand with no more self-consciousness than a child and discoursed spiritedly on Henry James's *The Golden Bowl*. At the theater, Camus shook hands warmly and said how glad he was to meet Fergusson: *The Idea of a Theater*, he declared, was the best book on tragedy he had ever read.

Fergusson's reputation in Europe is enormous, perhaps greater than in his own country, where learned academics sometimes look askance at any colleague who tends to have truly fresh and—for students—persuasive ideas. Effortlessly, Fergusson has managed never to be absorbed into the establishment. But once in Venice, for example, I ran into an internationally renowned professor of Italian literature and expert on Dante who was clutching and exulting over Fergusson's book *Dante's Drama of the Mind*. Later that same year, in Rome, I spent an afternoon with Alberto Moravia and Giorgio Bassani, who was at that time director of the Rome School of Drama. I happened to mention Francis Fergusson, and the other two immediately exclaimed that *L'Idea del Teatro* was an absolutely exceptional book and for Bassani in his professional work a kind of bible. I am told that it is not unheard of to elicit similar responses in Japan.

There are, needless to say, a great many more memories, all happy to contemplate, in a friendship that has lasted for more than fifteen years. There was the winter evening when my wife and I went to dine at the Fergussons, who had also invited the Jason Epsteins down from New York. (When Epstein was given free reign to begin the epochal Anchor paperback series, the second book he selected for publication was *The Idea of a Theater*.) It was snowing when we arrived, and before dinner was over drifts had completely blocked the Fergussons' driveway. Bunks were found for all of us, and Fergusson had just enough bourbon on hand to keep us satisfied till we had exhausted ourselves in talk, mainly, as I recall, about current literary periodicals and the feasibility of starting a new one. I was struck then, as I always am, by Fergusson's combination of quiet serenity and utter muscularity of intellect. He would no more compromise a literary opinion than he would cut off his own hand. Not that there is ever a question of imposing his views on others; he is much too good a teacher for that. A couple of years ago, he came up to Yale to see the production of Robert Lowell's *Prometheus,* and we asked Robert Brustein and his wife to join us for dinner. Brustein, the exceedingly tough-minded and vigorously forward-looking dean of the Yale Drama School, said that nothing on earth would keep him from the opportunity of meeting Francis Fergusson, who had been his literary idol for years. There was much harmonious and sociable talk about the performance the Fergussons were about to see; but Fergusson's account of the play later, in the *New York Review of Books,* did not conceal behind its courteous and elegant rhetoric the fact that he considered it a dramatic mess, a wild flailing of sometimes brilliant language around (to Fergusson's stern critical sense) an inertness of action.

But perhaps my most enduring recollection of Francis Fergusson is in his garden, tending the flower beds and pointing out the tracks of the foxes and deer that sometimes stray out of the woods at the foot of the slope. It is no bit of fancy to say that this is what Fergusson has always been doing. Unconcerned with the establishment and the academic literary fashions of the moment, almost unaware of them, he has gone on steadily cultivating his garden.

Francis Fergusson's key critical concepts are strikingly prehensile. Carefully applied to any work of literature that has a germ of the dramatic in it, they permit us to *take hold* in the most convincing manner. They work a kind of magic in the classroom; they are indeed teaching instruments, the product of a strenuously active mind that is persistently concerned with the process of learning and of teaching. And yet they do not come to us easily; if they are, so to speak, ideas that grasp, they are curiously difficult to grasp themselves. Nothing more straightforward, theoretically, than Fergusson's proposition that the first stage of a dramatic action is best identified by an infinitive of purpose: "to find the killer of the former king"; "to avenge the murder of one's father." Yet it took me, at least, no few years before I could make critical use of that principle with any assurance.

One reason, I think, is that American criticism and the minds of our best students have been pretty thoroughly romanticized in recent decades, while the intellectual temper of Francis Fergusson (like that of most others of his critical generation) is essentially classical—as, in his case, classicism was modified and thickened by the medieval vision of reality, and as the latter was thereafter modified and to some extent secularized by Shakespeare. Fergusson's critical eye looks and invites us to look at human motives, at the human spirit in purposeful motion, at human personalities thrusting against one another in a significant and illuminating clash of cross-purposes; but the romantic eye watches the human spirit examining itself, descending into itself, experiencing itself; and the romantic imagination, whether creative or critical, is most aroused by the spectacle of its own workings. Fergusson, or shall we say the Fergussonian critic, inspecting *The Scarlet Letter,* observes an austere conflict between Dimmesdale's impulse to confess, Chillingworth's will to discover, and Hester Prynne's determination to conceal. For the romantic critic, all this is very nearly beside the point; what he perceives as central is Hawthorne's imagination manipulating characters and incidents in a painful effort to wrest meaning out of the indecipherable and to invest phenomena with symbolic significance.

The analysis of action in a novel like *The Wings of the Dove* permits us to penetrate the thick and initially baffling haze of oblique allusion and get at the source of the novel's momentum—the ailing Milly Theale's anguished desire *to live,* essentially to experience the most fully rewarding relationship with another human being; as that purpose runs up against the strategically concealed counter motives of Kate Croy, her Aunt Maude, Lord Mark, and the ineffectual but slowly maturing Merton Densher. We marvel at the rich play of what Fergusson would call Henry James's "histrionic imagination," leading as it does and all so convincingly at last to the very nearly religious vision entertained by Densher, that moment of "perception" which, according to Fergusson, the purposes and the passions serve to beget in the thoroughly dramatized literary work. Henry James is of course the most avowedly dramatic of novelists; but even with a writer less vigorously histrionic, the analysis of action can be an indispensable approach. With Edith Wharton, for example, as we search the handsomely detailed settings and the meticulous description of women's wear to see just what kind of an action is being started and by what means, we come rather quickly to realize how limited and uncertain is the will power of most of her male characters, and how easily their dim gentle aspirations are defeated by smaller minded but stronger willed young ladies. The actions in Edith Wharton's best novels are, I suppose, what Fergusson would identify as "pathetic"; and just as the initiating purpose is usually vague and wistful and the passions muted, so the ensuing perception remains blurred and ambiguous, a general sense of the pathos of the human condition.

Fergusson's application of Dante's theory of the fourfold meaning of poetry deserves a paper in itself; since I do not have at hand his book on Dante and his other pertinent discussions, I can do no more than mention it. Nor indeed do I fully understand it. But perhaps I can refer to a part of Fergusson's theory of dramatic meaning—namely what I take to be his view that the *allegorical* level of any literary work that rises thereto is a certain revelation about the secret drift of human history, or, as the case may be, of the working out of God's purposes and promises within human history. Now this is not only unromantic; it is downright un-American. History as an object of scientific study may have great appeal to intelligent Americans; but when it comes to literature, the American critical mind is usually immune to such hints as may be bodied forth—the larger, remoter historical, or historico-mythic developments the main action may be representing.

And yet, when we concentrate on this aspect, how much that had gone unnoticed in major American novels (to stay with them) becomes visible. *The Scarlet Letter,* in one perspective, is a dramatic essay on the evolution of the New England temper from Elizabethan days to Hawthorne's time, with subtle apprehensive insinuations about the future. *Billy Budd,* or one version of it, surreptitiously adumbrates a theory about the nature of modern revolution. In *The Wings of the Dove,* the anagogic moment of vision is preceded and made possible by the subtly gathering image of a Europe, an entire human community (the Western world, we feel in retrospect, on the eve of the First World War), fatally succumbing to some implacable corroding force; and Francis Fergusson himself has compared the dark grandeur of the historical vision in *The Golden Bowl* to that of Vergil's *Aeneid.* If Edith Wharton's fiction resolutely and significantly holds back from anything like the anagogic, the small but perfectly understood social and moral history her actions imply shows itself only to greater effect—a movement exactly towards the ambiguous and the morally confused.

xvii

And we need only mention *Absalom, Absalom!* to become aware not only how important the historical dimension of a novel can be, but how cautious our assumptions must be about the relationship implied by a writer of genius between the historical on the one hand and the dramatic and individual on the other. Is Sutpen's finally disastrous career a synecdoche as it were of Southern history? Of American history? Of modern history? Is there a cause and effect relation—is Sutpen the product and victim of Southern history; or is the South the victim of men like Sutpen? No one of these questions can be answered confidently in the affirmative. But they are among the questions Francis Fergusson would have us ask; and no reader who believes that what *Absalom, Absalom!* is really about, first and last, is the struggling process of the creative or myth-making imagination will even come to them.

They are crucial questions because they make our minds stand up and ask about ourselves: where do *we* stand, with our habits and actions and beliefs, on the long, menacing, hope-arousing arc of history? They are sources of identity. Francis Fergusson's critical theories and practices have a kind of severely beautiful purity to them. They are uncontaminated by private idiosyncrasies, and they are not distracted by the clamor of *immediate* history. But they are profoundly, organically implicated in the processes of life—that is, with the allegory that, knowingly or not, we are all caught up in.

Yale University

SOME IDEAS OF A THEATER

ERIC BENTLEY

Ibsen, Shaw, Brecht: Three Stages[*]

Matthew Arnold expected from poets in general a "criticism of life," and many today would not only agree but add that this criticism should be a social one. Some will even argue that it *must* be a social one, since literature, in their view, is by nature social. Society, that is, can be regarded as providing both the source and substance of literature. It can also be maintained that to communicate a thought to another person—even more, to a group of other persons—is to socialize it.

As for the drama, it has often been regarded as, in several senses, yet more social than other kinds of literature. Sense one: the theater appeals most strongly and helpfully *to* society.

The theater is the most potent and direct means of strengthening human reason and enlightening the whole nation.

Mercier, *Du Théâtre,* 1773

Sense two: the theater has an especially close connection with the social conditions of the moment.

No portion of literature is connected by closer or more numerous ties with the present condition of society than the drama.

De Tocqueville, *Democracy in America,* 1835

Sense three: drama is pre-eminently the genre in which what is currently the characteristic type of relation of man to man is represented.

[*] Copyright © 1970, by Eric Bentley.

Thus investigation as to which type of man is suited to dramatic art coincides with the investigation of the problem of man's relation to other men.

George Lukács, *The Sociology of Modern Drama*, 1909

Finally, modern drama, drama beginning with Ibsen, has frequently been regarded as more social than earlier drama, as peculiarly concerned with social problems, a thesis which can best be documented in the lives of the three dramatists to be commented on here.

Though Henrik Ibsen would seem to us today to have been concerned with modern social problems from the very beginning, he did not in his early works seem so to the leading Scandinavian critic of the time, George Brandes, who criticized *Brand* (1865) as reactionary and read the playwright (as well as the rest of the world) this lesson:

What keeps a literature alive in our day is that it submits problems for debate. Thus, for example, George Sand debates the problem of the relations between the sexes, Byron and Feuerbach religion, John Stuart Mill and Proudhon property, Turgenev, Spielhagen and Emile Augier social conditions . . .

Inaugural Lecture, 1871

To which Ibsen replied: "Your work is a great, shattering, and emancipating outbreak of genius," and: "What cannot withstand the ideas of the times must succumb." Undoubtedly Brandes' writings, which, as Ibsen said, disturbed his sleep, also led him towards his great "modern period." Some fifteen years after Brandes' Inaugural Lecture, Henrik Ibsen's plays disturbed the sleep of George Bernard Shaw and led him to modernism and to the theater. In 1886 he took the part of Krogstad in a reading of *A Doll's House* (1879) staged by Karl Marx's daughter Eleanor. In 1890 he gave a Fabian lecture about that play. In the next year appeared the first book on Ibsen in English: Shaw's *Quintessence of Ibsenism*. One year more and Shaw's first play, *Widowers' Houses*, was ready. "It deals," Shaw said in a preface, "with a burning social question, and is deliberately intended to induce people to vote on the Progressive side at the next County Council election in London." It will be noted that Shaw is pushing the idea of problem literature further than Brandes had. Not debate now, but political pressure, if on a modest municipal scale. The scale would be enlarged later. In May 1895, a magazine called *The Humanitarian* asked a number of public men to answer the question: "Should social problems be freely dealt with in the drama?" Shaw answered:

We are . . . witnessing a steady intensification in the hold of social questions on the larger poetic imagination. . . . If people are rotting and starving in all directions, and nobody else has the heart or brains to make a disturbance about it, the great writers must. In short, what is forcing our poets to follow Shelley in becoming political and social agitators, and to turn the theatre into a platform for propaganda and an arena for discussion, is that whilst social questions are being thrown up for solution almost daily by the fierce rapidity with which industrial processes change and supersede one another . . . the political machinery by which alone our institutions can be kept abreast of these changes is so old-fashioned . . . that social questions never get solved until the pressure becomes so desperate that even governments recognize the necessity for moving. And to bring the pressure to this point, the poets must lend a hand . . .

If Shaw pushed the idea of problem drama further than Ibsen, Bertolt Brecht pushed it further than Shaw. The changes correspond, of course, to stages of history—and disillusionment. In 1871 there still seemed time for debate. In the 1890s it still seemed worthwhile to put pressure on government, local and national. All Brecht's mature playwriting came after the definitive collapse of nineteenth-century civilization in World War I. By that token, it also came after a crucial attempt to build a new civilization by means other than parliamentary debate and propagandist pressure: by revolution. The question that arose then was whether the theater could be of any use at all. Could the modern world even be portrayed in it? Brecht answered that it could, if it was portrayed as alterable. And for him, to portray it as alterable was to help to alter it, beginning with an alteration of the means of portrayal, namely, of the theater itself:

Half a century's experiments . . . had won the theatre brand new fields of subject matter and types of problem, and made it a factor of marked social importance. At the same time they had brought the theatre to a point where any further development of the intellectual, social (political) experience must wreck the artistic experience.

"On Experimental Theatre," 1939

. . . The Mother is a piece of anti-metaphysical, materialistic, non-Aristotelian drama. This makes nothing like such a free use as the Aristotelian theatre does of the passive empathy of the spectator; it also relates differently to certain psychological effects, such as catharsis. Just as it refrains from handing its hero over to the world as if it were his inescapable fate, so it would not dream of handing over the spectator to an inspiring theatrical experience. Anxious to teach the spectator a quite different practical attitude, directed towards changing the world, it must begin by making him adopt in the theater a quite different attitude from what he is used to.

Notes to The Mother, 1933

By means of a new kind of theater, Brecht would work on audiences in a new way and, by changing them, would help to change the world.

So far, so good. The quotations just made from our three authors are unequivocal and suggest accurately enough three clear phases of recent history. What they hardly begin to suggest is the actual tenor of the three writers' creative work. I have only been citing, really, the official stance of each man: the quotations are all from theoretical works, not from plays. If we wanted to document from actual theater what has here been cited as principle, it would be easier to document the Brandes-Ibsen position from plays by Alexandre Dumas *fils;* the Shaw position from plays by Eugène Brieux; and the Brecht position, perhaps from Erwin Piscator's production experiments, perhaps from Brecht plays which most critics would regard as his weakest efforts. Here, for example, are the first and last speeches of Brieux's *Damaged Goods (Les Avariés)*, cited in the translation for which Shaw wrote a preface:

I. [Before the play begins, the manager appears upon the stage and says:]
Ladies and Gentlemen, I beg leave to inform you, on behalf of the author and of the management, that the object of this play is a study of the disease of syphilis in its bearing on marriage.

II. DOCTOR: This poor girl is typical. The whole problem is summed up in her: she is at once the product and the cause. We set the ball rolling, others keep it up, and it runs back to bruise our own shins. I have nothing more to say. [He shakes hands with Loches as he conducts him to the door, and adds in a lighter tone:] But if you give a thought or two to what you have just seen when you are sitting in the Chamber [of Deputies], we shall not have wasted our time.

These passages correspond exactly to the young Shaw's idea that drama should put pressure on the people's parliamentary representatives. The significant thing is that no such passages occur in any play by Shaw. Even if they did, we could be sure they would have an entirely different tone. Even where the theoretical remarks of our three authors are consistent with their respective practice, such remarks really give no idea

6

what that practice is. Were the plays to disappear, the prefatory remarks to survive, posterity would receive a wholly misleading impression of what the plays had been like. Which ought not to amaze us. An author's official positions are one thing; his creative achievements are another. Secondly, it is minor authors who make movements and are content to exemplify their principles. Major authors may start movements or join them; they don't become submerged in them. To read Zola's proclamations, you would gather that novel-writing was a science and that once you've mastered the latest teaching on heredity and environment, you can put a novel together. Perhaps. But it wouldn't be a Zola novel, which is a remarkably "unscientific" work, compounded of Gothic imagination, great human warmth, and even a macabre sense of humor.

But I am not going to argue that Ibsen, Shaw, and Brecht are *not* social dramatists, only that the definition of the word *social* may need enlargement if it is to fit them and that, in any case, each must be regarded not as a member of a school or an example of a trend, but as an individual genius, making his own peculiar and wondrous explorations. Though all three have had imitators, the results do not show that any of the qualities for which we value them are imitable. Their criticisms of social phenomena may not be unique in the form in which we can abstract them from the work, but they are unique in the emphasis and color given to them in the setting of the work. Which is why it is to that setting that we must pursue them.

"The object of this play is a study of the disease of syphilis in its bearing on marriage." Nine out of ten students, questioned about this sentence, would guess that it referred to Ibsen's *Ghosts* (1881). Captain Alving had syphilis, and as a result his son Oswald is becoming an idiot in front of our eyes. Brieux would use this story as a pretext for urging us to have all possible measures taken to combat venereal disease. We get no hint whatsoever as to whether Ibsen would urge anything of this kind. What is *his* interest in the story? To be sure, Oswald's collapse is the central happening. What does Ibsen do with it?

The question can only be answered in terms of the whole play, a fact which is in itself significant and, as it turns out, a tribute to Ibsen's genius. Oswald is an Orestes for whom the Furies (Erinyes) do not turn into Wellwishers (Eumenides) in accord with a poet's desire to

7

affirm life and, by implication, the phase of life which his culture is passing through. He is irreclaimably doomed by "ghosts." Ibsen generally knew what he was doing and never more so than in his choice of title for this play. Not *The House of Alving*, not *Mrs. Alving*, not *Oswald*, though any of these titles would have been in the classical tradition. Rather, he chooses a title in the tradition of *The Eumenides* and *The Bacchae*. In classical tradition these are unusual titles because they stress extrahuman forces normally left in the background. Such forces come into the foreground at certain crises of history: Aeschylus celebrated the creation of the democratic city state, Euripides pronounces a doom upon the whole Hellenic experiment. Ibsen is a Euripidean playwright dramatizing the crisis of middle-class culture in his own day and somewhat beyond. Accordingly, his "ghosts" are neither furies nor bacchantes. What they are is very precisely, if complexly, worked out. They are ghosts, to begin with, in the most ordinary sense, that of superstition. Overheard in the next room by Mrs. Alving, Oswald and Regina sound like the ghosts (*revenants*, returned spirits, spooks) of Captain Alving and Regina's mother. *Sound like*: the word "ghosts" is in the first instance a simile. In the second, it is a metaphor for Captain Alving's legacy of disease: this is how syphilis enters into Ibsen's scheme of things. But it is not where he leaves his presentation of ghosts. They are more than superstition and more than physiology. They are cultural and social: they are a matter of the characters' beliefs and attitudes, their decisive and therefore dramatic beliefs and attitudes.

When Mrs. Alving hears the ghosts in the next room, she is brought that much nearer telling Oswald what she at that point believes to be the whole truth about his father. The simile drives her to explain the metaphor. And that would be where a conventional nineteenth-century play would have ended. But Ibsen's last and greatest act is still to come. In the process of telling this truth, Mrs. Alving finds that it is *not* the whole truth. Under the traumatic influence of those events or discoveries which are Ibsen's plot, she finds herself telling a different story and discovering a different truth: that not only Alving but she herself was responsible for the debacle. For she was a victim of the third kind of ghost, the ideological ghost. When she had tried, as a young wife, to flee from her husband to Parson Manders, who loved her, Manders had turned her away from the door, and she had consented to be turned away and to return to Alving. Not all the reading she then did in modern literature could erase the facts of her nonmodern actions. In her fantasy life she wants liberation from bourgeois culture. In actuality, she cannot defy the marriage laws; cannot contemplate the incestuous union of her son with his half sister; cannot practice mercy killing.

Corresponding to this double twist whereby Mrs. Alving's narrative turns from husband-denunciation to self-discovery, there is doubleness, too, in the main narrative line. Oswald's collapse, it has just been ventured, is the central happening. We could even say it is the only thing that happens on this stage and that once it *has* happened the play is over, the play of the superstition simile and the physiological metaphor. But this is to overlook the happenings within the breast of Mrs. Alving. *Ghosts,* finally, is the story of Oswald *as witnessed by his mother,* and the final effect is the effect upon her. She is the onstage audience. Such had been her fate from the beginning. What she now does or fails to do with her son she had previously done or failed to do with her husband: both times she reduces herself to the position of helpless, agonized onlooker. Oswald's paralysis, physical, unaccompanied by suffering, and exceptional, is as nothing to hers as she stands there holding the lethal pills and not using them: with a life still to live, in unbearable agony, and typical of a whole class of people, a whole phase of history. At this point we see just how different from furies or bacchantes and how much more modern Ibsenian ghosts are. Pale as they are by comparison, they are also far more negative because they have no possibility of transformation into Eumenides. They are inertia, where what is needed is movement. They are regression, where what is called for is progress. They are imprisonment and death where what is "desired" is liberation and life. I put the word desired in quotation marks because the authenticity of the desire is in question. In the situation depicted, hope is mere cultured fantasy and modish liberalism. Wherever the seeds of life are shown to be still faintly alive, as in Oswald's hankering after joy *and after his half sister,* they are precipitately, hysterically exterminated by Ibsen's enlightened abortionists.

It is tempting to call Ibsen the most ironical dramatist since Sophocles for, with him, nothing that glitters is gold. Now such irony would not be interesting if it were a merely technical fact, if it had the impact of a mere trick or mannerism, but only (a) if it seems the author's

authentic mode of vision and (b) if it succeeds in redefining the author's subject for us, the public. To establish that it is indeed Ibsen's
mode of vision we need only refer to his work. On the redefinition of
subject, we might cite yet again the notion of ghosts. Persons who have
noticed that Ibsen's ghosts are not furies may have failed to notice that
they are also not a curse rooted in real crimes, as in Greek drama and
the mythology on which it is based, or on original sin, as in much
Christian literature including, say T. S. Eliot's *Family Reunion,* based
as it is on the Orestes legend. In *Ghosts* there is a clear reference to the
Old Testament idea of the sins of the fathers being visited upon the
children, yet it would be disingenuous to cite this idea without noting
that Ibsen exactly inverts it. The idea that emerges from *Ghosts* is that
what Alving did was not sin after all; it was the unfortunate result
of his legitimate joy in life. Can we conclude then that Mrs. Alving
was the sinner? Not that either. What was wrong was that she *believed*
Alving sinned. What was wrong was what gave her this belief: her
education, her culture, her background, her epoch, and her class, in a
word, her society. Here we have the deeper sense in which Ibsenite
drama may truly be called social. Since the values of his society are not
the values of the play, but only the rejected values *in* the play, the
vision of the whole is a much broader one. In other words, Ibsen presupposes alternatives to his society.

We need not be surprised that he has generally been regarded as a
pessimist. Clearly, his spirit is shot through, like the spirit of tragic
artists in the past, with a sense of *curse* and *doom*—a curse upon the
life he sees around him, the doom of his fellow men and of the form of
noncommunity they have wrought. That the Judge Bracks in his audience find him totally negative is entirely correct from where they sit
and not entirely incorrect from where anyone else sits, since Ibsen put
down on paper what he saw, not what he would have liked to see.
Nonetheless, what he would have liked to see is present as something
more than a fantasy of the impossible. The "ghosts" that in fact doom
Mrs. Alving, the fear of scandal that in fact dooms Hedda Gabler, are
not divine or diabolical, nor do they partake of any necessity other
than the historical, which is to say they are necessary only for a time.
They have their day and cease to be. They are *un*necessary.

10

Ibsen made tragedy modern by infusing it with his sense of society as fate. In comedy, society has always been fate; and Ibsen can also be seen as fusing the tragic and comic traditions in his own essentially tragicomic vision. But the "society" of older comedy had been as immutable as the fate of older tragedy. Shaw and Brecht followed Ibsen in presenting an evolving, historical fate, of which the theatrical form might best be expressed in some words of Chekhov's: "You live badly, my friends. It is shameful to live like that." For people don't have to live like that. It need not be necessary for people to live like that.

But how shall it come about that they *won't* live like that? Bernard Shaw's simplest (but by no means only) answer is that he will talk them out of it. "I write plays with the deliberate object of converting the nation to my opinion . . ." (Preface to *Blanco Posnet*). And Shaw was also inclined to see Ibsen as engaged in that kind of effort. "Every one of them [Ibsen's plays]," he continued, "is a deliberate act of war on society as at present constituted. . . . [Ibsen undertook] a task of no less magnitude than changing the mind of Europe with a view to changing its morals." Brecht once said that for Shaw a man's most precious possession was his opinions, and it should be added that part of Shaw remained ever hopeful of robbing people of their most precious possession, offering them his own by way of reparations. Behind Shaw's remarks in this vein is the Victorian liberal tradition which sees culture as the final locus of free trade. Presupposed are open ears and sympathetic souls. Not presupposed are conflicts of interest along class lines or "false consciousness" as a mode of intelligently deceiving the self. Shaw himself learned to be highly critical of this liberalism, yet it played a part in putting together his own conception of a drama in which all characters can genuinely claim to have something to offer. "They are all right from their several points of view; and their points of view are, for the dramatic moment, mine also. This may puzzle the people who believe there is such a thing as an absolutely right point of view . . . nobody who agrees with them can possibly be a dramatist . . ." (Epistle Dedicatory to *Man and Superman*). We need not be scornful of Shaw's wish to "convert the nation." During the first half of the twentieth century the English nation was converted to many socialistic notions, and Bernard Shaw could take a great deal of credit for this. But another idea of drama is implicit in his description of the several points of view

11

which all embody part of the truth. Also there is hyperbole as well as humor in the idea that the whole nation was Shaw's audience. In fact, his plays were addressed to the educated bourgeoisie of all nations and were about that class, whether his characters wore the tailcoat or the toga, the pinstripe trousers or the doublet and hose. Shaw came to manhood in the century of the second great wave of *philosophes*, and, with the others, he helped the educated middle class to criticize itself. Ibsen had touched their guilt feelings. Shaw touched their funny bone. Which is to say that Ibsen showed their complicity in crime, while Shaw showed incongruities, inconsistencies, absurdities, both in the crimes and the complicity. What comedy may lack in depth, it can make up in scope. The subject matter of Ibsen's tragic plays is limited—is forever the same. In his comedies, on the other hand, Shaw would "cover the field": war and peace, the capitalist system, education, biology, religion, metaphysics, penal law, the Irish Question, the family, the various professions (medical, martial, clerical)—anything and everything.

More precisely speaking, it is in the prefaces and attendant pamphlets, articles, and treatises that the field was covered *in extenso*. The plays did what plays more characteristically do: brought certain crucial conflicts into sharp focus. Indeed we might well say that it was in the prefaces and the like that Shaw did his best to convert the nation, while in the plays he provided comic relief. But it was a comic relief of a highly ironical kind for, in it, the subjects of the prefaces are seen, not in a simpler form, but in a form which is even more complex, being more human and concrete. The difference between preface and play has sometimes been viewed as one between the propagandist and the artist, the latter, in turn, being considered "universally human." Shaw's critics are free to choose their terms and even to invoke shibboleths. To the present writer, however, it seems mistaken to think of the plays as any less social in their commentary than the prefaces. Surely comedy was always the principal vehicle of social criticism until academic men had the unhappy idea that the comic sense was not necessary in this field and founded the science of sociology. In any event, Shaw's comedies bring social principles to the final test, asking what they mean in the lives of human beings. Some critics will perhaps see a claim to the "universally human," a claim to be asocial, parasocial, metasocial, in Shaw's own statement that his plays present a conflict of free vitality with

12

various abstract principles and impersonal institutions. But just as the principles and institutions are specific ones and Shaw's satirical thrusts are directed at them, so the free vitality is seldom merely the life force in the abstract but is to be found in the actual life generated in a character by Shaw the comic artist.

A recurring type in Shaw's comedies is what, with apologies to Nietzsche, we may call the superman: a human being who is not divided against himself but is all of a piece and lives directly and happily from the primal vital spring. Caesar, Undershaft, and Joan are examples. There are no such people in the comedies of Aristophanes or Plautus, Machiavelli or Jonson, Shakespeare or Molière. Superior people stem from the epic and tragic tradition; and so, if Ibsen can be said to have given tragedy a comic twist, Shaw can be said to have given comedy a tragic one. Yet even tragic heroes are traditionally supposed to have a flaw, whereas the Shavian superman is flawless, an Achilles invulnerable even in the heel. Perhaps only one great tragic writer had regularly risked such protagonists: Corneille. And paradoxically the risk he ran was that of becoming ridiculous, which is to say, comic.

Invulnerable in himself, as a dramatic creation the Shavian superman has not proven invulnerable to dramatic criticism. There are obvious dangers to the comic art in the presence, at its center, of a man like Undershaft who knows all the answers, especially since it is not just verbal answers he knows but practical ones. For drama is *praxis*. The plot of *Saint Joan* is not helped by the fact our heroine couldn't do wrong if she tried. That she at one point pleads guilty in the trial is only a momentary hesitation that makes her final position the more heroic. Similarly, the Shavian Caesar's vanity is only the charming, humanizing foible of a great man, not a flaw undermining his greatness.

But has criticism been as ready to see why Shaw went in for this sort of hero as it has to note the reasons why he shouldn't have? Such a "why" might not be specially significant if explored in biographical, psychological terms, citing factors in Shaw's life that impelled him to seek flawless heroes, but it surely has much interest in relation to modern social drama. It relates to what Ernst Bloch has called *das Prinzip Hoffnung*—the principle of hope as the very foundation of the modern radical outlook, as of the religions and mythologies in the eras of their full vitality. And, as the religions and mythologies had a golden age in

13

the past which it was possible to hope for the return of or a heaven in the sky which was eternally there, so modern radical philosophy has a future in which this earth is a home for men.

When society is fate, a historical fate, then the dialectic of drama, it has been suggested, will be found in an interplay between epochs. We see this first, as Ibsen did, as an interplay between past and present: the theater exhibits a present into which the past ("ghosts") erupt. But, as Ibsen also knew, this is a simplification. There is a third factor: the future. And if art has a normative function—"it is always a writer's duty to make the world better" (Samuel Johnson)—the future is suffused by a definite sentiment, namely, hope. Indeed, in the modern situation, we must perhaps say that, if art is to have something positive about it, the most likely locus of the positive will be the future, past golden ages having become as inconceivable as heavens in the skies. The past, so far from being golden, hangs like lead about the necks of modern characters. The past is the dead weight of failure pressing upon the present and tending to kill the future. Such is the characteristically modern view of the past, personal and neurotic, social and historical. Thus, unless the modern artist is to acquiesce in a blank future, a future murdered by the past, he *has* to postulate and imagine a positive future. Which is to say that he has to work directly with his hopes; he has to build upon such actual and vital hope as he can find within himself.

This Ibsen the thinker certainly believed. Ibsen the artist felt on firmer ground with the past and present; hence the fact that most of his plays provide a far more desolate image of life than his proclaimed philosophy. Shaw and Brecht, if they lived in a time of yet greater public catastrophes, by that very token felt themselves also closer to whatever positive solutions were to be found. They clearly resolved, at whatever cost to their art as art, to inject a far larger positive element into their work than Ibsen had usually done. For them, even more than for him, art was not for its own sake but for the sake of the future. Like Ibsen's, their art would help exorcise the ghosts of the past—"let the dead bury their dead"—and help terminate the life-in-death of the present. Less ambiguously than Ibsen's, their art would help "us dead" to "awaken."

This in itself would have been sufficient reason for them to discontinue Ibsen's investigations of neurotic weakness. If they can be significantly referred to him at all, it would be to his one or two attempts at a simply positive hero, notably Dr. Stockmann in *An Enemy of the People* (1883). Such a superman was to find a place in both Shavian and Brechtian drama, though in different guises, corresponding to different nationalities and generations. Shaw's most characteristic and impressive superman is Undershaft, a radical critic of normal bourgeois procedures and shibboleths, yet himself a hero of bourgeois civilization— and a scintillating bourgeois intellectual to boot. If we look in the plays of Brecht for characters who are solid and all of a piece, who always are right and always do what is right, we shall find them only in the guise of the rebel as revolutionary: examples are Pavel in *The Mother* (1932), and several of the Communards in *Days of the Commune* (1949).

There are not many such supermen in Brecht or even in Shaw. Both playwrights remained Ibsenites to the extent that they dealt primarily, if not with neurotic weakness, with divided characters. Pavel is a revolutionary from the outset, but the protagonist is his mother who is not a revolutionary till near the end: meanwhile the play has shown her inner divisions. Particularly the Brecht characters who have universally been found most human and interesting—Mother Courage, Galileo, Azdak—are divided people, brave and cowardly, passive and active, good and bad. Even in Shaw, the superman didn't always have to be protagonist. He could fill a character role such as that of General Burgoyne in *The Devil's Disciple* (1897) or Sergeant Meek in *Too True to be Good* (1932).

Shaw generally placed his supermen over against men who were all-too-human, average products of a given epoch and class. In these encounters he was able to give the age-old contrast of ironist and impostor a thoroughly actual and relevant treatment. And his own divided nature preserved him from supermanic dramaturgy on a Cornelian scale: the ironist did not defeat the impostor too easily. Some plays—*Heartbreak House* (1919), for instance—are principally about impostors and contain no outright supermen. In some, such as *John Bull's Other Island* (1904), the emphasis is strongly on a single impostor (Broadbent). Again, a favorite Shavian device and achievement is the ironist-superman who ironically turns out not to be a superman after all but human-all-too-human. Such are Bluntschli (*Arms and the Man*, 1894) and Tanner (*Man and Superman*, 1901–1903). Nor is it true that a Shavian character who embodies free vitality must have superhuman capabilities. He may be an impotent priest like Father Keegan (*John Bull's Other Island*) or a senile crackpot like Captain Shotover (*Heartbreak House*).

He may be a she. Shaw was a feminist, not only after the more political and abstract fashion, but in his human and artistic instincts. He tended to identify both himself and free vitality with the Eternal Feminine and to identify the enemy with the society-ridden male. Hence, if we are looking for the positive element, for bridges to the future, for foundations of a socialist humanism, his women are just as important as his supermen. And this can be true in the least political of his comedies. *Pygmalion* (1913), for instance, is the tale of the incubation and liberation of a woman. With Tanner and the rest, Henry Higgins is a superman *manqué*, a clever ironist who proves to be an impostor, a Pygmalion who is only a Frankenstein.

The social drama, as practiced by nongeniuses like Brieux, ran into fatal clichés. That Bernard Shaw just did not notice the limitations of a Brieux is an index to his missionary zeal and to the strength of his commitment to a social criterion in drama. "Incomparably the greatest writer France has produced since Molière" (Preface to *Three Plays by Brieux*, 1909), Brieux was the kind of playwright that the propagandist-in-a-hurry within the breast of Shaw could not help envying, yet some deep intuition as to where his own calling lay kept the envy from growing into emulation. Let those who once considered that, as against Shaw, Brieux really came to grips with social problems take note that today Brieux cannot be seen as coming to grips with anything, whereas the playful Shaw must be seen to have come to grips, in play as well as preface, with the main problems of the era.

Widowers' Houses (1885–1892) and *Mrs. Warren's Profession* (1893–1894), Shaw's first and third plays, present capitalism in miniature and in this could be regarded as models for Brecht's *Threepenny Opera* (1928) and *The Rise and Fall of the City of Mahagonny* (1930). The perspective of all four comedies is suggested in some lines of Simon O. Lesser (*Fiction and the Unconscious*, 1957):

The attitude of most comedies is that of an urbane and tolerant friend, amused rather than censorious about that blonde he saw us out with the night before . . . Other

16

comedies are caustic and the reverse of indulgent, but they suggest a scale of values against which the shortcomings and misdeeds of the characters seem trivial . . . granted that the little people [this kind of comedy] sets before us are far from admirable, they, and by inference we ourselves are no worse than anyone else.

Bernard Shaw called the two types here adumbrated *Plays: Pleasant and Unpleasant,* a phrase he used as the title for all his early plays (1892–1898). The "unpleasant" play, as exemplified by *Widowers' Houses* and *Mrs. Warren's Profession,* was certainly a precision tool in social criticism, for which their author has scarcely yet received due credit, a dialectical tool. You can smile all evening at the amusing crimes of Sartorius and Mrs. Warren but when, on your way home, you realize that the whole social order is run this way you will smile on the wrong side of your face.

Shaw, for his part, seems to have found the "unpleasant" mode constricting. Like Swift, he "served human liberty," and the schematic early plays afforded his enterprise far too little elbow room. They had, for example, no room for his supermen, and, if they had room for rebellious women like Blanche Sartorius and Vivie Warren, they kept the rebellion within too narrow bounds. Even the impostors were miniatures compared with those to follow. Shaw once spoke of the need a dramatist has to let his characters rip. That is what he was not able to do in the earliest plays; the mold in which the plays were cast seemed to forbid it. There is far more freedom later, and this in two respects: first, there is the growing freedom of the playwright as he learns his craft and gives his genius its head; second, characters are placed in situations in which *they* have freedom in its ultimate form, namely, real freedom of choice on crucial issues. Both kinds of freedom had been lacking in *Widowers' Houses.* Not only had the journeyman playwright acquired no kind of ease or daring in handling the structure; inside the box of his plot structure and in the box (with one side missing) of the Victorian stage-scene, he presented a version of humanity boxed in by the capitalist system. It was clear, cutting, even devastating writing, but no wind of freedom blew from that stage to that audience. One thing needed was that the characters should work on the circumstances: they should not just be worked upon by the circumstances. History, by all means, can determine their mode of existence; but they in turn must work upon history.

17

Saint Joan (1923), for example, could not have been written by the playwright of the early 1890s. He wouldn't have known how to let his heroine "rip." In this play we do breathe the air of human freedom, and again it is both an artistic, technical matter and a matter of the outlook defined by the art and technique. The closed, box-like form of the nineteenth-century well-made play was progressively abandoned by Shaw. As a chronicle, *Saint Joan* is rather compact, but that it is a chronicle at all means open windows, fresh air, amplitude.

The essence of Shavianism in dramaturgy was the assumption that the modern world could best be placed onstage in the form of serious parody, a double form of parody as it turned out, for Shaw consistently parodied both the behavior of men and the patterns of dramatic art. In his mind, the two were so closely related as to be at essential points identical.

The truth is that dramatic invention is the first effort of man to become intellectually conscious. No frontier can be marked between drama and history or religion, or between acting and conduct.

> *Plays, Pleasant and Unpleasant,*
> 1898, preface to the Pleasant Plays.

Just as Marx proposed to stand Hegel on his feet, so Shaw proposed to stand all the nineteenth century's idealisms on their feet. Hence, notably, his subjection of melodrama, in theater or in life, to the test of reality. For such purposes, already in the 1890s, he was demanding a nonillusionistic stage.

For him [William Archer] there is illusion in the theatre: for me there is none . . . To me the play is only the means, the end being the expression of feeling by the arts of the actor, the poet, the musician. Anything that makes this expression more vivid, whether it be versification, or an orchestra, or a deliberately artificial delivery of the lines, is so much to the good for me, even though it may destroy all the verisimilitude of the scene.

> *The Saturday Review,* April 13, 1895.

Now what has just been called the essence of Shavianism was never challenged by Brecht. On the contrary, his plays, like Shaw's, are to a very large extent parodies both of more conventional plays and of conventional behavior. In the passage just quoted, Brecht would no doubt have been dissatisfied with the phrase "expression of feeling" while at the same time enthusiastically accepting Shaw's invitation to a non-illusionistic theater in which "versification, or an orchestra, or a deliberately artificial delivery" would not be out of place.

It was with such ends in view that so many of the treasured devices of traditional theater were dropped in Brecht's productions. The lighting, for example, was to be plain white and diffused over the whole stage. In this way the cult of *Stimmung* (mood) would be countered. To the same end, illusionistic scenery must go, for the paradox of scenery that "looked like the real thing" was that it induced dream-states in the audience. What was needed instead of a hypnotic trance was alertness. Actors would have to change their ways. Instead of attempting an hallucination of unrealities suddenly present ("I am Dracula") they must exhibit realities that can be recognized as such and have thus belonged to our past ("This was a man"). In place of the Stanislavsky actor who worked so hard to give a sense of the first person and the present tense and to absorb all stage directions into a living illusion of the actual thing, Brecht proposed an Epic actor who seemed to be using the third person and the past tense; as for the stage directions, at least as an exercise, they could be read aloud.

This is not the place to itemize every feature of Brechtian theater either in its early or Epic phase or in the final phase when Brecht was beginning to substitute the term Dialectical Theater. Too much theory would be misleading, at least if accompanied by too few looks at the practice. We must even take care, as was suggested above, not to·assume that Brecht's theories correspond exactly and in all ways to his practices. Even if they did, practice is no more deducible from theory than the beauty of an Italian landscape is deducible from the map. Just as the Ibsenite drama could never be deduced from existing notions of social theater, and Shavian comedy could never be deduced from free-floating notions like discussion plays and propaganda, nor yet from Shaw's own prefaces, so Brecht's achievement as a playwright, even as a social playwright, could not be deduced from theoretical writings, even his own. On the contrary, it is possible to make bad mistakes about the plays by too readily assuming they must be what the theories describe, no more and no less.

Whenever active artistry is at work, many concrete elements come into being which escape the net of general intentions. We may read in Ibsen's workbooks that "marriage for external reasons . . . brings a nemesis upon the offspring," and this idea is obviously in *Ghosts*: yet it neither makes *Ghosts* a good play nor gives it its particular tone, style, character—its mode of being. This latter stems—if indeed the source may be isolated in a single phrase—from Ibsen's *ironical use* of the idea and of all his other materials. So with Shaw. Many of the ideas of, say, *The Intelligent Woman's Guide to Socialism* (1928) are also to be found in the plays, sometimes in similar phrasing, but they neither constitute the merit of the plays nor give them their life as theater, as art. *A dramatic context ironizes,* and to say "dramatic irony" is often a little like saying "dramatic drama." A Shavian dramatic context sometimes ironizes to the point of conflict with the presumably intended idea. Thus it is not clear that, in the final act of *Major Barbara,* Shaw solved all his problems. One may feel that Undershaft is so strong a character that an intended balance is upset and a desired synthesis is missed.

Of Brecht, it has been said that, though his views were communist, his concrete existence contradicted those views. Even if this formulation is correct, it need not be taken as so damaging either to Brecht or to communism as has been assumed. Some tension between existence and idea is surely inevitable. What Christian is simply an embodiment of Christianity? If such a person existed, he would not, in any case, turn out to be a Christian *artist*. Always more concrete than theory, art must give a different account of the world, unless by sheer lack of merit (as with Brieux) it fails to be art. To the political artist, art presents a particular opportunity, which is not, as is commonly thought, simply to restate his political views and thus extend the political battle to another front, but, instead, to *test abstract principles in concrete situations,* to show what politics means in the lives of people. Contradictions enter the picture automatically, for, since the concretely human is the writer's special field, when he brings it into play it brings with it the contradictoriness of its people. Bertolt Brecht was a contradictory man, so is the present writer, and so are you, dear reader. Why not, also, Brecht's Galileo?

Es kommt: ich bin kein ausgeklügelt Buch
Ich bin ein Mensch mit seinem Widerspruch.
C. F. Meyer, *Huttens Letzte Tage.*

It should therefore come as no surprise that the socialist humanism of Brecht is more adequately rendered in a many-sided and problematic work like *The Caucasian Chalk Circle* (1945) than in the more explicit presentations, closer to Marx and Lenin, such as *The Mother* or *Days of the Commune*. Again the author's sense of humor—and specifically his ironizing of everything—is our best clue. When, as in the two plays just mentioned, Brecht writes of class-comrades he abandons this irony—understandably, to be sure, as it was likely to turn against them. Yet it was evidently hard to find anything to take its place: a friendly attitude, however commendable morally and politically, has no particular aesthetic merit, no energy as art. Another author might perhaps have found another solution. Brecht the artist, like Shaw the artist, is inseparable from his sense of humor. By his lyric gift, eked out with Hanns Eisler's musical genius, Brecht was able to raise both *The Mother* and the *Commune* well above the average level of political plays. It is just that to see his full range—and, at that, writing on socialism itself—we must turn to works that are steeped in his irony.

Ernst Bloch has written that, in the work of all the great poets and philosophers, there is a window that opens upon Utopia. One might add that sometimes (as for example in Shaw's *Back to Methuselah*) it is open too wide. What is engaging about *The Caucasian Chalk Circle* is the irony in the utopianism, particularly in the wake of a prologue that presents the Soviet Union as much closer to Utopia than it actually was. In this play Brecht used the idea of the Lord of Misrule, who for a brief interregnum turns the existing society and its values upside down. Which, if the existing society is an antihuman one, would mean substituting a genuine humanism. To be human for a day: that is the formula. But there is a catch in it. What we are likely to get is a flat, unbelievable virtuousness. Brecht does not give us this, arguing, as it were, that if the whole society was monstrous then the misrule would be grotesque: in its origin a fluke, it is by nature a freak. The fact that by definition it will have no future affects its character: it is only a truancy, not a liberation. All of which would have remained so much theorizing except that Brecht was able to create the poetry and the comedy, the narrative and the character, by which the word became flesh—by which, signally, the Lord of Misrule became "ein Mensch mit

21

seinem Widerspruch": Azdak, the disenchanted philosopher as quasi-revolutionary activist.

Does the irony undercut the author's activism? As with Shaw, there are those who think it does and with this much justification: that as they read or see the play, they find themselves responding more fully to the despair than to the hope. And it is always likely, a priori, that despair will outweigh hope in a work of art, since despair is an established fact that tends to pervade the past and the present, whereas hope tends to be just a project, devised as it is, for that frail, as yet merely imagined spot, the future. But it seems to the present writer that Brecht has linked despair and hope in lively dialectical interplay; and that, while there are many moments when despair predominates, hope remains at the end. Which is all that hope need do. It need not bring in the kingdom. It need only survive.

The question is whether the good society is felt, nostalgically, to be in the past (that is, to be over) or whether it is felt to be in the future, that is, in the making, felt to be a possibility and "up to us," something we can work on, a matter of *praxis*. The old notion of the Age of Gold has little meaning in *The Caucasian Chalk Circle* until it is inverted. We, the audience, return to the Age of Gold when we see Azdak inverting our rules and laws. In thought Azdak returns to an Age of Gold when he nostalgically recalls the popular revolt of a former generation. On the other hand, the age of Azdak himself is no Age of Gold but an age of war and oppression in which by a fluke a little justice can be done. That for Azdak himself revolutions are identified with the past is what is wrong with him. The era of Azdak has the transitory character of the Saturnalia, in which, after the brief interregnum is over, a Mock King goes back into anonymity. But the important Prologue suggests a *regnum* that is not *inter*. The ultimate ironic inversion, among many in the play, is that an Age of Gold should be envisaged, not in Arcadia, but in Georgia. Thus, what is planted in the minds of at least a sympathetic audience is not a memory, a fantasy, or a dream but a possibility. That this should be open to doubt, and that certain audiences respond differently, is a tribute to the dialectical complexity of the piece, the subtlety of its method.

"What is a modern problem play but a clinical lecture on society?" Bernard Shaw asked in 1901. If the works of Ibsen, Shaw, and Brecht

22

may fairly be described as modern problem plays, then our answer must be that they are *much* besides being clinical lectures on society. They are tragedies or comedies or tragicomedies of so special a kind that only close analysis can bring out their peculiarity, let alone their merit. They are dramatic art, and they are dramatic art in motion: we see the "problem play" developing from one Ibsen play to another, from one Shaw play to another, from one Brecht play to another. There is also a development from author to author. And since people are individuals and unique, geniuses, if an Irishism may be permitted, are even more individual and unique: the problem play, ultimately, was whatever Ibsen or Shaw or Brecht made of it. Yet there is reason, too, to say that it remained a problem play. If it has been the aim of this essay, on the one hand, to suggest that far more art and artifice went into this form of play than has usually been assumed, it has equally been its aim to confirm that the social drama was indeed social.

New York, New York

MAURICE CHARNEY

"This Mist, My Friend, Is Mystical": Place and Time in Elizabethan Plays

Aristotle's *Poetics* is a seminal book, so seminal, in fact, that it has not yet stopped fathering offspring of doubtful paternity. It is well known that of the three unities attributed to him, Aristotle discusses only unity of action, by which he means no more than the coherence and integrity demanded by all works of the imagination. Of the unities of place and time he has little to say, although later commentators seemed to feel that they were only expatiating on Aristotle's true intent.

The development of the unities of place and time is more properly related to the Renaissance revival of interest in the Roman theater, especially as it was represented in Vitruvius' influential treatise on architecture. There is an interesting set of stage designs by Sebastiano Serlio from the middle of the sixteenth century, in which Serlio depicts comic, tragic, and satyric (or pastoral) scenes. The settings are fixed and unchangeable, so that unity of place in the written play becomes a necessity of the staging. Unity of time follows as a corollary, since the restriction of the dramatic action to a single place also demands an unbroken time sequence. The two unities of place and time work together to produce a characteristically neoclassical effect of concentration.

In Serlio's comic scene, each side of the stage shows the houses of an ordinary street, built at an angle and projecting toward an imaginary vanishing point. A painted shutter at the back of the stage completes the perspective. Serlio is thinking of the actual houses one might find on a representative street, although he pleasantly mixes up Roman and Christian examples: "But specially there must not want a brothel or bawdy house, and a great inn, and a church." All the action takes place on what is imagined to be the street or square separating the houses on either side of the stage, and entrances and exits are made through the doors of these houses. In this static and carefully visualized setting, unity of place is a natural assumption.

Unity of time is not a direct product of these fixed settings, but unity of place tends to draw the play into the magic circle of a single day, either the natural day of twelve hours or the artificial clock-time of twenty-four. Thus, our ideal neoclassical play shows a conflict between characters and families who live on opposite sides of the stage. Whatever the magnitude of the difficulties confronting these characters in the morning, we are assured that they will be resolved by late afternoon or at least before night falls.

The unities of place and time provide a rational system for organizing the dramatic action. They concentrate and simplify that action in order to make it meaningful to an audience. If plays are an imitation of life, then the unities of place and time help to make the mimesis convincing. Violators of place and time are usually pursued by critics because they offend the obvious dictates of reason and common sense. Thus, Sidney's *Apology for Poetry*, which is certainly the best-known critical work in the Elizabethan period, ridicules the licentiousness of place and time in the contemporary English theater:

you shall have Asia of the one side, and Affrick of the other, and so many other under-kingdoms, that the Player, when he commeth in, must ever begin with telling where he is, or else the tale will not be conceived. Now ye shall have three ladies walk to gather flowers, and then we must believe the stage to be a garden. By and by, we hear news of shipwrack in the same place, and then we are to blame if we accept it not for a rock. Upon the back of that, comes out a hideous monster, with fire and smoke, and then the miserable beholders are bound to take it for a cave. While in the meantime two armies fly in, represented with four swords and bucklers, and then what hard heart will not receive it for a pitched field? Now, of time they are much more liberal, for ordinary it is that two young princes fall in love. After many traverses, she is got with child, delivered of a fair boy; he is lost, groweth a man, falls in love, and is ready to get another child; and all this in two hours space: which how absurd it is in sense even sense may imagine, and art hath taught, and all ancient examples justified, and, at this day, the ordinary players in Italy will not err in.

The Italian scrupulousness about place and time is set against an English indifference, and Sidney appeals to the indisputable good sense of his readers. In historical perspective, however, one could say that Sidney was blind to everything that was most distinctive in Elizabethan drama. It is hard to believe that *An Apology for Poetry*, written about 1583, was published in 1595, the very year in which *Romeo and Juliet* and *Richard II* were probably first being produced.

The most powerful attack on the assumptions about place and time from which Sidney is working is in Samuel Johnson's Preface to his edition of Shakespeare of 1765, and it is curious that Johnson should appeal to the same common sense of audiences as Sidney does in order to draw opposite conclusions. Shakespeare shows no regard to the unities of time and place because these unities are derived from a false notion of dramatic illusion. This is the basis of Johnson's argument, which he pursues with all the Socratic relish of practical examples:

The objection arising from the impossibility of passing the first hour at Alexandria and the next at Rome, supposes that when the play opens the spectator really imagines himself at Alexandria and believes that his walk to the theater has been a voyage to Egypt, and that he lives in the days of Antony and Cleopatra. Surely he that imagines this may imagine more. He that can take the stage at one time for the palace of the Ptolemies may take it in half an hour for the promontory of Actium. Delusion, if delusion be admitted, has no certain limitation; if the spectator can be once persuaded that his old acquaintance are Alexander and Caesar, that a room illuminated with candles is the plain of Pharsalia or the bank of Granicus, he is in a state of elevation above the reach of reason or of truth, and from the heights of empyrean poetry may despise the circumscriptions of terrestrial nature. There is no reason why a mind thus wandering in ecstasy should count the clock, or why an hour should not be a century in that calenture of the brains that can make the stage a field.

The truth is that the spectators are always in their senses and know, from the first act to the last that the stage is only a stage, and that the players are only players. They come to hear a certain number of lines recited with just gesture and elegant modulation. The lines relate to some action, and an action must be in some place; but the different actions that complete a story may be in places very remote from each other; and where is the absurdity of allowing that space to represent first Athens and then Sicily which was always known to be neither Sicily nor Athens, but a modern theater.

In exploding the unities of place and time, Johnson is "almost frighted at my own temerity and, when I estimate the fame and the strength of those that maintain the contrary opinion, am ready to sink down in reverential silence." This is not a familiar posture for Johnson, but he is not often attacking the pieties of neoclassical criticism. He understood, as Sidney did not, that the unities of place and time are irrelevant to the kind of theater in which Shakespeare and his fellow dramatists were working.

One of the commonplaces about the Elizabethan public theater is that the plays were presented on a bare stage without any attempt at scenic illusion. In recent years, we have come to believe that the stage was not so bare as was previously thought, especially by those who derive Elizabethan theaters from quaint Tudor innyards set up for makeshift plays. This is a pleasant theory that harmonizes well with our feelings about Merry England, but it may well be that Elizabethan theaters had a showy, baroque grandeur like contemporary theaters in Europe and other public buildings in England. We know from the contract for the Fortune that very exacting carpentry was demanded, including the carving of satyrs and the painting of imitation marble. It is likely that Elizabethan theaters had an impressive, architectural stage façade that could represent the walls of a city or the exterior of a castle. It is also likely that the theater itself was decorated with appropriate tapestries and pennons and that playgoing was a colorful and festive occasion. The stage was bare only in the sense that no attempt was made to provide painted settings, but the costumes of the actors were gorgeous and expensive, and a great variety of stage properties—thrones, arbors, swords, jewels, hell mouths, and decapitated heads—were in constant use.

Unity of place is difficult to achieve on a stage in which our sense of place is weak. If the stage does not represent one fixed place, as in the designs of Serlio, then it may represent any place at all, or, to put it in another way, the stage represents whatever place the dramatic action demands. If the action is not confined to a particular place, then we have an unlocalized scene. This is, of course, impossible with the designs of Serlio, since the scene is always set before the play begins. The audience knows where it is supposed to be at any point in the action, and the scene may be verified visually. This fixed setting could not function for most Elizabethan plays.

We may demonstrate the practical implications of place and time on stage in Shakespeare's *Antony and Cleopatra*, which happens to be one

27

of the plays that Johnson uses to support his argument. The conflict between Egypt and Rome is central to the meaning of this play, and the existence of at least two locales immediately dissolves any possibility of unity of place. If Shakespeare had restricted his action to Rome or to Egypt alone, he would have had to provide an extensive narration for the scenes imagined to occur in the other place. In *Antony and Cleopatra*, the Egyptian and the Roman scenes are directly presented, and, although there are no stage settings to strengthen the illusion, there is no difficulty in distinguishing between the two locales. Where Cleopatra is is Egypt, where Caesar is is Rome. These two characters and their followers define symbolic place by their costumes, imagery, and general style. Thus, in the use of characteristic properties, Caesar's sword may be set against Cleopatra's fan. The tragic conflict is generated by Antony's movements between Egypt and Rome, so that it is important for us to know where Antony is at any particular moment. But we do not need to know about any places more specific than Egypt and Rome. The old stage locations in Cleopatra's palace and Caesar's house— or another room in Cleopatra's palace and another room in Caesar's house—are superfluous.

There are some scenes imagined to be in other locations, and we might look at these for a moment to test the Elizabethan dramatic notion of place. The scenes in the houses of Pompey and Lepidus and aboard Pompey's galley would all be taken as Roman because of the characters involved. There is no special geographical feeling in the Pompey scenes that we are near Misenum, the promontory at the northern end of the Bay of Naples. Similarly, Ventidius' scene in Syria that opens Act 3 does not strain our spatial credulity for the simple reason that there is no effort made to convince us that we really are in Syria or in any other place except the stage itself. There is a geographical Syria and there is a Syria of the mind. The ten lines of Act 2, Scene iv, are located in "Rome, a Street," but the scene is actually located nowhere in particular. It could just as conveniently have been ticketed "The Bankside, a Stage," since there is not the slightest indication of where the brief dialogue of Lepidus, Maecenas, and Agrippa takes place. In our era of the movies, it is difficult to imagine a placeless and unlocated scene, and it may well be that the movies have permanently disabled us from understanding Elizabethan staging, although the new dislocated and disorienting style of Michelangelo Antonioni, Jean-Luc Godard, and others returns us to a freer and more expressive sense of place and of language, too.

Antony and Cleopatra has forty-two separate scenes in most editions, which seems to make it a sprawling and discontinuous play. But the forty-two scenes are calculated on the modern principle that each scene represents a different place. This is obviously not true for Elizabethan staging, where a series of quick, unlocated scenes might be used for a panoramic effect. There are four scenes to represent the battle of Actium, one only four lines long, and three scenes for the final naval battle. The locating stage directions—"A plain near Actium," "Another part of the plain," and "Between the two camps"—give us a wrong idea of what is happening. From the point of view of the audience, we have a series of quickly moving, fragmentary glimpses of battle, presented in terms of persons and not happening in any clearly defined places. The succession or juxtaposition of short scenes is meant to compress the amount of time involved and to create a sense of urgency.

We may agree that the representation of specific place was not one of the aims of Elizabethan staging, and, even if it were, the theater itself was not well equipped to provide "a local habitation and a name." This does not mean that Elizabethan dramatists did not use descriptions of places, sometimes scrupulously minute, in their plays, but they made a distinction between what could be accomplished by the staging and what could be evoked imaginatively. The sense of geographical extravaganza in Marlowe's *Tamburlaine*, for example, is almost entirely a product of the rhetoric rather than of the staging. How could Tamburlaine's ever-mounting succession of international triumphs be adequately rendered in visual and aural terms? The staging supports the hyperbole, but the real force of the persuasion is in those catalogues of exotic and polysyllabic place names.

When he discovers that he is dying at the end of Part II, Tamburlaine calls for a map, which is unfolded on stage to illustrate the triumphs of his military career:

> Here I began to march towards Persia,
> Along Armenia and the Caspian Sea,
> And thence unto Bithynia, where I took
> The Turk and his great Empress prisoners.

Then march'd I into Egypt and Arabia,
And here, not far from Alexandria,
Whereas the Terrene and the Red Sea meet,
Being distant less than full a hundred leagues,
I meant to cut a channel to them both
That men might quickly sail to India.
From thence to Nubia near Borno lake,
And so along the Ethiopian sea,
Cutting the Tropic line of Capricorn,
I conquered all as far as Zanzibar.
Then, by the northern part of Africa,
I came at last to Graecia, and from thence
To Asia, where I stay against my will
—Which is from Scythia, where I first began,
Backwards and forwards near five thousand leagues.
Look here, my boys, see what a world of ground
Lies westward from the midst of Cancer's line
Unto the rising of this earthly globe
Whereas the sun, declining from our sight,
Begins the day with our Antipodes.
And shall I die, and this unconquered? (5.3.126–150)

Like an experienced lecturer, Tamburlaine keeps close to his map, but the stage property can by no means be an objective correlative for the words of his speech.

The best known example of precise localization is Edgar's speech in *King Lear,* in which he describes to the blinded Gloucester the awesome view down Dover Cliffs:

Come on, sir; here's the place. Stand still. How fearful
And dizzy 'tis to cast one's eyes so low!
The crows and choughs that wing the midway air
Show scarce so gross as beetles. Half-way down
Hangs one that gathers samphire—dreadful trade!
Methinks he seems no bigger than his head.
The fishermen that walk upon the beach
Appear like mice; and yond tall anchoring bark
Diminish'd to her cock; her cock, a buoy
Almost too small for sight. The murmuring surge
That on th' unnumb'red idle pebble chafes
Cannot be heard so high. I'll look no more;
Lest my brain turn, and the deficient sight
Topple down headlong. (4.6.11–24)

Edgar's most convincing trick is to present everything in exact perspective, so that he seems to be the cinematic narrator for a travelling shot down the side of the cliff. The ability of Edgar to evoke a sense of place is heightened by the fact that his lyric and wondering speech is not in competition with any stage effects, and the audience is not tempted to make a comparison between the words and what they can plainly see and hear for themselves. In a movie, Edgar would be the narrator who would call our attention to significant details, and his words would be subordinate to the visual and aural imagery.

Usually, however, the words and the staging work together to produce a single impression. In *The Atheist's Tragedy,* for example, the elaborate plot to kill Montferrers is carried both by the language and by the stage directions. The murder is located in a gravel pit, represented by that area in front of and surrounding the stage that is also called the "pit" (or "orchestra" in modern parlance), where the groundlings stood. Montferrers is thrust off one side of the stage into the imagined gravel pit, where Borachio, the Machiavellian villain, can murder him at leisure. A few lines earlier we saw Borachio enter, as the stage direction tells us, *"warily and hastily over the stage, with a stone in either hand"* (2. iv). He immediately descends from the stage platform into the pit in order to lie in wait for Montferrers. By our willing suspension of disbelief, we agree that the pit of the theater shall be a gravel pit, but we do not have an exact description of the murder until Borachio's narration:

> I lay so fitly underneath the bank
> From whence he fell, that ere his falt'ring tongue
> Could utter double O, I knock'd out's brains
> With this fair ruby [*Borachio shows the bloody stone*],
>   and had another stone
> Just of this form and bigness ready; that
> I laid i' the broken skull upon the ground
> For's pillow, against the which they thought he fell
> And perish'd.   (2.4.91–98)

We need these additional details in order to explain what we thought we saw, and this example is interesting for the interplay between the narrative account and the stage business.

Another aspect of place in the Elizabethan theater is the representation of actual places in and around London that the audience would immediately recognize. These kinds of scenes depend upon the audience's willingness to supply the missing details, which it invariably does with a feeling of participatory pleasure. Dekker's *The Honest Whore, Part I*, ends with a scene in Bedlam, the familiar name for the psychiatric wards of the Hospital of St. Mary of Bethlehem in Bishopsgate, London. Although the play is set in Milan, the noble characters go to visit the madmen of Bedlam, which was a popular Elizabethan excursion, especially on weekends. We are shown a set of representative lunatics, as well as some disguised madmen, whose unmasking will unwind the plot. This scene must have pleased contemporary audiences, because we find Dekker imitating it in the sequel, *The Honest Whore, Part II*. Here the play ends with a vivid scene in Bridewell, a woman's prison of London where whores were traditionally sent to beat hemp and to mend their ways. We actually see two correction officers, one carrying the hemp, and the other a "beetle," or heavy mallet, and we meet such worthies as Dorothea Target, Mistress Horseleech, and Penelope Whorehound. The ostensible scene of the play is again Milan, but this illustrated tour to Bridewell convinces us that Dekker is not to be held back by his foreign settings.

On the vast subject of time in Elizabethan drama, I shall only add a few notes, since the representation of time is much better understood than the representation of place, and there is much valuable commentary on the distinction between clock time and emotional time, between chronological time and the emphasized, distorted, and foreshortened time out of which plays are built.

In Marlowe's *Dr. Faustus,* the twenty-four-year term of Faustus' pact with the devil passes with alarming rapidity. Marlowe makes no attempt to describe an orderly progression, but we are suddenly aware of the intense agony of Faustus' final soliloquy. The clock strikes eleven, and he has only one more hour to live. The solemnly tolling bell that marks the hours—and half-hours, too—begins a painfully slow time sequence, in which Faustus becomes conscious of time as the image of death. It is the striking clock that shatters his omnipotence and makes him feel the mortality from which he has been trying to escape:

> Ah, Faustus,
> Now hast thou but one bare hour to live,
> And then thou must be damn'd perpetually.

32

Stand still, you ever-moving spheres of heaven,
That time may cease, and midnight never come;
Fair nature's eye, rise, rise again, and make
Perpetual day; or let this hour be but
A year, a month, a week, a natural day,
That Faustus may repent and save his soul.
O *lente lente currite noctis equi!*
The stars move still, time runs, the clock will strike,
The devil will come, and Faustus must be damn'd.
(Scene 19. 133–144)

The steeds of the night cannot run more slowly, but the dramatist can deliberately slow down his action and use the passage of time as a theatrical metaphor.

Dr. Faustus violates unity of time, since the tragic action does not take place within a single day. The play could have been rewritten so that Faustus' career is presented in a series of narrative flashbacks, but this would have destroyed any sense of inevitable and fateful progression. It would also necessarily have limited the dramatic scope. There is an element of restraint and constriction in the unity of time that is foreign to Elizabethan exuberance and the appetite for large effects. Imagine *Hamlet* compressed into a twelve-hour mold. Time is so loosely developed in that play that the hero, after a brief and abortive sea voyage to England, suddenly seems to be thirty years old, an impossible age for the youthful, melancholy prince of the first act. We are not supposed to draw up a calendar of the action in order to show how slack a performer Shakespeare really was, but rather to accept the time scheme as a projection of dramatic emphasis. Both Dr. Faustus and Hamlet have aged over the course of the play. They have lost their innocence, and they are now, at the end, better able to deal with the experiences that generated their tragic doom.

Time is a crucial factor in revenge plays, partly because the logic of revenge demands a certain duration between cause and effect. It will not do to have the villain murdered directly after he is discovered, since the time that elapses between the discovery and the revenge seems to be a maturation period, and its intensity promotes the feeling of magnitude in the dramatic action. Critics with a psychological bent have tended to shift their interest from the inevitable but slow workings of revenge onto the element of delay, as if there were a curious network of subconscious reasons inhibiting the revenger from the simple task of murder. In *Hamlet,* delay has become the most important pseudotopic in the abundant criticism of this play, so that revenge is no longer the public act of justice, but a private debate between the revenger and his conscience. This seems to me a distortion because it puts an excessive emphasis on the motivations of the protagonist and detracts from the obvious intentions of the dramatic action.

In *Arden of Feversham,* the murder is protracted by a series of almost comic coincidences and ineptitudes on the part of Black Will and Shake-bag. "This mist, my friend, is mystical" (Scene 11, line 7), says Arden, speaking with ironic gratitude to the powers that are protecting his charmed life. *Arden of Feversham* is a naive murder play, not properly in the revenge tradition, but *The Spanish Tragedy* uses delay in the execution of revenge as a conscious device for developing the scope of the action. It seems to take Hieronimo an unconscionably long time to discover the murderers of his son and to put his brilliant plot into effect. This time lag, however, allows Kyd to develop Hieronimo as a character, especially through his madness, and to give the issues of the play a fuller realization.

Even beyond the halfway point in the action, Hieronimo will not believe Bel-Imperia's letter writ in blood, which plainly tells him who murdered Horatio:

> Hieronimo beware, thou art betray'd,
> And to entrap thy life this train is laid.
> Advise thee therefore, be not credulous:
> This is devised to endanger thee. (3.2.37–40)

And he resolves to try to verify the letter "by circumstances" (48). This kind of circumspection tends to disappoint modern audiences, especially in a father nearly crazed with passionate grief, but the revenge has a life of its own above and beyond human time, and it must be brought slowly and deliberately to the perfect fruition of a work of art. The process of revenge is unhurried in order that it may have the proper feeling of inevitability. *Hamlet, Hoffman, The Atheist's Tragedy, Titus Andronicus, The Revenge of Bussy D'Ambois,* and other bloody plays all emphasize duration as an essential aspect of revenge.

I have not been trying to defend the Elizabethan freedom of time and place as inherently better suited to drama than the unities. It all depends on what effects the playwright is trying to achieve. Ben Jonson was vigorously committed to the unities, and his comedies, especially *The Alchemist*, show that a playwright can create a powerful sense of coherence, concentration, controlled inventiveness, and beautiful logic by restricting his freedom to range widely in place and time. One feels that Jonson has made a characteristically neoclassical triumph over intractable and disordered materials. But these same rich and miscellaneous materials offered Shakespeare and other Elizabethan dramatists wonderful opportunities for developing contrasts, analogies, unlooked-for parallels, and a basically metaphoric and symbolic attitude to their subject matter. One approach is not better than another, although it should be obvious that one set of excellences tends to exclude the other: as we develop the free play of episodic inventiveness, we tend to lose that clarity and consecutive lucidity associated with the unities of place and time.

Rutgers University

NICOLA CHIAROMONTE

The Political Theater

In a certain sense, the first known example of political theater dates very nearly from the birth of theater in the West. It is the famous case of the *Capture of Miletus* by Phrynichus, a contemporary of Aeschylus', whose play was staged in Athens in 493 B.C. The tragedy, as Herodotus says, enacted the fall of the great Ionian colony into the hands of the Medes, who massacred the male inhabitants and made slaves of the women and children. The production, Herodotus also reports, roused the Athenian audience to wild displays of collective grief; the tragedy was banned at once, the poet was sentenced to pay a fine of a thousand drachmas, and the ban on his play was extended for all time.

We have here, it seems, a perfect example of political theater: the subject of a public nature and a burning topicality, since Miletus had fallen the year before; the violent emotion of the audience; the interference of censorship first and trial afterwards; finally, the sentencing of a dramatic poet for having dared to make a play out of a national disaster, for "defeatism," so to speak.

The history of the Greek theater, moreover, offers numerous examples of political theater. Aeschylus' *Persians* is a political tragedy; the Peloponnesian War is present in the form of allusions, sometimes quite transparent ones at that, in those of Euripides' plays which have the Trojan War as their subject; and, finally, the comedies of Aristophanes are openly political, so that he too had to pay in person for his opposition to Cleon, the demagogue whom he persisted in ridiculing so fiercely in the *Knights,* although he had already been the victim of Cleon's persecutions in court. And, as we know, the production of the *Knights* brought about the expulsion of Cleon by the enraged populace.

Even Shakespeare's history plays can be considered great examples of political theater; for some people, even *Hamlet* and *King Lear* are in substance political tragedies: for *Hamlet,* Francis Fergusson has quite dazzlingly argued just such an interpretation in *The Idea of a Theater.* The romantic theater in the last century is, from Schiller to Victor Hugo, surely political; we can say of it (and this applies in part to the plays of Vittorio Alfieri as well) that the true protagonist is History, or, to be exact, the struggle is between the free individual and the forces of Evil, Darkness, and Tyranny. A still more political drama—indeed, perhaps the drama to place at the origin of the modern political theater —is *Danton's Death* by Georg Büchner.

If, however, we speak of political theater, the name nine out of ten people today will pronounce is Bertolt Brecht's. This is unjust: the creator of the formula and the founder of a theater wanting to be, explicitly and radically, not only political in the broad sense but immediately at the service of a course of political action—the communist course determined by the Bolsheviks—is Erwin Piscator, the director with whom Brecht collaborated for some time and by whom he was more than merely influenced, at least as to theory.

For Piscator, a Bavarian like Brecht and three years Brecht's senior, as well as for Brecht (and, besides, for what we can call the first communist generation) the crucial experience was that of the First World War, in which Piscator had taken part as a simple soldier. The horror at that unheard-of slaughter and at the blindness of those who caused it, stubbornly going on with it nearly to the exhaustion of "human resources," was the prime reason for the ferment that followed the war in Europe. Along with the Bolshevik accession to power in Russia, that horror was also the point of departure for the political theater of Piscator. In this theater (as, on the whole, in Brecht's as well), pacifism and revolutionary ideology blur into a single protest in the name of the individual crushed by brute force, whether of political power or of money.

"My personal epoch begins on the 4th of August, 1914." With these words the memoirs of Piscator, precisely entitled *The Political Theater,* open. The sense of his career as a man of the theater and of the firmly preconceived ideas (rather than theories) that were the basis of his theater, is all in that sentence. It expresses, besides the foundation of Piscator's communism (which he himself dates from the reading of the message for immediate peace issued by Lenin and Trotsky on the 28th of November 1917), the idea that he formed of the theater as a means of breaking with the entirety of the art of the past, with the aim of making the problems of current history evident and urging action to "solve" them. The outgrowth of such an idea from the one which inspired the romantic theater seems direct enough, let us add parenthetically. The romantic idea of the theater is pushed here to its extreme. From such extremism derives as well the conception Piscator had of the relation between director, actors, and authors, a relation which was in his view entirely subordinate to the political (i.e., revolutionary) task in which the contemporary theater was bound, inevitably, to engage itself. Just as it was taken for granted then that the war and the Bolshevik Revolution had opened the era of the proletariat and closed the era of the bourgeoisie, so the political task of the theater was nothing else than the duty to reduce every theatrical theme of any kind to the most unimaginative topicality, represented in the most sensational way, with the aim not of moving the feelings, but of provoking action.

According to Piscator, the theater had to be revolutionary because it was eminently the art of the present and the topical. Conversely, no one could conceive of a topical art that would not be revolutionary. To bring about an authentic theater, it was not necessary to set out with this or that aesthetics, this or that idea of art, but rather to reject them all and be prompted solely by the will to transform the stage into a political forum (rather, into a "Tribunal," as the first of Piscator's theaters was called), to participate in political events and influence them through polemics, accusations, and praise. This ought to be done even at the risk of turning productions into sheer propaganda pieces. But, argues Piscator with sophistical naïveté, the best work—art— makes the most effective propaganda: bad art is not only bad propaganda but misguided politics as well, undermining and counterrevolutionary. Communism frees the theater insofar as it furnishes it with an ideology and thus opens up for the theater the paths of what Piscator calls "constructive thinking," denied to bourgeois culture, which is by nature utilitarian and so incapable of true thinking.

This is a convenient point to digress for a bit, in order to clarify the difference between what we might mean when we call Aeschylus' *Persians* or Aristophanes' *Knights* "political theater" and the meaning the expression takes on for Piscator and, after him, for Brecht and his more or less direct followers.

The difference is far from complicated: in the *Persians* and in the *Knights* the politics comes in naturally: the choice of a public subject on the author's part is a spontaneous one. In Piscator, instead, the intervention is willful, and the choice of a subject is based upon a fixed ideology. Or, to put it differently, the Athenian playwrights bring politics into their tragedies and comedies the way, in Molière, Monsieur Jordan brings in prose: without knowing it, simply because they were creating theater. "Politics," for them, meant "what concerns the *polis*," and the *polis* was not only the place of everyone, a free space protected by sacred laws, but also of *everything,* that is, of all that concerns man insofar as he is human, and not his private affairs only; but by the same token, not only the public events of the moment. In this sense, the Greek theater was political by nature. For the *Oresteia* no less than for the *Persians,* Aeschylus was inspired by the history of Greece and of Athens; but there was no ideology, no power, and no party that led him to deal with that subject rather than another. The story of the House of Atreus and of the Trojan War were no less "political," they were of no less concern to the moral life of the community than the victory of Salamis or the expedition of Cleon to Pylus. If anything, they were of greater concern, inasmuch as the plot of those ancient legends and stories allowed the community to recall and commemorate more extraordinary events and more significant characters than those of the present time. A current or recent event, such indeed as the victory over the great fleet of Xerxes, had dramatic value to the extent that the poet was truly able to "give it distance," to contemplate it by raising himself above the emotions and passions of the moment.

The *Persians* is a splendid proof of that ability, the loftiest example of civic poetry that we know of. "Our geometry applies only to mat-

39

ter, but the Greeks practised it first of all in learning virtue," wrote Simone Weil in *The Iliad; or, The Poem of Force*. Eight years after the triumph at Salamis, an Athenian poet caused his own townspeople not to contemplate the grandeur of their deed, but solely and strictly the law of the gods which had led to the ruin of the huge Persian force, the punishment of Xerxes' *hybris*, the harvest of sorrow reaped by a people because of the rashness of their king.

This is the highest note of the tragedy: the triumph of the poet's mind over the victory of his country and (if it is true that Aeschylus himself fought at Salamis) over his own victory. The victory with arms appears, in the drama, less important than its moral rightness. There is, to be sure, the famous account of the Messenger, and when he arrives at the point where the Greeks in fury strike their beaten enemies in the sea "like tuna spilled from the nets," the savage thrill of victory in battle must have run through the audience. But the words in which the pride of Aeschylus the Athenian resounds are not those of the account of the battle of Salamis (whose function in the tragedy is rather to show with full emphasis the disaster of the Persians), but the meager bits of dialogue between Queen Atossa and the Leader of the Chorus when she asks where Athens is and how armed and how rich and who commands the Athenians as their lord and master. The Leader of the Chorus replies: "They are no one's slaves or subjects"; at which the astonished Queen says: "How then could they resist the enemy invasion?" It is in this astonishment that Aeschylus causes the sense of the Nemesis that has struck the barbarians to flare up and at the same time the most truly liberating and purifying joy of the victory: the one of being in the right, of agreeing with more powerful laws than those which rule the world of material force. The largest force on earth has in fact been routed not by an equal and opposite force, but by that imponderable and sacred element which rules the course of human events and with which the Athenians were miraculously in harmony. The meaning of the victory and its merit consist in this.

We can measure the darkness of our present situation (darker than that of the time before Marathon and Salamis, when no Greek community felt protected from external violence) from the answer given today, in high and low places, to Atossa's question, an answer which is completely and always in favor of force.

As a final comment in this digression on the *Persians* and on the lesson that Aeschylus wished to bestow upon his townspeople in order to celebrate the victory against Xerxes, perhaps it is not out of place to recall that the choregus, the citizen called on as a public honor to pay the expenses of mounting the production, was Pericles, not yet twenty years old: the same man who, forty years later, with the aid of the most lucid, even faultless arguments, would persuade the Athenians to wage a war to the death against Sparta and therefore would lead Athens on a path of *hybris* just as ruinous as Xerxes' had been.

To my citing the example of Aeschylus, a Marxist could respond that it does not apply to our case, since the Athenian poet was in moral agreement with a society that in its turn conceived of dramaturgy as a civic function; whereas what distinguishes the capitalist society in which we are living is the impossibility of such an agreement, the inevitable alienation of the individual (and with all the more reason of the individual artist) not only from the constituted social order, but from his own work and from himself as a human being. Hence the inevitably unhappy and as a result inevitably negative and embattled situation of the modern individual.

The objection has a basis of truth, but on a quite different level and for reasons a lot more complex than those a Marxist is likely to adduce. First of all, what matters in the example of Aeschylus is not the case of a poet "integrated" in his society and of a society capable of "integrating" the poet naturally, but the fact that in the dramaturgy of Aeschylus (as, moreover, in that of Sophocles and Euripides), the real political or civic element is an organic part of a definite view of the meaning of existence, does not prevail over that view, and even less does it exhaust it. In the second place, if we are speaking of art, it is evident that what Marxists call "alienation" can be expressed in many and diverse ways: there is no imperative which forces us to give it the form of political or social polemics. And this for the simple reason that nothing can force anyone (even less, a poet) to *feel* a certain condition of things in a fixed way and to begin his discourse from a point established in advance. An imperative of this sort can only come from outside and from above, from the will to urge a definite type of political action. Such a will implies the conviction that the world ought to be

41

considered from a given viewpoint and not from others, which amounts to possessing an absolute and absolutely authoritative truth. Such a will expresses as well the belief that political action is, until further notice, a categorical imperative, an absolute, the truest form of the relation between man and the world.

It is on this point that we ought to be arguing and not on the nature of the Athenian social order, in regard to which we can surely grant that now there remains no other relation with it except memory and that therefore it would be absurd to take Greek tragedy as a model for the dramaturgy of today.

On the other hand, the modern political theater is not only a theater inspired by a definite ideology and by a definite polemical cause (anti-bourgeois, anticapitalist, anti-imperialist), but it relies on a conception of theatrical spectacle which is the opposite not only of the Greek conception, but also of the one from which the modern theater from the end of the last century until recently—the theater of Ibsen, Strindberg, Chekhov, Shaw, Pirandello—has drawn its inspiration. And we could go on to the very present, mentioning Witkiewicz, Ionesco, Beckett, Genet, Gombrowicz. More than on the poetic word and on the dramatic or comic conflict, the political theater rests on the visual and auditory emotions: this is one of its salient features. In Piscator's productions, as in Brecht's theatrical inventions, it is a question of pointing and showing by way of plastic example, not of logically developing the contrast between opposed moral situations. Thus drama turns into fable. Hence the importance which the staging takes on, even when, as in Brecht, it has apparently been reduced to the minimum.

It should suffice to mention here Mother Courage's wagon, of which we can say that it contains in itself the entire significance of the series of scenes imagined by Brecht on the theme of war.

In short, in the political theater, it is the theater of stagecraft, the theater-as-spectacle, which asserts itself, finding in the aim of political edification support for the aestheticism which characterizes it. Why aestheticism? Because, by its nature, this theater transforms into a more or less phantasmagorical scenic image the incitement to action it intends to produce, so that the formal element naturally gains the upper hand. Speaking of Piscator, we should not forget the influence that directors like Vsevolod Meyerhold and Alexander Tairov exercised on him—men

42

who distinguish themselves by the attempt to translate the revolutionary idea into a language of scenic design derived from the aesthetics of the Russian artistic and literary avant-garde of their time.

Erwin Piscator's ideas are a mixture of just intuitions and far-fetched concepts, of a genuine sense of theatrical spectacle and of a superstructure of ideology and advertising, of creative imagination and of pedantry. From such a mixture sprang a form of theater as original as it was ephemeral. Ephemeral not because it has had no disciples, since indeed it still has some, but for the intrinsic superficiality of the effects it seeks to obtain. Piscator's originality derives on the other hand from the unperturbed logic with which he breached the baroque and eighteenth-century theatrical patterns through every sort of staging device and technical resource, going from actors scattered on purpose amid the audience to the introduction of film not only as background, but as an integral part of the production.

But, as we have already hinted, the idea which Piscator carried to the extreme was not so much the one of political theater as it was the one of absolute supremacy for the production and inventions of scene design over every other element of the spectacle, and, above all, over the word. The director, according to Piscator, had to be a sort of emissary (or commissary) of historical forces, the supreme arbitrator of the total *effect* of the spectacle. And that effect, naturally, would have to be upsetting and revolutionary. But, in reality, it was an effect, pure and simple; and to this effect every other element of the spectacle had to be subordinate. All of which meant, to put it briefly, that everything would have to be subordinate to the success that the spectacle would have thanks to the sensation of novelty it provoked. Setting out from an extreme preoccupation with ideological content, Piscator thus arrived at the most extreme and self-defeating of formalisms. "The director and the author both have a single purpose: the success of the work," he proclaimed. He did not realize that, in making such pronouncements, he was giving a dogmatic form to the law which rules artistic production in a mass society. And, in fact, it is the advent of the mass media of communication (photography, movies, radio, yellow journalism), not of socialism, which the theater of Piscator really foretold.

As for Bertolt Brecht, it is well to remember that he began to put his conception of the theater into theoretical formulas only in 1934, when his career as a playwright was already established. We can, incidentally, note that the expression "epic theater" and the theory attached to it, which usually are considered Brecht's original ideas, not only were in the air, but had also been written down well before him. And it is not useless to stress another detail: "epic" in German simply means "narrative." In such a definition the meaning of Brecht's theater is already contained; it is in fact a narrative theater or, if you like, a theater of demonstration, not drama. The distinction is important.

For Brecht, in fact, it is the dramatic theater (no more or less than the Western theater from the fifth century B.C. to our times) which, in giving the spectator the illusion of witnessing a real action, involves him in the very action and fascinates him like a day dream, so that he loses his capacity for judgment. What distinguishes Brecht's "epic theater" is the fact that it consists of a series of objective illustrations of the "morality" that the author has in mind, produced on a bare stage and "distanced" (*entfremdet*) by an ironic performance. It ought therefore to leave the spectator aware of looking upon a fictive work and free to draw his own conclusions from what is being performed. But we are still dealing with a "morality," or a "fable" if you prefer. Brecht's dice are loaded and are meant to be. For example, it is understood in advance that in watching *Mother Courage* the spectator will not be able not to conclude in favor of proletarian revolution and against warmongering capitalism. Which does not, luckily for Brecht the artist, turn out in fact to be the case: *Mother Courage* is in reality a pessimistic fable, indeed nihilistic and misanthropic much more than pacifist or anticapitalist. What is shown in it is not so much the degradation caused by war as the abjectness to which the human animal is willing to stoop just to survive the storms of history. If we imagine it taking place in Russia between 1919 and 1921, during the Revolution and the Civil War, the costumes would be different but the meaning would remain the same. The moral of another renowned epic composition of Brecht's, *Galileo,* is substantially no different from that of *Mother Courage*: in the final analysis it still deals with the baseness of man; and the baseness is not condemned; it is rather considered a legitimate defense of the individual against the violence of arms or the implacable force of institutions.

44

The theory of the epic theater is therefore specious. No discussion shows this better than one by Brecht himself in a famous passage, quoted as classically convincing by his admirers, in which he defines the difference between the moral situation of the spectator before dramatic theater and before epic theater:

> The spectator of dramatic theater says: "Yes, I too have experienced this feeling—Yes, I too am like that—Well, this is natural—It will always be like that—The suffering of this man moves me, because there is no other outcome for it—This is great art: all here is obvious, is evident—I weep with whoever is weeping, I laugh with whoever is laughing."
>
> The spectator of epic theater says: "I would never have thought of this—You ought not to do this like that—It's surprising, almost inconceivable—It can't go on like that—The suffering of this man moves me, because it might have turned out differently!—This is great art: nothing here is obvious—I laugh with whoever is weeping, I weep with whoever is laughing."

Now, it seems obvious that, in Brecht's discussion, various kinds of theater and of possible reactions of the spectator in the theater are deliberately confused. For example, the observations on dramatic theater could apply to bourgeois comedy, but certainly not to Sophocles, to Ibsen, or to Shaw. On the other hand, there is nothing particularly bourgeois in a play (like *Philoctetes* or *King Lear*) which makes the spectator say: "The suffering of this man moves me, because there is no other outcome for it." Whereas it is a very ordinary bit of sarcasm to imagine that watching a beautiful play (say Kleist's *The Prince of Homburg*) makes him observe that it is "great art" because "all here is obvious, is evident." Again, almost all of Brecht's observations on what he defines as "dramatic theater" apply as well to certain scenes by Brecht himself: to the episode of Dumb Kattrin in *Mother Courage*, which is moving; but that is a poetic virtue, not a fault. Whereas everyone sees, conversely, how much distance or "distanc*ing*" or, more simply, reflection, not only a tragedy by Aeschylus or Euripides imposes with complete naturalness on the spectator, but a play by Strindberg or Pirandello as well.

More specious still than the theory of the epic theater (though no one would deny that, as applied by Brecht himself and by the actors of the Berliner Ensemble, it has yielded theatrically outstanding results) is Brecht's theory of the political theater. We can sum it up from the response the playwright-director gave in 1955, a year before he died, to the question: "Is it possible to express the world of today by means of the theater?" The response was: "The world of today can be described to the men of today only if one describes it as a world that can be changed." And Brecht added: "For the men of today, the value of today's problems can be measured by the answers they get. The men of today are interested in situations faced with which they can act in some way."

Now (and it is characteristic of Brecht's personality), this opinion of his contains more truth than it seems to at first glance, if we don't balk at the banality of the formulas; but at the same time, it is a lot more false than a devotee of pure art might find it.

The truth is a truth of fact: it is true, that is, that the men of today, taken in the mass, are not interested in contemplated action (that is, in *drama*, in the true root sense of the word) but in action or potential action. Which means a succession of images, movements, gestures, and (secondarily) words that arouse overwhelming emotion and possibly active participation (or physical imitation). This corresponds, in the most significant instance, to a ritual action, a dance or collective frenzy, in which we participate with the limbs and nerves but not the mind. And this occurs because what we look for in such actions is to submerge our self-consciousness in frenzied movement. In Greek, this was called *dromenon*, which indeed means "action," in opposition to *drama*, which is the action seen from outside, contemplated.

This means, however, that taken in the mass, the men of today are not interested in the theater, epic or dramatic as the case may be. At the theater the individual cannot help participating with his mind as well as with the emotion of his nerves and his visual, auditory, and plastic sensibility. After all, Brecht said he wished to attain just this with epic theater: that the audience, remaining outside the action, not charmed or roused to frenzy, might judge it and draw reasoned conclusions from it. In this, let it be clear, Brecht's conception is nothing new: surely every dramatist of any importance, from Aeschylus to Molière, from Molière to Strindberg, Chekhov, and Pirandello, understood theater in this way.

On the other hand, Brecht's thesis is false for a very simple reason, which recalls the answer T. S. Eliot gave to those who spoke of the theater as a religious event: "If I wish to participate in a rite, I go to Mass, not to the theater." Similarly, if it is true as Brecht asserted that the men of today are interested in the theater only insofar as the theater may describe the world as a world which can be changed, we shall note in the first place how the Marxist notion—already arguable in itself—becomes, applied to the world of theatrical fiction, quite obscure. Fiction is fiction, and such it remains despite every edifying or didactic intention. A work of fiction never refers to the so-called "real" world, much less to this or that action one must perform, but always and only to the world of feelings, thoughts, meanings: the world of the spirit and of communication on a spiritual level, whose connection with the real world and in a particular way with the world of actions, remains indefinite by nature. What sort of action, for example, is suggested by, let us say, not *Oedipus the King* or *Rosmersholm,* but by *The Threepenny Opera* or *The Caucasian Chalk Circle?*

In the second place, if it is true as Brecht asserted that the men of today are interested in the theater only insofar as the theater describes the world as a world which can be changed (which, please note, presupposes a fundamental optimism as regards the world itself and human nature), then instead of going to the theater they should go to "change the world," whatever may be the meaning of such a notion in theory and whatever may be the practical consequences which might possibly be drawn from it.

Dramatic or epic as the case may be, we go to the theater in order to *contemplate* the world (that is, to find a possible meaning in men's apparently meaningless actions and not to change it nor to get from the theater the urge to change it. The moral and practical consequences of such contemplation are something else again: something having to do with the metamorphoses of the individual mind, which follow unforeseeable paths, never traced in advance.

To which we can add that if it is Marxist in form, in substance Brecht's opinion matches the conservative's and the philistine's: it is in fact typical of the conservative and the philistine that they are interested "only in situations faced with which they can act," as Brecht put it. This is exactly the reason why the conservative and the philistine really dislike either the serious theater or any form of unbiased thought or of free art.

Naturally, to impugn Brecht's theories does not mean to deny his talent as a writer and a man of the theater. As a writer and a man of the theater, Bertolt Brecht remains one of the most significant personalities of our time; but not for the reasons he gives, much less for those his adulators cite.

The limitations of directors like Piscator and of director-dramatists like Brecht, on the other hand, do not stem from their desire to create a political theater, but from their rigid, pre-established idea of politics. This contradicts both the nature of theater and the nature of politics. To begin with, a theatrical action, however unreal, is an objective fact and the preconceived opinions or didactic aims of the director or even the author cannot reduce it to the single meaning he would like it to have. This, let us add parenthetically, is the reef on which some presumptuous contemporary directors have foundered, insisting as they have on tendentious interpretations and over-elaborate productions. The best inventions by Brecht (who tended, as a director, toward literal fidelity)— *The Threepenny Opera, Mother Courage, The Caucasian Chalk Circle* —are vitriolic, picturesque and (I am tempted to add) picaresque fables about the elementary simplicity, hardness, and lowness of the human instincts, therefore about the rather distressing nature of human history. No effort on the part of ideologists can cause them to mean incitement to revolution or to be a demonstration of the class struggle.

There is no partisanship in the theater, whether of ideologist or of director, which can change the meaning of a theatrical situation, because once this has been defined, it resists even its author's solicitations; in fact, the quality of a play more often than not can be appraised by the clarity with which the author was able to recognize the essential in the situation with which he began and to stick to it without allowing himself to be distracted by secondary ideas or rhetorical temptations. In the same way, there is in politics no ideology that can change the nature of the real situation which is recognized by common sense even before politicians recognize it, and the best politician is not the one who persists in demonstrating that he was right but the one whom the present state of things seems to prove right. In one instance as in the other, in theater as in politics, it is we citizen-spectators who are the arbiters. The dramatist who does not touch in us what we know is a common moral situation interests us as little as the politician who can impose his power and the power of his party, but does not care about the lot of real people. They are both remote personages, or, if you like, specialists whose language has validity only for their fellow specialists.

The contemporary political theater follows an entirely different direction from that marked by Ibsen first and then by Shaw. It is a theater which goes not from the situation towards its logical outcome through a more or less dialectical development, from action towards lyrical expression, or from emotion towards meaning, but on the contrary from a certain theme drawn more or less directly from current events towards the most spectacular and violent effect of stagecraft possible and from a certain pre-established idea towards a mimed symbol of it, plastic or vocal. And we say "vocal" to indicate that, in such a theater, the word tends to have a purely functional role, not unlike what it has in sound movies.

This is evident in Piscator and quite clear in Brecht; it becomes explicitly programmatic in what today is called the "theater of confrontation," running from the "Living Theater" to Peter Brook's productions, passing through various minor American, French, and Italian efforts. The fact that many of these men of the theater go back to Artaud and interpret as they do the heterogeneous and contradictory ideas included in his formula of the "theater of cruelty" serves only to emphasize this tendency, which, all considered, abandons drama for a form of theater that is often called a theater of "gesture."

Such a tendency appears clearly already in Brecht, whose inventions, as we have already noted, have nothing of the dramatic, but are rather plastic symbols of a definite idea. This idea takes the form in the best pieces by the theoretician of "epic theater" of a ballet with a script to it. The script is almost always too long and wordy, almost always overburdened by the moral the author wants to force on it, which then remains truly hanging there, outside the theatrical image in which it ought to be embodied. Brecht's originality consisted in his ability to invent strongly expressive images for the stage, like the already mentioned wagon of Mother Courage.

In short, as regards Brecht's theater, there are two facts to stress here: the first is that the "epic theater" is really a theater of stage effects, not of the word or of dialogue; therefore it not only is not

49

dramatic but it is not even ideological, since the concrete image on stage goes inevitably beyond any ideological intention and remains fatally ambiguous in that respect. The second fact to stress is that a theater like Brecht's ends in a sort of performance in which the political intention is transformed into a bantering fable whose meaning is essentially nihilistic. After all, it is really the nihilism—that mixture of dry cynicism and discomfort expressed better perhaps in some poems than in the theater—which constitutes Brecht's originality and modernity. It is to the nihilism and to the basic unbelief that his success in this postwar period is due and not to the banal didacticism of his declared intentions.

The importance of Brecht's work as a playwright and director in the contemporary theater lies in his having contributed in an outstanding way to the transformation (that had already begun long before him, let us not forget) of the stage from the realm of the incarnate word to the site of more or less picturesque scenic effects and of polemical illustrations of preconceived notions. The forms of theater based on gesture, on realistic effects, on orgiastic frenzy, which are presented just about everywhere today, owe much to the author of *The Threepenny Opera*. "Performances ought to let the thing being performed take precedence," Brecht had written. It is true that he added that the "thing being performed" would have to be "the common life of men"; but, theatrically speaking, this is a hollow phrase. The "thing" really being performed by Brecht is the concrete image which corresponds to the intention of his fable, and his method is the one of montage in the movies, which he himself contrasts with the principle of dramatic development.

Today, in the phraseology of a certain *avant-garde*, the political theater has become the "theater of confrontation" or of "protest" (or even "guerilla theater"). We cannot, to be sure, see wherein the difference in subject matter really lies, except for the usually lesser talent of the new authors and directors. The attacks on the bourgeois mentality, the "affluent society" with its advertising, imperialism, racism, the American way of life, war in general, and the war in Vietnam in particular, which are modish today on the stage of Europe and America, have this peculiarity: on the one hand they smash doors that were open, "confronting" ideas and facts which wear their weaknesses on their sleeve, while on the other they are simply rather weak forms of political theater, since they are reduced to turning in a circle around the thesis that evil is evil, good is good, war is ugly, peace is beautiful, and so on. The "confrontation" of Piscator and of Brecht, besides stemming from less simpleminded ideas, was in any case a great deal more artful and had quite a different charge of virulence.

But if we look carefully, we see that the so-called theater of "confrontation" has no ideological intentions; it is addressed not to the mind but to the nerves. It aims at striking the spectator from the outside, with stage effects and pantomimes so shocking and violent as to force him (so the belief goes) to recognize himself as an alienated individual in a world void of meaning. In reality, however, it does not escape the aestheticism of which it is intended to be the absolute antithesis. Faced with the most provocative effects, the most orgiastic and realistic frenzies, the spectator still remains a spectator; the more frenzied the acts which seek to involve him, the more unrelated and the more rigid is his situation as a simple onlooker. A confrontation which is not moral but physical (which, that is, addresses itself to the nerves rather than the consciousness) confronts nothing. At most it causes a temporary thrill, and the illusion of participating through such a thrill in the struggle of good against evil.

The fact is that an authentic return from *drama* to *dromenon,* from contemplated action to enacted action, would imply that we had to deal with a real rite, not with theater; and this in turn would presuppose no more nor less than the existence of a new religion. Now, neither in the individual soul nor in the life of society can political ideology take the place of religious belief. Grown inflexible, it can only transform itself into fanaticism. And fanaticism for its part can surely mobilize the spirit of sacrifice and of conquest in man, but as to moral life and artistic creativity it is sterile by nature. Particularly sterile, in this regard, is the still dominant and basically fanatical idea which holds that the meaning of human life is accomplished in the succession of historical events, that its substance is politics, so that the destiny of humanity will be decided on the terrain of political struggle. In such a case, naturally, political ideology—which taken by itself, has to do with the field of action, the very terrain of the contingent and the relative—becomes an absolute of a religious type, and with it the state, the nation, the society, the party become ultimate and absolute realities. Such a belief is hostile by nature not only to artistic creativity, but to every kind of human activity which refuses to become its instrument: indeed the divinities of this religion call for ruling hierarchies and rank slavery, not ritual ceremonies, liturgies, and festive celebrations.

Now, it is precisely from an ideology of this type that the contemporary political theater draws its inspiration. This explains its limits; and it explains as well how such a theater, even if it is almost inspired by genuine artistic intentions, ends by transforming itself into something which goes beyond ideological intentions: into a theater of gesture and of orgiastic realism. That such forms of spectacle can still be called theater is doubtful. But that is a question to take up somewhere else.

The discussion we are engaged in here does not at all imply the rejection of the idea of political theater. In a certain sense no great theater is unpolitical: all great theater is concerned with the life of the community by way of individual cases. In particular, there is no doubt that, given the way we live now, plays and comedies based on family affairs, unhappy loves, and things of this sort have become impossible rather than intolerable; as with realistic stories, their place by now is in screen and television plays, not in the theater. The only themes which withstand the test of the live stage are the ones concerned with the common fate, with the situation of man as such, today. To use a slightly abused word, we can say that the contemporary theater tends to be a metaphysical theater: the few examples of original dramaturgy which we have, from Beckett to Ionesco, to Genet, to Harold Pinter's best work, to the most recent Polish, Czechoslovakian, and Hungarian theater, move in this direction. But that does not deny that the formation of theatrical companies composed of writers, actors, and directors who dedicate themselves to transforming the political events of the moment into drama or farce would be an excellent thing.

The first, paradoxical, purpose of a political theater today would be to struggle against the tyranny of politics (of the absolutism of the state or party) over the life of society. But, paradox aside, the purposes of such a theater would be essentially two. The first of these is the necessity to fight that deadly sophistry of our time according to which the only valid judgments on politics are those made by the experts, by the professional Machiavellians, and by the professors of Machiavellianism: in short, "inside" judgments, while the rest are vain intellectualism and moralism. Since we want to banish them from the "stage" of politics, it would be extremely proper to have the intellectuals and moralists take the theatrical stage. There, they would play the role of that animal, man, which is in essence political, but neither expert nor Machiavellian (at least in Aristotle's view). This man, being the one who suffers the politics of the experts and the Machiavellians, will have at least the right to discuss it behind a mask and by way of theatrical fiction.

On the other hand, while it would give a certain satisfaction to the individual in question, such a theater would also try to do justice to the politician, the expert, and Machiavellian, who are not, as we are often led to believe, only monsters, dolts, or egomaniacs, but, if looked at closely, men as well.

The second purpose of such a political theater is more strictly theatrical. It ought to be completely different from the one conceived by a Piscator or a Brecht inasmuch as it is inspired by no damaging ideology, but simply by liberty to judge and satirize. To bring politics to the theater, to bring it there seriously, not smuggled in as if an advertisement, means (as we have already noted) to bring ideas there and drive out anecdotes, family affairs, psychological clichés drawn from daily newspapers, false spiritualism, and false moralism. An authentic political theater, something other than a cabaret theater, would not deal in a more or less journalistic way with the affairs of the day; on the contrary, starting out with the political and social events of the moment, it would bring to light the conflicts of passions, interests, and ideas which underlie them, while portraying them in a convincing manner.

Our time has had and continues to have, in the tremendous ways we know, the experience of force, with everything which force, violence, power exercised by man upon man without pity contain that we might call genuinely numinous. Such an experience has so far been impoverished by stereotyped ideas, by ideological sentimentality, and by demagogy. Therefore it is legitimate to imagine a political theater which, among other things, restored the sense of the tragic conflict, the awareness deep down that there are insoluble conflicts and insurmountable limits in life, and that on this very awareness the dignity of man's lot is based. From such an awareness could spring a sense of life a little less degrading than the one evinced in the ways of thinking and acting which are widespread today.

For such a theater, the difficulty would be to avoid the banal realism which still controls, although in strange forms, the writing of the present. A political theater which rejects realism may seem a contradiction in terms. But it is not. There are two ways, both servile ones, of facing current events: the first is to follow, to copy even, their "plot," simplifying it only insofar as deemed useful to the stage effect. This is the way of propaganda, more or less sophisticated. The second way, more intelligent, is to transpose them by means of ideology, replacing the real sequence of events with a more or less prefabricated logic: this is Brecht's theoretical principle, and it has the inconvenience of establishing an intellectually, morally, and aesthetically specious link with reality; which leads, by the way, to doubts as to the authenticity of the ideological intention of such work.

But perhaps there is a third way: one which begins with rejecting the first axiom of realism, according to which the significance of events and of human actions is exactly parallel to the occurrence of the events and the performance of the actions themselves and, so to speak, is parallel in time as well, so that any intervention of the imagination, the intellect, the symbol, would lead to a weakening of the significance. Naturally the contrary is true: it is truly impossible to render the *real* significance of a fact without having come to conceive it in the imagination. The *Persians* of Aeschylus, the comedies of Aristophanes, the history plays of Shakespeare, and the comedies of Shaw are surely outstanding examples of political theater which is not realistic or even ideological and yet is genuine.

Here, to sum up, is the problem that the theater of Piscator, the theater of Brecht, and the present-day theater of "confrontation" do not solve, but obscure instead. Yet we have to admit that such forms of theater have the merit, if no other, of posing this problem. And that, after all, is the crucial problem of the creation of a dramatic theater that is contemporary not with the events of the day, but with our sensibility and with the questions which, in the depths of our awareness, we address to ourselves and to the world we live in.

Rome, Italy

Translated by Richard Koffler

STANLEY EDGAR HYMAN

Untuning the Othello Music: Iago as Stage Villain*

One solution to the problem of Iago's motivation is the approach of genre criticism, which deals with Iago as traditional stage villain. In these terms, what motivates him is the need to war perpetually against love and happiness, trust and virtue, harmony and beauty, and all other manifestations of order and value; this perpetual war is the theatrical convention of his role. This role goes back at least as far as the earliest medieval mystery and miracle plays and continues beyond Elizabethan times well into Jacobean.

The traditional villain of the English stage has a number of fixed and easily recognizable characteristics. The basic one is the deceit and hypocrisy with which he misleads his dupes. We can see this as early as Mak the sheep stealer in the Towneley Second Shepherd's play, assuring the shepherds

> As I am true and lele, to God here I pray,
> That this be the fyrst mele that I shalle ete this day.

The villain Dissimulation in Bale's *King John*, who intends to poison the king, addresses him thus:

> Now Jesus preserve your worthye and excellent grace,
> For doubtless there is a very angelyck face.

* Adapted from *Iago: Some Approaches to the Illusion of His Motivation*, by Stanley Edgar Hyman. Copyright © 1970 by Stanley Edgar Hyman. Reprinted by permission of Atheneum Publishers.

Now forsoth and God, I woulde thynke my self in heaven,
If I myght remayne with yow but yeares alevyn.
I woulde covete here none other felicyte.

In Thomas Kyd's *The Spanish Tragedie,* the chief villain, Lorenzo, who has prevented Hieronimo from getting to the king to tell him of Lorenzo's wicked murder of Hieronimo's son, assures his father:

> Your-selfe, my lord, hath seene his passions,
> That ill beseemde the presence of a king;
> And, for I pittied him in his distresse,
> I helde him thence with kinde and curteous words,
> As free from malice to Hieronimo
> As to my soule, my lord.

As late as Marlowe's *The Jew of Malta,* Barabas tells Mathias, who will soon be one of his victims,

> Oh, heaven forbid I should have such a thought,
> Pardon me though I weepe.

Accompanying this falsity to the victims and dupes there is the villain's proud candor regarding his real nature and intentions in asides or soliloquies to the audience. Again Mak furnishes a ready example, in a boast to his wife:

> I am worthy my mete,
> For in a strate can I gett
> More then thay that swynke and swette
>   All the long day.
> Thus it felle to my lotte, Gylle, I had sich grace.

Politick Persuasion, the Vice in *Patient and Meek Grissell,* announces:

> I will not cease prively her confusion to worke,
> For under Honnie the proverbe saith poyson maye lurke:
> So though I simulate externally love to pretend,
> My love shall turne to mischife, I warrant you
>   in the end.

Villuppo, the secondary villain in *The Spanish Tragedie,* after he has told his brazen lie that gets Alexandro sentenced to death, remarks amiably to the audience:

> Thus have I with an envious forged tale
> Deceived the king, betraid mine enemy,
> And hope for guerdon of my villany.

Lorenzo, the principal villain, explains in an aside,

> Why, so! this fits our former pollicie;
> And thus experience bids the wise to deale.
> I lay the plot, he prosecutes the point;
> I set the trap, he breakes the worthles twigs,
> And sees not wherewith the bird was limde.

Finally, Barabas the Jew has any number of long monologues in which he proudly proclaims his crimes, of which the single line, "Sometimes I goe about and poyson wells," should be adequate illustration.

These two characteristics of the traditional stage villain are central to Iago (although he is only candid with the audience about his nature and purposes, not his motives—since he has no motives which are not onto-logical). Other features of the traditional role which he does not share (because they were largely extinct by 1604) need detain us only briefly. The stage villain is a ranter and a roarer, like Erode in the Coventry Corpus Christi play dealing with the Slaughter of the Innocents, who rages typically:

> A-nothur wey? owt! owt! owtt!
> Hath those fawls trayturs done me *this* ded?
> I stampe! I stare! I loke all abowtt!
> Myght I them take, I schuld them bren at a glede!

In other cases they degenerate into burlesque figures, such as the Beelze-bub who enters the Lutterworth St. George play announcing cheerily

> In comes I, old Beelzebub;
> Over my shoulder I carry my club,
> And in my hand a frying-pan
> Pleased to get all the money I can.

(A parallel development evolves into the villain's comic sneering aside, which we see on occasion with Iago, at least in regard to Roderigo.)

Like these traditional figures, Iago exposes his villainy to the audience in boastful soliloquies. A classic example comes near the end of the first scene, just before Iago leaves the stage. He says, of Othello:

> Though I do hate him as I do hell paines,
> Yet, for necessitie of present life,
> I must show out a Flag, and signe of Love,
> (Which is indeed but signe) . . .

This not only exposes Iago to the audience, but does so with gusto and wit, since he is Othello's flag-bearer or *ensign* ("ancient" in the play), and Iago is raising his flag or sign of hatred to the audience as he dissembles love for Othello.

Two principal characteristics of the stage villain, as these soliloquies make clear, are exaggerated wickedness and hypocrisy. The extreme wickedness is early revealed in the first scene in a simile Iago uses when instructing Roderigo how to cry out to rouse Brabantio. He says

> Doe, with like timerous accent, and dire yell,
> As when (by Night and Negligence) the Fire
> is spied in populous Citties.

Gould's account in *The Tragedian* of how the actor Junius Brutus Booth performed this speech gives a good sense of the aura of stage villainy in the imagery. He writes:

J. B. Booth uttered these words, without heat, with a devilish unconcern, as if pleased with the fancy of terror and dismay; and playing, meanwhile, with his sword-hilt or pulling at his gauntlets. He then strikes on the door of Brabantio's house, and speaking through the key-hole, sounds the resonant alarm, "What ho, Brabantio." Yet in saying this, we felt his mind was "playing with some inward bait." The duplicity, the double nature, the devil in him, was subtly manifest.

The stage villain's excess of duplicity and hypocrisy are revealed to Roderigo (and the audience) all through the first scene. The earliest revelation is a bold pun on "service," when Iago says "I follow him, to serve my turne upon him." It is all summed up in an early speech of self-revelation. Iago says

Were I the Moore, I would not be Iago:
In following him, I follow but my self.
Heaven is my Judge, not I for love and dutie,
But seeming so, for my peculiar end:
For when my outward action doth demonstrate
The native act, and figure of my heart
In Complement externe, 'tis not long after
But I will weare my heart upon my sleeve
For Dawes to pecke at; I am not what I am.

When Othello enters in the second scene, we observe Iago's duplicity in action. Although later in the play we see him as a cold-blooded assassin, a smiler with a knife, he begins the scene by proclaiming to Othello his scruples against killing. Iago says of Brabantio:

Though in the trade of Warre I have slaine men,
Yet do I hold it very stuffe o'th'conscience
To do no contriv'd Murder: I lack Iniquitie
Sometimes to do me service. Nine, or ten times
I had thought t'have yerk'd him here under the Ribbes.

Iago goes on to explain that when Brabantio insulted Othello, Iago restrained himself "with the little godlinesse I have." This latter is a lovely phrase, since it disclaims all but a minimum of godliness in Shakespeare's familiar character of the honest, bluff soldier; beneath that it proclaims that he is in fact too godly to kill; and it simultaneously assures the audience that he is in fact quite ungodly enough to kill on the instant. Later in the scene Iago swears "By Janus," quite the proper god for the double-faced stage villain, and perhaps Janus is all the godliness he has.

In the third scene, the confrontation with the Duke and the Venetian senators, Iago, quite properly, is mostly silent. When Othello finally introduces him to the Duke it is with heavy unconscious irony: "A man he is of honesty and trust." Just before he exits, Othello addresses Iago in the first of many such salutations as "Honest Iago." That leaves Iago alone on the stage with Roderigo; and after Roderigo has been instructed and has departed, Iago remains for another villainous soliloquy to the audience, and we hear him develop his plot further. Iago muses

Cassio's a proper man: Let me see now,
To get his Place, and to plume up my will
In double Knavery. How? How? Let's see,
After some time, to abuse Othello's eares,
That he is too familiar with his wife:
He hath a person, and a smooth dispose
To be suspected: fram'd to make women false.
The Moore is of a free, and open Nature,
That thinkes men honest, that but seeme to be so,
And will as tenderly be lead by th'Nose
As Asses are:
I have't: it is engendred: Hell, and Night,
Must bring this monstrous Birth, to the world's light.

When Iago enters with Desdemona in the first scene of the second act, Cassio addresses him as "Good Ancient" and "good Iago," with the adjective carrying the same heavy irony as "honest." When Othello enters shortly afterwards, he proclaims his great love to Desdemona, and, as they kiss, he expresses the hope that the kisses will "the greatest discords be/That ere our hearts shall make." Iago immediately proclaims in a prose stage whisper, in what G. Wilson Knight has shown is the central image of the play, his plan for the untuning of the Othello music:

Oh you are well tun'd now. But Ile set downe the peggs that make this Musicke, as honest as I am.

This is a particularly interesting use of "honest," among what William Empson has counted as fifty-two uses of "honest" and "honesty" in the play, in his brilliant chapter "Honest in Othello" in *The Structure of Complex Words*. Among other things it means: that he will untune the Othello music however honest (that is, faithful) Othello thinks him; that he will do so by means of his hypocritical "honesty"; and that he can honestly assure the audience that it will honestly be done. Later in the scene, Iago gives another description of Othello's goodness, along the lines of his soliloquy at the end of Act I, which further defines his own villainy by contrast. He says

The Moore (howbeit that I endure him not)
Is of a constant, loving, Noble Nature.

60

If Othello is Iago's vulnerable antithesis, Roderigo is his despised tool, whom he describes as "this poore Trash of Venice." He concludes the scene with a characteristic ringing couplet of the stage villain, about his unformed plot, proclaiming

> 'Tis heere: but yet confus'd,
> Knaveries plaine face, is never seene, till us'd.

In the second scene of the act, Othello again describes Iago as "most honest," and Cassio again addresses him as "good Iago." Iago, as soon as he is alone on the stage once more, sneers villainously at "my sicke Foole Roderigo," and as Cassio and Montano, the governor of Cyprus, approach (with Cassio made drunk by Iago's doing), Iago soliloquizes grandiloquently:

> If Consequence do but approve my dreame,
> My Boate sailes freely, both with winde and Streame.

As the two fight, and Montano is wounded, Iago pretends to try to calm them, and when Othello and his attendants enter, Iago lectures them both, with repulsive hypocrisy:

> Have you forgot all place of sense and dutie?
> Hold. The Generall speaks to you: hold for shame.

(We have only to recall Iago's cynical definitions of both "sense" and "duty.") Othello then addresses Iago:

> Honest Iago, that lookes dead with greeving,
> Speake; who began this? On thy love I charge thee?

In the ensuing discussion (foreshadowing the Desdemona main plot) Iago manages to indict Cassio in the guise of defending him, and Othello concludes

> I know Iago
> Thy honestie and love doth mince this matter,
> Making it light to Cassio:

In his next words, Othello dismisses Cassio summarily. When he is next alone on the stage with Cassio, Iago says to him ambiguously, "And good

Lieutenant, I thinke, you thinke I love you," and advises him to plead his suit to Desdemona, dismissing Cassio's praise for his advice with "I protest in the sinceritie of Love, and honest kindnesse." When Cassio exits, again saluting his treacherous undoer as "honest Iago," Iago is left alone on the stage for another of his villainous self-revelations to the audience. He first asks rhetorically:

> And what's he then,
> That sayes I play the Villaine?
> When this advise is free I give, and honest,
> Proball to thinking, and indeed the course
> To win the Moore againe.

As he continues, he asks again "How am I then a Villaine?" and goes on to expose his real intentions:

> For whiles this honest Foole
> Plies Desdemona, to repaire his Fortune,
> And she for him, pleades strongly to the Moore,
> Ile powre this pestilence into his eare:
> That she repeales him, for her bodies Lust . . .

After Roderigo has entered to complain and been sent off with more glowing promises, Iago is left onstage to conclude the act with still another traditional soliloquy of the stage villain. He says:

> Two things are to be done:
> My Wife must move for Cassio to her Mistris:
> Ile set her on my self, a while, to draw the Moor apart,
> And bring him jumpe, when he may Cassio finde
> Soliciting his wife: Aye, that's the way:
> Dull not Device, by coldnesse and delay.

In the third scene of Act III, when Æmilia assures Desdemona that her husband is grieved by Cassio's fate, Desdemona adopts the general view of Iago and comments, "Oh that's an honest Fellow." Later in the scene, Iago begins the serious business of his principal villainy, the destruction of Desdemona by arousing Othello's jealousy. He begins it with the characteristic hypocrisy of his traditional role, warning

> Oh, beware my Lord, of jealousie,
> It is the greene-ey'd Monster, which doth mocke
> The meate it feeds on.

(The critical debate on these famous lines is probably the fullest, and certainly the funniest, for *Othello*—Zachary Jackson's explanation that what is meant is a green-eyed mouse or mouster is one of the high points of nitwit scholarship—but there has been no agreement about the key words: whether "mock" means "sneers at," "toys with," or what; whether "the meat it feeds on" is the victim, suspicion, or what. As is usual with Shakespeare, however absurd it is to say, the purport of the passage is perfectly clear even where many of the words mystify.) Iago goes on in the scene to warn Othello, "Looke to your wife, observe her well with Cassio," and, turning on her his own ambiguous label (here meaning "chaste"), assures Othello (with a wonderful double negative) "I do not think but Desdemona's honest." As Iago separates from Othello to leave, Othello picks up the word, musing

> This honest Creature (doubtlesse)
> Sees, and knowes more, much more than he unfolds.

When Iago has left the stage, Othello continues, "This Fellow's of exceeding honesty." Later in the scene, after Æmilia has given Desdemona's lost handkerchief to Iago and been dismissed, he proclaims to the audience,

> I will in Cassio's Lodging loose this Napkin,
> And let him finde it.

He then adds gleefully, "The Moore already changes with my poyson." When Othello re-enters, momentarily less gullible, and demands some evidence of Desdemona's betrayal, Iago goes all melodramatic about the hard fate of the truthful in this world, crying out, "Take note, take note (O World) / To be direct and honest is not safe," and announces that he will never again try to help a friend with the loving truth. Othello immediately backs down: "Nay stay: thou should'st be honest." Iago again denies that he wishes to say any more, but explains that he is "Prick'd to't by foolish Honesty, and Love." The scene ends with Othello entirely convinced.

Iago appears only briefly in the fourth scene, to bring Cassio to Desdemona, egg him on to plead his case to her, and then leave, on the pretext that Othello is so rarely angry that if he is so now, Iago must go to mollify him.

In the first scene of the fourth act, Iago finally succeeds in untuning the Othello music, and Othello, babbling madly, falls into a trance. Iago stands over him to make the most bombastic, didactic, and melodramatic of all his stage villain speeches. He cries out,

> Worke on,
> My Medicine workes. Thus credulous Fooles are caught,
> And many worthy, and chast Dames even thus,
> (All guiltlesse) meete reproach.

Othello revives, and Iago sends him off to prepare for the next revelation, which will set the pegs down a turn or two more. Iago then soliloquizes, "Now will I question Cassio of Bianca," while Othello watches from concealment, thinking the questioning is about Desdemona, and Iago announces triumphantly of Cassio: "As he shall smile, Othello shall go mad." Convinced, Othello resolves to poison Desdemona, and Iago proposes, in a height of melodramatic villainy,

> Do it not with poyson, strangle her in her bed,
> Even the bed she hath contaminated.

At the end of the scene, when Lodovico, the emissary from Venice, inquires about Othello's mad ranting and raving, Iago answers with his usual loyal reticence that charges more than any charge could:

> Alas, alas:
> It is not honestie in me to speake
> What I have seene, and knowne.

In the second scene, with the most revolting hypocrisy, he reassures Desdemona: "Go in, and weepe not: all things shall be well." (Shakespeare may have been familiar with *Revelations of Divine Love* by Dame Julian of Norwich, whose "Sin is behovely, but all shall be well, and all manner of thing shall be well," has been popularized in our time by T. S.

Eliot.) Iago's next move as stage villain is to encourage Roderigo to kill Cassio. He proposes "the removing of Cassio," explains, in answer to Roderigo's query, "Why, by making him uncapable of Othello's place: Knocking out his braines," and then instructs and assures Roderigo: "if you will watch his going thence (which I will fashion to fall out betweene twelve and one) you may take him at your pleasure. I will be neere to second your Attempt, and he shall fall betweene us."

In the first scene of the fifth act, the attempted assassination is set up. Roderigo is left in his hiding-place with unsheathed rapier, but, not quite a model of bravery, he implores Iago, "Be neere at hand, I may miscarry in't." Iago assures him, with his familiar hypocrisy, "Heere, at thy hand," and then in a soliloquy to the audience, reveals his nasty contempt for Roderigo and the utter ruthlessness of his real hopes. He says

> I have rub'd this yong Quat almost to the sense,
> And he grows angry. Now, whether he kill Cassio,
> Or Cassio him, or each do kill the other,
> Every way makes my gaine.

("Quat" is a pimple.) Iago wishes Roderigo dead because he will want back all the money he has given Iago to win Desdemona for him. As for Cassio:

> If Cassio do remaine,
> He hath a dayly beauty in his life,
> That makes me ugly: and besides, the Moore
> May unfold me to him: there stand I in much perill:
> No, he must dye.

When Cassio enters, and he and Roderigo have wounded each other (or Iago has wounded Cassio), Othello appears as instructed by Iago, whom he now calls "O brave Iago, honest, and just," under the impression that Iago has slain Cassio on Othello's behalf. When Iago, who has temporarily left the stage, returns, he is about to dispatch Cassio (in a reading of Booth's to which I subscribe) when he sees Lodovico and Gratiano approach and instead talks sympathetically to the wounded Cassio, learns that his attacker lies nearby wounded, and piously crying, "Oh murd'rous Slave! O Villaine!" he stabs Roderigo to death. Iago concludes the scene with the standard crisis image of his tradition (Lorenzo says "how stands our fortune on a tickle point"):

> This is the night
> That either makes me, or foredoes me quight.

In the second scene of the act, and the play's last scene, the final confrontation of Othello and Desdemona, in which he smothers her, Othello tells Desdemona that Cassio can no longer admit or deny anything, since his mouth has been stopped by "Honest Iago." After the murder, Othello informs Æmilia that he learned of Desdemona's adultery with Cassio from her husband, "An honest man he is," and adds, more desperately, "My Friend, thy Husband; honest, honest Iago." We see no more of Iago as traditional stage villain in the play. When he returns for the last time, to be exposed, judged, and sentenced, he is in another role.

There can be no doubt that Shakespeare was familiar with the stock villain of the religious plays, which were the principal drama of England for two centuries. The great local cycles of miracle plays were still being performed at least past the death of Elizabeth. There is a clear reminiscence of *The Harrowing of Hell* in the Porter scene in *Macbeth*, and Falstaff's attributes are openly borrowed from the Vices of a number of different morality plays. Shakespeare was almost unique, however, in using the tradition of the stage villain without humor or comic ranting (at least here: the Bastard in *Lear* has plenty of humor, and Richard III rants like any medieval Herod), as he wrote in *King Lear* the only version of the "Cinderella" story (in the "Love Like Salt" variant) which has an unhappy ending.

Little has been written about Iago as traditional stage villain, although every critic has been aware of this aspect of the character (emphasis on it was the dominant acting tradition for the role until our century), because it is usual to think of the convention as a style in which Iago's otherwise-motivated villainy is expressed, rather than as the motivation itself. However, as A. C. Bradley says, "Iago's plot is Iago's character in action." Since he is, in one of his aspects, a stage villain, so must he do and say stagily villainous things. Beyond that lurks Shakespeare's own motivation: he must unfold his dramatic action, the untuning of the Othello music.*

Bennington College

---

* The only comprehensive treatment of the subject with which I am familiar appears in *Shakespeare and the Allegory of Evil* (New York, 1958), by Bernard Spivack, although this suggestive work has certain limitations which I will take up elsewhere.

BERNARD KNOX

Euripidean Comedy

"The most tragic of the poets" Aristotle called him (whatever he may have meant by it),[1] and succeeding ages have agreed; the great Euripidean tragedies, *Hippolytus, Medea, Bacchae, Trojan Women,* show us a world torn asunder by blind, disruptive forces, which affords no consolation, no compensation for suffering, no way to face it except resigned endurance, a world which reduces man from the status of hero to that of victim. But Euripides had another side to his genius: he introduced to the theater of Dionysus new forms of drama, the *Iphigenia in Tauris,* the *Helen,* the *Ion,* plays which critics and scholars have labored in vain to define. They are clearly a radical departure from Euripidean tragedy (from any of our notions of tragedy, for that matter), but the search for a term which adequately describes them has resulted only in a confusing assortment of vague categories: they have been called romantic tragedy, romantic melodrama, tragicomedy, romances, romantic comedy, *drames romanesques, Intrigenstücke,* to list only the most influential attempts at nomenclature. One cannot help suspecting that what everyone would really like to call these plays (at least the *Ion*) is comedy (though no one, to my knowledge, has taken the plunge).[2] There are, of course, good reasons for such hesitation. But I should like to suggest that they are not good enough, that provided the word "comedy" is understood in modern, not ancient terms, Euripides, in these plays but especially in their culmination, the *Ion,* is the inventor, for the stage, of what we know as comedy.

One reason for stopping short of this word is of course the certainty that Euripides himself would have repudiated it with some indignation. "Comedy," he would have said, "is an entirely different kettle of fish: it is what my friend Aristophanes writes." In fifth-century Athens the two genres were rigidly separate, and comedy—a high-spirited combination of unbridled personal lampoon, literary burlesque, indecent buffoonery, brilliant wit, and lyric poetry of the highest order—had its own recognizable conventions of plot, language, dance, and meter, which were quite distinct from those of tragedy. When at the end of a long night of revelry, drinking, and conversation Socrates in Plato's *Symposium* proposed and defended the thesis that the same man could be capable of composing both tragedy and comedy, we are left in no doubt that his hearers, a comic and a tragic poet, are reluctant to accept this surprising idea. "They were being forced [ἀναγκαζομένους] to this conclusion," says Plato, "but they could not follow his argument too well, for they kept drowsing off—Aristophanes went right off to sleep first, and Agathon went the same way just as dawn was breaking." [3] Only Socrates could have proposed such a paradox; for the fifth-century Athenian, tragedy was tragedy and comedy comedy, and never the twain should meet.

But Aristophanic comedy has had no descendants, and comedy for us is something different. It comes to us from the Greeks all right, but not from Old Comedy; it descends through Plautus and Terence to the Renaissance dramatists from Menander, the Athenian comic poet of the fourth century, and his plays in turn derive from those plays of Euripides in which the prototype of modern comedy is to be found. In this, as in so many ways, Euripides is prophetic, the poet of the future; what he invents is the prevailing drama of the next century, the domestic comedy of manners and situation, of family misunderstandings —between father and son, husband and wife—of mistaken identity and recognition, of lost children reclaimed and angry fathers reconciled to spurned suitors finally revealed as long lost sons of wealthy friends, the comedy of misapprehension, recognition, and restoration, of Menander and Philemon—which is also the main tradition of modern European comedy from Shakespeare to Oscar Wilde.

Of course, the mere fact that these Euripidean plays have a happy ending is not enough to justify the term "comedy." Aristotle preferred tragedies which end in misfortune, but his statement clearly implies that some sort of happy ending was far from rare and did not disqualify a play as tragedy. And this would have been clear even without Aristotle, for the *Oresteia* of Aeschylus and the *Philoctetes* of Sophocles, to take only two examples, do not end in misfortune, and yet no one has ever thought of them as comedies. Such a term for these Euripidean plays could be justified only by the appearance in them of a treatment of situation and character differing sharply from the tragic norm. And Euripides does indeed in these plays (and, for that matter, in others) introduce to the tragic stage an entirely new attitude to human nature and action. It has been called "realistic," but it is not hard to show that the term is inadequate. To avoid begging the question, it is perhaps better to demonstrate the nature of Euripides' untragic tone, not from one of the plays in question, but by reference to the opening scenes of a play which, taken as a whole, clearly belongs to the tragic canon, the savage *Electra*. It is a shocking play. What in Aeschylus was the just punishment of a father's assassins by a god-driven son, in Sophocles the crowning achievement of a heroic daughter's lonely endurance, becomes in Euripides a pair of sordid murders: Aegisthus ignominiously butchered by the guest he had invited to the sacrificial feast, Clytemnestra lured to her death through her solicitude for her daughter's feigned pregnancy. These actions are of course the climax of the play and are written in Euripides' grimmest mood. But the opening scenes are a surprising contrast.

The prologue speech is delivered by an unnamed character, a small farmer, who gives us the astonishing news that he is Electra's husband. Not that he has presumed to exercise his marital rights, he goes on: he has too much respect for Agamemnon's line (lines 43 ff.). The situation is piquant, to say the least, but we have no hint yet of a real departure from the heroic mode which has always been appropriate for this particular story. Except one. Aegisthus, the farmer tells us, forbade Electra's marriage to a noble suitor, for fear of a son who would avenge Agamemnon (22 ff.). But then he decided to kill her anyway because of a fear "that she would bear children to one of them secretly" (26).[4] This slight hint of scandalous possibilities is all we are given to prepare us for the shock provided by Electra's entrance. She comes on stage as no tragic heroine we know of ever did before—balancing a jug

70

on her head in the immemorial fashion of Greek village women on their way to the spring. "O dark night," she sings, "keeper of the golden stars, in which carrying this jug balanced on my head, I go to fetch water from the river" (54 ff.). Perhaps, we think, we are meant to be moved to pity at the depths of poverty to which this princess has been reduced: this is one more pathetic prop—like the rags of Telephus, Oeneus, Phoenix, and many another Euripidean hero.[5] But Electra goes on: "Not that I have reached any such degree of poverty—it is so that I may show the gods the savagery of Aegisthus" (57–58). Just in case we don't get the point, her husband asks her why she goes to all this trouble "even though I tell you not to" (66). She replies that she wishes to repay his kindness by helping him, by sharing his labors. "You have work enough in the fields. It is *my* duty to prepare everything inside the house. When the workman comes home, it is pleasant for him to find everything shipshape inside." "Well," says her husband, "go ahead, if you insist. The spring is not far from the house in any case" (71 ff.). And in any case, Electra has a servant with her.[6] "Take this jar off my head and put it down," she commands later (140), as she sings her solo aria recounting the sorrows of her life. Quite apart from the extraordinary visual detail of the water jug, the tone of this scene is unmistakable. It is *domestic:* we are being invited, not to identify ourselves with the passions and destinies of heroic souls, but to detach ourselves and observe the actions and reactions of ordinary human beings in a social situation with norms and customs we are only too well acquainted with. And this domestic realism, which might have served simply to deepen the pathos of the heroine's situation, is made, by ironic comment and juxtaposition, to expose not merely the sordid details of Electra's misery, but also her pretenses and affectations.

This scene is only the beginning; there is much more to come. To the chorus which invites her to accompany them to the great festival of Hera, Electra replies not only with a recital of her wrongs and a repetition of her determination to mourn Agamemnon's death forever, but also with a more mundane excuse. "Look at my hair; it's dirty. Look at these rags of clothes. Are they fit for Agamemnon's royal daughter?" (184 ff.). These sentiments are couched in faultless glyconics but they still mean nothing more than "I haven't a thing to wear," and in case we had any doubt the chorus offers to lend her something.

71

"Borrow from me fine-woven dresses to wear and these golden ornaments to go with them—do please accept" (191–193).

Less than two hundred lines later Electra is standing at the door of
the house talking to Orestes and Pylades (she does not yet know who
they are) when her husband comes back from his work (for his lunch
presumably). He is certainly a patient husband, but even he is upset.
"It's disgraceful—a wife standing around with men." "Dearest," replies
Electra, "don't get suspicious of me." The strangers are emissaries of
Orestes come to see the sorrows of her life. "Well," says her husband,
"some of them they can see, and I'm sure you are telling them the
rest"; [7] he is, of course, quite right. He invites the strangers into his
house. Orestes, in a long speech, admires his nobility, but Electra takes
a different view. When husband and wife are alone together, she proceeds as follows: "You rash fool, you *know* how poor your house is;
why did you invite in these strangers who are of a higher station than
you?" "Why not?" says the farmer reasonably. "If they are as noble
as they seem, they will be as content in humble circumstances as in
high." "Humble's the word," says Electra.[8] "You made a mistake. Now
go off and find the old man who used to look after my father . . . tell
him to bring some food for my guests." "All right," says her long-
suffering husband, "I'll go. Now *you* go inside, and fix things up. You
know very well that a woman, if she wants to, can always find something extra to piece out [προσφορήματα]," a word which occurs nowhere
else in Greek literature. And in the next scene the old man, complaining
about his bent back and wobbly knee, comes in loaded with food and
drink (487 ff.). "Here, daughter, I've brought you a newborn lamb
from my flocks, and garlands for the guests, and cheeses I took out of
the buckets and this wine—vintage stock of Dionysus—such a bouquet
—not much of it, but sweet stuff—just pour a cup of this into some
weaker brew . . ."

The comic effect of much of this is unmistakable; [9] but the play of
course does not continue long in this vein. True, there is still the burlesque of Aeschylus' recognition scene to come,[10] with the old man plead-
ing for one after the other of the three traditional recognition tokens
only to have them all contemptuously dismissed by Electra as foolish-
ness. But Orestes finally *is* recognized by a scar on his forehead, and after
that brother and sister plan and carry out the two treacherous, brutal

murders. The effect of the domestic atmosphere of the first half of the play is to strip every last shred of heroic stature from Electra and Orestes, so that we see their subsequent actions, not as heroic fulfillment, not as the working of some destiny or curse, not as the fulfillment of a god's command, but rather as crimes committed by "men as they are," to use Sophocles' description of Euripides' characters, by people like ourselves. After we have seen a shrewish and snobbish Electra scold her husband for not knowing his place in society, we are not likely to see her murder of her mother as anything else than what it is, an unnecessary act of paranoiac jealous hatred.

The comic tone is used here for a purpose which has nothing to do with comedy. But as social comedy the opening scenes of the play are brilliant,[11] and since they are the first extant appearance of such scenes on the tragic stage, they invite careful examination. The most novel and incongruous element in them is the repeated emphasis on the everyday details of domestic life, on meals and their preparation, the need to carry water and bring food, not to mention wine. This is a new note. In Greek tragedy before this (what we have of it) references to food and drink are scarce, short, incidental, and frequently negative;[12] certainly no tragic heroines before Electra balance water pitchers on their heads, quarrel with their husbands about whether there is enough food for the guests, and send them off to procure cheese, lamb, and wine. All this smacks of comedy, where people eat and drink with gusto, prepare enormous meals and drink gigantic quantities of wine, where menial tasks (from pouring gravy on a pancake to feeding a giant dung beetle) are the order of the day. But such matters also bulk large in satyr plays,[13] and, although Euripides did not write comedies in the ancient sense of the word, he did, like Aeschylus and Sophocles, write satyr plays. In the only specimen of this extraordinary genre which has survived complete, the *Cyclops* of Euripides, food, drink, and domestic chores are very much to the fore. "Here I am at my work," says the prologue-speaker, Silenus, "filling sheep troughs and sweeping floors. I wait on that godless Cyclops at his unholy meals. And now I must follow orders, and scrape out the cave with this iron rake . . ." Odysseus arrives; thinking he is in Book 9 of the *Odyssey*, he begins in heroic style, but breaks off at the sight of the satyr chorus. Soon he is exchanging his wine for the Cyclops' food—meat, cheese, and milk. And so it goes on, including,

73

before the climax (the blinding of Polyphemus), a drunken symposium, with Silenus stealing the drunken Cyclops' wine, which ends as Polyphemus, announcing that Silenus is his Ganymede, carries him off protesting into the cave.

We have, of course, one other Euripidean play which, if not strictly satyric, was at any rate performed fourth after three tragedies, the *Alcestis*. It has no chorus of satyrs, and, though it has a contrived happy ending, it is a poignant and bitter play. In fact, the only thing which reminds us that this is a substitute for Silenus and the "foreheads villainous low" of the satyr chorus is the scene in which, after the servant describes the difficulty of waiting on Heracles at table (he is an importunate guest who, not content with what is offered, demands more, and a hard-drinking guest as well), the hero himself emerges to berate the servant for his gloomy looks and expound his philosophy of eat, drink, and be merry in almost the same terms Cyclops uses to Odysseus.[14] Here we are for a moment back in the world of food and drink and domestic detail, but it is only a moment, and we cannot help wondering what the Athenian audience thought of this Euripidean experiment, the first of many. What he has done in *Alcestis* is to present a satyr play completely transformed by the introduction of tragic situation, character, chorus, and style. And if he could do that, why could he not do the opposite? In the *Electra*, I suggest, he has completely transformed the first half of the tragedy by the introduction of situation, character, and style proper to a satyric play.

This transformation of the tragic atmosphere by the introduction of domestic detail did not, of course, escape the keen eye of Euripides' constant critic. Aristophanes, in the *Frogs*, puts into his mouth the boast that he had improved tragedy by "bringing in household matters, things we use and live with"—οἰκεῖα πράγματ' εἰσάγων, οἷς χρώμεθ' οἷς σύνεσμεν (959–960)—and taught the Athenians to "run their houses better than before." Dionysus' reply to this claim dots the i's and crosses the t's.

> So now the Athenian hears a pome
> of yours and watch him come stomping home
> to yell at his servants every one
> "Where oh where are my pitchers gone?
> Where is the maid who has betrayed
> my heads of fish to the garbage trade?

Where are the pots of yesteryear?
Where is the garlic of yesterday?
Who hath ravished my oil away?" [15]

In the opening scenes of the *Electra*, the domestic, light tone prevails, but they are an introduction to the grim horrors of the denouement. It is in such plays as *Iphigenia in Tauris* and *Helen*, which present not tragic catastrophe but hairsbreadth escape from it, that the new spirit achieves its full expression and dominates the whole play. These two plays are generally admitted to be a new departure. They are the ancestors of a whole genre of Western melodrama in which captured white adventurers avoid a gruesome death by playing on the ignorance and superstition of the savages. They have a neat formula: part one, the recognition; part two, the escape by trickery (in both plays the woman provides the brainwork).[16] But the only thing that puts these plays in the tragic category is the fact that they were entries in the tragic competition at the festival of Dionysus.

What Euripides has done in them is to eliminate from tragedy what previously had been its essence: τὸ ἀνήκεστον—"the incurable" (it is Aristotle's word, and Nietzsche's).[17] He has suppressed the action which cannot be recalled, which allows no escape from the consequences—the meeting of the hero and the absolute situation and his decisive act which changes, "incurably," his world. If Iphigenia had actually sacrificed Orestes, that would have been incurable and could have been tragic. If all three of the protagonists had been recaptured and killed, that would have been incurable and possibly tragic. But Athena intervenes, they all get away, and furthermore the chorus of captured Greek girls get to go home too.

The essence of this new dramatic form is that the characters are set to walk on the thin ice which separates them from the dark tragic waters; though they may crack the surface, they never quite break through. The genre is a virtuoso exercise in the creation of suspense, which ends with a happy escape from the incurable tragic act and suffering. But this new dramatic purpose is still expressed in and to some extent hampered by tragic form. There is still a chorus, for example (which has to be rescued *en masse* in *Iphigenia in Tauris*). But if the main purpose of the dramatist is to generate excitement from the danger

75

and eventual escape of the protagonists, how can the chorus do what it has always done? [18] How can it illuminate the deeper meaning of the action, trace its roots in the mythic past, explore its wider significance as a paradigm of man's condition, his relationship to his city and his gods? What has it to sing about? Nothing. And that is what it does sing about, very beautifully, with late-Euripidean lyric elegance, but it is still singing about nothing at all.[19] "Why should I dance the choral song?" the chorus of *Oedipus the King* asks. That question raises the main issue of the play and is answered in unmistakable terms by the outcome of the action. But this is a question which the choruses of the *Iphigenia in Tauris* and *Helen* had better not ask; it would only remind us that their choral songs are on the way to becoming mere musical interludes, the ἐμβόλιμα of Agathon, which could be put anywhere in the play or for that matter in any play.

The chorus is not the only awkward impediment to Euripides' new dramatic design; there is also the myth. The end of the road on which he has taken the first step, suppressing the dignity and terror of the tragic action, is the abandonment of myth altogether. This was of course the achievement of his younger contemporary, Agathon, who produced the first tragedy based on invented characters. But Euripides puts his new wine in the old bottles and though he chooses his myths carefully for their outlandishness (among Taurians, Egyptians, and, in the *Andromeda*, Ethiopians) and for their unfamiliarity to the audience (both Iphigenia and Helen have to explain their situation at length and with precision), the mythical figures and their associations keep suggesting that there are greater dimensions to the action—a suggestion which true tragedy can exploit, on which, in fact, it relies, but which now saddles Euripides with an incongruous element, a hint of seriousness clashing with the bright swiftness of his plot and the wit that distances us from his characters. In the *Helen* the heroic aspects of the Trojan myth are played down as much as possible except where they are used to pose a comic contrast; Menelaus, ordered off by an old gatekeeper woman who talks to him as if he were a beggar, recalls with regret his "famous armies," only to be told: "you may have been an important figure *there,* but you're not *here*" (453–454). And in the *Iphigenia* Euripides allows the myth to add a sort of false profundity to the action, false because unrelated: the themes of Greek versus barbarian ideas of morality, of human sacrifice and divinity and so on, like the antiquarian disquisitions on the Athenian Choës or the Artemis cult at Brauron, are grace notes, not a tragic bass.

Though these two plays brilliantly exploit the new tone and techniques, their exotic setting works against too heavy an emphasis on the domestic detail, the everyday round. But this is well to the fore in the *Ion,* a play which, in a sense still to be defined, is fully-fledged comedy —a work of genius in which the theater of Menander, almost a hundred years in the future, stands before us in firm outline.

Like the *Iphigenia* and the *Helen,* its plot depends on ignorance of identity, *agnoia,* and recognition, *anagnorisis.* A man comes from ignorance to knowledge, solves the mystery of his birth, and knows for the first time who he is. That is the plot of the *Ion* and also of Sophocles' *Oedipus the King.* The resemblances between these two plays are, in fact, remarkable.[20] Both turn on oracles of Apollo, both contain a mother who exposed the child which she has now every reason to think is dead (but is alive); in both the hero fears that his unknown mother may turn out to be a slave (but in fact she is a queen); Oedipus killed his father and Ion threatens to kill his (supposed) father Xuthus. But between the two plays there is all the difference in the world. For the recognition, which is the catastrophe of the one, is in the other the happy solution of the potentially tragic deadlock. *Oedipus the King* presents the tragic spectacle of man's recognition of his real status, not god but man, not ruler but ruled, blind, not all-seeing. But the *Ion* presents a similar situation in fundamentally different terms: the recognition, the hero's realization of his identity, is not a tragic climax but a happy ending—what made Oedipus the King an outcast makes Ion the slave a king.

The play begins with a prologue spoken by a god, Hermes. But this is not the dread Hermes, conductor of the dead, invoked by Orestes in the *Choëphoroe*: he introduces himself as "manservant of the gods [δαιμόνων λάτριν]" (4) as he recounts the background events in which he played a part—the part of "manservant" to his elder brother Apollo. He carried off the child of Apollo and Creusa (whom its mother had abandoned) and "doing my brother a favor," as he puts it, left the child on the steps of the temple at Delphi, where it was rescued by the priestess and brought up as a temple servant. Creusa (who returned to find the child missing) was later married to a foreign prince, Xuthus.

77

But the marriage is childless, and they are on their way to Delphi to consult Apollo, Xuthus hoping for a son of his own to be born to Creusa, while she hopes that in some miraculous fashion Apollo will restore to her the vanished child. And that, Hermes tells us, is just what Apollo plans to do; he will give Ion to Xuthus as his own son (Hermes does not tell us how this delicate operation will be performed—Euripides holds that in reserve), Creusa will be told the truth when she gets home to Athens, Creusa's (and Apollo's) indiscretion will remain concealed from the world (and especially from Xuthus), and everything will be for the best. But here comes the boy himself, Hermes tells us: "I'll step aside into the laurel grove here, to find out what happens to him." And so he does, as Ion, a temple slave equipped with a broom made of laurel branches (103), some kind of water container (105–106), and a bow and arrows (108), comes out of the temple.

This is a very unusual beginning. Gods as prologue-speakers are no strangers to the Euripidean stage, but this Hermes is a world away from the menacing Aphrodite of the *Hippolytus,* the vengeful Dionysus of the *Bacchae,* the august figures of Poseidon and Athena who in the *Trojan Women* prologue plan the destruction of the Greek fleet. For one thing, unlike all these deities, who have urgent personal motives for appearing, Hermes has no business here at all. "I have come [ἥκω] to Delphi," he says, echoing similar formulas used by Poseidon and Dionysus, but unlike them, he does not tell us why; the only reason suggested (faintly) is curiosity about the outcome, "to learn what happens to the boy" (77)—an interesting statement in view of the fact that Apollo has planned everything down to the last detail. But even this suggestion is a mere dramatic pretext, for like his successors in New Comedy (Pan in the *Dyscolus,* for example and Tyche in the *Aspis*) Hermes has no part in the action and promptly vanishes from the play. His sole function is to explain the situation, and for that purpose, since the situation involves rape (11), concealment (14), and deceit (71), no better spokesman could be imagined than the "manservant of the gods"—λάτριν, a word which Aeschylus' *Prometheus* (966) used to insult him, but which this Hermes complacently applies to himself.[21]

Ion's monody opens with a brilliant evocation of sunrise at Delphi which is justly famous, but as it proceeds we learn that his duties, which he is performing, are to sweep the approach to the temple, water down the dust, and keep the birds away from the statues. He even sings a lyrical address to his broom (112 ff.), in which phrases like "O fresh-blooming instrument of service made of beautiful laurel . . . with which I sweep the floor of Phoebus all day long" remind us irresistibly of Aristophanes' merciless parody of Euripidean monody (*Frogs,* 1331 ff.), the point of which is precisely the ludicrous effect produced by the combination of high-flying lyric form and earth-bound content. The resemblance of all this to Electra and her water jug and still more to Silenus and his rake is only too clear, and the dithyrambic grace of Ion's warnings to the various birds he threatens with his arrows does not disguise the obvious fact that if he fails to keep them away from the statues he will soon be cleaning up bird droppings just as surely as Silenus is raking out sheep dung.

It might be expected that the entry of the chorus would at last strike the solemn note appropriate to tragedy, but this chorus, maidservants of Creusa, reinforces the holiday mood which has so far prevailed. Delphi was a tourist center in the ancient world as it is in the modern, and the girls are sightseers,[22] excitedly calling each other's attention to the pedimental sculptures, identifying the figures for all the world as if one of them had a *Guide Bleu* in hand. Finally in an inspired bit of byplay, they ask the museum attendant, Ion, if they can go inside, and like so many of their modern counterparts, get a short negative answer.[23]

Creusa and Ion feel an immediate sympathy; he admires her nobility of appearance, and she his courteous manner. She tells him, in answer to his questions, the story of her marriage to Xuthus, a foreigner (he expresses polite surprise, 293), and of their childlessness; Ion, questioned in turn, confesses that he has no name, no known parents, and is a temple slave—his mother must have abandoned him. Which reminds Creusa of a friend of hers, who abandoned her child; he would now have been about the same age as Ion, and his father—well, his father was Apollo. Suddenly the real purpose of her presence here is revealed: while Xuthus is off making preliminary enquiries at the oracle of Trophonius, she has come to make a secret enquiry about the child—her friend's child—and asks Ion to take the matter up with the Pythia. He points out that such a request would put Apollo in an awkward position and no

79

servant of the god will run the risk of doing that. As Xuthus comes on stage, Creusa hurriedly begs Ion not to say a word about the matter; Xuthus might not approve, and the thing might get out of hand. She is afraid that "the story might develop along lines other than those we have pursued" (396–397)—an admirably diplomatic formula.

Xuthus goes in to consult the oracle and comes out wild with excitement to meet Ion, whom he rushes forward to embrace, for, as we learn later, he has been told by Apollo that the first man he meets will be his own true son. The ensuing dialogue, in racing tetrameters, here for the first time employed in tragedy for undeniably comic effect, is one of Euripides' most brilliant scenes. One feature of it which has not been sufficiently emphasized (in fact it has often been suppressed) is the ambiguity of the word Xuthus uses to address Ion in the opening lines, τέκνον. It can mean "son" but it can also mean simply "child" or "boy." [24] Since in the dramatic circumstances it cannot possibly occur to Ion that it means "son," the only explanation of Xuthus' conduct likely to recommend itself to him is that this middle-aged man is making vigorous sexual advances to him. This too is the only valid explanation of the violence of Ion's reaction (524); if an older man rushes towards you asking to kiss your hand and embrace you, you might well think him crazy and push him away if he also addresses you as "my son," but it is only if he calls you "boy" that you will threaten him with a weapon. The ambiguity is essential to an understanding of the opening lines, and yet it is ignored in most commentaries [25] and suppressed by translators, who consistently have Xuthus hail Ion as his son in the opening line. There is no excuse for this; it was clearly explained by Wilamowitz long ago,[26] and he is certainly right; no one conversant with fifth-century Athenian ways can doubt it, and the art of the period is rich in apposite illustrations, from the red-figure vases on which bearded men court boys with gifts of tame birds and unmistakable gestures, to the self-satisfied smile on the face of the terracotta Zeus at Olympia as he carries Ganymede off in his arms.

But let the scene speak for itself. The rough translation which follows, far from exaggerating the comic element, falls far short of it for want of a modern English tragic style to accentuate the contrast between form and content.

Xuthus.   Boy, be happy. That's the only
        formula that fits the case.
Ion (retreating).   I'm quite happy. You be quiet
          and we'll both be better off.
X.   Let me kiss your hand, enfold you
   in my arms in fond embrace.
I.   Are you in your right mind, stranger?
   Has the god deranged your wits?
X.   Right mind? I've just found my dearest.
   Why not rush into his arms?
I.   (still retreating). Stop it! Don't you paw me. You'll
         destroy Apollo's laurel wreaths.
X.   I *will* touch you. I'm not stealing;
   you're my dearest, found at last.
I.   (picks up bow and arrow).
   Get your hands off me or you'll get
   arrows in those lungs of yours!
X.   Why do you repel me? Don't you
   recognize your dearest love?
I.   One thing I *don't* love is putting
   crazy foreigners in their place.
X.   Kill me, burn me, then, your father,
   that's who you'll be murdering.
I.   You my father? How can that be?
   You my father? What a laugh! [27]
X.   Wait. If you'll just listen to me
   I'll explain my point of view.
I.   What have you to say?
                  X.   Your father—
I'm your father, you're my son.
I.   Who says so?
           X.   The god Apollo
brought you up, but you're my son.
I.   Don't you need another witness?
X.   Just Apollo's oracle.
I.   You misunderstood some riddle.
X.   Not if I can trust my ears.
I.   Exactly what *did* Phoebus tell you?
X.   That the first man I should meet—
I.   Where and when?
           X.   Coming from the temple,
   from the oracle of the god—
I.   Well, and what's supposed to happen?

X. —that man is my own true son.

I. Yours by birth or a gift in some way?

X. A gift, and yet my very own.

I. And I'm the first one you ran into?
No one else? X. Just you, my child.

I. That's a curious combination.

X. Yes. I'm overwhelmed myself.

I. Yes, but, in that case, who's my mother?

X. There you have me, I don't know.

I. Phoebus didn't tell you? X. I was
so delighted I didn't ask.

I. Earth must be my mother. X. Hm.
The earth does not bear children, though.

I. How *can* I be yours? X. I don't know,
I refer it to the god.

I. Well, let's try investigation.

X. Anything you say, my son.

I. Did you have an affair with someone?

X. Yes, when I was young and wild.

I. Before you married Erechtheus' daughter?

X. Naturally. I've since reformed.

I. That was when you got me, was it?

X. Yes . . . the times *do* coincide.

I. In that case how did I get to Delphi?

X. I don't have the slightest clue.

I. It's a long way from Achaea.

X. Yes, that's what is puzzling *me*.

I. Did you ever come here to Delphi?

X. Yes, for Bacchus' festival.

I. And you stayed with one of the locals?

X. Yes. There were some Delphian girls . . .

I. He introduced you to their circle?

X. Yes, and to their Bacchic rites.

I. And you, how were you, drunk or sober?

X. Well, I wasn't feeling pain.

I. That's *it*—the hour of my conception!

X. Fate has found you out, my son.

Ion, rather reluctantly, accepts his new father, but when told he is to come to Athens, he speculates gloomily on his status there as an outsider, the base-born son of a foreigner, and on the fact that his situation vis-à-vis Creusa will be, to put it mildly, delicate. But Xuthus has it all figured out (like Apollo). He will take Ion along with him "as

82

a sightseer [θεατὴν]" (656) and then, on some propitious occasion, he'll tell Creusa the truth. He's sure he can bring her around. He orders the chorus, on pain of death, to keep Creusa in the dark and rushes off to prepare a huge feast. But the chorus does tell Creusa, and there is nothing comic about the tormented aria in which she blurts out the whole story of her lost child and reproaches Apollo for his heartlessness. The chorus and the old man she has brought with her—the tutor of Erechtheus, a fierce guardian of the blood-purity of the royal line—are appalled. But the old man, though he had trouble climbing the steep approach to the temple, is not slow to urge action ("I may be slow in the foot," he says, "but I'm quick in the head," 742), and proposes revenge on the god who has acted unjustly. "I am a mere mortal," Creusa replies. "How shall I prevail against higher powers?" The old man's answer suggests that we are not to take all this too seriously. "Burn down the holy oracle of Apollo!" "I am afraid," she says. "I've got trouble enough already"—καὶ νῦν πημάτων ἅδην ἔχω (975). The suggestion that she kill Xuthus she rejects, for he was good to her once, but she accepts with alacrity the idea of killing the boy; Ion, the bastard son of a foreign interloper, shall never reign in Athens. The old man is sent off to poison Ion's wine at the feast Xuthus has prepared.

The attempt fails, the old man confesses, and Ion leads the hue and cry after Creusa, who takes refuge at the altar. The deadlock is resolved by the priestess who once found the child on the temple steps; hearing that Ion is leaving for Athens, she comes to bring him the cradle in which he was left—it may help him some day to find his mother. Creusa recognizes it, and by describing its contents convinces Ion that he is her child. But it is not so easy to convince him that Apollo is his father; he knows that Apollo told Xuthus a different story. He goes toward the temple to resolve his doubts "whether the god is a true prophet or a false" (1537). But this potentially embarrassing interview never takes place; Athena appears, to speak for Apollo, since, she says, the god himself thought it better not to face them "lest blame for things past should come into the open." But all will be well. Ion will go to Athens, succeed to the throne, and become the ancestor of all the Ionians. Xuthus will never know the truth about Ion, but Creusa will bear him sons, Dorus and Achaeus, who will be the ancestors of the rest of the Hellenic nation.

This play is clearly a step beyond the plays of recognition in far-off lands and escape from the barbarians. The scene is Delphi, the background Athens and Athenian patriotic myth; the familiarity of the surroundings is emphasized by insistence on domestic detail. And the pattern of recognition followed by deceit has been transformed: here the recognition is delayed until near the end of the play,[28] while deceit, used not by Greeks against barbarians, but by husband against wife, wife against husband, son against father, mother against son, and Apollo against them all, winds its complex threads throughout the entire play. There is only one reminiscence of the old pattern; in the end one character remains deceived—Xuthus, and he is, if not a barbarian, at least a foreigner.

It is time to document the claim that this extraordinary play is the prototype of comedy in the modern sense of the word. Definitions of comedy are notoriously inadequate, and I do not propose to attempt a new one; I shall be content if I can demonstrate that the *Ion* is the first drama we know of which contains in combination those elements which characterize the standard comic form as we see it in Menander, Plautus, Shakespeare, Molière, and all the way to Oscar Wilde.

First and foremost, the undeniably comic element of scenes which provoke laughter. No matter how ambitious or intellectual comedy may aim to be, it cannot dispense with this element; even the *Tempest* has its drunken butler and mooncalf, *Dom Juan* its Sganarelle, *Tartuffe* its Orgon. The *Ion* has not only its broadly comic Xuthus-Ion scene but a score of light touches here and there which must have caused, if not outright laughter, at least a smile. This laugh, even the smile, is something tragedy at its most intense dare not risk; there is no humor in *Oedipus the King*; one smile would have dissipated the almost unbearable tension on which Sophocles relies to sustain belief in the hopelessly improbable situation and one good laugh would have shattered the illusion once and for all.

Secondly, the action is set in a context which emphasizes domestic realities—food and drink, clothing and shelter, cooking and cleaning, the normal human round. Ion's humble duties are emphasized not merely in the opening scene but throughout: the chorus identifies him for Creusa as "that young man who was sweeping the temple" (794–795), and the play contains a long description of a feast (Ion's birthday party) at which the wine flows freely. This emphasis is constant in comedy: Caliban has to "scrape trenchering" and "wash dish," and his reply to Prospero's threats is "I must eat my dinner"; Falstaff's tavern bill shows "one half-penny-worth of bread to this intolerable deal of sack," and in *The Merry Wives* he is hidden in a laundry basket and covered with foul linen; Dom Juan is eating (and Sganarelle is trying to) when the statue knocks on the door; and no one is likely to forget the cucumber sandwiches of *The Importance of Being Earnest*.

These two elements of comedy, broad humor and the emphasis on mundane detail, are Euripides' most striking innovations, and their source is not in doubt; they are both regular ingredients of the satyr play. The next feature of this prototype of comedy, the hairsbreadth escape from catastrophe, appears also in the plays of recognition and escape, the *Iphigenia in Tauris* and the *Helen*. This close brush with the incurable tragic act—Ion and Creusa narrowly avoid the fates of Orestes and Medea—becomes a standard feature of comedy, which generates the excitement of tragic potentiality but spares us the pity and fear caused by its fulfillment. Hegio in Plautus' *Captives* is on the point of killing his son Tyndareus, but relents and sends him off to the quarries to be recognized and welcomed later; Antonio and Sebastian are about to kill Alonso—"then let us both be sudden"—when Ariel intervenes; Tartuffe's triumph is complete, but the police official, to his surprise (and ours) arrests *him* instead of Orgon; Macheath is led off to be hanged, but the Player objects—"Why then, friend, this is a downright deep tragedy. The catastrophe is manifestly wrong"—and Macheath is spared; Tom Jones tumbles into bed with one Mrs. Waters and it turns out that she is probably his mother and Tom a sort of Gloucestershire Oedipus, but it's all right—she's not. Comedy skirts the edge of the tragic frontier, but retreats just in time.

The next significant feature of the *Ion*, the presentation of the recognition not as catastrophe (*Oedipus the King*), nor as the prelude to the tragic action (the three Electra plays), or escape (*Iphigenia in Tauris* and *Helen*), but as the happy ending, seems to have no precedent in drama but becomes, from this point on, through Menander, Plautus, Terence, *Twelfth Night, Cymbeline, L'Avare,* and *The Importance of Being Earnest,* the stock comic solution, "la fin d'une vraie et pure comédie," as Mascarille introduces the double recognition which ends Molière's *L'Étourdi*. The delayed prologue of Menander's *Perikeiromene* is delivered by a goddess who had neither temple nor priest—Agnoia, mistaken identity; she mercifully explains the extremely complicated situation for which she is responsible. In Greek society exposure of unwanted children and enslavement by war or piracy gave a certain plausibility to the recognition of a slave girl as an heiress or a temple slave as a prince; in modern comedy the effect is usually obtained by disguise, as with Viola and Sebastian in *Twelfth Night* (they almost kill each other in a duel), or by robbing the cradle (as in *Cymbeline*). It takes an Oscar Wilde to have his hero left by the charwoman in a bag at the Victoria Station cloakroom. Of course, to bring about the recognition there must be some stage property left with the baby to be brought out at the critical moment, like the cradle and the snake-bracelet in the *Ion*, or, as in *Cymbeline*, "a most curious mantle, wrought by the hand of his queen mother, which, for more probation, I can with ease produce." (Act V, Scene 5).

In the *Ion* ignorance of identity is dramatically exploited in virtuoso fashion. The unknown identity is that of Ion—only Apollo and Hermes know it. Before the play is over we have seen a false as well as a true recognition; Ion has been taken for the son of three different mothers and two fathers. The happy solution has an ironic twist: both Xuthus and Creusa accept Ion as their son, each one thinking (correctly, in Creusa's case) that the other is deceived. This ending is like that of *Tom Jones*. Is Tom a bastard or a true man? He ends up a squire, but he is still a bastard. Only, like Ion, he happens to be the bastard son of the right person.[29]

The happy ending of comedy is, as in the *Ion*, a restoration of normalcy, an "integration of society," as Northrop Frye puts it, "which usually takes the form of incorporating a central character into it." [30] Ion is restored to his proper station, in his family (son returns to mother) and his city (from slavery to freedom, indeed to royalty). This characteristic of comedy was long ago remarked by Euanthius (*illic prima turbulenta, tranquilla ultima*) [31] and the restoration may take many forms: of individual to proper status, of balance between the sexes (*The Taming of the Shrew*), of order in the state (the return of the

Duke in *Measure for Measure*), or a deeper spiritual restoration as in the finale of *The Tempest*—

> In one voyage
> did Claribel her husband find in Tunis
> and Ferdinand her brother found a wife
> where he himself was lost; Prospero his dukedom
> in a poor isle, and all of us ourselves
> where no man was his own.

Further, this restoration of normalcy reaffirms, as in the *Ion,* the traditional values of society. Tragedy presents the hero overthrown, though he is magnificent in defeat; a world collapses in and with him, never to be restored. It is the rejection of all normal standards of success, of all comforting moralities, the naked exposure of the fault in things, a view of the abyss. But comedy leaves us with a sense that the standards of this world, though not perfect, are sound: there is no flaw in the universe, only misunderstandings, maladjustments; once restoration is achieved, all is peaceful, *tranquilla ultima,* and everyone gets his just deserts. "Voilà par sa mort un chacun satisfait," says Sganarelle as Dom Juan goes down in flames. "Ciel offensé, lois violées, filles séduites, familles déshonorées . . . maris poussés à bout—tout le monde est content." The chorus closes the *Ion* with a similar assurance that justice governs the universe:

> In the end the good and noble all enjoy their just reward,
> but the low and evil natures never prosper in this world.

This uninspired jingle (translation, for once, offers no insoluble problem) is a far cry from the lines that end the *Bacchae*:

> Many are the shapes of divine dispensation
> many the unexpected decisions of the gods.
> What we expected is not fulfilled
> for what we never thought of the god found a way.

Furthermore, in comedy as in the *Ion,* the traditional values which are reaffirmed are those of an exclusive group, social, racial, or national. Comedy depends on a feeling (shared by the audience) of cohesion and exclusiveness, of a common identity which resents and repels outsiders; part of the pattern of restoration, in fact, is the expulsion of the intruder, balancing the readmission of the lost or disguised group member. This intruder is of course the most comic figure in the cast, the pretender, the *alazon,* and at the end of the play he is restored to his proper (lower) station, like Parolles, the "gallant militarist," who is exposed as a "past-saving slave," Malvolio, who, believing that greatness is thrust upon him, is "most notoriously abused," and Falstaff, who cried, "The laws of England are at my commandment!" but was greeted by his "sweet boy," now king, with the words, "fool and jester." In the *Ion* this figure is, of course, Xuthus, the only character who is presented in broadly comic vein; he is a foreigner in an Athenian society which jealously guarded the privileges of hereditary citizenship (therein lies the relevance of Ion's long speech about the trials that await him in Athens), and Xuthus' final deception is accepted as just return for his presumption—his plan to put what he thinks is his illegitimate son on the throne of Athens. Xuthus' foreignness is emphasized by Creusa, the old man, Ion, and by Xuthus himself, who quickly dismisses Ion's suggestion that the earth may have been his mother, though Athenian tradition (recited not once but almost *ad nauseam* in the play) claimed just such a birth for Erichthonius, Creusa's grandfather.

Xuthus, the intruder, the comic butt, has one more characteristic which is to become a standard ingredient of the comic recipe—his wife is the mother of someone else's child. The real father is a god, and of course many tragic husbands found themselves in the same position, Amphitryon, for example, in the *Heracles.* But Amphitryon knew that he was "the bed-fellow of Zeus" and was proud of it. Xuthus is ignorant of Ion's true paternity, and, what is more, he is tricked by the real father (who has an oracle at his disposal) into believing (though everyone else in the play finally knows the truth) that Ion is his own flesh and blood. Such a situation of blissful ignorance is a constant fear of the comedy father, in Athens as elsewhere; "we none of us know whose son we are," runs a fragment from Menander's *Carthaginian*; "we just suspect or believe." [32] And a fragment attributed to both Euripides and Menander runs: "The mother loves her child more than the father; she knows it's hers and he just thinks it's his." [33] The Athenian marriage formula ran, "for the begetting of legitimate children" [34]—a formula which Molière could not have known but which sounds very like Mascarille's prayer before his marriage: "que les Cieux prospères/nous donnent des enfants dont nous sommes les pères." Around the head of Xuthus, the deceived but happy husband, floats a prophetic aura of things to come; he is the prototype of the farcical St. Joseph of the medieval mystery plays and of Machiavelli's Messer Nicia.

All this, taken together, seems to justify the claim that in the *Ion* Euripides invented what was to become the master pattern of Western comedy. The ingredients of the comic mixture come from different sources: from tragedy, from satyr play, from his own invention. The real originality lies in their combination, and the success of that combination can be judged from the fact that down through the centuries comic dramatists have returned to the formula time and again.

And yet Euripides did have a model, a predecessor, though he was not a dramatist. As in almost every field of Greek poetry the great original is Homer. The *Iliad* is the model for tragedy (especially for Sophocles) and the *Odyssey* contains almost all of the elements Euripides combined to create dramatic comedy. The emphasis on domestic routine and food is remarkable throughout; Eumaeus tends swine, Eurycleia washes the beggar's feet, while Odysseus himself announces frequently that man's hungry belly is what drives him on,[35] and as for the meals, Fielding called the *Odyssey*, not without justice, the "eatingest epic." The hairsbreadth escapes are many and various, though the crucial one stems from Odysseus' decision not to go straight to the palace; he goes disguised as a beggar and mistaken identity is followed by recognition, which is the happy ending—the slaughter of the suitors and Odysseus' restoration as husband and king. The suitors are upstart intruders, usurping the place of a hero of the Trojan war, and they are very definitely put in their places, though they are not treated comically. But there is an occasional touch of broad humor, the most remarkable being the song of Demodocus about Ares and Aphrodite trapped in the golden web, and this even presents us with a deceived husband. Finally, the normal, popular standards of justice are reaffirmed; everyone gets his just deserts. And on this point Aristotle remarked: "The poem has a double plot and also an opposite catastrophe for the good and the bad . . . the pleasure, however, derived from this is not that of tragedy. It is proper rather to comedy . . ."[36]

There is, of course, one aspect of the *Ion* which I have neglected entirely, an important one—for some critics, in fact, it is the most important one of all. I mean the religious problem posed by the play: what are we to make of Apollo? The play begins with a description of a god's intention and plan, a clear, logical design. So does the *Hippolytus*. But in that play the plan works inexorably through to its hideous end. In the *Ion* it comes completely unstuck: everything goes wrong. Mother and son come within an ace of killing each other, and though this unforeseen calamity is avoided, the whole story of Creusa and Apollo is published to the world, whereas its continued suppression, Hermes told us, was one of Apollo's principal objectives—γάμοι τε Λοξίου κρυπτοὶ γένωνται (72–73). And in the end, when Ion goes to the temple to demand the truth from Apollo, Athena prevents the confrontation: Apollo, for fear of "blame for the past," does not appear.

Explanations of this treatment, unique in tragedy, of a major Olympian figure [37] fall into three main groups. Verrall and many who follow his lead but avoid his excesses see Euripides the Rationalist at his most trenchant, exposing the absurdity not only of the myth but also of the Olympian religion. Wilamowitz and many after him see political factors involved; Apollo had predicted a Spartan victory in the war and was a safe target. A modern school of interpreters, stressing the emphasis on religious and mythical motifs in the play, tries to reclaim it as religious in feeling; Apollo's divine benevolence is almost foiled by human ignorance and folly.[38]

These explanations remain unconvincing: each is a partial solution which only throws more emphasis on those aspects of the play it fails to explain. But once we regard the play as an entirely new medium, a tragedy written in the comic mode, the whole problem disappears. For in comedy the gods are neither attacked nor defended; they take their place with human beings in a world where nothing too much is expected except that things shall turn out right in the end—*tranquilla ultima*. Aristophanes can present Dionysus in his own theater as a coward and buffoon, a blasphemous buffoon at that,[39] or Zeus overthrown by a couple of Athenian tax dodgers in the *Birds*, without anyone's believing that he is trying to undermine religion. On the contrary, Aristophanes is always given full marks, not always deserved, for religious and political conservatism. Here again Euripides seems to have taken a hint from

90

the comic poets. Ironic, but also sympathetic, his new vision embraces gods as well as men: the acceptance of limitations, weakness, passions, and mistakes extends even to Olympus. To err may be human, but in the *Ion* it is also divine.

In a papyrus fragment, discovered early in this century, of a life of Euripides by Satyrus, the following headless sentence occurs: "towards wife, and father towards son, and servant towards master and also the whole business of vicissitudes, raping of young women, substitutions of children, recognitions by means of rings and necklaces. For these are of course the main elements of the New Comedy, and Euripides brought them to perfection." Denys Page, with that confidence we cannot help but admire, once proposed a correction—"Menander" for "Euripides" [40] —but no one seems to have followed his lead. And Philemon, who in the fourth century put into the mouth of one of his characters the lines,

> If I were sure of life beyond the grave
> I'd hang myself—to meet Euripides,[41]

was not a tragic, but a comic poet.

The Center for Hellenic Studies
Washington, D.C.

NOTES

1. In the context it would seem to refer to the prevalence of unhappy endings in his plays: αἱ πολλαὶ αὐτοῦ εἰς δυστυχίαν τελευτῶσιν (1453ᵃ25). But, as D. W. Lucas (Aristotle, *Poetics*, Oxford, 1968) points out (p. 147): "it is not clear that Euripides was addicted specially to the unhappy ending." (He quotes Gudemann's computation: "unhappy Soph. 43, Eur. 46; happy Soph. 16, Eur. 24".) Lucas himself thinks that "taken in its context this famous aphorism must mean that Euripides excels in arousing pity and fear" and interprets: "most tragic in the sense that he is the most heart-rending of the poets." He rejects R. C. Jebb's "most sensational" (*Attic Orators*, I, ci) on the grounds that this meaning of τραγικώτατος is "unexampled at this date." But Jebb cites Hyperides 3, col. 37, τραγῳδίας (which J. O. Burtt in the Loeb edition renders as "theatrical complaints"), and he might have added the similar [τραγ]ω(ι)δίας γράψαι in 2, col. 10, as well as Demosthenes 18. 13, ἐτραγῴδει; 19. 189, τραγῳδεῖ.
2. Some critics have come close to the edge. L. Parmentier, *Euripide* IV (Paris, 1925), p. 186 (preface to the *Electra*): "Euripide . . . a écrit pour ses contemporains

les plus épris de la nouveauté, et, pressentant la sorte de théâtre que réclamerait bientôt
son peuple, il a introduit dans certains de ses drames le genre d'intérêt et le ton qui
devaient aboutir bientôt à la comédie moyenne et à la comédie nouvelle." Wolf H.
Friedrich, *Euripides und Diphilos* (Munich, 1953), Zetemata V, p. 10: "Keine der
erhaltenen attischen Tragödien ist geeigneter als diese [i.e., the *Ion*] den Übergang zur
Komödie, insbesondere zu Menander, zu bilden."

3. Cf. J. P. Mahaffy, *A History of Classical Literature* (London, 1891), I,
part II, 5: "Plato hazards as a mere drunken fantasy what Shakespeare has realized for
us—the compatibility of tragic and comic genius in the same poet."

4. The new *Aspis* of Menander gives us a comic parallel for this phrase: the cook
lists among the kinds of domestic events which cancel feasts and deprive him of a job,
ἢ τέτοκε τῶν ἔνδον κυοῦσά τις λάθρα (*Menandri Aspis et Samia I*, ed. C. Austin
[Berlin, 1969], p. 12, l. 218).

5. Aristophanes, *Acharnians*, ll. 418 ff.

6. Even if the other imperatives are thought of as addressed by Electra to herself,
θές with ἐμῆς in l. 140 must be addressed to someone else. J. D. Denniston in
Euripides, Electra (Oxford, 1939), pp. 64–65, presents the opposing views on this
point and comes (reluctantly) to the conclusion that Electra does have an attendant.
"Certainly, an attendant is somewhat superfluous in this scene, and the presence of one
impairs the emotional force of Electra's outburst. But these considerations cannot
outweigh the linguistic intractability of ἐμῆς. Θές, then, must be addressed to the
attendant."

7. L. 355, οὐκοῦν τὰ μὲν λεύσσουσι, τὰ δὲ σύ που λέγεις.

8. The translation attempts to reproduce the effect of ἔν τε μικροῖς (l. 407) ἐν
σμικροῖσιν (l. 408).

9. It has, however, been variously appraised. Denniston, *Euripides, Electra*, p. xxxi,
finds the scene in which Electra scolds her husband "charmingly done" and the farmer's
comment at ll. 77–78 a "delightful touch," but Keene's commentary, *The Electra of
Euripides* (London, 1893), is unrelievedly serious throughout, as is that of G. Schiassi,
Euripide, Elettra (Bologna, 1955). H. D. F. Kitto, *Greek Tragedy*, 3d ed. (London,
1961), p. 333, n.1, refers under the heading "Realism" to "the invitation to the festival (167 ff.), Electra's nagging of her husband (404 ff.), and the general atmosphere
of domesticity." Parmentier, *Euripide* IV, p. 179, speaks of "un ton de parodie . . .
nous avons la fille acariâtre qui se trouve si malheureuse d'être mal mariée, mal vêtue, mal
parée et mal coiffée . . . nous avons la martyre avouant qu'elle va sans nécessité
puiser elle-même l'eau à la rivière . . ." Schlegel, of course, thought the *Electra* the
"allerschlechteste" Euripidean tragedy precisely because of the untragic treatment of
the situation: "Durch seine Absichten ist es wenigstens keine Tragödie geworden, er
hat es vielmehr auf alle Weise zum Familiengemälde, in der heutigen Bedeutung des
Wortes, heruntergearbeitet" (*Vorlesungen über dramatische Kunst and Literatur*,
Erster Teil (Stuttgart, 1966), p. 120.

10. This scene has alway been a stumbling block for admirers of Euripidean tragedy
and in many an embarrassed defense of it we can almost read between the lines

Goethe's fervent wish for *Antigone*, ll. 904 ff.: "I would give a good deal if some qualified philologist could prove to us that it is an interpolation." A learned and powerful attempt to do so was made by E. Fraenkel in an appendix to his edition of Aeschylus' *Agamemnon* (Oxford, 1950), 3. 815–826; he revives and reinforces a suggestion by A. Mau as a necessary corollary of his own condemnation of the corresponding portion of the recognition-scene in the *Choëphoroe*. His arguments are respectfully but efficiently countered by H. Lloyd-Jones in the *Classical Quarterly*, n.s. XI (1961), 171–181. F. Solmsen, in a careful and enlightening analysis, "Electra and Orestes. Three Recognitions in Greek Tragedy," *Mededelingen der Koninkluke nederlandse Akademie van Wetenschappen, AFD.* Letterkunde, Nieuwe Reeks Deel XXX, no. 2 (Amsterdam, 1967), demonstrates the dramatic appropriateness of the three tokens of recognition in each of the two scenes.

11. I have mentioned only the high-points, but of course there is much more: the farmer's down-to-earth reflections on the uses of wealth, ll. 426 ff., for example; Electra's fierce rejection of the idea that Orestes would come back in disguise for fear of Aegisthus (ll. 524 ff.); Orestes' enquiry about the old man (ll. 553–554) which runs (the translation is Denniston's): "To which of your friends, Electra, does this ancient relic of humanity belong?"

12. Aeschylus, *Persians*, l. 490 (the Persians short of food on the retreat), *Agamemnon*, l. 331 (the Greeks breakfast in Troy), l. 1597 (the banquet of Thyestes), ll. 1621–1622 (Aegisthus threatens the chorus with starvation), Sophocles, *Antigone*, l. 775 (the food to be left in Antigone's prison-tomb), Euripides, *Hippolytus*, l. 112 (H. will eat before feeding the horses), l. 275 (Phaedra will not eat; cf. *Medea*, l. 24), *Suppliants*, ll. 864–866 (Capaneus a moderate eater).

13. Cf. V. Steffen, *Satyrographorum Graecorum Fragmenta* (Poznan, 1952): Aristias, frs. 3, 4; Aeschylus, frs. 39, 46, 47, 75–76; Sophocles, frs. 8, 40, 42, 47, 89, 123, 130, 131, 147, 158; Euripides, frs. 12, 31, 39, 43; Ion, frs. 10, 11, 18; Achaeus, frs. 1, 5, 7, 12, 14, 21, 31.

14. *Alcestis*, ll. 780 ff., *Cyclops*, ll. 336 ff.

15. Aristophanes, *Frogs*, ll. 980 ff., tr. Richmond Lattimore.

16. See the fundamental article of F. Solmsen, "Zur Gestaltung des Intrigenmotivs in den Tragödien des Sophokles und Euripides," *Philologus* LXXXVII (1932), 1–17, reprinted in *Euripides*, ed. Ernst-Richard Schwinge, Wege der Forschung LXXXIX (Darmstadt, 1968).

17. Aristotle, *Poetics*, 1453[b] 35. Nietzsche, *Menschliches Allzumenschliches* II, 23 "unheilbar."

18. Cf. Kitto, *Greek Tragedy*, 3d ed., pp. 339 ff.: "The Chorus in New Tragedy."

19. In *Helen* the first regular stasimon is not sung until l. 1107. Its last stanza (ll. 1151 ff.) speaks of the folly of the war at Troy, but the connection of this sentiment with the events witnessed on stage is artificial, to say the least. The next stasimon (ll. 1301 ff.), which describes the sorrows of Demeter (Cybele), makes some kind of connection between this theme and Helen's situation, but the text is corrupt and obscure, and we do not know and cannot guess what it was. Much has been made

93

of this vexed passage but the most recent comment on it, by A.M. Dale, *Euripides.
Helen* (Oxford, 1967), p. 147, seems the soundest: "There is no room for more than a
hint, and indeed more would only have emphasized the complete irrelevance of this
motif to all the rest of the play. . . . The ode is in fact introduced for its own
sake." The third and last stasimon is elegant embroidery. In the *Iphigenia in Tauris* the
first two stasima express in varied ways the nostalgia of the chorus; the third and last
tells how Apollo slew the dragon Python and took over the oracle at Delphi. The
relevance of this is far to seek; arguments that begin like Seidler's (summarized by
Paley) "as the plot of the play turns on Apollo's oracle being proved right . . ."
only serve to point up the contrast between this play and the *Oedipus the King,* where
the truth of Apolline prophecy really is an issue and is so treated.

20. Cf. D. J. Conacher, "Some Profane Variations on a Tragic Theme," *Phoenix* 23,
I (1969), 26–33.

21. The same word is twice applied to Hermes in Sophocles' *Inachus,* where he helps
Zeus in his love-affair with Io. Cf. D. L. Page, *Greek Literary Papyri* (Cambridge,
Mass., and London, 1941), p. 24, Διὸς . . . λάτρις and V. Steffen S. *Gr. Fr.,* p. 170,
Ζηνὸς . . . λάτριν. Whether the *Inachus* was a tragedy or a satyr play is still a
question; cf. W. M. Calder III, "The Dramaturgy of Sophocles' *Inachos,*" *Greek and
Byzantine Studies,* 1. 2 (1958), 137 ff., and R. Pfeiffer "Ein neues Inachos-Fragment des
Sophokles," *Bayerische Akademie der Wissenschaften Philosophisch-Historische Klasse*
(Sitzungsberichte-Jahrgang 1958), heft 6, who thinks that the new fragment reinforces
his earlier opinion (*Bay. Ak.* etc., II [1938], 26–62) that it was a satyr play. Pfeiffer's
view is reinforced (by reference to vase-paintings) by C. Pavese, "L'Inaco di Sofocle,"
Quaderni Urbinati di Cultura Classica, III (1967), 31–50.

22. Euripides repeats this device in *Iphigenia in Aulis:* the chorus consists of wives
(l. 176) from Chalcis (l. 168) who have come over to see the Greek fleet in which
their husbands will go to Troy. They give an exhaustive account (some critics have
thought it exhausting—and interpolated) of their sightseeing.

23. L. 221, οὐ θέμις, ὦ ξέναι.

24. For τέχνον used as a simple form of address by an older man to a younger, cf.
Sophocles, *Philoctetes,* l. 130 (Odysseus to Neoptolemus), l. 141 (chorus to Neoptole-
mus), l. 300 (Philoctetes to Neoptolemus), Euripides, *Electra,* l. 605 (old man to
Orestes).

25. An exception is G. M. Grube, *The Drama of Euripides* (New York, 1941), p.
266.

26. *Euripides. Ion* (Berlin, 1926), p. 111.

27. L. 528, ταῦτ' οὖν οὐ γέλως κλύειν ἐμοί;

28. See F. Solmsen "Euripides' *Ion* im Vergleich mit anderen Tragödien" *Hermes*
LXIX (1934), 390 ff. (Also reprinted in *Euripides,* ed. Schwinge, Wege der Forschung
LXXXIX).

29. Cf. Friedrich, *Euripides und Diphilos,* Zetemata V, p. 10: "Die Handlung . . .
endet schliesslich in Eironeia—in Vorsicht, Verschwiegenheit und sanftem Betrug."
He compares the ending of *Hecyra*

30. *Anatomy of Criticism* (Princeton, 1957; Atheneum ed., 1965), p. 43.

31. Euanthius, *Excerpta de Comoedia*, pp. 13–31 of Donatus, *Commentum Terenti*, ed. P. Wessner (Leipzig, 1902), vol. 1. The citation is on p. 21 and is worth quoting in full. "Inter tragoediam autem et comoediam cum multa tum imprimis hoc distat quod in comoedia mediocres fortunae hominum, parvi impetus periculorum laetique sunt exitus actionum, at in tragoedia omnia contra, ingentes personae, magni timores, exitus funesti habentur; et illic prima turbulenta tranquilla ultima, in tragoedia contrario ordine res aguntur; tum quod in tragoedia fugienda vita in comoedia capessenda exprimitur . . ."

32. Ed. Koerte-Thierfelder, *Menander, Reliquiae*, 2, fr. 227,

αὐτὸν γὰρ οὐθεὶς οἶδε τοῦ ποτ' ἐγένετο
ἀλλ' ὑπονοοῦμεν πάντες ἢ πιστεύομεν

33. A. Nauck, *Fragmenta tragicorum graecorum*, 2d ed., fr. 1015,

αἰεὶ δὲ μήτηρ φιλότεκνος μᾶλλον πατρός·
ἢ μὲν γὰρ αὐτῆς οἶδεν ὄνθ', ὃ δ' οἴεται.

34. Koerte-Thierfelder, *Menander*, 2, fr. 682, παίδων ἐπ' ἀρότῳ γνησίων and elsewhere. (It now turns up again in the new papyrus of the *Samia*—l. 727 in Austin's edition).

35. Odyssey, 15. 344; 18. 53–4; 17. 286. This last example,

γαστέρα δ' οὔ πως ἔστιν ἀποκρύψαι μεμαυῖαν
οὐλομένην, ἣ πολλὰ κάκ' ἀνθρώποισι δίδωσι,

was closely imitated by Euripides in an unknown play. (Nauck, *Fragmenta*, 2d. ed., fr. 915),

νικᾷ δὲ χρεία μ' ἡ κακῶς τ' ὀλουμένη
γαστὴρ ἀφ' ἧς δὴ πάντα γίγνεται κακά.

And this passage in turn was quoted with approval:

εὖ γ' ὁ κατάχρυσος εἶπε πολλ' Εὐριπίδης
νικᾷ κτλ.

by the comic poet Diphilus (ed. T. Kock, *Comicorum atticorum fragmenta*, fr. 60).

36. Aristotle, *Poetics*, 1453a 30 ff.

37. Apollo's oracle is condemned by the Dioscuri in *Electra*, ll. 1245 ff., but the tone and the occasion are serious. In the *Eumenides* he is outmaneuvered in the trial-scene by the Furies (ll. 640 ff.), but there is no loss of dignity comparable to that presented by the finale of the *Ion*. There Apollo is challenged in his own house of prophecy by his own dedicated servant but fails to appear. Instead, Athena comes "at a run" (l. 1556) to speak for him: Apollo "did not think it right [the word could also mean "did not deign" or simply "refused"] to come before your sight, lest blame for things past should come into the open" [or "come between you and him"—less likely]. Athena's statement that Apollo "has done all things well" (l. 1595) is followed by a justification which cannot gloss over that fact that the prophetic god par excellence failed to foresee the reactions of the human beings concerned to his plan for their welfare.

95

38. F. M. Wassermann, "Divine Violence and Providence in Euripides' *Ion*," *Transactions and Proceedings of the American Philological Association*, LXXI (1940), pp. 587–604. Anne Pippin Burnett, "Human Resistance and Divine Persuasion in Euripides' *Ion*," *Classical Philology*, LVII (1962), 89–103. Burnett's article, though it speaks of "man-made tragedy . . . transformed into providential comedy" (p. 101) takes the role of Apollo very seriously; he is "the one god who could embody the idea of mercy" and who "is chosen to represent the divinity which can restore life where death is threatened, and change guilt to blessedness" (p. 101). Even for those who cannot accept this conclusion the article is valuable for its perceptive discussion of individual passages, its subtle analysis of the dramatic structure, and also for the magisterial way in which it finally disposes of those Victorian moralistic attitudes towards Apollo's way of a god with a maid, which still, after all these years, confuse the issue.

39. Aristophanes, *Frogs*, l. 479, is the most obvious example.

40. D. L. Page, *Actors' Interpolations in Greek Tragedy* (Oxford, 1934), p. 220. ". . . Εὐριπίδης appears to be an error for Μένανδρος."

41. Ed. Kock, *Comicorum atticorum fragmenta*, 2, fr. 130.

RICHARD SCHECHNER

Actuals: A Look into Performance Theory

Tiwi society is established on what we would consider an absurdity. These north Australians make no connection between intercourse and pregnancy. The mother is the sole biological source of the child. The mother's husband controls his wives and his children; and of these he particularly values his daughters. Women, like money with us, are the main means of exchange. It is not necessary to detail the system. The result is that old men have young wives and young men, if they are lucky, marry crones.

Where there are old men with young wives and young men without sex mates there will be adultery. A Tiwi elder accuses a young man of adultery by coming to the center of the village, preferably on a feast day so he can be sure of a large crowd, and calling the offender out. The old man is painted white from head to toe. In one hand he carries some ceremonial spears and in the other hunting spears. A crowd arranges itself in an ellipse with the old man at one elongated end and the young man at the other. Everyone in the village and often out-groupers too, are present—men, women, children, dogs. They sit, stand, move about, according to their excitement. The young man is naked, except for a few strokes of white. The more white he wears the more defiant he declares himself to be. Perhaps he carries a spear or two or only a throwing stick. The old man begins a harangue of about twenty minutes' duration. He details the young man's worthlessness and ingratitude— talking not only of the offense at hand but the whole life of the young man. The old man stamps his feet and chews his beard: he puts on a

97

good show. The young man takes this verbal assault in silence. When the harangue is over the old man throws a hunting spear at the young man. The young man dodges—which is not hard to do because the old man is throwing from forty or fifty feet away. If the young man moves too far from the end of the ellipse the crowd jeers him. If the old man is wild in his throws, he is jeered. The trial/duel continues until the young man has dodged enough spears to prove his prowess, but not so many that he appears insolent. Allowing himself to be hit takes great skill, and the crowd enjoys a young man who takes a spear in the fleshy part of the thigh or the upper arm. There is much blood and no permanent harm. The young man is wounded, the crowd happily applauds both parties to the dispute. The old man's authority and dignity have been repaired and the young man's bravery and humility have been demonstrated.

Such is the Tiwi ritual combat according to the rules. But sometimes a young man is extremely defiant. He dodges too many of the old man's spears or he answers the harangue or he returns the old man's fire. In such cases the old man is joined by other old men, while still others restrain the relatives of the young man. Spears are thrown in volleys and the young man is driven from the village permanently, seriously wounded, or killed.

The Tiwi "trial" does not determine "right" or "wrong." It doesn't matter whether in fact the young man is guilty of adultery or whether there are extenuating circumstances. The trial is a test of the young man's willingness to confirm the authority of the old man. Whenever that authority offers itself for confirmation, Tiwi custom demands submission. Tiwi society rests on the authority of the old, and the only capital offense is defiance of that authority. The crowd enjoys the spectacle which makes the law tangible. If the ceremony were a true trial with a doubtful outcome, Tiwi society would collapse.

In 1967, Allan Kaprow composed *Fluids*, "a single event done in many places over a three-day period. It consists simply in building huge, blank, rectangular ice structures 30 feet long, 10 feet wide, and 8 feet high. The structures are built by people who decide to meet a truck carrying 650 ice blocks per structure. They set this thing up using rock salt as a binder—which hastens melting and fuses the blocks together. The structures are to be built [and were] in about 20 places throughout Los Angeles. If you were crossing the city you might suddenly be confronted by these mute and meaningless blank structures which have been left to melt. Obviously, what's taking place is a mystery of sorts." [1]

I could multiply examples of similar "mysteries." The tradition of happenings, from the Italian Futurists through the dadaists, surrealists, and on to practitioners of Earth Art [2] and other kinds of avant-gardists, introduces us to the idea that art is not a way of imitating reality or expressing states of mind. At the heart of what Kaprow calls mystery is the simple but altogether upsetting idea of art as an event—an "actual."

Plato in Book X of the *Republic* attacks the arts. "The tragic poet, too, is an artist who represents things; so this will apply to him; he and all other artists are, as it were, third in succession from the throne of truth." Art is an imitation of life and life merely a shadow of the ideal Forms. Thus "the work of the artist is at third remove from the essential nature of things." Cornford comments that "the view that a work of art is an image or likeness (*eikon*) of some original, or holds up a mirror to nature, became prominent towards the end of the fifth century together with the realistic drama of Euripides and the illusionistic painting of Zeuxis. Plato's attack adopts this theory." [3]

Plato's student Aristotle agrees that art is mimetic but asks what precisely does art imitate and how? Art does not imitate things or even experience, but "action." Action is a problematical idea and, at best, I can only sketch an interpretation of what Aristotle might have meant. Art imitates patterns, rhythms, and developments. In art, as in nature, things are born, they grow, they flourish, they decline, they die. Form, which is crystalline in Plato, is fluid in Aristotle. Each organism (animate, natural, artistic [4]) conceals a determining pattern-factor that governs its development. This DNA-like factor determines the rate of growth, shape, rhythm, and life span of every organism. Everything has its own life plan, its own "indwelling form." It is this form which art imitates.

Aristotle's idea is sublime. It imparts to everything—from thought to the slow unwinding of a galaxy to the lives of men to the grain of sand—a living, intrinsic, and dynamic participation in creating, being, becoming, and ceasing. From the Aristotelian perspective "individuality" is seen in its original meaning: not divisible. Things are integral both inherently and in their relationship to their environments. Destiny is the interplay between what is inborn and what is met. Every acorn is an oak-in-process. But between acorn and oak is sun, rain, wind, lightning, and men with axes. "Count no man happy until the day of his death," intones the chorus of *Oedipus*. That tragedy is fulfilled, and ended, but not so Oedipus, who goes on to other adventures. "Tragedy, then, is the imitation of an action that is serious, complete, and of a certain magnitude." Of an action, not of a man's life. Oedipus offered to Sophocles two complete actions—*Oedipus the King* and *Oedipus at Colonus*.

From a naive biographical vantage, tragedies are about broken lives, early death, unfulfilled promises, remorse, maimed ambitions, and tricks of fate. What has a "beginning, middle, and end" is the artwork. At the deepest level a play is about itself. Aristotle suggests that the playwright takes from life an impulse—a story, an idea, an image, a sense of person. This impulse is the kernel of the artwork whose process is a twisting and transformation of the impulse until, at a decisive moment, the artwork breaks off and becomes itself. From then on, the artwork makes its own demands in accord with its indwelling form or action. These, as artists know, may be stubbornly unlike those of the original impulse or conscious plan.

Thus an Aristotelian artwork lives a double life. It is mimetic in the Platonic sense, but it is also itself. As Fergusson points out, the relationship between artwork and experience is one of "analogy." The root idea of *mimesis* is sophisticated by Aristotle, but not transmuted. Art always "comes after" experience; the separation between art and life is built into the idea of *mimesis*. It is this coming after and separation that has been so decisive in the development of Western theater.

An analogy will make clear exactly what I mean by "coming after." Cooked food "comes after" raw food. Cooking is something that is done to raw food to change it and (apparently) to make it purer. All cooked food was once raw; all raw food is cookable. There is no way for raw food to "come after" cooked food. So it is with art and life. Art is cooked and life is raw. Art is the process of transforming raw experience into palatable forms. This transformation is a mimetic one, a representation. Such, at any rate, is the heart of the mimetic theory.

The hot interest in anthropology over the past generation or so has not been all good. Artists and critics alike have turned to "primitive" man with embarrassing yearning. Leslie (1960) said "There is . . . a fashionable modern conception of 'primitive man' as inhabiting a 'mystical' world of 'timeless,' 'cosmological,' metaphorical,' and 'magical' presences. Costumed in the 'archetypal' masks of tribal art, and possessed of a special 'primitive mentality,' this phantasmagoria is said to perform 'ritual dramas' of 'mythic reality.' This particular conception of primitive man enjoys greatest currency in artistic and literary circles [where] primitive cultures are to modern thought what classical antiquity was to the Renaissance." [5] But it is no better to think of the Tiwi as the guys next door. Leslie thinks this countercurrent attributing an urban pragmatism to primitive men an apologia for that kind of rationality which many anthropologists feel is in jeopardy. What makes *The Savage Mind* so satisfying is Levi-Strauss's ability to uphold the claim of what is special in primitive peoples while not denying what is common to all men. The logic of Aristotle is not universal, but an appetite for classification is. Peoples think differently, but every people thinks systematically in its own terms. Levi-Strauss does not resurrect the noble savage or blur differences with an archetypal smear.

We live under terrible stress. Politically, intellectually, artistically, personally, and epistemologically we are at breaking points. It is a cliché to say that a society is in crisis. But ours, particularly here on this North American continent, seems to be gripped by total crisis and faced with either disintegration or brutal, sanctioned repression. The yearnings of the young may be a combination of infantile wishes for the wholeness of mama's breast and a thrashing towards an impossible utopian socialism. Or these yearnings may indicate a genuine alternative to our horrific destiny. I cannot distinguish between the true and the false. But I can identify yearnings which have triggered not only an interest in primitive peoples but artistic movements that concretize that interest and start to satisfy those yearnings:

(1) *Wholeness*. Participatory democracy, self-determination on the local, national, and international levels. Therapies which start from the oneness of mind/body/feelings. "Getting it together." Total theater, environmental theater, intermedia, integrated electronic systems, McLuhanism. An end to the dichotomies:

101

a whole person	not mind/body
families	not fragmented individuals
communities	not government *vs.* governed
jobs like play	not alienated work
art where we are	not in museums far away
one world in peace	not wars and international rivalries
man one with nature	not ecological warfare

(2) *Process. Organic Growth.* An end to the assembly line, both for the production of goods and the conformism of people. Animosity to the police, the military-industrial complex. "Process, not product." "Do your own thing." "Turn people into artists, not onto art." Turbulence and discontinuity, not artificial smoothness. Organic foods. Kicking out your feelings. Ritual art, all-night dances.

(3) *Concreteness.* Down with theories, abstractions, generalizations, the "biggies" of art, industry, education, government, etc. Make your demands known, act them out, and get an answer now. Radicalize the students. Street and guerrilla theater, Provo action, marches on Washington, demonstrations on campus. Arm the blacks, urban warfare in the ghettoes. Dig the physicality of experience. Sensory awareness, involvement, and expression. Happenings, earth art, concrete poetry and music, porno.

(4) *Religious/Transcendental Experience.* Mysticism, shamanism, Messianism, psychedelics, epiphanies. Zen, yoga, and other ways to truth through participation or formulation, as in macrobiotics and yoga exercises. Eschatological yearnings: what is the meaning of life? Make all experience meaningful. Sacralize everyday living. Sung poetry, encounter theater, marathons, T-groups, theater made in and by communities, tribalism, rock festivals, drugs, trips, freak-outs, ecstasies.

The four categories are inseparable. They overlap, interpenetrate, feed on each other, exchange with and transform into one another. Any separation is artificial. In many cultures the very separations that make this essay possible would be impossible.

Wholeness, process and organic growth, concreteness, and religious/transcendental experience are fundamental to primitive cultures. The terms differ from culture to culture and those of any primitive culture differ radically from our own. But we have uncovered links between us and them. These links, or metaphors, are strongest and clearest between what we call art, particularly new theater, and what they call by names ranging from play to dancing to doing.

A try to explain "actuals" involves a survey of anthropological, sociological, psychological, and historical material. But these are not organized to promote the search. And the scope of this essay prohibits me from taking anything but a quick glance at the sources. There I find an incipient theory for a special kind of behaving, thinking, relating, and doing. This special way of handling experience and jumping the gaps between past and present, individual and group, inner and outer, I call "actualizing" (perhaps no better than Eliade's "reactualizing," but at least shorter). Actualizing is plain among rural, primitive peoples and it is becoming plainer among our own young and in their avant-garde art. The question is not polemical, but structural. Not whether the new theater (and life style) is good, but how it is built and what, precisely, are its bases. Then, what are its functions and how do these relate to the life we live individually and collectively. I think we will find that the new theater is very old, and that our localized urban avant-garde belongs next to a worldwide, rural tradition.

What might we make of the possible etymological link between the word "drama"—from the Greek *dran*: to do, to act, to make—and the word "dream"—from the Old English and the Old Frisian *drām*: a dream, a shout of joy? Somewhere in that pretty connection is the feel of actualizing. "According to the [Australian] aborigines," says Lommel, "in the dream state man has a share in the creativity of nature, and if he were to be creatively active in this state he would really, as the painter Baumeister expressed it, 'not create after nature, but like nature.'" [6]

Understanding actualization means understanding both the creative condition and the artwork, the actual. Among primitive peoples the creative condition is identical with trances, dances, ecstasies; in short, shamanism.[7] Shamanism is "a method, a psychic technique" [8] of which the "fundamental characteristic . . . is ecstasy, interpreted as the soul forsaking the body." [9] This technique is very ancient, with roots among Central Asian peoples during the Alpine Palaeolithic period, some 30,000 to 50,000 years ago. "No one has yet shown that the ecstatic experience is the creation of a particular historical civilization or a particular culture cycle. In all probability the ecstatic experience, in its many aspects, is coexistent with the human condition." [10] What is an ecstatic experience? Eliade and Lommel quote examples. And Rothenberg cites Isaac Tens's own account of how he became a shaman.

Then my heart started to beat fast, and I began to tremble, just as had happened before. . . . My flesh seemed to be boiling. . . . My body was quivering. While I remained in this state, I began to sing. A chant was coming out of me without my being able to do anything to stop it. Many things appeared to me presently: huge birds and other animals. . . . These were visible only to me, not to the others in my house. Such visions happen when a man is about to become a shaman; they occur of their own accord. The songs force themselves out complete without any attempt to compose them. But I learned and memorized those songs by repeating them.[11]

Rothenberg thinks that Tens's experience is "typical of (1) the psychology of shamanism, (2) the shaman's 'initiation' through dream & vision, (3) transformation of vision into song." [12] Eliade and Lommel cite similar examples. Eliade says there are three ways of becoming a shaman: as Tens did through the "call"; by inheritance; and by personal ambition or the will of the tribe. A shaman is authenticated "only after having received two kinds of instruction. The first is ecstatic (e.g., dreams, visions, trances); the second is traditional (e.g., shamanic techniques, names and functions of the spirits, mythology and genealogy of the clan, secret language." [13] The instruction of the fledgling shaman first by older shamans and then by the spirits is a universal aspect of shamanism. Its structure is much like Dante's travels with Vergil through the Christian other worlds. Lommel describes an Australian shamanic instruction.

At sunset the shaman's soul meets somewhere the shadow of a dead ancestor. The shadow asks the soul whether it shall go with it. The shaman's soul answers yes. . . . Then they go on together, either at once into the kingdom of the dead or to a place in this world at which the spirits of the dead have gathered. . . . The spirits begin to sing and dance. . . . When the dance is over the spirits release the shaman's soul and his helping spirit brings it back to his body. When the shaman wakes his experiences with the spirits seem to him like a dream. From now on he thinks of nothing but the dances which he has seen and his soul keeps on going back to the spirits to learn more and more about the dances. . . . Then he will first explain the dances to his wife and sing them to her, and after that he will teach them to everyone else.[14]

The shaman's journeys are neither gratuitous nor for private use. He goes to get something and he must deliver what he gets to his people—he must teach them what he learns. His work is social work.

The shaman is prized by his people. He is "the exemplar and model for all those who seek to acquire power; [he] is the man who *knows* and remembers." [15] But sometimes his powers fail him, his link with the other world breaks. This is a crisis for the entire community. (I am reminded forcefully of the plague which starts the search for Laius's murderer. King Oedipus is a shaman. His sacrifice cures Thebes, and his search, assisted by the townsfolk, is a paradigm of shamanic quest. The story is overlaid with other things, but its roots go deep into pre-Aristotelian patterns of feeling and doing.) Lommel says that in Australia when a shaman loses touch with the other world "his poetic gift for creating songs and dances vanishes." All the men of the community sit in a circle around the shaman. They sing for hours a "regularly rising and falling note" and rub his body. The shaman goes into trance. He seeks a spirit of a dead ancestor, whom he tells that he "cannot 'find' any more songs." The spirit promises help and the shaman comes out of trance. Several days later the shaman "hears a distant call. It is his helping spirit calling him. He goes off by himself and converses for a while with the spirit." A few days later his soul leaves his body. "Many spirits now come up from the underworld [and] tear the [shaman's] soul to pieces and each spirit carries a piece into the underworld. There, deep under the earth, they put the shaman's soul together again. They show him the dances again and sing songs to him." [16] The shaman is whole; his link is repaired. Everyone helped him get it together.

What are we to make of these experiences? It has been customary to "interpret" reports like these—to find in our way of thinking analogues that make such experiences rationally acceptable. Thus Lommel says that the quest for the missing ceremonial link is "an authentic account of the nature of artistic creativity [which shows vividly] the connection of an artist's creative potency with tradition—with the ancestors." [17] Eliade never tires of showing that shamanic experiences are prototypes of our own religious beliefs. Psychoanalysts interpret in the direction of instinctual needs and unconscious processes. I accept these interpretations. But they are not complete. Shamanic experiences are real and whole. Our interpretations diminish and fragment them—we want to make the experiences "otherworldly," "transcendental," or "fantasies." But these experiences are the result of something which Cassirer noted about primitive thought. "By a sudden metamorphosis everything may be turned into everything. [There is] the deep conviction of a fundamental and indelible *solidarity of life* that bridges over the multiplicity and variety of its single forms." [18] Everywhere there are overlaps, exchanges, and transformations. For example,

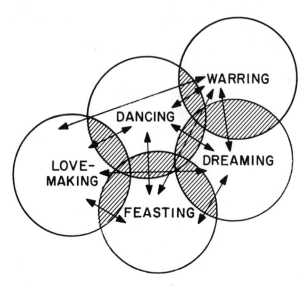

Figure 1

Experience is not segregated on hierarchical planes. It is not that every-thing is the same, but that all things are part of one wholeness and that among things unlimited exchanges and transformations are possible.

Artists among us use experience the way the Australians do. Artists treat experience as something indivisible but exchangeable; as endlessly varied but on the same plane; as here and now but other-worldly. It is this hard-to-talk-about-in-our-language thing that Levi-Strauss (1966) means when he says that "there are still zones in which savage thought, like savage species, is relatively protected. This is the case of art. . . . Savage thought is definable both by a consuming symbolic ambition such as humanity has never again seen rivalled, and by scrupulous at-tention directed entirely towards the concrete, and finally by the im-plicit conviction that these two attitudes are but one." [19] From here it is just a short step to understanding actualization.

Eliade does not define reactualization. Instead he gives examples of it. An initiation is a ceremony in which "a new generation is instructed, is made fit to be integrated into the community of adults. And on this occasion, through the repetition, the *reactualization*, of the traditional rites, the entire community is regenerated." [20] The actualization is the

106

making present a past time or event. Eliade describes a puberty initiation of eastern Australia called a *bora*. The initiates are surprised at home, "kidnapped," and taken to the place of initiation. There they are secluded and instructed in the lore, dances, and songs of their tribe. This schooling lasts for months. During it, the initiates are kept under strict discipline. The ceremonial area is a "sacred space" within which ordinary time has been abolished and Dream Time is. Dream Time is the time of the first initiation rite performed by Baiamai, the supreme being. Finally, amid dancing and singing, the initiates are circumcised: their bodies irrevocably marked with a sign of belonging to the tribe. The *bora* ground is Baiamai's first camp and the initiators are those who were with Baiamai when he inaugurated these ceremonies. This reintegration of time and place is not peculiar to the Australians. It is true "for the entire primitive world. For what is involved here is a fundamental concept in archaic religions—the repetition of a ritual founded by Divine Beings implies the reactualization of the original Time when the rite was first performed. This is why a rite has efficacy—it participates in the completeness of the sacred primordial Time. The rite makes the myth present. Everything that the myth tells of the Time of beginning, the *bugari* times [Dream Time], the rite reactualizes, shows it as happening, *here and now*." [21]

This is true not only of compact rites but of those which are narrative and of long duration. The Elema of New Guinea celebrate a cycle called the *hevehe*, after the majestic thirty-foot-high mask-spirits whose appearance and dances climax a process that takes from six to twenty years or more to complete. The masks are built in the men's ceremonial house, the *eravo*, which is lengthened and heightened to accommodate the painstaking work. A number of ceremonies mark the *hevehe* over the years—there is a close knitting of the *eravo*, the masks being built in it, the political and economic life of the people, the life cycle of individuals in the community, and the *hevehe* which gives to both individual and social life meaning and continuity. Some cycles which Williams (1940) observed were started in 1914 but not finished by 1937 when he gathered his data. Others, begun at about the same time, were completed in 1920, 1932, and 1934. "It may be thought that this dragging out of the cycle is the result of modern influences, as if the *hevehe* were drawing a series of long, dying gasps. [But] there is ample evidence to show that formerly, as well as now, the *hevehe* cycles occupied very long periods." [22] A man with a full life might participate in three, possibly four, *hevehe*.

In a cycle that takes as long to complete as the *hevehe* things are not so strict from moment to moment as they are in the *bora*. The cycle develops in bursts, with intensive activities surrounding particular ceremonies and long periods of inactivity between. The ceremonies all take place in and around the village, and many involve the women and children. In one, the *eharo*, people from neighboring villages wearing small dancing masks, invade the host village. Bunched around the *eharo* are enthusiastic women and children, and resisting the invaders are hundreds of people who shower the invaders with coconut flakes. A mock battle is fought on the beach and then the invaders sweep into the village. Erotic pantomimes vie with more staid dancing, and children run about the village armed with toy bows and arrows which they shoot at bunches of banana or sago. Throughout all of this some of the village elders lounge on the veranda of the *eravo*, seemingly disinterested and certainly unperturbed. This carnival mock war dance seems altogether different from the *bora*. There the ceremony is formal, far from the village in total seclusion, and no women or children are permitted to watch or even know of the rituals; the elders are the most important participants. In the *hevehe*, everything is the opposite; but the differences are not of an essential kind.

The climax of the cycle is the month-long dancing of the *hevehe* masks. Months of hard preparation have laid away stores of food, and inside the *eravo* the last touches have been completed on the masks. The night before the emergence drumming begins from the upper level of the *eravo*. Before dawn a large crowd of women and children gather before the *eravo's* thirty-foot double doors. The drumming suddenly stops and the pushing and shoving of the crowd reaches a "perfect fury of joy and excitement."

There are many dramatic situations in the cycle, but none can compare with this supreme moment when the *hevehe*, after wellnigh twenty years of confinement, issue forth to commence the brief fulfillment of their existence. In the grey light of early morning the first of them, "Koraia," stood framed against the blackness of the open door—a tall, fantastic figure, silvery white, its coloured patterns in the atmosphere of dawn appearing pale and very delicate. . . . For a brief moment "Koraia" stood there, the great crowd of spectators gazing in silence. Then, with a thump of the drum and a prodigious rattling of harau, it started down the gangway. Immediately behind it came "Pekeaupe"; and after that, in crowded succession, 120 others.[23]

As each mask starts dancing, groups of women and children detach themselves from the large crowd and dance around masks worn by fathers, husbands, brothers, and sons. The women carry green twigs and they flick the legs of the mask-dancers.

In the centre are the portentous figures of the *hevehe,* with their staring eyes and their fierce jaws abristle with teeth, their mantles rising and falling, and their human arms vigorously belabouring the drums and kicking up the dust. Though they are 20 feet high and more they dance, not lightly (that would be a sheer impossibility) but with amazing animation.[24]

The *hevehe* dance throughout the village and on the beach. They dance all day and part of the night for a month. It is hot, and a man dances his mask for from fifteen minutes to an hour. Then he returns to the *eravo* and attaches his mask to its hook.

Streaming with perspiration, the last wearer sits down to cool off; but presently he will be seen fitting some other mask over his head, shuffling a little to get it balanced to his satisfaction, and then making his way towards the door, fully prepared for a further tour. Any man, in fact, may wear any mask with its owner's permission; nor is the owner likely to refuse it, since he is flattered to see his *hevehe* in frequent use.[25]

The dancing is a performance, but of a special kind. It is thought that when a man wears a mask he is "animated by the spirits which are derived from the myths." Each *hevehe* has a name because each is a spirit. The spirit moves only when a man is in the mask. Conversely a man dances well only when he is moved by the spirit. Two autonomous, symbiotic existences interpenetrate each other. The women and children know who are in the masks—they accompany their close relatives and tease them into more vigorous dancing. Men freely exchange masks, animating and being animated by many spirits in one day. Here is a clear example of the exchange between two realities which the Elema put on one plane: (1) the masks which are living things; (2) the men who wear the masks. The masks do not represent the spirits or contain the spirits; the masks *are* the spirits.

At the end of the month of dancing the *hevehe* make their way to the beach for the last time. The women "rush to the giant masks and embrace their projecting jaws and kiss their faces, while not a few were shedding tears." [26] Some beat their breasts and others try to stop the *hevehe* from reaching the beach. But the masks get there and dance. Then one by one, in no set order, each gives up its drum and slowly they form into two lines. These lines start a solemn procession back from the beach to the *eravo*. Soon all but eight of the 122 *hevehe* have gone into the *eravo*. The last eight masks are intercepted by some young women and a ritual combat begins. The men have arranged that the last eight masks should be small and light and the men in them strong.

Next moment they were circled about by a score of robust females clasping one another's hands. Almost immediately the circle broke up into two, one for either *eravo*-side and each imprisoning four *hevehe*. . . . The *hevehe* try again and again to burst through the circle. They turn side on and hurl themselves on the outstretched arms of the women. But the women are strong, and they are reinforced by others, standing outside the ring, who clamp their hands together. They easily hold their own and send the *hevehe* staggering back into the centre; but after repeated charges the wall begins to break and one after another the prisoners escape.[27]

When the last *hevehe* enters the *eravo* the 200 women turn towards the *eravo*, raise their arms over their heads, and chant. Some hours later, after a feast, four of the masks re-emerge. A shaman arms his bow and says, "I, Aku-akore, stand here and am about to kill you. I am taking all you possess." He shoots through the face of a mask. "Very realistically, as if mortally wounded, the *hevehe* staggered and fell." [28] The women cry out in grief and flee from the village. The three other masks are shot.

With the fall of the four *hevehe* and the exodus of the women there began a scene of deliberate destruction. Masks, no longer worn but carried, came pouring out of the door to be propped against the house-walls or thrown carelessly on the ground. Without the slightest trace of reverence or regret their owners proceeded to strip them of their *mae* mantles and their feathers.[29]

Parts of the masks are kept for the next cycle; parts are lent to neighboring villages. The dead hulks are taken to the stream and thrown into three piles. "It seemed as if the masks were to be disposed of without any touch of ceremony whatever, so keen was every one on the practical side of the business." But, before the masks are burned, the shaman says, "Now I am going to burn you. Look kindly on the men of my *eravo*. When they hunt let not the arrow stick in the ground, but in the eye of the pig. I do no harm to you. Constantly, from long ago I have fed and fostered you. Do not be angry with us." Or, "I have called you up because of my pigs and sago. I have fed you constantly. In the future some other strong men will call you. Do not be angry." Or, "The man of pigs, the man of dogs, calls you. But now I burn you. Ivo and Leravea, our women, girls, and little boys—let no centipede sting them, no thorns pierce them, no snakes or sharks bite them. Guard them well." [30] There is personal variation and style in the invocations. The masks have life and must be killed. When they are burnt the *hevehe* spirits go back to the bush. "Why the *hevehe* should be killed at all is a question which no native was ever able to answer." [31] The spirits are immortal and they will be re-created in the next cycle. The *eravo* is empty.

Gradually the great grey building falls into decay; the floor-boards rot; thatching, ripped off by the wind, goes unrepaired and rain falls miserably upon deserted hearth-sides. One by one the members seek other sleeping quarters, and at last the *eravo* is a ruin. Then, when it threatens to collapse . . . the community will make a strenuous effort and demolish it. For some years, perhaps, they will content themselves with humbler lodgings; but at last, if spirit is willing and flesh is strong, they will set to and build themselves another *eravo,* and with that the long *hevehe* cycle will start all over again.[32]

The cycle is majestic. Its duration, the harmony among its many parts, and the close-fitting, almost symbiotic ties between it and other aspects of the life of the Elema make it one of mankind's great creations. But along with its solemnity and grandeur come a joviality and irreverence that at first glance seems to jar.

The women are not supposed to see parts of the cycle or the masks hanging dead inside the *eravo*. Eliade says that when men swinging bull-roarers enter the village "they have the right to kill any woman or non-initiate who tries to discover their identity." [33] But Williams tells of many times when concealment is treated casually. The doors of the *eravo* are often left open and the women see "quite enough to dispel their curiosity." [34] If a woman dances with the *hevehe* of a son rather than a husband the offended man may become violently angry. During the "cutting off" combat the women are strong enough to keep the eight masks trapped indefinitely. But Williams heard one young man brag how he told his sister, "Isn't it time you let me go?" and at the next charge he was free.[35]

The *hevehe* cycle mixes the ceremonial and the personal without diluting or blending either. A mask dances because it is alive. A man dances because he is animated by the mask. A mask dies when its face is shot through by an arrow. Parts of its hulk can be used again. The spirits may suffer as they are killed. Yet they do not die but go to the bush and wait to be recalled. After the audience of weeping women leave the village, the masks are killed simply by being thrown down. Both the dancing and the dying are performances—and all performances are vis-à-vis someone. There is an absolute separation between the performance and the performer. A separation that encourages exchange and transformation. Bravado, joking, rehearsing, and special backstage behavior are possible because the Elema know when they are onstage and when they are off. Their performances are not impersonations, but possessions and exchanges; the spirit and the man interpenetrate each other without either losing his identity. The dancing of the *hevehe* lifts the whole community to a month of exaltation. When the *hevehe* are killed and the spirits gone the *eravo* falls to shambles.

What is the relationship between the mask and the masker? At every moment during each ceremony in the long *hevehe* cycle the people know two independent but reciprocating realities. (1) The reality of the *hevehe* masks and autonomously unfolding cycle. These spirits are not abstract or generalized. They move in space, can be touched and seen, and are known *personally* by the men building them. Slowly they are built in the *eravo*, and each phase of building is marked by celebration. The masks are never half-alive, but like embryos they are not ready for independent dancing life outside the *eravo* until they are complete and whole. When they emerge they dance among all the people for a month. The spirits can be heard in the roar of the bull-roarers and the clamor of the gongs. They do not die, but they must be killed anyway, and not mysteriously but by bow and arrow, and then burnt by fire. (2) The reality of the villagers' everyday lives—of hunting and farming, feasting, sharing, exchanging, marrying, child-rearing, politicking, fighting, ageing, sickening, dying. In theatrical terms neither the performed (masks) nor the performers (villagers) are absorbed into one another; one does not "play the role" of the other. They stand whole and yet autonomous. Their relationship is what Grotowski calls "confrontation." It is not that one reality reflects, represents, or distills the other. Both move freely through the same time/space. The realities confront, overlap, interpenetrate each other in a relationship that is extraordinarily dynamic and fluid.

The burning of the *hevehe* masks and the circumcising of the initiates at the *bora* are culminating irrevocable acts proclaiming that there can be no turning back. The Australians mark off a special place where the men bring the boys into the whole community. The initiation is relatively swift and certainly intense, convulsive, and isolated. Contrarily, the Elema cycle unfolds among the villagers' homes, meeting places, and playgrounds. After the masks are burned the village is only half alive until the start of the next cycle. But the apparently opposite actuals of Australia and New Guinea are founded on the same belief in multiple, valid, equivalent, and reciprocating realities. The actuals are here and now, efficacious, and irrevocable.

Joan MacIntosh, playing Dionysus in *Dionysus in 69*, had to start her performance each night by emerging naked amid an audience of 250 and saying, "Good evening, my name is Joan MacIntosh, and I am a god." Only by finding, releasing, and showing her deepest impulses of fear, hilarity, fraud, and humiliation could she begin to cope with the actuality of her preposterous situation. Her claim to divinity is thinkable only in the terms of the trapped *hevehe* mask who said to his sister, "Isn't it time you let me go?"

When a performer does not "play a character" what does he do? Stand-up comics play aspects of themselves. Essential are "in-joking" and a straight man who leads the comic into traps or kids him about that aspect of himself that is the core of his act. Disclosure is the heart of the comic's art. He carefully keeps to the edge—just a little too much and his act is embarrassing and painful. The audience teeters between knowing it is being put on and glimpsing brief but deep looks into the "real man." Like a Malibu Beach muscleman, the comic overdevelops parts of his personality and displays these shamelessly.

The movie star wears a different story and costume in each film. But he is groomed for one limited set of traits and these vivify all his roles. The cynical, easy violence of Bogart; the austere integrity of Cooper; the slurred, rough goodness of Wayne; the virgin-who-will-fuck of Doris Day; the slut-who-is-good of Marilyn Monroe. The star has his own thing that organizes the filmic "vehicle" around it. We are never sure how much of the "star personality" is genuine, and how much put on. The star is usually not sure either. A stereotyped mask thickens and freezes—a mask worn publicly and privately throughout life.

Circus performers are like performers of actuals—except that at a circus everything is made to look more glamorous and dangerous than it is. The motive of the circus is "I dare you" and this is blatantly stimulated in the audience by the performers and ringmaster. The great circus performers are those who go to the utmost limit, seem about to fail, recover, and succeed brilliantly. Hokum and skill—coming out of a near fall with a perfect landing capped by a superbly graceful bow to the cheering house: that's the essential circus.

Athletes, like circus performers, display their skills. The rules of games are designed to show prowess, quick judgment, speed, endurance, strength, and teamwork. Also the rules encourage spectators to measure performance against some objective standard. Athletics are embellished by the ballyhoo and excitement natural to large crowds and focussed by the intense competitiveness of our way of sporting. But competition is dispensable. Among Mexico's Tarahumaras racing is participatory— men, women, and children, old and young, race together. It doesn't matter who finishes first—to arrive last is as honorable as to arrive first. The whole race is of interest to all spectators who measure performance against ability. What counts is that everyone who participates does his best. To be a laggard brings shame on you and your family.

The idea of danger is exploited by the circus; that of excellence is the kernel of athletics. This combination of risk and mastery is asked of the performer of actuals. He is not a shaman or an acrobat or an athlete— but he is very close to all of these.

An actual has five basic elements, and each is found both in our own actuals and those of primitive peoples: (1) *organic growth*, something happens *here and now*; (2) *consequential, irremediable,* and *irrevocable* acts, exchanges, or situations; (3) *contest*, something is *at stake* for the performers and often for the spectators; (4) *initiation,* a *change in status* for participants; (5) space is used *concretely* and *organically.* Each of these basic elements deserves extensive explication. I shall be able only to skim what is available.

(1) Process, something happens here and now. This is largely a matter of emphasis. Even the most conventional actor affirms that something goes on inside him during a performance. But most training and rehearsals are designed to hide this process or to bring it entirely in line with the playwright's intentions as envisioned by the director so that the performance reveals not the actor but the character he is playing. The goal of conventional acting and the basis of Stanislavski's great work is to enable the actor to "really live" his character. Nature ought to be so skillfully imitated that it seems to to be re-presented on stage. The tendency of an actual is the opposite. Instead of the smooth "professionalism" of the "good actor," there are rough and unexpected turbulences, troubled interruptions. These are not stylistic, but a genuine meeting between performer and problem.

Two processes unfold simultaneously. The first is the one shaped by author and director, the play and the *mise en scène.* But just as important is the more evanescent process of the performer. The play and *mise en scène* have a quality of having been lived, while the performance has the quality of living now. The play will be completed only if the performer is able to carry through the process he starts afresh each night. That process cannot be rehearsed.

Perhaps this will be clearer if I cite an analogy given me by Ryszard Cieslak of the Polish *Teatr Laboratorium.* I did not understand what Cieslak meant by "score" and asked him to explain.

We work in rehearsals to find an objective set of actions and relationships that, understood apart from anything we the performers might feel, communicate to the audience the images, actions, and meanings we want to communicate. This process takes months and it is a *via negativa*—that is, we reject more than we accept and we search so that we can remove obstacles to our creativity. We play out the actions at hand, the associations that offer themselves to us. Grotowski watches. He helps us remove blocks, things that prevent us from fully confronting and experiencing the actions at hand. Finally we construct a coherent score. This score, which grows minutely day by day, includes all the objective things a spectator sees from night to night. For example, in *Akropolis* my score includes how my body lies in the wheelbarrow, what tone my voice has, how I breathe, how my fingers move. The score even includes the associations I have, what I think about from moment to moment. These associations I change from time to time, as they get stale. And as it is for me, so it is for everyone else. Ideally the score is whole and does not need completion or revision. In practice, it is never that way. Only a percentage of each production is scored when we begin performing it for audiences. After four years of performing *Akropolis* about 80% of it is scored for me.

The score is like the glass inside which a candle is burning. The glass is solid, it is there, you can depend on it. It contains and guides the flame. But it is not the flame. The flame is my inner process each night. The flame is what illuminates the score, what the spectators see through the score. The flame is alive. Just as the flame in the candle-glass moves, flutters, rises, falls, almost goes out, suddenly glows brightly, responds to each breath of wind—so my inner life varies from night to night, from moment to moment. The way I feel an association, the interior sense of my voice or a movement of my finger. I begin each night without anticipations. This is the hardest thing to learn. I do not prepare myself to feel anything. I do not say, "Last night this scene was extraordinary, I will try to do that again." I want only to be receptive to what will happen. And I am ready to take what happens if I am secure in my score, knowing that even if I feel a minimum, the glass will not break, the objective structure worked out over the months will help me through. But when a night comes that I can glow, shine, live, reveal—I am ready for it by not anticipating it. The score remains the same, but everything is different because I am different.

Grotowski describes the score as the "two banks of a river" and the performer's process as the "water flowing between those banks." [36]

We conventionally think of "process" as the sequence of events in the script—if these were "really happening" the story would be "inevitable." Thus the "death" of Hamlet or the "blinding" of Oedipus. When I think of process I think of something that occurs in fact here and now: the melting of the ice-liths in *Fluids*, the dodging and ultimate taking of spears in the Tiwi trial, the dancing of the *hevehe*. These processes are not gimmicks, but fundamental elements of the performance structure.

The whole of the Living Theatre's *Paradise Now* is a process. The audience is given a program which is a map of the event (see page 117). The performance passes through eight phases from "The Rite of Guerrilla Theatre" to "The Street." There is no time-limit, and many performances take six hours or more. To my knowledge all eight steps have never been genuinely accomplished—that is, the permanent revolution has not happened. (It is, of course, an error to think that it could.

116

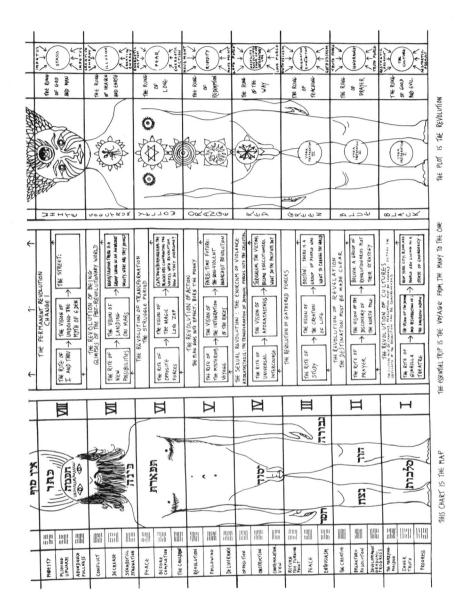

THIS CHART IS THE MAP

THE ESSENTIAL TRIP IS THE VOYAGE FROM THE MANY TO THE ONE

THE PLOT IS THE REVOLUTION

117

The Australians are more modest and successful with their ceremonies. And insofar as *Paradise Now* is a "demonstration," it is mimetic.) *Paradise Now* is built so that the performance incorporates disruptions the spectators act out. *Paradise Now* is pushed and pulled this way and that, seemingly in total disarray, until you realize that the performers are like tour guides—they want to move the thing along, but only after most of the audience is ready to move on. If anyone wants to stop off here or there, to examine a detail, to "put on a show," to shout, protest, or in any way detour the performance, that is fine. *Paradise Now* develops through random movement towards goals and through phases. It distends and collapses, intensifies and slackens, coheres and fragments. But still it does move, as the performers decide when one phase has been sufficiently explored and then initiate another. Many spectators cannot adapt themselves to a structure that appears so disorderly. But *Paradise Now* is very well organized if diversion, disruption, and side-tripping are recognized as part of that organization. It is much briefer than most primitive ceremonies—many of which also include side-trips in the guise of new dances and stories and disruptions when the community runs out of wealth or is threatened by hostile out-groups. Our sense of smooth time is jolted by *Paradise Now*, which treats time as lumpy, malleable, and turbulent.

The performers in *Paradise Now* have two tasks. They act things and they nudge the audience along. Like shamans they are the principal performers and the masters of ceremony. Throughout the performance spectators wisecrack and taunt the performers. This is not irrelevant— each phase must pass through ordeals to achieve the next step. Taunts and mockery are also part of many primitive ceremonies. Even the not-paying-attention is part of some solemn occasions—like the Yom Kippur service of Hasidic Jews, from which the Living Theatre took elements of *Paradise Now*. Eventually *Paradise Now* is at the eighth phase and the performers, accompanied by many spectators, confront the police outside the theater. I am reminded of Irma's little speech at the end of *The Balcony*. "You must now go home, where everything—you can be quite sure—will be even falser than here." The Living Theatre turns Genet on his head.

(2) Consequential, irremediable, and irrevocable acts. There are almost none of these in our theater. Irrevocability is finely expressed in

the circumcision of initiates. But it could also be taken from the exchanges of goods and people that vivify primitive life. Mauss calls these each "a total social fact." Levi-Strauss interprets them as events which have "significance that is at once social and religious, magic and economic, utilitarian and sentimental, jural and moral." [37] Even at Christmas and on birthdays or anniversaries we are not likely to involve ourselves in such whole exchanges. To demonstrate this I devised a classroom exercise. I asked everyone to choose a partner and to exchange something for fun. Men gave their wallets, shoes, pens; women their rings, cosmetics, handbags. Then I said, "Now exchange something for real." People gave each other empty cigarette packages, blank paper, matches.

Ralph Ortiz's *The Sky Is Falling* includes elements that are irrevocable. In it mice and chickens are killed, a piano axed to bits, and participants doused with blood. Participants are divided into a small number of Initiators and a larger number of Initiates. The scenario is written in the terminology of primitive ceremony, with free use of words like "ritual" and "shaman." Initiates are interrogated by the Initiators and verbally abused when they refuse to participate in any detail of the piece. Violence is combined with sexuality and scatology. The violence increases through a series of overlapping and simultaneous "rituals" culminating in the "Piano Destruction Rite" and "The Birth of Henny Penny Rite." Preparatory events include breaking eggs, killing mice, cutting paper screens on which images of human dissections are projected, burning clothes, burning food, ripping and kicking apart overstuffed furniture, dismembering dead chickens, tearing clothes off participants, and throwing blood at each other. The piano destruction is carefully orchestrated and precisely performed by Ortiz. He is exact about how the demolition should be done. "One hundred live mice in a wire screen and two gallons of blood in plastic bags are to be placed inside the piano behind the panel above the keys." The ax must be "brand new," the piano "pushed on its back to the floor—the key board and hammer sections smashed away so that the harp is completely exposed," and so on. The "Birth of Henny Penny" has two "men Initiators wearing maternity full length dresses . . . under spotlights ten feet apart. Each has a live chicken tied between their legs under the dresses. There is also fifteen feet of tubing connected to a balloon tied low on their waist under the dresses which extends to an upright tire pump." Initiates are "ha-rangued into pumping the pumps." The dresses inflate, all participants "join in the sighing moaning groaning and sexual motions" which continue until the balloons explode and the chickens are "delivered." Two Initiators (now called Shamans) raise the birds "victoriously . . . then waving the chickens like flags they race through the Ritual Room shouting irrational violent sounds" which convert into a "Henny Penny" chant. The other Initiators pick up the chant and then attack the Shamans, grabbing the chickens and bringing them to the demolished piano. The chickens are spread-eagled over the piano harp. The Initiators form a tight circle. The Shamans, outside the circle, start chanting "The sky is falling!" They take the ax, the circle admits them, and each Shaman decapitates the other's chicken. As this happens, everyone cries like children, "Mommy!" The decapitated heads are worn in plastic baggies "taped inside the fly" of each Shaman's pants. The cry changes to "Mousie" as the tight circle opens and the Initiators go to "zones" where the Initiates have watched the sacrifice. The Initiators shout at the Initiates, "You're just a bunch of fucking voyeurs!" Then the Shamans give each Initiator a live mouse. The Initiators surround the mousetrap area and throw the live mice in. Led by one of the Shamans, the Initiators begin to leave the room, "seeking out Initiates and seductively and lovingly telling them 'You love me, you love me.' "[38] The room after the performance was strewn with guts, living, dead, and half-dead mice. The floor was about an inch deep in blood. Bits of furniture, tatters of clothes, mashed food, a student vomiting—and on a platform to one side and fifteen feet high were ten observers, some with cameras. The room stank of guts and blood. The effect was hideous.

Eliade comments that modern "so-called initiation rites frequently betoken a deplorable spiritual poverty. . . . But the success of these enterprises likewise proves man's profound need for initiation, that is, for regeneration, for participation in the life of the spirit."[39] *The Sky Is Falling* is a moralizing piece founded on a belief in Artaud's dictum that violence will purge violent feelings. This, in turn, is Aristotelian catharsis escalated towards the Roman reality games of gladiators and armies in deadly combat for "fun." There is, however, another frame for Ortiz's piece. Those who did not choose to participate or watch from the platform saw everything on closed-circuit television. During a discussion which followed the performance a woman berated Ortiz for "promoting such things. How can you kill animals?" she asked. Ortiz answered, "You were watching on TV, you knew where it was happening, why didn't you stop it?" This converted *The Sky Is Falling* into a political parable: the room was Vietnam, the television viewers were American citizens, the Initiates were draftees, the Initiators were the regular army, the Shamans were the military brass and top government officials. But I don't think we can leave it at that. *The Sky Is Falling* raises the question, what *kind* of irrevocable acts?

Roman reality games and mimes are the ultimate mimetic spectacle. Ortiz's work shares that mimetic ambition. His mirror is distorted and the stakes are not so high—animals, not people. Unlike the Maori of Australia, who press earth down on an initiate's chest to make him understand death, Ortiz takes animal blood and chops off the heads of chickens. The "symbolic ambition" Levi-Strauss detects as the motor of savage thinking is converted into reductive imitation. Irrevocability is understood as something which happens to the objects of the drama—the chickens and mice, the pianos and furniture—not to the subjects of the piece, the initiates and spectators. At best these are put through a harrowing hour and left with scalding memories. Or, perhaps, like soldiers, they finally weary and are blunted to bloodshed. When violence, cruelty, sacrifice, even ritual murder and combat (as among the Dani of New Guinea)[40] are incorporated into authentic ceremonies, they are always part of a *known system*. Violence without the system is meaningless and destructive. Ortiz tries to invent a system as he goes; or maybe he's trying to fight a system through miniviolent homeopathic demonstration. His scenario is rich with the terminology of primitive religion, but without a link to a system. Irrevocable acts are rare in our theater. They can't be made by magic. When they happen they usually manifest themselves as metaphors. And they act on the people, not the props.

(3) Contest, something is at stake for the performers and often for the spectators. In *Dionysus in 69* there is a scene about halfway through that starts when Dionysus offers Pentheus "any woman in this room." Pentheus says he can have his pick without Dionysus's help. "OK," says Dionysus, "try it yourself." Pentheus is left alone in the center of the room. Almost every night some woman comes to him and offers help. The scene plays privately between them, and ends with the woman

going back to her place. The performance resumes and Pentheus, defeated, is sacrificed. Once it did not happen that way. In the words of William Shephard who played Pentheus:

> The one time the sequence was completed was when Katherine Turner came out into the room. . . . The confrontation between us was irrational. Her concern for me was not based on the play, my playing a role, whether or not I was going to die, or any of that. What happened was that I recognized in one moment that the emotional energy Katherine was spending on me literally lifted me out of the play, as though someone had grabbed me by the hair and pulled me up to the ceiling. I looked around and I saw the garage and the other actors and I said, "It finally happened." The play fell away, like shackles being struck from my hands. The way the play is set up Pentheus is trapped inside its structure. But on that night it all seemed to fall away and I walked out the door.[41]

Joan MacIntosh was playing Dionysus that night. Her reactions were different.

> Bill got up and left the theatre with the woman. I announced that the play was over. "Ladies and gentlemen, tonight for the first time since the play has been running, Pentheus, a man, has won over Dionysus, the god. The play is over." Cheers and cries and celebrations. . . . I felt betrayed. I was hurt and angry at Shephard. . . . I learned something corny but true: that if you invest all of yourself in the work, the risks are very great.[41]

On only one other occasion was the performance similarly torn from its rehearsed path. But many times people came into the play challenging performers, participating in the "death ritual" (where Pentheus is "killed"). Some of this participation was naive, but much of it came from people who had seen *Dionysus* more than once. In June 1969, Shephard was "kidnapped" by five students from Queens College who planned to stop the "killing" of Pentheus and had spent an afternoon working out their strategy. Many of the performers felt that the play should not stop because Pentheus was not "genuinely" rescued. I agreed and asked for a substitute Pentheus from the audience. A young man of seventeen volunteered—he did very well: he had seen the play five times and knew what was expected of him.

It is hard to build into a performance both narrative power and the tensions of a sporting match. The two ambitions cross each other. Suspense does not describe the tensions of sports, which come not from the spectators being in doubt about the outcome but from the doubt and resulting struggle among the players. There is some doubt like this in all performances because actors seek the unknown in their partners. In conventional theater an actor's creativity is most powerfully engaged in the narrow band between the details of the *mise en scène* and the obligation not to throw his partner by doing something wholly unexpected.

The band is much wider in *Dionysus* and theater like it. Those in the audience who know the performance can enter it at any of several places and change the flow of the action. In the scene cited the play can end abruptly. Mostly, however, the changes are modular—in tone, speed, intensity. Even those who are at the performance for the first time can participate, if they stick to the rules. These are implicit: you can do anything that will not prevent the performers from performing. What varies wildly from night to night is not the text or the story but the quality of the action. If we expand Cieslak's analogy, the gestures and text are the candle-glass and the action is the flame.

Grotowski (1968) thinks that Artaud's proclamation that "actors should be like martyrs burnt alive, still signalling through the flames" contains the "whole problem of spontaneity and discipline, this conjunction of opposites which gives birth to the total act [which is] the very crux of the actor's art." [42] Both spontaneity and discipline are *risks* for the performer. His entire effort is to make his body-voice-mind-spirit whole. Then he risks this wholeness here and now in front of others. Like the moves of the tightrope walker on the high wire, each move is spontaneous and part of an endless discipline. The kind of performer I am talking about—like the Shaman, Artaud's martyr, and Grotowski's Cieslak—discards the buffer of "character." Cieslak does not "play" the Constant Prince; MacIntosh does not "play" Dionysus. Neither "are" they the characters. During rehearsals the performer searches his personal experiences and associations, selects those elements which reveal him and also make an autonomous narrative and/or action structure, strips away irrelevancies and cop-outs, hones what remains until everything is necessary and sufficient. What results is a double structure, not unlike that of the *hevehe*. The first is the narrative and/or action-structure of

123

The Constant Prince or *Dionysus in 69.* The second is the vulnerability and openness of the performer. In each performance he risks freshly not only his dignity and craft, but his life-in-process. Decisions made and actions done during a performance may change the performer's life. The performance is a set of exchanges between the performer and the action. And of course among all the performers and between them and the audience. "The theatrical reality is instantaneous, not an illustration of life but something linked to life *only by analogy.*" [43]

(4) Initiation, a change in status for the participants. This change in who you are flows from the first three elements. If something has happened here and now, if the actual is made of consequential, irremediable, and irrevocable acts and exchanges, and if these involve risk for the performers (and maybe for the spectators too), then there will be changes, new dimensions of integration and wholeness. Change will either be bunched, troubled, difficult—an initiation; or smooth and continuous.

Initiation can be the kernel of a performance. The structure of events parallel the process stimulated by the events. For example, *The Constant Prince* is a set of initiations both for the Prince and for Cieslak. The performance is made of climactic bursts leading Cieslak from resistance to resignation to sacrifice. The Prince goes one step more, to apotheosis. At each of the first two crossings Cieslak is in crisis and surrenders to it. His role is passive—to take in all that happens to him. The more he gives up the farther he progresses. When he "dies" he does not move. Other performers apotheosize the Prince but nothing more happens to Cieslak, who merely lends his body to the work of the others. Cieslak's inner movements from night to night are not as radical as those proposed for the Prince; but the Prince is a fiction. The narrative of the Prince is a whole and Cieslak is a metaphor. But this does not mean that Cieslak is less whole than the Prince. Cassirer says:

Whoever has brought any part of a whole into his power has thereby acquired power, in the magical sense, over the whole itself. . . . The very nature of this magic shows that the concept in question is not one of mere analogy, but of real identification. If, for instance, a rain-making ceremony consists of sprinkling water on the ground to attract rain, or rain-stopping magic is made by pouring water on red hot stones where it is consumed amid hissing noise, both ceremonies owe their true magical sense to the fact that the rain is not just represented, but is felt to be really present in each drop of water. . . . The rain is actually there, whole and undivided, in the sprinkled or evaporated water.[44]

Thus, and in precisely that way, Cieslak is there.

The question of efficacy goes to the very heart of theater's function. The dynamics of ritual have been nicely put by Levi-Strauss:

There is an asymmetry which is postulated in advance between profane and sacred, faithful and officiating, dead and living, initiated and uninitiated, etc., and the "game" consists in making all the participants pass to the winning side by means of events.[45]

Events are the ritual. When it is over the initiates have been initiated and everyone is together. If theater could be an initiatory participatory game, it could be at once entertaining and fateful. But, as Cassirer notes, "word and mythic image, which once confronted the human mind as hard realistic powers, have now cast off all reality and effectuality." Cassirer welcomes this "liberation," hoping that now art will attain "its own self-realization." [46] Artaud wanted to make language "spatial and significant . . . to manipulate it like a solid object." [47] Language is a particularly heated focus of a more general conflict. The ambition to make theater into ritual is nothing other than a wish to make performance efficacious, to use events to change people. Cassirer's analysis seems old-fashioned and Artaud's prophetic.

(5) Space is used concretely and organically. Eliade describes a Fiji initiation called *nanda*. For this ceremony a stone enclosure 100x50x3 feet is built a long way from the village. This is the *nanda* (which means "bed"). Two years pass between the building of the *nanda* and the first ceremonies, which do not use it. Two more years pass before the second and final ceremony. For weeks before the second ceremony large quantities of food are stored in cabins built near the *nanda*.

On a particular day the novices, led by a priest, proceed to the *nanda* in single file, with a club in one hand and a lance in the other. The old men await them in front of the walls, singing. The novices drop their weapons at the old men's feet, as symbols of gifts, and then withdraw to the cabins. On the fifth day, again led by the priests, they once more proceed to the sacred enclosure, but this time the old men are not awaiting them by the walls. They are then taken into the *nanda*. There "lie a row of dead men, covered with blood, their bodies apparently cut open and their entrails

125

protruding." The priest-guide walks over the corpses and the terrified novices follow him to the other end of the enclosure. "Suddenly he blurts out a great yell, whereupon the dead men start to their feet, and run down to the river to cleanse themselves." [48]

Obviously the mysteries of death and rebirth animate the *nanda*. But what interests me here is the building of a simple space for one ceremony. This *ad hoc* theater is built four years before its use. Somehow the elapsed time "prepares" the space. The space is designed by the event performed in it. The walls are high enough to conceal the corpses until the last minute; the *nanda* is large enough to engulf the initiates in the bloody field of death. When the dead rise and race to the river, the initiates are alone in a large fenced-in space.

The *eravo* of the Elema is made for the *hevehe* masks. It grows over the years from rear to front as the masks grow taller. At the culminating moment of the cycle the huge *eravo* doors open and the masks dance out to fulfill their lives. The *eravo* is a womb, and the doors the passageway to life. The *eravo* doors open just once. When the *eravo* is empty of masks it is left to deteriorate. But while the masks are under construction in the *eravo* the building serves as the men's living-quarters and the village meeting-house. The womb is comfortable enough to welcome the men easily and naturally.

When the *hevehe* dance through the village and on the beaches, bands of women and children (about twenty-five in each band) weave around them so that the whole scene is made up of as many as fifty dancing groups, each orbiting around a gigantic dancing mask. The space and feel of the *hevehe* cycle is dynamic and expansive. It moves freely through the village and in spaces around the village. Other elements of the cycle include scaling walls, mock battles fought with lighted torches at night and coconut flakes and sticks during the day. The burning of the *hevehe* takes place near the river, which is tidal. High tide washes the remains of the masks out to sea. Throughout the cycle there is an interplay between the village, the beach, the river, the sea, and the bush. There is no special stage such as the *nanda*. The *eravo* is backstage, shop, office, and dormitory. Bateson (1958) describes how

the ceremonial house [of the Iatmul people] serves as a Green Room for the preparation of the show. The men put on their masks and their ornaments in its privacy and thence

An *Eravo* at Orokolo

(From F. E. Williams, *The Drama of the Orokolo*, Oxford, 1940. Reproduced by permission of The Clarendon Press.)

sally forth to dance and perform before the women, who are assembled on the banks at the sides of the dancing ground. Even such purely male affairs as initiations are so staged that parts of the ceremony are visible to the women who form an audience and who can hear issuing from the ceremonial house the mysterious and beautiful sounds made by the various secret musical instruments—flutes, gongs, bullroarers, etc. Inside, behind screens or in the upper story of the ceremonial house, the men who are producing these sounds are exceedingly conscious of that unseen audience of women. They think of the women as admiring their music, and if they make a technical blunder in the performance, it is the laughter of the women that they fear.[49]

Wherever we turn in the primitive world we find theater—the interplay among space, time, performers, action, and audience. Space is used concretely, as something to be molded, changed, dealt with. The simplest arrangement is, of course, an open area with a performance in the center and the audience on all sides. That is the shape of the Tiwi trial. Or a musical performance from inside for a gathering outside randomly standing, sitting, or moving. Or the multiple simultaneous performances of the *hevehe,* which cohere into a whole that no one person can see all of. Or the construction of special places as in the *nanda.* Or the building of an entire camp away from the village as in the *bora.* Often space is articulated by the deployment of props or elements, such as a large fire or a hollow log on which the initiates to be circumcised are put or a throne or an animal pen where a beast for a sacrificial feast is kept. Examples of different spaces can be multiplied at will. Each is made for and as part of a particular ceremony, event, or ritual.

Nowhere do we find a permanent theater or ceremonial place—a single structure whose shape is "neutral" and "adaptable" to all uses. The closest we come to that is an open space for dancing, debating, trading, dueling, trying. Or the whole village, which is a stage for everything that goes on in and around it. Throughout the primitive world events make shapes. In many ceremonies the principal architectural element is people—how many there are, how and where they move, what their interactions are, whether they participate or watch or do both. Mead and Bateson's film *Dance and Trance in Bali* (1938) shows some people keenly watching the show, others lounging disinterestedly, and several walking through the performance on their way to other business. Our culture is almost alone in demanding uniform behavior from audiences and in clearly segregating audience from performers and audience from others in the area who are neither audience nor performers.

We are also almost alone in using ready-made spaces for theaters. Possibly the development of a modern theater as a special place which can accommodate many different kinds of performances is tied to urban cultures where space is expensive and must be clearly marked out for uses. Surely the need for scene design in our theaters is an attempt to overcome the limitations of ready-made space as well as an outlet for mimetic impulses. A strong current of the new theater is to allow the event to flow freely through space and to design whole spaces entirely for specific performances. Grotowski is a master of this, using simple elements and combining these with deployment of the audience and precise movement of the performers so that the spatial dynamics of the production metaphorize the drama. Thus the audience peeps down at the sacrificial planks on which the Constant Prince is immolated or sits amid the proliferating crematorium pipes of *Akropolis* or only slightly fills the large open volume of *Apocalypsis*. *Paradise Now* stumbled through the Brooklyn Academy because that large proscenium theater blocked the flow of the performance.

In The Performance Group's *Makbeth* (1969) I experimented with audience movement through a complicated space. The environment (designer, Jerry Rojo) is not easy to describe. It is an interlocked arrangement of cubic spaces, ladders, a stairway, and a long curved ramp. The whole space is 50x40x20 feet. The lowest level is a trench six feet deep and thirty-five feet long cut below floor level on one side of the space's fifty-foot axis. Over it a vertical grandstand of five stories rises from floor to ceiling. On the floor level is a table 25x12 feet, around which the audience can sit and on which scenes are played. In three corners of the room are similar but not identical two- and three-story cubes rising to the ceiling. Along the wall opposite the grandstand is a long ramp rising from the head of the stairs to the top of a corner structure. All the space is open—there are no interior walls, doors, or hangings. At the edge of most of the platforms are narrow strips of carpet on which the audience sits. The floor is concrete and the walls of the room white.

The performance occurs throughout the space, often with three or four scenes playing simultaneously. There is no place a spectator can see everything from. On several occasions I met with audiences of around seventy-five before the show and told them they could move during the performance. "If you are noisy or block the performers' movements you can bust this thing up. If you take off your shoes so that you are absolutely silent and move from carpeted area to carpeted area, you can intensify your own and our experience. Try to understand the action and go with it. Think of yourselves as witnesses, or people in the street. Something happens—you go to see what. But you can't interfere or change what's happening." The audiences were beautifully co-operative and some impressive things occurred. During the banquet scene the empty table swiftly filled with people who became guests at Dunsinane. The murder of Banquo under a platform was witnessed by a few. During the prophecy scene in the trench where Makbeth learns of Macduff and Birnam Wood, fifty spectators stood or crouched, as around a bear-pit, while Makbeth talked to the Dark Powers who dangled upside down from pipes. Duncan's funeral cortege and Makbeth's coronation parade were augmented by people lining the ramp and joining in the processions. The soldiers advancing through Birnam Wood found allies. In many ways the performance found focus as crowds condensed and dispersed; as a few people showed up here and there; as many silently and swiftly tiptoed stocking-footed through this open but secretive castle. The audience became the soldiers, the guests, the witnesses, the crowds—the powerless but present and compliant public.

Figure 1 (page 106) is a model of experience that shows each element as different dimensions of the same plane. Elements exchange, interpenetrate, and transform—but there is no hierarchy that permanently or a priori puts any life process "above" any other. To dream is as "real" and as "vital" as to eat or dance or make love or war. Different contexts will of course make one activity more important within a given circumstance and time. The model is not ethical or personal—that is, it does not distinguish between right and wrong, good and bad, your taste and mine. Ethics, values, and tastes are always making hierarchies—but these are contingent, not fundamental. It has been customary to view theater hierarchically. For the writer the text is first and most important; to the performer his own presence on stage is the center of the event; the director knows that the theater would be impossible without him; and every technician will tell you that lights, sets, and costumes can make or break a show. Production has been thought of as a blend of many arts and as the "realization" of a text. A different view is one adapted from Figure 1 to the theater:

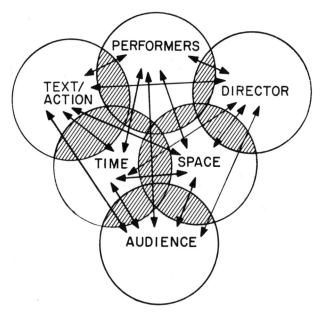

Figure 2

A complicated picture that gets more so the more elements there are. Perhaps an absurd model—for how can the director "transform" or "interpenetrate" or "exchange" with time or space; how can the audience do likewise; and so on? And if I do not mean these operations literally, what do I mean? First I mean that all elements of the theater are (like experience generally) on the same plane—there is no a priori hierarchy, no way of determining before rehearsal what will be the dominating element, if any. Secondly, *all* elements need rehearsal—which means that all elements are capable of radical, total change. Thirdly, in a way that is difficult to explain but which I have experienced, "by a sudden metamorphosis everything may be turned into everything." That is, the director finds himself deeply and personally enmeshed with the performers and their life problems; the environmentalist recognizes that action shapes space and space shapes action; the writer sees his text

131

signify things he never intended; the audience is plunged into the difficulties of the performance so completely that its reactions regulate the tone and flow of the action; the amount of time spent in rehearsals and the immediate time-span of a performance condition the performers' way of working and their interactions with each other. These are only a few of the many combinations and outcomes possible.

Mimetic theater has given us great masterpieces. Mimetic acting is a major tradition. There are other kinds of performances, however. Of these, "actuals" relate practices among primitive "whole-seeking" peoples and parts of our own population, particularly the young. Parallels can be misleadingly overdrawn. But I think our young are whole-seeking, and in a way and of a scope not experienced in our culture for hundreds of years. What we are undergoing is not a neoprimitive movement, but a postindustrial one. I think it will not be long before we know whether this is a passing phase or a genuine development of lasting power.

New York University

NOTES

1. Allan Kaprow, "Extensions in Time and Space," in *The Drama Review*, XII, No. 3, 154. Kaprow's work more than any other I know has the simple quality of "happening"—of something that is. By ever so slight a change or heightening he converts everyday actions into "mysteries." See his *Assemblages, Environments, and Happenings*, (New York, 1966), and his "poster-scenarios"—announcements of his pieces that are also the scenarios.

2. For a popular explanation of Earth Art see Roy Bongartz's "It's Called Earth Art—and Balderdash," *New York Times Magazine*, 1 February 1970, pp. 16 ff. Earth Art develops from some old impulses and is based on two principles: (1) art includes the arrangement of natural objects or the confrontation between a natural object and a man-made object—for example, draping a cliff for one mile with cloth; (2) art is autonomous and can therefore be "displayed" anywhere, even where it is not likely to be seen by human beings, such as under water or deep in a desert.

3. Francis M. Cornford, notes to Plato's *Republic* (New York, 1945), pp. 323–324.

4. Aristotle's view of the world is organic—he sees all growth and development modelled after what he observed in plants and animals. He believed that every event contains at the beginning the virtuality of its entire career. He believed in "fulfillment" rather than "transformation."

5. Charles Leslie, Intro. to *Anthropology of Folk Religion* (New York, 1960), p. xi.

6. Andreas Lommel, *Shamanism. The Beginnings of Art* (New York, 1967), p. 146.

7. Shamanism has both a technical and a broader meaning. Its technical meaning is that of a certain kind of magico-religious leadership originating with hunting peoples in Central Asia. The word is of Siberian origin. The techniques of shamanism spread westward across the northern tier of Europe and to the north shores of the Mediterranean and eastward across Siberia into Alaska and down the west coasts of both North and South America. Shamanism in its more general meaning includes all kinds of ceremonial leadership, and it is in this wider sense that I use the word.

8. Lommel, *Shamanism*, p. 148. Shamanism is not "magic" in our debased sense of that word. It is a rigorous technique that assumes communication and transformation among several kinds of experiences, including the reintegration of the past and present, conscious and unconscious, dead and living, dream and waking, individual and group. See Claude Levi-Strauss's "The Sorcerer and his Magic" in *Structural Anthropology* (New York, 1963), pp. 167–185, and Mircea Eliade's *Shamanism: Archaic Techniques of Ecstasy*, Bollingen Series LXXVI (New York, 1964).

9. Mircea Eliade, *Rites and Symbols of Initiation* (New York, 1965), p. 100.

10. *Ibid.*, pp. 100–101.

11. *Technicians of the Sacred*, ed. Jerome Rothenberg (New York, 1968), pp. 51–52.

12. *Ibid.*, p. 424.

13. Eliade, *Rites*, p. 87.

14. Lommel, *Shamanism*, pp. 138–139.

15. Eliade, *Rites*, p. 102.

16. Lommel, *Shamanism*, p. 139. The techniques of repairing the broken link are not improvised. An identification is made between word and body power and the spirits. Rothenberg, *Technicians of the Sacred*, comments (in regard to another but similar ceremony): "What's of interest here isn't the matter of myth but the power of repetition and naming (monotony too) to establish the presence of a situation-in-its-entirety. This involves the acceptance (by poet & hearers) of an indefinite extension of narrative time, & the belief that language (i.e., poetry) can make-things-present by naming them," p. 385. This is a fundamental part of actualizing.

17. Lommel, *Shamanism*, p. 139.

18. Quoted by Rothenberg, *Technicians of the Sacred*, p. 417. It is very hard to show this way of thinking to those who have not thought this way. It is a very fluid way of thinking. All experiences are virtually equal in their claim for attention, combination, transformation, overlap, and interpenetration. The distinctions which we make automatically and absolutely, say, between a mental event (e.g., a dream) and a physical event (e.g., snow falling) are not made. Each situation possibly can equate *any* two (or more) events. This is the "concrete" thinking Levi-Strauss admires and the "poetic" thinking Rothenberg admires.

19. Claude Levi-Strauss, *The Savage Mind* (Chicago, 1966), pp. 219–220.

20. Eliade, *Rites*, p. 4.

21. *Ibid.*, pp. 5–6. The implications of an event happening here and now that is an actualization of a situation which occurred "there and then" are widespread and complicated. There is no doubt that such phenomena are universal. In our own culture,

psychoanalysts call these things "acting out" and "abreaction." There is a rich literature from that point of view—see especially the special issue on "acting out" of the *Journal of the American Psychoanalytic Association,* Vol. 5, No. 4 (1957). What is involved is treating time concretely and being able to manipulate it so that any time may be any other time. This takes two forms—(1) the living of time A at time B; (2) making time T omnipresent. In both cases an integration of time is accomplished and linear unidirectional time abolished. This ability to manipulate time is essential for performing. We may also have a metaphorical actualizing—that is, the event actualized is not the "original" event, but a substitute (a displacement or a *pars pro toto*). Or there may be no "original" event but rather a series of events none of which "came first" and all of which are "available," given the right techniques to evoke them.

22. F. E. Williams, *The Drama of the Orokolo* (New York, 1940), p. 188. Williams' excellent book is unfortunately out of print. It details the whole *hevehe* cycle.

23. *Ibid.,* pp. 356–357.

24. *Ibid.,* p. 361.

25. *Ibid.,* p. 360.

26. *Ibid.,* p. 365.

27. *Ibid.,* p. 367.

28. *Ibid.,* p. 373.

29. *Ibid.,* p. 375.

30. *Ibid.,* pp. 376–377.

31. *Ibid.,* p. 373.

32. *Ibid.,* pp. 390–391.

33. Eliade, *Rites,* p. 33.

34. Williams, *The Drama of the Orokolo,* p. 364.

35. *Ibid.,* p. 367.

36. Lecture at the Brooklyn Academy, 1969.

37. Claude Levi-Strauss, *The Elementary Structures of Kinship* (Boston, 1969), p. 52.

38. All quotations and descriptions of *The Sky Is Falling* are taken from the manuscript scenario which Ortiz distributed about two weeks before an event which took place at the Middle Atlantic States regional meeting of the American Educational Theatre Association held at Temple University in January 1970. The event itself was modified the night before performance, and some changes were made improvisationally during the performance. I arrived too late to see it. I walked through the aftermath in the Ritual Destruction Room and took part in a discussion of the performance. Ortiz told me of the changes made from scenario to performance. Most important of these were: (1) Songmy atrocity posters were distributed on the campus, and the piece took on a definite war tone. Interrogations were focussed on killing and atrocities; the eggs were called "enemy foetuses"; each preliminary act of destruction was identified with killing Vietnamese; Initiates were treated as draftees, and their participation in the event called "a tour of duty"; the Destruction of the piano was identified with the destruction of a Vietnamese village—and the Indian god of destruction, Kali, was identified with Lt. Calley. (2) When the chickens/babies were delivered the partici-

pants divided into two groups, one shouting "Kill the enemy!" and the other, "Let them live!" The chickens were identified as Vietcong babies. The Shamans left the theater and ran through the campus pursued by the two groups. The goal was to run through the city streets and then back into the Ritual Destruction Room—this goal was achieved and the chickens were not killed. (3) The audience sat in the large Temple University theater and watched the event over TV—the "six o'clock news," Ortiz calls it. The pursuit of the Shamans with the chickens/babies included climbing over and through the audience watching on TV. Just prior to this a man was brought out and dumped on the stage. He was bloody, and his role was to create empathy for his plight as a victim of brutalization. He dragged himself to the edge of the stage. He vomited, drooled, writhed. Brutalizers returned from time to time to lift this man's face, spit in it, throw blood on him. People in the audience thought the man had freaked out. Several demanded that a doctor be called. But no one acted. And when the man tried to crawl off the stage and sit with the audience he was pushed back by people from the audience who said, "There's something wrong with this man—don't let him get off the stage."

Since writing my impressions of *The Sky Is Falling* I have spoken at length to Ortiz. He is interested in provoking "schizoid" reactions in participants in his events—he believes that the "palaeologic" of schizoid ritual-making is basic to "visceral acting." He feels that the individual is capable of producing his own private *system;* he makes distinctions between societies that are whole and have social ritual systems and societies, like ours, that are alienating and force people to make their own ritual systems. I hope to examine Ortiz's work in detail soon. I have let my original impressions stand here— but I now believe I undervalued Ortiz's work.

39. Eliade, *Rites*, pp. 134–135.

40. The Dani engage in ritual warfare. See Robert Gardner and Karl G. Heider, *The Gardens of War* (New York, 1968), and the excellent movie *Dead Birds*.

41. Both Shephard's and MacIntosh's comments are from *Dionysus in 69*, a book of photographs, text, variations, and commentaries (New York, 1970), ed. Richard Schechner.

42. Jerzy Grotowski, *Towards a Poor Theatre* (New York, 1969), pp. 123, 125.

43. *Ibid.*, p. 118.

44. Ernst Cassirer, *Language and Myth* (New York, 1946), pp. 92–93.

45. Levi-Strauss, *The Savage Mind*, *p.* 32.

46. Cassirer, *Language and Myth*, p. 99.

47. Antonin Artaud, *The Theatre and Its Double* (New York, 1958), p. 72.

48. Eliade, *Rites*, pp. 33–34.

49. Gregory Bateson, *Naven* (Stanford, 1958), p. 128.

PURGATORY AND OTHER VOYAGES

STRINGFELLOW BARR

Leaves from an Asian Diary

Sunday, December 20, 1953
Bangkok, Thailand

Beneath this hotel balcony the river slides quietly, gracefully past, blue under the cloudless Siamese sky. Now and then a huge heap of water hyacinth hurries silently by. Far out in midstream a number of freighters, flying the flags of many nations, lie at anchor—far out, for this is a mighty river, this is the Menam, the Mother of Waters, and today it looks as broad as the Mississippi did, forty years ago—the Father of Waters, muddy, brown, hurrying between its levees. I have not seen the lower Mississippi since except from the air; but can it possibly be broader than this Menam looks today?

Friday night, when we found this room, it was already dark and I simply could not make out what these mounds were that floated silently past. Then, in the morning, I found them floating in the other direction, and realized that ebb and flood, flux and reflux, compelled or permitted these dark green living islands to start downstream towards the Gulf of Thailand and then, without apology or remorse, to start upstream again towards those graceful pagoda spires I can see from here where I sit. At the moment, the water hyacinth hurries downstream, pretends to be putting off to sea again.

But there is a kind of transverse rhythm on the Menam that has come to fascinate me more than the water hyacinth. There are small ferries, shaped not unlike Venetian gondolas and sculled by a single female Charon. She stands in the back, managing her sweep, and she wears a sort of lampshade hat to shelter her from the hot sun. She can work her way across even this river in a matter of ten minutes, and our guide this morning claimed she could collect the Thai equivalent of two and a half cents U.S. for doing it. The sculling looks strenuous, but the guide says it is woman's work and too light to attract manpower. To the Western spectator, sitting in the shade of the Hotel Oriental, this woman's work certainly seems light—as light as ballet. Each little female gondolier, sheltered from the burning sun by her lampshade hat, takes two light steps forward. Then, on the third step, the foot never descends: it points into space, long enough to furnish a subtle balance, the pendulum moment between ebb and flood, between flux and reflux, then back swings the extended leg, and two steps backward trips the little gondolier, when the other leg swings, this time backwards into space. The leg swings straight, but not rigid; and the sarong is worn loosely enough to permit a really wide swing. It is the purest ballet and I can hardly take my eyes off the ferry woman long enough to write these words. Arno has promised me a good movie film of one of them sculling.

I am more sensitive to ballet than I was twenty-four hours ago, because of what I saw last night. When I was thirteen or fourteen years old, I saw Nijinsky dance, but it only half awakened me from the clumsiness and awkwardness of daily life. Then, around 1920, when I was at Oxford, I used to dash down to London, leaving my bike at the railway station at Oxford so I could make the porter's lodge at Balliol by the time Big Tom finished striking twelve—to see Karsavina dance. Was last night even more releasing?

We found out that the Royal Fine Arts Department of Thailand was to present at the Silpakorn Theater a *khon*, or masked play, so we went. The *khon* was based on several episodes from the great Indian epic, the *Ramayana*, especially on the fire-ordeal of Sita and the battle with the demon Banlaiyakalp. Siamese theatrical art is highly formalized and presents, as it were, the abstract essence of human life, which is normally too cluttered with the particular, the singular, the special, to be truly intelligible. It is an art that grew out of shadow-shows or that was certainly very much modified by shadow-shows. This play, for example, could present in a sort of entr'acte two characters engaged in earnest dialogue. But not only did their masks present stylized faces to the audience; not only did their highly artificial gestures preserve the style the masks had set; but readers sat with the small orchestra in front of the audience to the right and read these actors' speeches to each other as if the actors were speechless puppets. When wise words come out of a man's mouth, is it not always because some god put them there, as Athene put them in the mouth of Telemachus, son of Odysseus? Why should these live puppets before us use their own tongues to speak? I suddenly remembered that the English word *person* came from the Latin word *persona,* signifying a mask worn by a character in a play; and that some etymologists claimed *persona* came from *personare,* to sound through, as the actor's voice sounded through his mask.

The puppet must speak for himself if he would have his voice sound through his mask. But the voices I listened to last night, in the little theater, came from the small group of readers, singers, and players of instruments who sat in front of me but to the right. The faces I watched were unchanging masks that expressed the lasting character and not the fleeting moment's thought—the character of Rama, who was certainly a king and presumably a god; the character of Sita, his queen, whose fidelity to him was both genuine and ambiguous, as Penelope's was to Odysseus; the character of the demon Banlaiyakalp and that of his conqueror, Rama's monkey ally, Hanuman. Even the gestures, though eloquent and fluid, were still highly conventionalized, the eternal gestures of love and hate, of loyalty and suspicion, of hope and fear. For this is the epic of Rama, this is one of the great religious poems of all time, and liturgy there must be, if certain high matters are to be spoken of at all. The high, quavering, nasal voices of the singers to our right had the same liturgical quality, and so had the musicians who played on the xylophone, and those who beat out the rhythms with their fingers on the lovely slender drums. The conventions, the formalities, the abstractions, the quintessences were all there, the things that make civilizations possible, themselves the distillates of great cultures, things moving in patterns and rhythms that have through the long centuries baffled or dazzled or angered the barbarian who could not read them or love them. Even the dramatic narrative is the familiar one of the beloved epic, known all over Asia. There could be no "element of surprise" to distract the audience from the work of understanding afresh the oft-narrated events. The audience would be like the peasants of medieval

141

Europe who stood in awe before the frescos or statues of a cathedral, frescos that told once more the long familiar tale of an incarnate God who walked among men.

The episodes we saw included Rama's reception of his wife Sita at his camp in Lanka—the Ceylon we had so recently visited—just outside the royal citadel; Rama's doubts of his wife's chastity; Sita's ordeal by fire, her blessing by the gods, and her reunion with her husband in his bedchamber in the camp. It included also the story of the demon Banlaiyakalp and his death at the hands of Rama's ally, Hanuman, the monkey general of a monkey army. But the parts that remain most vividly in my memory are, first, Rama on his throne with some of his own army sitting at his feet and to his left and some of the army of monkey allies sitting also at his feet but to his right; and, second, the bedchamber reunion of Rama and Sita. In the first scene, the immobility of Rama, sitting on his throne, with the tall pagoda of gems towering from the top of his head, reminded me of something old Hermann Keyserling once quoted from the Chinese: "The Emperor turned to the East, and the Empire had peace." And the actors who played the roles of the monkeys at his feet were superb: their restlessness, their ostentatious scratching at themselves, their inattentiveness were all conveyed to the audience by the most highly formalized gestures: these people can extract the permanent formal element even from restlessness, as if they were conveying the unchanging principle of change itself.

In the second scene that has most stayed with me Rama has led Sita to his bed. They are king and queen, but they are also husband and wife—why do they so often remind me of Odysseus and Penelope?—and, though Sita is also a Helen of Troy for whom an entire war has just been fought and won, is she not necessarily another Sita and he another Rama, after the passage of these long years? And since they are, each one, both same and other, the relation of one to the other must be both same and other too, as the river that flows below my window here is always both the same river and another river. This ambivalent relation expresses itself as a love that is strong and deep and tender and a love at the same time that is tentative, modest, hovering, and gently asking. And all this their subtle gestures convey, above all, the turned-back, half-contorted gestures of the little Siamese hands. Their spiritual love play illumines the darkest paradox in human love: the unity their

142

love has made of them and the duality that keeps that love taut and alive. No wonder their pantomime contains both passion and wit. Now, as I look back on those two little glittering figures, with the towering pagodas springing from their headdress, with their bodies both interlaced and at the same time strenuously detached, I feel both horror and mortification that at this instant Hollywood love scenes are showing in nearly every movie theater in Bangkok. Those love scenes strive to be so strong and so significant and, measured by what happened last night between Rama and his queen-wife Sita, they are so curiously weak and incoherent. They achieve neither the simple dignity of the mounting stallion or the coupling bull nor yet the half-godlike encounter of Rama and Sita, seeking each other, finding, and seeking.

In the entr'acte the ushers vended bottled Coca-Cola, and some of us wandered through a side exit onto a terrace and smoked in the soft Siamese night, and from our darkness discreetly watched the faces of the audience in the now brightly lighted theater.

Sunday, January 17, 1954
Patna, State of Bihar, India

My meeting with Jayaprakash Narayan occurred on my first morning in Patna, as soon as I had washed up and settled in. Singh drove me to his house, where I found in his sitting room, seated in chairs, Western style, a group of Indian and American journalists sent to Patna to cover the Conference. Suddenly, from another room, Jayaprakash entered, looking incredibly tall—he actually is six feet—and dressed in Indian costume. He wore a dhoti of homespun cotton (Gandhi's inevitable *khadi*) and a gray woolen jacket, also homespun. His bare feet were sandaled. He advanced toward me and offered his hand, Western style, and murmured some sort of greeting in a low voice. Then he sat, but we said little. Of a sudden he crossed the room and laid before me a copy of *Citizens of the World*. "Do you recognize this book?" he asked, with a twinkle in his dark, hitherto melancholy eyes. "With shame," I answered. He laughed pleasantly.

I had been prepared to find Jayaprakash an imposing person, but he felt like even more of a person than Natsir in Java, which meant the most of a person I had met in Asia. This is the sort of question I have never in my whole life been able to answer. A few men are persons,

143

a lot are robots, and even more of us seem to be a mixture of person and robot. You feel yourself in the presence of a person, but merely in the vicinity of a robot. Why? Sitting in Jayaprakash's living room, I suddenly thought of Martin Buber's *I and Thou*. Apparently you encounter persons, where you merely collide with robots—or more often, you use small talk to prevent collision with them.

I had two talks alone with Jayaprakash—or J. P., as everybody calls him. In the first, he recounted his political odyssey. He had gone to America as a youngster, had studied for eight years in four successive universities, and during the depression had joined the American Communist Party. But he was also interested in Gandhi's nonviolence. Stalin's purges were more than he could take, and he fell back on Lenin. But in Lenin's writings he found the same strain of violence, and that drove him back to Marx. The violence reappeared. He returned to India, became a hero of resistance to the British, served his time in jail, tried to work in the Congress Party with Nehru, and finally founded the Indian Socialist Party, which he headed for several years. Now he has withdrawn from all practical politics to follow Vinoba and work for Bhoodan. I gather that he, like millions of non-Americans all over the world, agrees basically with Marx's diagnosis of the weaknesses of capitalism but that he does not accept the therapy. "Of course, I am still a Socialist," he said, "but I don't think India can solve her political problems without a moral revolution." Before we were through, the Associated Press appeared, in the person of Zig Harris. The conversation became more informational and, for me, less informative.

Our second conversation occurred at my hotel, where he had come to escape interruption: there was a perfect throng at his house. I said his withdrawal from Party leadership must have placed a heavy strain on his relation with Ram Lohia, who had remained an activist. I said also that I thought Ram showed signs of needing a withdrawal to reflect. And I spoke of Ben-Gurion's resigning the prime ministership of Israel to go down into the Negev, to tend sheep, and to think. He agreed that withdrawals were essential. Then he added, very simply:

"I did not leave practical politics until I had made a twenty-one-day water-fast."

J. P. left with me a pamphlet containing a recent exchange of letters between himself and Nehru. Nehru has been trying to coax him back

144

into the Congress Party. J. P. believes Nehru's purposes are basically his own. "But Jawaharlal lacks a sense of the urgency of the social problem," he declared gently. So the prodigal has not returned.

Sunday, January 31, 1954
New Delhi, India

We saw the Independence Day dances at the stadium, in some ways the most exciting experience since the National Theater at Bangkok. Cliff and I went at sunrise to the memorial services for Gandhi at Rajghat. And that afternoon all three of us heard Prime Minister Nehru address an open-air mass meeting in New Delhi, with some twenty-five thousand Indians sitting cross-legged, or standing, in a grassy common in New Delhi.

Nehru of course spoke in Hindi, although my Indian friends tell me that when he does that, he is thinking in English. Although we had nobody with us to interpret, the rapport between Nehru and his audience was something anybody could catch, whether he understood the words or not. Hindi is sprinkled with English technical terms, as Anglo-Saxon once became sprinkled with Norman French; and the words "atom bomb," pronounced in a staccato, Frenchified way, occurred repeatedly. Every time it occurred, the audience chuckled appreciatively. I had the impression that Nehru was scoffing at atom-bomb diplomacy and that his audience shared both his dislike and his amusement.

In the morning Cliff and I, at Rajghat, where the murdered Gandhi's body had been cremated, watched and listened while a large crowd sat cross-legged on rugs and read in unison Gandhi's beloved *Gita,* as one would read the psalms. After the reading there was "mass spinning" in a nearby pavilion. Gandhi of course had made mass spinning a sort of sacrament, or anyhow a sacramental; and rows of Gandhians sat at their little charkhas, spinning thread from raw cotton, in a sort of Quakerlike silence. As a matter of course, Nehru joined the spinning for a decent interval, but the malicious tell us he does not spin very skillfully. Rajghat demonstrated one thing: his dramatic sense of ceremony.

But the dances were the real event. We sat at the stadium under a starlit sky. At the center of the arena was a large stage, far enough off for the dancers to look somewhat puppet-sized. One by one the troupes from the far-flung states of the Indian Union filed into the arena, ac-

145

companied by their musicians, took their places on the dark stage, and then the stage lights came on and they began their local dances. The variety in the dances and in the spirit behind them was extraordinary. I remarked on the variety to an unknown neighbor and on the ability of his nation to produce such variety. "We Indians," he said gravely, "are not a nation. We are a subcontinent." He made the statement without a shadow of either apology or boast. He was just trying to help me understand.

One by one, the troupes came on. A group of women dancers from Bombay performed a Goan dance from Portuguese India. Their full skirts and bodices did indeed look like costumes I had seen in Portugal, and through opera glasses we could see the gold crosses hung from their necks. The music was Indian and yet—it was Mediterranean too. Then a troupe from Hyderabad did me a personal favor. They performed a dance around a village well. And, joy of joys, they all wore dark red saris and carried brass waterpots on their heads as I had seen the village women do a few mornings before on the long drive up from Bombay. They presented me with the formal quintessence of that riverside processional minus all the accidental, the trivial, the irrelevant. And to it they added what the riverside processional had lacked: the profound meaning of the common well where women go for water in a dry land but also to commune after the dryness of household solitude.

The last number of the evening started for me as a puzzle. The stage lights had gone off, and the preceding troupe could be dimly descried filing off the stage and out of the arena. And then through the darkness came the troupe from Manipur, that province that borders Burma, that province where Mongoloid features appear even in Aryan-Dravidian India. They took their places in the darkness, the women ready to dance, the men sitting in the back cross-legged, with their unfamiliar musical instruments and their inevitable, gracefully elongated Indian drums. And then the music started, the light went on, and a slow, convoluted dance began. It was a grave dance. Certain musical phrases repeated themselves insistently. The sense of repetition grew. In fact it grew until I began to wonder whether this might not be the wrong number to finish a perfect evening on. If this dance had any dramatic structure, I was impervious to that structure. There seemed something a little childish about repeating things to this point. Repetition to this point suggested that what was being said was banal, was a dead formulary, dictated by an empty piety, a flagging conviction, a weakening imagination. If it was so worth saying, why did it not find several ways of asserting itself, something more like variations on a theme? But this strong rhythm, this saying it again and in the same way, would surely end in impotence.

And then the repeated thing, the reiterated emotion, the reasserted phrase, and the gravely turning dancers suddenly gripped me, and I thought: this must be said many times to be believed. Why should one fidget and invent? How many times has the *Gita* been chanted and in how many villages? If this is true, if Manipur remembers it is true, and if we others have forgotten, why should they not tell us again, with a strong beat, with a musical phrase that must be heard again and again to be believed? And we, of Manipur, who have lived for millennia— but where in India? or is it China again?—we who are neither Aryan conquerors from the mountainous north nor swarthy Dravidians from the south, we who are certainly not Moslems from the Western highlands and would never have built the Taj Mahal, we out of the East are trying to tell you something and are repeating it as one repeats things to a small child. In the end you will understand, not only you in all the villages of India, but you who come from Europe and beyond and who wonder about the economic development of underdeveloped countries and the military capabilities of Pakistan.

The stage went dark again, and the insistent, throbbing music was stilled, and the troupe from Manipur processed dimly like wraiths back to their dressing rooms, and we in the audience stumbled out of the magic and into the modern, somewhat Washingtonian, very cosmopolitan city of New Delhi, where the British Viceroy once reigned and near where the Grand Mogul reigned before that.

Thursday, February 11, 1954
Gaya, State of Bihar, India

That afternoon Bhoodan, the land-gift mission, provided us with guides and we started through the countryside on country roads, feeling our way and consulting peasants. But the one word "Jayaprakash"

147

always elicited enthusiastic help and even, once or twice, extra passengers. We arrived after dark, our Willys groaning under its passengers, in a remote village of mud huts. We stopped at a rather elaborate brick building, a zamindar's, or tax collector's house. Somebody came out into the starlit darkness to say that Jayaprakash and his followers were at prayers. Would we wait? Or would we prefer to join in them?

My mind flew to Ram Lohia in Calcutta, who claims he has never met God; to Asoka Mehta in Bombay, who knew that the peasants would believe J. P. because he is a religious man and not just a politician; to Acharyaji in Banaras, with his frail body, his ascetic face, his noble head, and his deep disapprobation for those who introduced Hindu religiosity into problems like the land question; and to the countless other leaders of the Socialist Party who must be baffled by Jayaprakash's present life.

I said that, if we might, we would join Jayaprakash at prayers.

We were shown through a door, across an open court, and into a bare room. The earth floor was covered with straw. A gasoline lantern stood in the middle of the room, casting long shadows on the walls and illumining in sharp chiaroscuro the faces of a dozen or so men, women, and children, who sat cross-legged on the straw with their backs to the walls. A little girl of about ten or twelve was chanting the prayers. Cliff and I lumberingly sat, on the straw, cross-legged. The chant went on, the worshippers, eyes closed, joining in the wailing, drifting melody. Then there would be a moment of silence, and the little girl who led the chant would start another prayer. Finally, she started one in which I could understand the one word, Rama; and, at a given point, the worshippers clapped their hands in unison, not too loudly. Again and again the words came around to Rama and to the clapping hands. Jayaprakash sat erect, the light of the lantern doing extraordinary things to the contours of his face, his eyes closed; but he was not singing. I made a quick guess that, like me, he wanted to sing but refrained for the same reason that holds me back in church, even when my favorite canticles are being sung—in short, that he flatted his notes, or that at least he had a bad ear.

The praise of Rama ended, and there was a moment's silence.

"I see you are here," said Jayaprakash, smiling, and pressing the palms of his upraised hands in salutation. I returned the greeting.

Wednesday, March 10, 1954
New Delhi, India

Tom Keehn had us to luncheon with Lakshmi, who is intelligent and delightful. Although he looks only about thirty, he is head of the All-India Cooperative Union. As a youngster, he was a Gandhian. I asked him what that felt like.

"Very few of my generation, at least of those I knew," he answered, "really believed that Gandhi's nonviolent methods would push the British out. But what alternative was there? Anything like armed insurrection seemed to make no sense at all. The British had the weapons. So we followed Gandhi." Supposing Washington succeeds in developing a workable hydrogen bomb. Could it be there would soon be so many "weapons" and such destructive ones, for both "sides," that men would say: "So we followed Gandhi"? And that we, like Lakshmi, would say: "What alternative was there?"

On Thursday I spent a half hour with Prime Minister Nehru in his office. Nothing happened, except that we bored each other. But I would have always thought, if I hadn't gone through with the engagement, that something might have happened, and I suspect that Nehru, if he had refused to see me, might have felt he had been graceless to Boyd Orr. I wish we could have connected up. He still makes more sense to me in the international field than any other head of state. This trip has convinced me that he has a firmer hold on the hearts of his people than the head of any other non-Communist state—or, more precisely, than the head of any other state with a free press. And, after all, he governs the second largest nation on earth. In short, our failure to communicate has not changed my opinion of him. And it is a pleasure these days to see an egghead, and not a mediocrity, at the head of a government.

I found him sitting at his desk, dressed in a burnt-orange "Nehru coat," made of heavy *khadi*. A portrait painter had set up an easel and was painting his portrait, a fact to which Mr. Nehru made no allusion. He rose, shook hands, and then settled back in his chair and waited, a little coldly. I had a sudden feeling that Mr. Dulles had already smashed this conversation with his Pakistan agreement. I reminded Mr. Nehru that Lord Boyd Orr had kindly given me an introduction to him and said that more Americans than he could perhaps guess from

149

our press were grateful to him for the thoughtful and sane influence he had exercised during these perilous years. He said nothing. I told him I had just returned from a week in the villages with Jayaprakash and Vinoba and had been much moved. He was still silent, so I concluded that he preferred to consider this meeting an "interview" and was waiting for questions. In effect, I asked what forces he discerned that could make for a just and peaceful world community; and his answer was on the whole as banal as the question. It was already clear we were boring one another. But we scuffled along somehow, and he began to talk more freely, at least in volume if not in candor. It was evident that he was merely being hospitable, and I soon rose to go. Again we shook hands. His manner throughout had been correctly British, courteous but cool.

My Indian friends assured me that this was almost standard treatment at the first meeting, whereas at the second, when there was a second, he often chatted easily and brilliantly. One of them asked me whether he had dozed off lightly at any time during the conversation and insisted that he often did at the first meeting. My own judgment was that, making some possible deduction for the fact that it was no moment for a visiting American to ask him for hospitality, I had quite simply bored him. I was not surprised: I had bored myself. And since the things he had told me, some of them with considerable animation, were things I already knew, I had to admit that he had bored me too. Turn about was certainly fair play.

Thursday, April 22, 1954
Teheran, Iran

This is my fourth day in bed: Delhi Belly, known in the American colony here as Teheran Trots, or just T. T. I think I was careless about drinking-water on the two-day drive from Meshed. It was such a vicious bout that Cliff called a doctor. The cure seems mostly a diet of boiled rice and yoghurt. Cliff has done what he could to see people here, and a number of people have been kind enough to come to our hotel to talk with me, but my T. T. has reduced considerably what I might have learned here.

Dick Bernhardt's show at Meshed turned out to be absorbingly interesting, and his home was an oasis. Dick has been most patient under questioning and most adroit at getting us around to see things. His work is primarily in agriculture, health, and education. Since this countryside is stock country, he got in some magnificent Brown Swiss bulls and Merino rams and two stud donkeys from Cyprus. Also some Hampshire chickens. He has established experimental farms. In the field of health there are malaria controls, sanitary water supply, public baths. Also Point Four has been helping with a local leprosarium, which we visited. We went out with the doctor in charge, who is Iranian, and with a young American nurse. It was my first leper colony, and it proved to be a heartbreak. The lepers live in rooms around a large patio, some 250 of them, men, women, and children. Some of the children were born there, and some of the married men first met their wives there. The doctor said that although they were supposed not to go to Meshed, around 170 of them did sneak in to buy opium to relieve their pain. Although some of the patients were horribly disfigured by the disease, and although most of them exhibited a kind of languor, there was considerable activity. Some few were even working in the fields nearby, growing a crop of—appropriately enough—poppies, to produce opium. Their attitude to the doctor was moving: he was their only hope. There was something Dantesque about this agglomeration of human misery in one spot. And yet, my most vivid memory of that terrible afternoon was the Mongoloid face of an old woman, her face frightfully disfigured, gazing blindly upwards while another leprous woman brushed her hair gently and arranged a scarf around her head—tenderly, as one would clothe a little child. It was like seeing one sufferer in the Inferno holding a cup of unexpected water to the lips of another sufferer. And the leprosarium suddenly felt like a microcosm of our tortured, baffled, hating world, in which love refuses to die wholly from the earth, and in which some help, though not much, is given. Mostly, I suppose, those of us who are not lepers or who have not discovered in what sense we are, just cry, "Unclean!" and avoid the gaze of those who undoubtedly are and know it.

Wednesday, May 19, 1954
Ramat Aviv, Israel

In the New City we tried to locate Leon, to get his advice on the most economical use of our time in Israel, but we couldn't get through to him. So we decided to drive straight to Ein Hashofet. We went down the Jerusalem Corridor towards Tel Aviv, and our eyes widened at the speed with which the naked, stony Palestinian hills had been clothed with evergreens. Three years ago, when I left Israel, I promised myself to come back in fifteen years, if I possibly could, to see what the government's heroic program of reforestation would have done to the scenery. But that familiar stretches of road should in three years have been rendered unfamiliar by the young forests everywhere—that, I was not prepared for. Even if we had arrived in Israel from New York, I think I would have been impressed. Arriving from the deforested Middle East, I was overwhelmed.

Entering Israel from the East is an adventure anyhow. The last time I was here, I had come via Portugal, Spain, Morocco, Algeria, Tunisia, and Greece. Now I come from six months of wandering in southern Asia, mostly in our Willys station wagon. And I share some of the Arab's astonishment and fear at this massive spear-thrust of Western technology into the flank of ancient Asia. It is true, Asia seeps over the line, or remains not wholly obliterated. We passed three camels—but they were riding in a truck! I experienced all over again an emotion I had felt the first time I saw in Virginia a horse riding in a truck. Man bites dog. For weeks we had seen so many camels, bearing so many burdens, including that baby camel in Afghanistan. There are still camels, but in Israel they ride in trucks. Here, though on Asian soil, we are in the West again.

Ein Hashofet's new sources of water make it look very green in the midst of the Galilean hills. Ein Hashofet, "the Well of the Judge," was so named for Justice Brandeis when it was founded by American and Polish immigrants some twenty years ago. Three years ago it was my first kibbutz, or communal settlement. There is the children's house, here is the common dining hall; but the little concrete houses for man and wife have multiplied at the fringes now. Ein Hashofet's forest looks really impressive: it has grown outward as well as upward until it meets the forest of a neighboring kibbutz, Mishmar Haemek. It is too late in the season for the wild cyclamen that Oak used to pick at the forest's edge.

I asked Josh whether he and his fellow farmers were in any different plight from farmers in every other country, capitalist or socialist, once they pass from subsistence living to a money economy. I challenged him to name a country in the world with a money economy of whatever type where the city population did not have the farmer by the throat, although I admitted that how hard you squeezed the farmer's throat was a matter the city decided differently according to circumstance. I ended by telling him a little about Gandhi's weird-sounding economics and at last about Vinoba's nonviolent but drastic agrarian revolution. He listened intently. We were sitting on the Mohills' little front porch, in the starlit darkness of a Galilean night, smoking and talking. After I had described the Bhoodan operation in some detail, Josh rose, stretched, and said, "I guess you have to be an Indian to understand that stuff." And he went home to bed.

There have, of course, been notable cases in which Jews did understand that stuff. In fact, the determination to use reason and not force wherever they possibly could was one of the things that struck me hardest when I came here in 1951. The attitude of the Jewish Israeli to the Arab Israeli really moved me then: the Jew was so deeply determined that the Arab citizen would get full and equal rights in the new state. But the border raids have gone on, and the Arab states that surround this tiny pioneering country have continued their economic boycott, and I find the Israeli's nerves are fraying a bit, much as the American's nerves are fraying in the cold war with Russia. I am told that some of the Israelis, especially the newcomers, are learning to hate Arabs.

Yet Sampson, when he was checking our car for a shimmy in the steering gear, spoke to Cliff with that candid eye for justice that you see in so many Jews, in Israel as elsewhere.

"Cliff," he said earnestly, "what I'm going to tell you now is not Mapam policy or Hashomer Hatzair policy. It is my own viewpoint. I know the Arabs. I speak three Arabic dialects and I served in the British Army in Egypt. You cannot trust the Arabs. Why? It's simple. If someone stole my land, I wouldn't sleep at night until I'd stuck a knife into his back."

"But Sampson," protested Cliff, "then you believe it inevitable the Arabs will attack again."

"No, not until they have enough strength to defeat us."

"You mean that some day they really will push you into the sea?"

"Over my dead body they will," replied Sampson, somewhat ambiguously.

I told Shmuel, who had asked me what "they" were saying about "us," that the Arabs insisted they would push "the Jewish invaders" into the sea.

"It will take a lot of pushing," he answered gravely.

So I told him what the Egyptian doctor had said in that village near Baghdad: that in another generation the Israelis would be Middle Easterners just like them, and then the Arabs would push them into the sea.

"He may have something there," muttered Shmuel.

We drove up to Jerusalem again and talked with Daniel Levin, head of the Asian desk in the Israeli Foreign Office. We discussed Vinoba's campaign for gifts of land for the landless; Jayaprakash's interest in getting some Israeli technicians to help him staff the institute, or ashram, that he wants to start; and Hacohen's plans in Rangoon to have Israeli technicians help Burma construct a tire factory. We find the Burmese are now asking for the technicians and are willing and able to pay transportation and salaries. They want technical aid from neutral and uncommitted countries. Israel is also inviting J. P. to visit and see the settlements and would be delighted if they could furnish technicians for India. Unlike Burma, India has not recognized Israel yet. However, Nehru sent the Tel Aviv zoo a baby tiger the other day. The Israelis are humorous about the ambiguous nature of this sort of gift.

I finally saw Martin Buber. I greatly admire his books and had missed him when I was still in New York and he was lecturing at Columbia. Now I was almost glad: I wanted to meet him here. I went to his home in Jerusalem, hoping I could stay for half an hour without a sense of intrusion. But we began talking. It was the best conversation I have had since those with Jayaprakash, if I except my endless ones with Gebran Magdalany. And Buber took his place promptly on my list with Natsir, J. P., and Jumblatt. Feeling I might be interrupting work—and that I should hate to interrupt the kind of work he does—I tried to leave several times. But apparently he likes to talk too and all but laid hands on me when I tried to go. I ended by staying three hours, when Cliff phoned to remind me we were due at Ernst Simon's in twenty minutes.

I told him on arrival how much his books had meant to me and that I had even quoted him, perhaps incorrectly, in a book of my own: how Peter had asked him how a man as deeply religious as his own books showed him to be could defend the Marxist kibbutzim with their devout atheism; and how Buber had quoted from the Talmud: "Would they had forgotten my name and done that which I commanded them." Sure enough, I had missed some of the subtlety of the remark, but so little of it that I can't now remember exactly where he caught me offside.

I told him about our trip through Asia, about how India had hit me harder than any other country we saw, and why Bhoodan hit me harder than anything we saw in India. He knew a little about the Indian Socialists, who sent him *Janata* regularly. He wanted to know more about Bhoodan.

But before we really discussed Bhoodan, he asked me whether somebody wasn't obligated to get together a dozen or so men from all over the world and take inventory of the Hydrogen Era. He was horrified by the insouciance with which we were entering that era. I told him about Robert Sarrazac's notion that we needed a *conscience mondiale* somewhere, permanently constituted, to speak for Man instead of for parochial national governments with their petty power politics and inevitably conflicting policies. I told him also of my urging Boyd Orr to call a meeting at his home in Scotland on the whole food problem of the world, as a start to some realistic political thinking in the world community. I agreed with Buber that no step of this kind could be fruitfully taken if it involved a fanfare of publicity and that this fact would make it hard to move on the problem in America in the Era of Public Relations. He is clearly much troubled, and just as clearly our stockpile of atomic weapons is at least the symbol of his anguish.

I remarked that my own country felt as near moral bankruptcy as at any time in my life span and that our growing self-righteousness seemed to point in that direction. I said Asia had felt nearly as bankrupt to me until I had collided unexpectedly with Bhoodan and found a source of really vast moral energy. I began to describe in detail what I had witnessed in the villages. Buber became visibly excited and kept crying out: "You must write about what you saw. Just as you have been telling it to me!" I said I doubted if I had the skill to convey to

American readers what I thought I had seen. Periodically, he would say, "I can see it! I can see it!"

I told him that Europe, which I had loved all my mature life, seemed to me spiritually exhausted too. But he insisted there were people in Europe living significant lives today.

"The worker priests, for instance," he said. "I know some of them. They are alive, like your Vinoba."

We talked more about America. He reported that, except for a few men he had met there, he had found it impossible to talk to American intellectuals. He could talk freely with taxi drivers and day laborers. He had not accepted their premises, which had a curious violence about them. But he believed they and he had actually communicated. The intellectuals had never seemed to him willing to talk as man to man, but always retreated into erudition—French eighteenth-century literature or nuclear physics or some other specialty. I suggested to him that the decay of general education in America and the seepage downward of specialization, even into the high school, ought to account for the sterility he had found.

His appearance interested me. Despite his long years in Jerusalem, he remains very much the Viennese Jew, physically as well as intellectually. He is short, slightly chunky, agile. I understand that he has been recently quite ill and that he is certainly in his mid-seventies. He does not look it. His face is pink and white, his eyes are a clear blue, and he has a childlike purity of expression. He is extremely alert in conversation. Although we were repeatedly interrupted by telephone calls, he returned each time to the thread of the conversation, instantly. This was a real feat, since the thread was not an obvious thread.

"The awful thing about the period we are passing through," he said to me sadly, "is the well-nigh universal distrust between persons. I don't mean the distrust I would feel if I met, on a lonely road, a man who showed every sign of being a highwayman. I mean a worse distrust: the feeling that the man you are talking to is not telling the truth and could not tell the truth if he wanted to. I am afraid that for that distrust two men bear primary responsibility. They are both men whom I admire intellectually, and one of them I knew personally and loved. They are Karl Marx and Sigmund Freud. How can you talk to your neighbor if you believe that it is not he who is really talking, but his economic interests or his sexual desires? How can I really encounter another man, if I find in him only class interests or rationalizations? If I never listen to the ideas he expresses because I am too busy analyzing his motives for entertaining such ideas? The Marxist tends to assume, not only that a bourgeois is lying, but that, being a bourgeois, no amount of good will on his part can save him from lying."

I replied that, unhappily, especially now in America, the anti-Marxist was behaving in the same way; and that never in my lifetime had so many Americans profoundly distrusted each other.

I told him how troubled I had been by the blind hatred for Israel we had encountered throughout our drive, once we had entered Iraq; and how even more troubled I was that some of my friends in Israel were themselves being so eroded by the Little Cold War out here that they were beginning to think in terms of violence. I said that three years ago I had found them free of this blindness, but that now they reminded me of the violence that had come to characterize so much of our thinking in America—perhaps under the constant erosion of the Big Cold War.

Buber became very grave. The Israeli-Arab problem obviously caused him deep pain. He spoke wistfully of the Arab friends he had had under the British mandate, here in Jerusalem.

"And yet," he added, as if anxious to tell the whole truth, "those friendships, much as I valued them, did lack something too. They lacked something that you and I would consider candor."

There was no iota of recrimination in the remark, so far as I could detect—only the sadness of a man who values the communion between human beings as the highest thing a man can attain, next to communion with God. It was as if he were trying to describe a psychic limitation he felt in a friend he truly loved, a psychic limitation which his very loyalty to his friend forbade him to gloss over sentimentally.

I do not remember what else we talked of especially. But I found conversation with him a kind of communing that went far beyond the particular topic that footnoted the communing at any given moment of the meeting. We exchanged addresses. I promised to send him certain books I thought would interest him. We said good-bye. I wish he could sit down with Vinoba and Jayaprakash of India, Natsir of Indonesia, and Jumblatt of Lebanon. And not because of the hydrogen bomb

157

either. I would want John Boyd Orr and Einstein to be present too. I offer that company no agenda: they would need none. I did not meet U Nu in Burma, but from what I can learn of him he ought to be present too. Between them—or, for that matter, individually—I think they represent more Power than the hydrogen bomb does.

The group contains interesting overlaps. Most of them are, quite clearly, deeply religious: Natsir, a devout Moslem; U Nu, a devout Buddhist; Vinoba, a devout Hindu; Jumblatt, a devout Druse; Buber, a devout Jew. Shall I add J. P. to that list? The question feels to me intrusive. Einstein? Yes, but he would smile. I remember, after I took Abbé Pierre to call on him, he said something smilingly to me that made me feel he considered himself an agnostic and would consider any other position a presumption on his part. Boyd Orr? "Jawn" is too busy doing "that which I commanded of you" to indulge in theology. Besides, he is a reticent Scot to whom I decline to apply a Test Act.

If they have, as a group, a common love of God, have they anything in common politically? Going over the list, I find that five of the eight are socialists: U Nu, Jayaprakash, Jumblatt, Buber, and Einstein. I don't know whether Natsir considers himself a socialist; but the Masjumi Party which he heads would certainly endorse measures we Americans would consider socialistic. Boyd Orr is deeply empirical: he is a member of the British Labor Party; a director of a bank; and a canny Scot with no doctrinaire preference for either capitalist solutions or socialist solutions. He merely wants to know, in a given case, what will work. Still, Anthony Eden chose to call the committee of British industrialists which he heads Communist-dominated; and Boyd Orr has visited both China and Russia—a naughty thing these days. I am afraid none of my list, except perhaps Natsir, would fare too well before a Congressional committee.

One of the eight, Jayaprakash, is an ex-Communist. Two of them, J. P. and Jumblatt, founded socialist parties. Jumblatt is the only Socialist member of the Lebanese parliament. One of them, U Nu, is a prime minister; another, Natsir, is an ex-prime minister. Even Boyd Orr, of course, sits in the House of Lords; but he is an unenthusiastic politician. So far as I know, three of them—Vinoba, Buber, and Einstein—have never run for political office.

Four of them certainly—Jayaprakash, Boyd Orr, Buber, and Einstein

—have publicly recognized mankind's crying need for a common government. I do not know how the other five think about this.

In the field of economics all of them are deeply committed to the need for economic aid to those countries that lack modern technology; but one of them, Vinoba—and I suppose J. P. too—is more than eclectic about what elements of that technology are needed.

Six of them are scholars. I do not think J. P. would admit that he was one, and I do not know what claims can be made for Natsir, though I suspect they would be good claims. The other six are scholarly men, of whom two, both scientists, Einstein and Boyd Orr, are holders of Nobel Prizes. One of them, Einstein, is passionately fond of music; I cannot speak for the others. So far as I know, there are no poets among them. One of them, Vinoba, is commonly considered a saint.

A sign of the times: All of them speak English well; Einstein, although born and educated in Germany, is an American citizen; Jayaprakash spent eight years in America; Boyd Orr has visited America often and knows it well; Jumblatt is there right now—for the first time. Five are Asians by birth; and one, Buber, by adoption—if, indeed, Israel really is in Asia. English—or Scottish—is the mother tongue of only one; but three of the list were born and brought up in Europe. There is no native American on the list, and I can think of none I ought to add. My generation of Americans is concerned with another sort of power than the Power I believe these eight men possess in eminent degree.

I suggest all eight acquired that Power by the well-known method of withdrawal and contemplation. I know that this is true of U Nu, Vinoba, J. P., Jumblatt, Buber, and Einstein. I should guess it to be true of Natsir; and again I decline to pry into a Scotsman's habits. All eight men are conspicuously undoctrinaire in a highly doctrinaire period of history. And I mean to include Vinoba, Gandhian economics and all.

Having arranged this conference, at least in my imagination, I would propose to them that they invite Scott Buchanan to chair their meetings. I would explain to them my two reasons for the nomination: he has a gentle spirit and a tough mind. Then I would secrete myself somehow in the conference room and really learn something. I am beginning to find this fantasy more than merely amusing. If the Foundation had adequate funds left, I would ask Buber if he would care to invite the other seven men to Jerusalem; he clearly thinks conferences of this sort should be taking place. But Jumblatt would, I suppose, wreck his political usefulness in Lebanon if he entered Israel. Natsir might share his Arab coreligionists' feelings towards Israel. U Nu is perhaps too busy running the Union of Burma—although Burma is one of only three Asian states that have recognized Israel—to come to Jerusalem. Vinoba is too busy collecting land for the landless, and might easily feel my conference was big-timing; Vinoba, like Gandhi, thinks every man should hoe his own garden. Einstein is pretty frail for so long a trip now. Better leave my conference in my own imagination as merely a picture of Power, in a power-hungry world in which moral energy is in signally short supply.

Kingston, New Jersey

E. D. BLODGETT

Dante's Purgatorio as Elegy

Forse in Parnaso . . .

Purgatory is where no one stays forever. Its fire, unlike the fire of Hell, is temporary. It is a fire that makes its joyful victims acutely aware of transience and suspension between different temporal conditions. This is one of the reasons why the figure of a mountain rising both from Hell and from an indeterminate sea and reaching toward the transparencies of Heaven is so eminently suitable to the various movements of Purgatory. The mountain itself is a figure for time and, once the climb is undertaken, it seems to lead almost unerringly to two great temporal climaxes. The first is the farewell to Vergil and the second is the final act of spiritual renewal, anticipated by Statius, in which the poet is changed

> come piante novelle
> rinovellate di novella fronda.
> (33. 143–144)

Vergil returns to the ancient shades and Dante rises to the shores of light. This is the frame within which we sense that Purgatory is a kind of vast drawing apart of things and, like many situations in which we are confronted with a widening gyre, making choices and distinctions becomes an act of overwhelming poignancy. Dante, of course, is unquestionably skillful at playing with such an emotional fact. Within an almost excessively doctrinal structure, the desire, we might say, to become transient gives the poetry its peculiar elegiac cast.

161

Dante's play, however, is also a form of discipline. The reader is lured by transience the same as Dante the pilgrim. The fact of the reader's weakness is what gives such a universal character to Beatrice's reproval of Dante when he first meets her again in the *Paradiso Terrestre*. Beatrice berates Dante because he yielded to time:

> Alcun tempo il sostenni col mio volto:
> mostrando gli occhi giovanetti a lui,
> meco il menava in dritta parte vòlto.
>   Sì tosto come in su la soglia fui
> di mia seconda etade e mutai vita,
> questi si tolse a me, e diessi altrui.
>   Quando di carne a spirto era salita,
> e bellezza e virtù cresciuta m'era,
> fu' io a lui men cara e men gradita;
>   e volse i passi suoi per via non vera,
> imagini di ben seguendo false,
> che nulla promession rendono intera.
>
>   (30. 121–132)

Because of Dante's failure to see beyond the mortal and transitory, he moved away from true *bellezza e virtù*, preferring the world of flesh to the world of the spirit. Thus Vergil is sent to draw him from a transient joy to show him how to see the spirit. The magnificence of Dante's notion of such a purgatorial process is that he knows that the search for liberty depends upon giving things up. It is a search which runs headlong into the solitude and second thoughts one might have reaching an unknown shore upon an uncharted sea. It may be intellectually true that freedom is salvation, but it does not always seem so to the pilgrim trying to get his first bearings:

> Io mi volsi dal lato con paura
> d'essere abbandonato, quand'io vidi
> solo dinanzi a me la terra oscura . . .
>   (3. 19–21)

Without the pilgrim's fear of being abandoned, the *Purgatorio* would have been merely didactic. Without the canticle's doctrine, the middle state of the *Commedia* could have become merely sentimental. As the poet, however, draws the pilgrim more steadily to himself, as Rome drew Statius, elegy is pervaded with joy and assumes a special meaning.

I have suggested that Dante plays with his persona of pilgrim in such a way as to point an elegiac contrast. His dramatization of place as well as his use of characters is equally elegiac. The farewell to Vergil, however, is the most obvious example of the kind of loss which is among the enduring characteristics of elegy.[1] His departure, in fact, is more than a farewell. It is a kind of failure, a testimony to the insufficiency of a particular way of life. If the insufficiency were not radical, it might be possible to compare his yielding of his role as a guide to other famous separations in Western literature. We think of Hector and Andromache, of Dido and Aeneas, of Roland and his sword, not to speak of all of Ovid's abandoned heroines. But Vergil's return to the fire

> ch'emisperio di tenebre vincia
> (*Inf.* 4. 69)

is symbolic of the ultimate failure of reason's uses once it has been employed to the greatest avail.[2]

Vergil's departure is mentioned in two places in the poem. The first is in the course of Canto 27; the second is the brief and poignant complaint that occurs in Canto 30. The latter dramatizes the fact of absence as it impinges upon the pilgrim's consciousness. It is enough to eclipse the greater loss of Eden:

> Ma Virgilio n'avea lasciati scemi
> di sé, Virgilio dolcissimo patre,
> Virgilio; a cui per mia salute die'mi
>   né quantunque perdeo l'antica matre,
> valse a le guance nette di rugiada
> che, lagrimando, non tornasser atre.
> (30. 49–54)

Dante's action here anticipates by analogy what Beatrice later accuses him of. He fails to distinguish significant process from loss. Just as he prefers to weep for Vergil rather than for Eve's loss at this point in his ethical education, so as a youth he failed to follow the transformation of Beatrice to spirit and followed the fleeting passage of another lady.[3] The awareness of absence on the part of the pilgrim is used to illuminate his acute appetite for transience and the passing away of human things. The process of Purgatory is the response to the process of loss, but one of the characteristics of purgation is to create conditions which impress upon us varieties of absence so that we learn to distinguish their values. It is in this manner and for this purpose that Dante's memory confronts Eden and Vergil, both symbols of loss, both aspects of gain.

The canto in which Vergil actually departs is punctuated by a number of remarks and allusions that cast suggestions of elegy. While the reader is carefully reminded of the times of day on earth, the setting of the canto is toward evening. Day was on the point of departure in Purgatory, but we are told that it was dawn over Jerusalem where the sun's Creator shed His blood. The imagery of time with which the canto opens points to a specific hour for the pilgrim who is about to lose Vergil, as well as to the other hour of darkness in which Christ died. Thus absence is woven into a temporal context. But what are signals to us are not yet seen by the pilgrim. Christ's blood was redemptive in a manner analogous to Vergil's failure as an illuminator. What faces the pilgrim is more painful than the memory of Christ's crucifixion. Vergil's immediate role is to turn Dante to other afflictions:

> Ricordati, ricordati! E se io
> sovresso Gerïon ti guidai salvo,
> che farò ora presso più a Dio?
> (27. 22–24)

Not only is Dante urged to remember in a manner at once hortatory and elegiac, but Vergil is also thrown into the ambiguous situation that may be noted in the canto's opening lines. What, indeed, will Vergil do now that he is nearer to God but begin to withdraw? This is the fire that will eventually sunder father from son, guide from pilgrim, teacher from student. But to encourage Dante, he freshens his charge's memory with the name of his youthful love and suggests, by calling the fire a wall, an older fairy tale of youthful heroism. As Dante notes in his brief simile, no wall prevented Pyramus from venturing to embrace death to reach his love, and thus the pilgrim overcame his scruples of conscience. But while the focus of the reference to Pyramus concerns how he could wake to love, the fact of how he died broods through the stanza: he committed suicide from a failure in perception. Love made him believe

that Thisbe was dead. Thus the presence of Pyramus in the canto participates in the types of ambiguity already noted. The wall of fire makes
everybody acutely aware of before and after.

Once through the fire, the poets arrive in the country of pastoral and
its timeless evenings. By poetic suggestion, Dante evokes Vergil's youth
at the same time as he is about to meet the Lady of his own early poetry.
But the timeless aspects of the passages are merely the environment for
a very gradual movement forward to sleep and the illumination of the
third dream. Thus the reminiscence of many of the endings of the
eclogues is ironic, for the pilgrim merely withdraws to new perceptions,
and the reader is not urged to see evening as a sign of a little drama
coming to close at a moment when

> maioresque cadunt altis de montibus umbrae.

Thus the final evening of Purgatory continues to shape a sense of transience by the modulations of recollection, imagery, and sound-shift:

> Sì ruminando e sì mirando in quelle,
> mi prese il sonno; il sonno che sovente,
> anzi che 'l fatto sia, sa le novelle.
> (27. 91–93)

Still a pilgrim, Dante continues to be suspended between a before and
after of temporal fire in a way that recalls the ambiguity of the canto's
opening lines. The dream, however, gives ambiguity a symbolic meaning
by presenting the dreamer with a vision of Leah and Rachel. The dream
and all the flow that prepares it brings the pilgrim to a kind of interior
climax that marks by anticipation the larger transition of the whole
canticle which is the movement from Vergil to Beatrice. And with the
close of that dream

> le tenebre fuggian da tutti i lati . . .
> (27. 112)

Such is the dawn of the most glorious day in Purgatory: darkness and
flight. The contrast between this morning and the morning of the First
Day (1. 13 ff.) could not be more sharply drawn. Here, then, is the
threshold of Vergil's falling away to shade. It is the moment, we are

led to believe, that all the albas of Provençal poetry point to. Here is the loss of shade as well as the loss of all earthly light. Here Dante is ready for fulfillment at a time when he can be no more fully alone.

Purgatory might be described, in fact, as the loss of Vergil, inasmuch as it makes Dante essentially alone. It is a process that began with Cato, whom Vergil addresses when explaining Dante's journey:

> libertà va cercando, ch'è sì cara,
> come sa chi per lei vita rifiuta.
>
> (1. 71–72)

What is marvelous, however, about Dante's conception of Purgatory is that he knows that it is a kind of refusal of earthly life, which is something not yielded with ease. Thus Cato is implicated in the beginning of the journey, for Purgatory, no matter how tender and joyful, is a kind of suicide. Like suicide, Purgatory is an existential crossroad that perceives events temporally in a framework of before and after. This kind of perception is most apparent in the speeches made by those suffering from particular sins. It is also part of the structure of the broad base of the mountain, the Ante-Purgatory.

The morning of the First Day, when Vergil and Dante stand confused upon the new shore, is marked by a peculiar ambivalence which is suffused through all the objects and characters at the mountain's foot. As Dante notes,

> Noi eravam lunghesso mare ancora,
> come gente che pensa a suo cammino,
> che va col cuore e col corpo dimora.
>
> (2. 10–12)

The shore is there to underscore the sense of division and separation that the poet's anabasis with Vergil dramatizes. While it is true, as Professor Fergusson has observed, that Dante the pilgrim in the Ante-Purgatory "is always aware of the same 'distant' or homesick scene," [4] I would hesitate to agree with him by characterizing Dante's homesickness as lyrical. The Ante-Purgatory defines an elegiac situation which involves distance in the manner in which it looks behind. The look behind is struck in the initial invocation to the Muse when he bids *la morta poesia* to rise again (1. 7). We are reminded of a more immediate past when the pilgrim remarks that he has just issued from Hell, *l'aura morta* (1. 17). A variation on the pilgrim's relief occurs in Cato's surprise that someone has risen from Hell, a surprise that suggests that God's laws have been violated in such a way that the old and enduring order has been changed (1. 43–48). Thus elegy is turned to an ironic vantage: the laws indeed endure while Vergil and Dante are allowed to wander without being *esperti d'esto loco* (2. 62). Events and encounters for the pilgrims become modes of recession and loss. As Dante reaches for Casella, he fails to grasp anything:

> Ohi ombre vane, fuor che ne l'aspetto!
> tre volte dietro a lei le mani avvinsi,
> e tante mi tornai con esse al petto.
>   Di maraviglia, credo, mi dipinsi;
> per che l'ombra sorrise, e si ritrasse;
> e io, seguendo lei, oltre mi pinsi.
>
> (2. 79–84)

What occurs in fact occurs as well in rhyme. As the suffix falls in the coupling of *pinsi* with *dipinsi*, a similar suggestion of loss occurs between *aspetto* and *petto*. Thus we might speak grammatically of the failure of first encounters in Purgatory, and the failure to grasp only anticipates the sudden departure of the *masnada fresca* at the end of the canto.

Of the many other types of loss and separation that characterize this region, I shall call attention to the two which most clearly illustrate my topic. One is the meeting with Manfred; the other is the encounter with Sordello. The Manfred episode is used to create a sense of both spatial and temporal recession. The meeting begins from a search for a way through *la terra oscura*, for the certainty of some *quia* that will take them to the steps of Purgatory. They see a new crowd of spirits and begin to move toward them, and the pilgrim notes:

> Ancora era quel popol di lontano,
> i' dico dopo nostri mille passi,
> quanto un buon gittator trarria con mano . . .
>
> (3. 67–69)

The same crowd had already tried to move toward Dante and Vergil—

> e non pareva, sì venïan lente.
>
> (3. 60)

167

Thus Dante's uncertainty is reflected by the crowd *chi va dubbiando,*
not only creating vast openings of space but also slowing down time.
It is precisely time's loss, figured in the hyperbole of the thousand steps
across the shore, that defines the special poignancy of the excommuni-
cated and the more general pathos of all that precedes Purgatory. Purgation depends upon time in order to reach God's time by the renunciation
of earthly time. And so, not knowing what to look forward to, the
souls of the shore can only look back and wait. It is a region filled with
the mood and pace of Richard II's speech as he awaits the arrival of
Bolingbroke and exclaims:

> For God's sake, let us sit upon the ground
> And tell sad stories of the death of kings—
> How some have been depos'd, some slain in war,
> Some haunted by the ghosts they have depos'd,
> Some poison'd by their wives, some sleeping kill'd,
> All murthur'd.
> (3. 2. 155–160)

Here, before Purgatory, doing nothing is not sweet,

> ché perder tempo a chi più sa più spiace.
> (3. 78)

Manfred's particular speech is very brief and focussed upon two major
points: his body, disinterred by the archbishop of Cosenza, and God's
love, which cannot be put out by papal malediction. It is a speech deliberately designed to avoid explaining *lo perchè* and, thus, rising from the
simplicity of the narration, is the striking solidity of his body's bones
that the rain washes and the wind moves. Manfred does not yet conceive
of himself as a spirit but as a body behind him, still enmeshed in process
and decay. It is a body, furthermore, that symbolizes the random weari-
ness of the long wait that the souls in the Ante-Purgatory have before
them. For them, time has stretched thin. For them, time seems merely
to go by without meaning, for these are souls who are literally stranded
between earth's time and God's time. What seems most important to
Manfred is the message he wishes Dante to take back to his *bella figlia.*
While the speech is hardly nostalgic, it is concerned with the past and
with the things of earth. To that extent it participates in the mood of

the opening lines of the eighth canto. Manfred's is the voice of one whose ear is still attuned to

> squilla di lontano,
> che paia il giorno pianger che si more.
> (8. 5–6)

Dante the pilgrim is also entranced, it would seem, by the same distant sound, for in the time that he took listening and gazing with wonder upon Manfred the sun rose fifty degrees from the horizon. Over such a stretch of time, even Manfred's bones would become ethereal. The speech, then, within the framework of the slow walk that precedes their meeting and the discussion on perception that begins the fourth canto seems to make earthly time dissolve:

> vassene 'l tempo e l'uom se n'avvede . . .
> (4. 9)

The encounter tends to break down the outlines of events and make the past recede to where the prior time appears, as one of the Old English elegists says, *swa hit no wære*,[5] as if it never were.

The encounter with Sordello is of a different order. It is at once more intimate and more political, springing from the almost magic mention of Vergil's birthplace. For the moment I should like to concentrate upon the seventh canto, in which Vergil identifies himself. It is remarkable self-description, for Vergil does not reveal himself as the author of the *Aeneid*, but rather as

> Virgilio; e per null' altro rio
> lo ciel perdei che per non aver fé.
> (7. 7–8)

It is upon such an accent of loss that the canto begins and proceeds. And the statement is particularly appropriate as an anticipation of the pilgrims' sojourn in the valley of the rulers, who neglected their duty and thus jeopardized their heritage. It is a canto of protracted lament which, in contrast to the Manfred episode, recedes into the future. It is an elegy of men whose failure ruined what they should have protected.

What I have spoken of as division or separation—the suspended state that may conduce to an idea of elegy—is suggested in this canto both thematically and rhetorically. When Sordello is told he has been speaking to Vergil, he acts as one

> che crede e non, dicendo "Ella è . . . non è . . ."
> (7. 12)

Sordello's implied doubt becomes a very painful echo of the short sounds of grief that harmonize Vergil's statement,

> lo ciel perdei che per non aver fé.

In a sense, this might be called the original speech of elegy, to say *è è*. Here, however, the dialectic of loss and gain is both the intellectual environment of the Ante-Purgatory and Vergil's own situation. Vergil has lost the sight of the high Sun:

> Non per far, ma per non fare . . .
> (7. 25)

Thus the sound of elegy is used to initiate a dramatization both of Vergil's loss and of the loss of the negligent kings.

The same kind of spatial and temporal vagueness that is apparent in the Manfred episode may also be noted here: it provides the background against which one is undone by not doing. As Sordello remarks,

> Loco certo non c'è posto . . .
> (7. 40)

It is a landscape whose uncertainty is reflected by the uncertainty of rulers who fail their duty. It is a place, finally, that calls for Sordello's pessimism when he states that

> Rade volte risurge per li rami
> l'umana probitate . . .
> (7. 121–122)

The valley suggests a receding future of failing heritage, a future which is seen as dimly as the kings seated at random in the twilight—

là dove più ch'a mezzo muore il lembo.

(7. 72)

Vergil participates in the failure of light and failure of doing, and it is this participation that gives the scene its pathos. For him as much as for the kings it may be said that

del retaggio miglior nessun possiede.

(7. 120)

This scene is analogous then with the later canto in which Dante is conscious of his loss of Vergil. It is part of the whole rhythm of the canticle, which forces characters and reader to look behind, to become attuned to different kinds of losses and withdrawals. It is a structural and thematic rhythm that is succinctly figured in Dante's early appeal to Vergil as they start to climb the mountain:

O dolce padre, volgiti, e rimira
com' io rimango sol, se non restai.

(4. 44–45)

Not only is the liberty Dante seeks fearful, but also the things behind constantly remain attractive. Reaching one of the first "viewpoints," the poet tells the reader,

A ceder ci ponemmo ivi ambedui
vòlti a levante ond' eravam saliti,
che suole a riguardar giovare altrui.

(4. 52–54)

As a consequence, one of the poetic pleasures of the Purgatory is the fact that looking back is not entirely painful. In fact, remorse of conscience seems effectively ambivalent as Vergil implies in his suggestion to Dante:

Volgi li occhi in giùe:
buon ti sarà, per tranquillar la via,
veder lo letto de le piante tue.

(12. 13–15)

171

But, as I indicated earlier, it is in such a manner that Dante uses poetry for theological effect. It is as if the reader were meant to enjoy the wrong thing, to follow Dante the pilgrim when he prefers to weep for the loss of Vergil rather than for the loss of Eden. As Dante the poet plays with the persona of the pilgrim, so he plays upon the misplaced sentiment of the reader. In this way, as the pilgrim's experience approaches the poet's wisdom, so, it is hoped, the reader's experience will undergo the same process.

The rhetoric with which Dante shapes contrition is employed precisely to give the reader a false theological pleasure and permit him to enjoy the wrong thing. To what other end are the anaphora and *exclamatio* directed when the pilgrim addresses the *exempla* of the punishments of the proud? Pride assumes an elegiac mask:

> O Nïobè, con che occhi dolenti
> vedea io te segnata in su la strada,
> tra sette e sette tuoi figliuoli spenti!
>   O Saùl, come in su la propria spada
> quivi parevi morto in Gelboè,
> che poi non sentì pioggia né rugiada!
>
> (12. 37–42)

If the reader does not wish to linger upon such portraits to the extent that the pilgrim does, then Vergil's admonition not to lose time has little effect. The point of presenting so attractively the many varieties of pathos is to force a kind of satiation of grief, in other words, to purge pathos, for a heaven where past and present do not seize the soul across an elegiac space. This is done by employing, if such a phrase is permitted, a rhetoric of purgation. It is rhetoric that urges the pilgrim, not to speak of the reader, to look back according to *la punctura della rimembranza*.

The same technique is used in Guido del Duca's appeal to the failure of Romagna:

> Ov' è 'l buon Lizio ed Arrigo Mainardi,
> Pier Traversaro e Guido di Carpigna?
> Oh Romagnuoli tornati in bastardi!
>   Quando in Bologna un Fabbro si ralligna?
> quando in Faenza un Bernadin di Fosco,
> verga gentil di picciola gramigna?

172

Non ti maravigliar s'io piango, Tosco,
quando rimembro, con Guido da Prata,
Ugolin d'Azzo che vivette nosco,
    Federico Tignoso e sua brigata,
la casa Traversara e li Anastagi
(e l'una gente e l'altra è diretata),
    le donne e ' cavalier, li affanni e li agi
che ne 'nvogliava amore e cortesia
là dove i cuor son fatti sì malvagi.
                                    (14. 97–111)

The reason that passages like these are so moving is not so much because of their structure, because of their questions and exclamations, because of the skill with which future and past are made to be psychologically the same thing, or because so much talent is used to attack the Romagnuoli turned to bastards. On the contrary, Guido's outburst is a cry of sadness, and the reader, as much as Dante, marvels at the grief. For against the prick of memory, the fact that hearts have become wicked only makes more pathetic those who felt that *è mestier di consorto divieto*. In spite of the sin for which the loss of so many is invoked, the character of the invocation runs contrapuntally against sin and gives the tirade a tone the same as that of Villon in his more famous ballades. The accent of the appeal falls upon its rhetoric, upon the nostalgia of memory, and, finally, upon the reader's memory of his own pain, brooding upon those who have gone before. It is the same kind of plaintive note that resides in Statius' query of Vergil:

dimmi dov' è Terrenzio nostro antico,
Cecilio e Plauto e Varro, se lo sai:
dimmi se son dannati, e in qual vico.
                                    (22. 97–99)

It participates, finally, in the same *moto spiritale* that urges Dante to weep over the loss of Vergil despite Eve's greater loss. It is a sorrow similar to that which punctuates the examples of anger when the pilgrim sees Lavina:

surse in mia visïone una fanciulla
piangendo forte, e dicea: "O regina,
perché per ira hai voluto esser nulla?

173

Ancisa t'hai per non perder Lavina;
or m'hai perduta! Io son essa che lutto,
madre, a la tua pria ch'a l'altrui ruina."

(17. 34–39)

Such an image seems to capture in microcosm what we have been examining as the elegiac aspect of Purgatory. It is loss implicated in other loss, in the process of which relationships are changed for the worse. The rhetorical skill is obvious to the point where it borders upon deliberate sentimentality, which eventually, like a form of homeopathic therapy, carries both pilgrim and patient reader to an awareness of order beyond personal loss.[6] Lavina's first word is *regina,* which is not only answered by *Lavina* and *ruina,* but also by another vocative that consummately defines domesticated tragedy:

madre, alla tua pria ch'al l'altrui ruina.

Loss as a kind of heritage is made rhetorically intimate in the change from *perder* to *perduta,* and it is not hard to sense an allusion here to the sons of the negligent rulers. Lavina, finally, underscores the elegiac character of the vision by sharing the sorrow of Amata's fate but at a distance, so that her grief becomes distilled and vaguely ironic. A similar technique may be seen in Ovid's version of Dido's epistle to Aeneas:

Facta fugis, facienda petis; quaerenda per orbem
    Altera, quaesita est altera terra tibi.
Ut terram invenias, quis eam tibi tradet habendam?
    Quis sua non notis arva tenenda dabit?
Alter amor tibi restat habendus et altera Dido:
    Quamque iterum fallas, alter danda fides.

(*Heroides* 7. 13–18)

Although the skill with which Hellenistic rhetoric is employed in this passage is obvious and forced, it throws into relief the same qualities I have been indicating in Dante. As the last line makes bitterly clear, separation continues to occur like a tragic curse. It is a sense of loss that seems to penetrate Vergil's poetry almost inevitably, and Orpheus' successive failure gives it an archetypal stamp. As Vergil tells us, after Orpheus looked back, Eurydice

174

fugit diversa, neque illum
prensantem nequiquam umbras et multa volentem
dicere praeterea vidit . . .

(Georgic 4. 500–502)

It is the sentiment that penetrates profoundly Forese Donati's question to Dante,[7]

Quando fia ch'io ti riveggia?
(14. 75)

I have purposefully devoted most of the space of this paper to the *Purgatorio* as a poem of loss inasmuch as its didactic structure and tone are more widely appreciated. But all elegy is not *flebilis,* even though it seems committed to change and process. The question, then, that we might ask, is whether only the kinds of things I have pointed to are elegiac. Is it possible to consider the rest of the canticle as elegy? Paradoxically, it can be, but in a manner that creates from the counterpoint of two kinds of elegy a genre of greater value than those which went into its composition.

The other kind of elegy which the didactic elements of the *Purgatorio* resemble is early Greek elegy, particularly the poetry of Tyrtaeus and Solon. What characterizes their poetry is an essentially ethical intent which encourages a young man to compete for the highest prize. For Tyrtaeus, the prize was valor in battle:

Hoûtos anèr agathòs gígnetai en polémoi
(This man becomes good in battle.)
(Diehl, fr. 9. 20)

For Solon, life was not merely a matter of community defense, but rather a contest that involved more complicated aspects of ethics. The city, as he observes in one of his central poems, is not a Spartan camp but a social organization beset by the ills of pride and surfeit (Diehl, fr. 3). From these psychological conditions develop sociological and political break-downs. The hope of the city lies in the concept of *Eunomía,* or Good Order. The poet's role is political; his style is analytical; his tone is hortatory. All of these characteristics are reflected in the didactic elements of Dante's poem, with certain significant differences.

175

Dante's politics are of course subsumed under theology. Nevertheless, Good Order—even if more profound than Solon's idea of it—is the hope which sends Beatrice after Dante. The exhortation to virtue is shared by both Dante and the Greek elegists of the seventh and sixth centuries B.C. Adjuration, in fact, is signaled by Eric Auerbach as one of the "three hallmarks of Dante's style," [8] and adjuration, as Jaeger remarks, is, if nothing else, "the one constant element in elegiac poetry." [9]

The major difference, however, between Dante's use of parainetic elegy and the Greeks' is the fact that Dante employs process and development when he teaches. Instead of the static moral exhortation of the type cited above from Tyrtaeus, Dante's whole notion of ethics as it is exposed in the *Purgatorio* depends upon love as a *moto spirituale*. It is with such a notion that Dante unifies ethics and poetry.[10] But to see the teaching of ethics, to understand paraineses to virtue as dependent upon process is the mark of Dante's understanding of Purgatory. The result of Dante's perception is that he never forsakes the sense of movement and process upon which Alexandrian elegy depends. But against the notion of things slowly receding from loss to loss, Dante poses another kind of movement that carries the renewed soul, like Statius (not to speak of Dante the pilgrim), closer to new gains. Thus, the didactic element of *Purgatorio* not only recalls the early Greek elegy, but also seems to spring directly from the later elegy of lament. The process of parainesis, then, connects both types of elegy in intellectual and poetic counterpoint. Their dual effect, as poetic movements, serve to carry out Cato's command

> a spogliarvi lo scoglio
> ch'esser non lascia a voi Dio manifesto.
> (2. 122–123)

An example of both kinds of elegy working toward such an end may be seen in Dante's brilliant cry of adjuration and despair beginning *"Ahi serva Italia . . ."* (6. 76 ff.). It is also what resides in the inversion of Statius' line, *"a sè mi trasse Roma"* (21. 89): as the poet returns to the source of his language, he approaches, unwittingly, what will be the new Rome of his conversion. Going backward, in the case of Statius, turns out to be a movement forward. The phrase *in nuce* seems to fix the effect of the double movement of the *Purgatorio*. While it seems as if much of the movement of the canticle is toward loss, the movement is a paradox. It suggests the drawing back of a bowstring whose purpose is to propel an arrow suddenly in an opposing direction.

It would be unwise to assert that Dante had a firsthand knowledge of the early Greek elegy. We might conjecture that his understanding of its effects developed from his knowledge of Aristotle's *Ethics* and the Provençal *sirventes*. The combined effect, however, of the kinds of elegy I have been examining seems to be his own discovery. One of its aspects is its similarity to Old English elegy. Space does not permit even the slightest analysis of this small body of poetry. Suffice it to say, however, that while it shares with Hellenistic elegy a sense of irremediable separation and loss, it is also characterized by an effort to come to grips with a new situation by doing more than lamenting. While not carrying parainesis to the point of invective, it often suggests an acceptance of new values by a subtle interplay of shifting perspectives.[11] The role of shift and contrast is to achieve some measure of understanding of the fact and implications of loss. As Leonard H. Frey has put it, "the likely movement is toward a general understanding of the nature of the world, beginning with contemplation of one's own situation." [12] And the situation is inevitably the problem of transience, which conduces to reflection upon things more permanent than what was. What makes the Old English elegies particularly persuasive is the use of the first person as a dramatic speaker. The lament is not for someone else but for the poem's speaker and through him all who are alienated or exiled. We might claim the same for Catullus 68 (*Quod mihi fortuna casuque oppressus acerbo . . .*) except for the fact that the design of loss in that great elegy protects the speaker from participating in loss. For Dante and Old English elegy, loss means in a very profound sense self-loss and self-re-evaluation. It is a purgatorial act.

No one, of course, need ask whether Dante had read or needed to read Old English elegy. It was an expression of medieval poetic consciousness and, to the extent that Dante participated in the "medieval spirit" (the studies of Karl Vossler and E. R. Curtius make this abundantly clear), a discovery of the effects of Old English elegy was possible. Thus Dante may be said to have completed the vision of these anonymous elegists in the process by which he adapted Hellenistic and, unwittingly, early Greek elegy.

University of Alberta

NOTES

1. As a working description of the kind of elegy the bulk of this paper discusses, Northrop Frye's is sufficient: "the elegiac is often accompanied by a diffused, resigned, melancholy sense of the passing of time, of the old order changing and yielding to a new one." See *Anatomy of Criticism* (Princeton, 1957), pp. 36–37.

2. See Francis Fergusson, *Dante's Drama of the Mind* (Princeton, 1953), p. 166.

3. Whether there was "another woman" is in historical doubt. What counts, nevertheless, is the fact of "falling-away," which Erich Auerbach has already discussed in *Dante: Poet of the Secular World,* ed. Theodore Silverstein, tr. R. Manheim (Chicago, 1961), p. 115.

4. *Dante's Drama,* p. 23.

5. "The Wife's Lament," 24. Cp. "The Wanderer," 95–96.

6. Although it would be imprudent to claim extremely early influences of Dante upon Chaucer, a similar use and understanding of sentimentality as necessary to purgation may be observed in the *Book of the Duchess.*

7. The dramatic context within which this question is uttered is one that establishes a rhythm of appeal without response. Here are souls *che pregano, e 'l pregato non risponde* . . . (109). Such an ambivalent situation is highly suggestive of Leo Spitzer's discussion of Jaufré Rudel's paradoxical *amor de lonh* in *L'amour lointain de Jaufré Rudel* (North Carolina Studies, 1944), repr. in *Romanische Literaturstudien 1936–1956* (Tübingen, 1959), pp. 363–417. Although Spitzer wishes to emphasize "le thème foncièrement chrétien 'possession-non-possession' de cette poésie séculière" (p. 404), I am inclined to doubt him. The same theme can be found in ancient poetry. It is one of Ovid's favorite rhetorical devices. Vergil was equally fond of it. It was hardly Christian in Dante's sense. It might be more accurate to say that Dante uses such a theme to overcome the pathos it engenders.

8. *Dante,* p. 59.

9. Werner Jaeger, *Paideia: the Ideals of Greek Culture,* tr. G. Highet, 3 vols. (New York, 1943–1945), 1. 89.

10. Fergusson, *Dante's Drama,* p. 92.

11. See Neil D. Isaacs, "Image, Metaphor, Irony, Allusion, and Moral: the Shifting Perspective of 'The Seafarer,'" *Neuphilologische Mitteilungen,* LXVII (1966), 266–282.

12. "Exile and Elegy in Anglo-Saxon Epic Poetry," *Journal of English and Germanic Philology,* LXII (1963), 294.

PHILIP PASTRAS

Unamuno's Romantic Tragedy

Suffering is the key to Unamuno's concept of tragedy. The epigraph of the seventh chapter of *The Tragic Sense of Life* is a passage from Byron's *Cain*:

> Cain: Let me, or happy or unhappy, learn
>   To anticipate my immortality.
> Lucifer: Thou didst before I came upon thee.
> Cain: How?
> Lucifer: By suffering.

Joaquín Monegro, the protagonist of *Abel Sanchez*, learns of the existence of his soul and anticipates his immortality by suffering, just as his Byronic prototype does. The basic conflict of the novel can be stated quite simply: Joaquín and Abel, who have known each other as long as they can remember, are almost like brothers, we are told at the beginning of the novel. A pleasant but rather insipid young man with a talent for painting, Abel Sanchez is honored by many friends and achieves a degree of fame for his work. Joaquín broods over his isolation and his anonymity as a practicing physician and dreams of the day when he will be able to devote his time to scientific research. The first crisis in the novel occurs when Abel wins the hand of Helena, whom Joaquín himself loves. Joaquín's brooding then turns to passionate hatred and envy of Abel. Through the rest of the novel, the suffering that his passion evokes varies in intensity as he is torn between revealing and concealing his hatred.

The mythical frame plays a symbolic role in the novel when Abel

179

decides to do a painting on the theme of Cain and Abel. When Abel reads the passage from Genesis, Joaquín stops him at the line in which God reveals his preference for Abel's offerings: "And why is that?"— Joaquín interrupted—"Why did God look with favor at Abel's offering and with scorn at Cain's?" Abel replies: "It is not explained here" (*Obras completas*, ed. Manuel Garcia Blanco, Madrid, 1958, 2. 1040). As it stands, the biblical account is not concerned with the reasons for God's preference: it is the story of Cain's guilt and punishment. Against this view, Joaquín evokes the Byronic view, in which the antagonist becomes the protagonist. The absence of rational motive for God's choice causes Joaquín to interpret the passage as the story of an injustice committed against Cain.

The irony of this scene lies in the fact that it is Abel who introduces Byron's *Cain* to Joaquín. Unamuno has already hinted at the Byronic prototype for Joaquín, not only in the dialogue on Genesis, but also in the personal mannerisms of his hero: the other characters sense traces of his passion and suspect the presence of an unnameable guilt; the narrator observes Joaquín's melancholy habits, his piercing eyes, and his pallid complexion; and Joaquín frequently turns pale in the middle of a conversation when he suspects that someone has discovered his secret passion.

The biblical and Byronic versions of the Cain myth within the novel represent Joaquín's awareness of his relation to Abel. On one level, Joaquín sees himself as the biblical Cain and fears that he, too, will murder his "brother." His hatred of Abel is hateful in itself; he struggles to rid himself of his passion, although he does not succeed. On another level, the intensity of Joaquín's passion and the intensity of his struggle against it give him a heroic dimension which evokes the Byronic Cain, the man whose crime and guilt are so enormous that he compels awe and even admiration. It is *because of*, not *in spite of*, his passion that Joaquín achieves the depth of his moral perspective, which is quite close to the moral perspective of the novel itself. Although Unamuno adopts the third-person point of view, we see the action of the novel unfold through the eyes of Joaquín. Through the device of interpolating pieces of the *Confession* that Joaquín wrote in the last years of his life, the narrator provides us with glimpses of his protagonist's internal struggle at significant points in the action. In fact, that device accounts for most of the moral and metaphysical dimensions that grow from Joaquín's hatred for Abel.

When Abel returns from his honeymoon with Helena, his life is threatened by a sudden illness. Joaquín realizes that it is in his power to let Abel die without arousing suspicion and thus to rid himself of his hated rival. But at a critical point, which is described in the *Confession,* Joaquín decides that he must save Abel. Joaquín arrives at his decision when he realizes that he needs to keep Abel alive. The meaning of the insight is not elaborated at this point in the novel. Joaquín senses its truth and acts without much further reflection. His exhilaration over his "victory" approaches delirium, and for the first time he sees himself in the grip of madness. The dialectic of Unamuno's tragic vision is nowhere more succinctly articulated: Joaquín's happiness grows out of his misery; and the fact that the two emotions are inextricably bound helps us to understand, by implication, why Joaquín feels that he needs Abel.

Earlier in the novel, we are told that Joaquín's depression over Abel's marriage brought him to "the discovery within myself that there is no soul." That statement prepares us for the further development of the theme of Joaquín's dependency on Abel. When Joaquín later reads Abel's copy of Byron's *Cain,* he records his reaction in his *Confession*:

Until I read and reread Byron's *Cain,* I, who had seen so many men suffer and die, did not think about death, did not discover it. And then I wondered if, at death, I would die with my hate, if it would die with me, or if it would survive me. I wondered if hate survives those who hate, if it is something substantial that is transmitted, if it is the soul, the very essence of the soul. And I began to believe in Hell, and that death is a being, is the Demon, is Hate personified, is the God of the soul. (*Obras,* 2. 1044.)

Just as Unamuno, the novelist, says in *Three Exemplary Novels* that an idea can become a person, Joaquín sees death as "Hate personified" (*Obras,* 2. 1044). The phrase that Unamuno uses habitually to describe the purpose of his fiction is "to undress the soul," and the action of Joaquín exemplifies that purpose. Joaquín not only reveals his soul, first to himself and then to others, he also discovers it: "What I had not found with the scalpel in others, I found in myself. A corruptible organism would not be able to hate as I hated." (*Obras,* 2. 1039–1040.)

In Byron's *Cain,* Joaquín finds a mirror in which he sees his own soul

181

reflected. In that mirror, he sees that his life has been defined by his hatred of Abel. He craves for a fame that will eclipse Abel's. He has married so that he, like Abel, can have a child to survive him: "perhaps I married only to create more hateful people like myself, to transmit my hatred, to immortalize it" (*Obras,* 2. 1045). Joaquín comes to understand what Unamuno says in *The Tragic Sense of Life*: "Consciousness is a sickness" (*Obras,* 16. 144). As a doctor, Joaquín frequently speaks of curing his passion, which he sees as a sickness, but he comes to realize that his sickness is his consciousness and his life. And if passion brings him to the point of madness, how can he be cured without denying his life? It is for this reason that he could not let Abel die. Joaquín's rational motive in the novel is to cure himself of his hatred. More often, however, that motive is expressed in his desire to kill Abel, and so to rid himself of the source from which he feels that his life has been poisoned. But he discovers that his hatred is "something substantial" within himself, a principle of his own being that he cannot destroy without also destroying himself.

The motive that arises from Joaquín's insight takes the form of a recognition of his tragic situation: his rational need to be cured of his passion and his knowledge that he cannot live without it represent the poles of the conflict within which Joaquín is to live his life. The conflict varies only in intensity. Joaquín wins a few victories, and for a time the conflict seems to have been stabilized. His lecture on Abel's painting is considered by the audience to be a greater triumph than the painting itself, and his desire to eclipse Abel is at least partially fulfilled. Abel's son takes up medicine rather than painting, becomes a disciple of Joaquín, and helps Joaquín to prepare the book that is to be the masterwork of his life and experience as a doctor. But in fact the conflict has never abated. After the triumph of the speech, Joaquín is aware only of defeat. He had hoped that he could cure himself of his envy by eclipsing Abel; instead, he finds that he dreams of dedicating himself to oratory in order to keep Abel constantly in the shadow of his glory. And when Joaquín's daughter marries Abel's son, the child that is born of the union favors Abel, who delights his grandson with his drawings; the child shuns the morose Joaquín.

The conflict over the grandson finally destroys Joaquín. When he asks Abel to leave and never return, Abel tells him that he is insane, and the argument that ensues reaches its climax when Joaquín attacks Abel physically. Although Joaquín does not literally kill Abel, the shock causes Abel's weak heart to give out, and Joaquín blames himself for the death of his friend. Less than a year later, Joaquín, suffering from "an obscure disease," is on his deathbed. When his wife tells him that he could live longer if he wished, he replies:

Why? So that I can come to be an old man? To truly old age? No, not old age! Egotistical old age is nothing more than an infancy in which there is consciousness of death. An old man is a child who knows that he must die. (*Obras*, 2. 1119.)

Unamuno deliberately obscures the facts concerning the "murder" of Abel and the death of Joaquín. To say that Joaquín considers himself morally responsible for Abel's death is not enough: Joaquín has been murdering Abel all of his life. Like the inhabitants of Dante's *Inferno*, Joaquín appears to us fixed at the moment of his crime. If we remember that the hunger for immortality is man's most vital impulse in Unamuno's world, we can see that Joaquín's desire for eternal oblivion indicates the dimensions of his final defeat. But the final irony of Joaquín's story appears in the title itself: the novel which tells his story is named after the man that he envied and hated all of his life.

The idea of tragedy that informs *Abel Sanchez* is foreshadowed in Unamuno's philosophical work, *The Tragic Sense of Life,* which preceded the novel by four years. Joaquín Monegro is "the man of flesh and bone" of the essays: the man "who is born, suffers and dies—above all, dies." Unamuno places Aristotle's definition of man as a "political animal" in the rationalist tradition and opposes to that definition the man of flesh and bone, who has a hunger for immortality which reason alone cannot appease. We might expect, therefore, to find Unamuno's concept of the tragic hero in conflict with Aristotle's. Aristotle advises against exhibiting the fall of either a perfectly good or a perfectly bad man, since the first is merely shocking, and the second inspires neither pity nor fear. The Aristotelian ideal is "a man like ourselves," the character between these two extremes (*Poetics*, 13. 2–3). Joaquín represents the opposite of the ethical norm by which Aristotle defines the tragic hero. He is not "a man like ourselves" in Aristotle's sense, but a man whose life is consumed by envy and hatred of his closest friend. Aristotle's definition does not encompass the fall of the "perfectly bad man" whose fall *does* arouse the emotions of pity and terror: that is, the satanic hero of the romantic tradition. Joaquín is able to arouse those emotions because he compels our admiration through the enormity of his guilt and suffering. If it can be said that Joaquín represents the norm in Unamuno's tragic vision, it is clearly not an Aristotelian norm, the mid-point between two extremes; rather, Unamuno tells us that extreme behavior is the "norm" of humanity.

A more significant departure can be seen in the value which Unamuno places implicitly on the three parts of the plot described by Aristotle: the reversal of the situation, the recognition, and the scene of suffering. Aristotle spends most of Chapter 11 of the *Poetics* defining the reversal and recognition and explaining why, in an ideal plot, reversal and recognition occur simultaneously. This emphasis is clearly owing to Aristotle's interest in the rational elements of plot-construction: that is, to use *Oedipus the King* as an example, in the manner in which the audience, as well as Oedipus himself, discovers the nature and outcome of Oedipus' action. Like Oedipus, we are driven through the play by a desire to know what actually happened. Only when all the pieces are in place, when the recognition has occurred, do we arrive at the scene of suffering, the third element of the tragic rhythm.

All three elements of plot-construction described by Aristotle are present in *Abel Sanchez*, but their qualitative and quantitative values have been radically altered. The reversal occurs when Joaquín discovers that he needs to keep alive the man whom he considers to be his mortal enemy; and the recognition occurs when he learns, through his hatred, of the existence of his soul. In fact, there are a number of minor reversals and recognitions which take place in the opening chapters of the novel. Their significance lies not in their number, but in their placement. In Aristotelian terms, *Abel Sanchez* begins with the recognition and the reversal, and the major portion of the novel is given over to the scene of suffering. Thus the salient details concerning the nature and dimensions of Joaquín's passion are at our disposal before the novel is half over. The only question that remains in our minds is whether or not Joaquín will finally kill Abel, and Unamuno does not bother to build much suspense over the issue.

Unamuno's idea of tragedy as the consciousness of suffering has a genealogy which was at least a century old when *Abel Sanchez* was published. As in the case of most modern artists, Unamuno's point of departure is romanticism. In fact, "point of departure" is the wrong phrase to use in his case: in many respects, Unamuno's romanticism is pure and unambiguous. We have already noted the fact that Joaquín represents, on one level, a variation on the Byronic hero. Unamuno himself defines the romantic impulse which most clearly characterizes his work. In *The Tragic Sense of Life,* he tells us that no paintings of the horrors of hell could move him when he was a child, because even then nothing seemed more horrible to him than nothing itself. At least in Hell there is consciousness, if only consciousness of suffering. Unamuno rejects the notion of beatitude as a mystical absorption and contemplation of the Godhead:

And the soul, my soul at least, desires something else; not absorption, not quietude, not peace, not to be extinguished, but to draw near eternally without ever arriving, interminable desire, eternal hope that is renewed eternally without ever being wholly exhausted. (*Obras,* 16. 381.)

The struggle cannot be resolved; it can only be renewed in a larger arena. A few sentences later, Unamuno describes that realm as "An eternal Purgatory rather than a heavenly glory; an eternal ascension." The phrase "to draw near eternally without ever arriving" defines with great concision the romantic fascination with process. That fascination underlies the most typical romantic formulas: both the organic metaphor in aesthetics and the metaphor of the spiral (that is, of cyclical patterns) in history, reveal the same focus on growth, movement, and the process of becoming. Unamuno's notion that the dichotomies of man's tragic existence can never be resolved is cut from the same pattern. The story of Joaquín Monegro belongs to Hell rather than to Purgatory because in Joaquín's attempts to resolve his conflict Unamuno sees a denial of the very process by which the human spirit acts and moves. Unamuno represents that denial as the tragedy of rationalism—that is, of the desire to impose a rational coherence to motives and actions. Joaquín's desire to cure himself implies a denial of suffering, which for Unamuno represents a denial of life itself.

At this point, however, we must ask an obvious question: if Unamuno rules Paradise out of his vision of the afterlife, how can he distinguish between Hell and Purgatory? There is only one clear distinction between the sufferings of the two realms: the sufferings of Purgatory are endured in expectation of a transformation, while those of Hell are eternal. It is for that reason that Purgatory in Dante's *Commedia* is the only realm in which time exists; the very concept of Purgatory implies movement in time and space toward the transformation that occurs in the Earthly Paradise. Unamuno does not want such a transformation. He wants survival, with consciousness and identity preserved intact. His "eternal Purgatory" seems in the end to be a thinly disguised version of Hell.

The "expectation of a transformation" is a phrase that Francis Fergusson uses in his book *The Idea of a Theater* to describe "the recurrent moment of pathos in the tragic rhythm." Since it is the moment of pathos (Aristotle's "scene of suffering") that absorbs Unamuno's attention as an artist, what Mr. Fergusson has to say in those pages about the nature of romantic art has a particular relevance to the *Historia de pasion* of Joaquín Monegro:

> It is this "concentration in expectation" . . . which gives form to the passion itself; places it in a wider rhythm of life and action, and in due time brings it to an end. It is evident that this passion of purgation is quite unlike the luxury of merely yielding to feeling, the gloomy satisfaction which does not look beyond the dissolution of the moral being; and the questions to ask about romantic art are whether dissolution or a new equilibrium is envisaged; and in the latter case, what the "new equilibrium" seems to be (p. 83).

These questions are properly asked concerning *Abel Sanchez*. In a sense, Joaquín Monegro discovers the reality of Unamuno's Eternal Purgatory. The "concentration in expectation" does not bring to Joaquín the transformation he so ardently desires when he tries to cure himself of his passion. His story is one of dissolution, madness and death; no new equilibrium is ever achieved. We may rightly wonder whether in fact anything but an infernal mode of existence is possible on Unamuno's terms.

I am not convinced, however, that romantic art which rules out the possibility of transformation "does not have much meaning except in relation to the psychology of the artist," as Mr. Fergusson suggests. On those terms, we should have to conclude that Unamuno's fiction fails aesthetically, for Unamuno explicitly denies the value of such a transformation. But *Abel Sanchez* is a perfect example of what Mr. Fergusson calls the univocal sense of form: that is, action as the expression of emotion. The art of the novel itself reveals the "idealist perfection of form" that the univocal concept of action demands (*Idea of a Theater*, pp. 107–109). We have noted earlier in this essay that the plot of the novel is almost entirely devoted to the scene of suffering, and that rational motivation accounts for very little. The narrator's role is severely restricted, and the action is rendered primarily through dialogue, as well as through excerpts from the *Confession*. And the almost total absence of scene-painting in the novel again reminds us that human passion is the only reality of significance for Unamuno.

Rutgers University

TRADITION AND TRANSLATION

GLAUCO CAMBON

Fairfax versus *Wiffen: Tasso's Clorinda in Elizabethan and in Romantic Garb*

I don't know if a metaphor suggested by the specific poetical context on hand can be usefully extrapolated to describe a translator's work and indeed his predicament vis-à-vis the original. In a sense, it does, considering the fact that a tailor is something of an artist in his own right (even without taking into account Carlyle's metaphysics). Besides, the metaphor does imply the translator's close dependence on his *donnée* (the original text) along with a basic incommensurability of his work to that *donnée*. As a consequence, a translator with artistic claims is far from disparaged by the sartorial comparison: the fabric of his own making may adhere to the living original body of poetry in such a way as to reveal its elegance. But this assumes that the translation cannot be appreciated apart from a close comparison with the original; which is clearly not the case. We don't really need to know Horace's Latin odes to respond to Ezra Pound's English version of three of them, nor does our ignorance of Chinese prevent us from savoring the style of his *Cathay* or of Klabund's German renditions of Chinese verse; and while an analytical collation of Homer's Greek and Robert Fitzgerald's English may contribute significantly to our appraisal of the latter's artistry, its first test will certainly come from a direct, continuous reading of Fitzgerald's *Odyssey* as an English poem in its own right.

The rationale for such a translation, as distinguished from a com-

191

pletely free treatment of the same subject, is that retelling a great story makes up a substantial part of a poet's traditional duties. The ancients held literary imitation in great esteem precisely because it afforded the poet a chance to prove himself in direct competition with an illustrious source; and the borderline between imitation and translation is at best unclear, as Catullus' *Ille mi par esse deo videtur* amply shows. On the other hand, the distinction between translating and creating work may turn out to tax the most discriminating critic, once he realizes that it corresponds to the highly questionable difference between craftsmanship and inspiration. The ancients were not unaware of the latter, as Plato's "divine madness" theory shows. Eighteenth-century aesthetics, with the polarization of *taste* and *genius,* fruitfully brought that issue up once again; it was Longinus *versus* Aristotle after all. But if Longinus and his modern reincarnations (Coleridge, Friedrich von Schlegel, Croce, among others) remind us that there is something unpredictable about literary work, Aristotle need not be interpreted mechanistically; Francis Fergusson has made this point rather conclusively. It is Aristotle after all who identifies genius with the aptitude for analogy ("metaphor")—a thesis shared by some of the most daring contemporary poets.

If we keep in mind how intrinsic to poetical creation the practice of poetical translation has been in our time, we may be able to refocus the whole question of imitation and originality—which is the real issue behind the problem of the possibility of such a thing as poetical translation. There is genius rather than mere taste in Pound's translations; a genius of a special kind if you like, as R. P. Blackmur pointed out when he said that Pound was at his best as a translator. This is also the kind of genius I feel inclined to recognize in Richard Wilbur when he translates Molière—a feat of the highest order, something which we can best describe as creative work starting from the hardest *donnée.* The analogical structure a translator of this type sets up in his own language both claims validity in its own right and bears the scrutiny in comparison to the original. This is where I have to discard the sartorial metaphor in favor of a more structural description; Harry Levin's "refraction" providing one alternative, and classical emulation another.

The *Encyclopaedia Britannica* article on translation acknowledges the importance of this kind of literary activity, which presided over the blossoming of such phases of Western literature as the Latin Golden

Age of the first century before Christ, the Elizabethan and the German romantic eras. But that article fails to do justice to Fairfax's, Wiffen's (and Arthur Golding's!) work. Even though Ugo Foscolo, as I gather from Professor E. R. Vincent's *Ugo Foscolo, an Italian in Regency England* (Cambridge, 1953), disliked Wiffen's work, its merits will be apparent upon close scrutiny. In the account of Wiffen in *The Dictionary of National Biography* (written by the late Alexander Gordon), it appears that Wiffen prepared himself for the task and that he had literary ambitions of his own. In his own time, Wiffen was considered respectfully by the *Quarterly Review*, even though that periodical made the point that Fairfax was still his superior; and Sir Walter Scott praised him very warmly.

One thing that the present article is meant to show, even if based on one limited sampling, is that Fairfax and Wiffen did two different things altogether, because the former felt toward his Italian text a cultural contiguity that the latter could not possibly have; Fairfax took liberties with Tasso precisely on account of the intimacy he had with his near contemporary; Wiffen approached Tasso from a historical distance and with the reverential attitude of romantic historicism—other components of his style here being easily identifiable with a taste for the then fashionable Gothic story and with Scott's own cult of the legendary past, as witness *Ivanhoe*, one of the obvious references. Fairfax (on whom see Henry Morley's judicious foreword to the Carisbrooke Library edition of *Jerusalem Delivered*, London, 1890) is charmingly naive even if at times embarrassingly so; he can afford to be that, for he somehow "prolongs" Tasso's original work in his own Spenserian-Elizabethan ambience, while Wiffen "revives" Tasso. For us today Fairfax is part of the Elizabethan landscape. Yet Professor Harold Hooper Blanchard chose Wiffen over Fairfax for his *Prose and Poetry of the Continental Renaissance, in Translation* (New York, 1949, 1955, 1959, 1962); and I no longer question the wisdom of this choice. Tasso is remote from us as he was not from Fairfax's age; Wiffen takes that remoteness into account and banks on it, so to speak, by making it a factor of his own poetical rendition. Some vital parts of Tasso's text undergo a reductive metamorphosis in the process, yet others survive transplantation, and the whole justifies itself as a literary feat of great merit; hence my attempt at revaluation, qualified though it has to be.

193

Any reader of Tasso knows the armor-clad virgin Clorinda needs no
additional clothing, whether of the literal or of the figurative kind. And
(to return to my initial cue) I wonder whether the sartorial metaphor
applies, by and large, to the remarkable work of the Spenserian Edward
Fairfax and of the Shelleyan Jeremiah Holmes Wiffen, each of whom
obeyed the call of a poetical instinct attuned to his own time. Yet when
we compare the Elizabethan and the romantic rendering of *La Gerusalemme liberata*'s Canto 3, Stanza 21, with Tasso's original text, we
may be inclined to consider these English versions two kinds of gar-
ments draped over the shining nakedness of the Italian poetry, which
they for all their elegance cannot help veiling at this particular point.
It is, of course, a crucial stanza in the poem because it shows the beauty
of the pagan maiden suddenly overwhelming her Christian lover, Prince
Tancred, who unintentionally frees her sunlike head from the helmet
with a spear blow, thereby hopelessly reopening the love wound that
this blond radiance had inflicted upon him at Antioch one day; and
here is Fairfax's rendition of it:

> This while forth pricked Clorinda from the throng
> And 'gainst Tancredi set her spear in rest,
> Upon their helms they cracked their lances long,
> And from her head her gilden casque he kest,
> For every lace he broke and every thong,
> And in the dust threw down her pluméd crest,
>> About her shoulders shone her golden locks,
>> Like sunny beams, on alabaster rocks.

That's pretty good, and whatever by now has become lexically archaic
is surely not in the way; Fairfax has a winsome directness which earned
him the reputation of being germane to the Italian song he transposed
into his own language. But now let's hear that song itself:

> Clorinda in tanto ad incontrar l'assalto
> va di Tancredi, e pon la lancia in resta.
> Ferîrsi a le visiere, e i tronchi in alto
> volaro, e parte nuda ella ne resta;
> ché, rotti i lacci a l'elmo suo, d'un salto
> (mirabil colpo!) ei le balzò di testa;
> e, le chiome dorate al vento sparse,
> giovane donna in mezzo al campo apparse.

Marked though it generally seems by what critics like Hugo Friedrich have come to envisage as a protobaroque sumptuousness, here Tasso's melodious style stands out for its spareness vis-à-vis its English counterpart. The final couplet is a miraculous climax of vision, with that verb *apparse* resolving in itself the movement of the whole tumultuous stanza. By comparison, Fairfax's "shone" sounds certainly felicitous, yet it is somewhat weakened by its inconspicuous placement in mid-line, and even more by the decorative bent of the whole couplet as against Tasso's emphasis on action and functional meaning: for with Tasso the culminant verb *apparire* (to appear) subsumes its predicate (*giovane donna*, a young woman), which in turn gives the verb body and substance. In this way a further heightening becomes possible at the outset of the next stanza, where Tasso shows Clorinda's beauty as an imperious light, before searching Tancred's love-struck heart with a flashback to their first meeting. What's more, the strategic use of *apparse* here raises the flashback to a verbal leitmotiv by echoing the *apparse* which, in Canto 1, Stanza 47, characterized the *coup-de-foudre* apparition of Clorinda to Tancred in the context of background narrative. The same verb, in the present tense (*appare*), will mark the apparition of the dead Clorinda in a dream to her grief-stricken lover and killer after the catastrophe of the final duel (12. 91).

We cannot expect even as resourceful an artist of translation as Wiffen to retain this structural hinge of a word, even though he does stay consistently closer to the phrasing and imagery of his Italian model than breezy Fairfax generally cares to. Thus Wiffen's Englishing of the momentous stanza I have been discussing (from Canto 3) turns out to be no more than a brilliant paraphrase, if we look for those pivotal words that make Tasso's specific text so striking in itself and so relevant to the whole story of Tancred and Clorinda:

> Meanwhile Clorinda rushes to assail
> The Prince, and level lays her spear renowned;
> Both lances strike, and on the barred ventayle
> In shivers fly, and she remains discrowned;
> For, burst its silver rivets, to the ground
> Her helmet leaped, (incomparable blow!)
> And by the rudeness of the shock unbound,
> Her sex to all the field emblazoning so,
> Loose to the charmed winds her golden tresses flow.

Tasso's *parte nuda ella ne resta* (literally, "she remains partly naked from the blow"), so sensitive a clue to the erotic overtones of the episode and of the whole story as such, loses any sexual charge in Wiffen's rephrasing ("she remains discrowned"), while the injection of the word "sex" in the eighth line, an obvious carry-over from Tasso's *giovane donna,* hardly makes up for the loss. Despite the fluency and melody attained by Wiffen in his difficult meter—the Spenserian stanza, which adds one long line to the eight of the original and compels him at times to write more ornately than Fairfax—we feel as if a lovely tapestry had been substituted for the live flesh; a damask stylization replaces the dramatic directness of Tasso. But Wiffen reads consistently well; he has Shelley in his ears (Shelley, who used the Spenserian stanza in *The Revolt of Islam* and the Italian *ottava rima* of Ariosto and Tasso in *The Witch of Atlas,* because he loved the fullness of these cognate meters and the *sfumato* effects they could yield; and let us not forget that Wiffen's translation of *Jerusalem Delivered* appeared in 1824, at the height of Shelley's vogue).

A good translation of poetry should be first of all an independent poem; and if I point out what elements of Tasso's poetry could not be transplanted in the Elizabethan climate of Fairfax or recaptured by the romantic-historical workmanship of Wiffen, it is only to confirm once again how inviolable true poetry is and yet how capable of provoking new poetry in the form of metrical, syntactical, and thematic analogy—which is what a translation really amounts to. In a way, Tasso's poetry is to its lovers Fairfax and Wiffen what the unpossessible Clorinda is to Tancred: he cannot have her, but he is permanently possessed by her image and thereby permanently changed, permanently bound to her. A Petrarchan situation actually underlies the love-and-death story of Tancred and Clorinda, and it partly colored the translators' style, at least in the matter of conceits—though of course nobody could expect them to have retained specific quotations like Tasso's *le chiome dorate a l'aura sparse* [1] in the stanza under consideration. This type of reference must be seen as intrinsic to Tasso's procedure, because he worked with a whole tradition in his blood, as his copious Petrarchan, Dantesque, Vergilian, and Homeric echoes show.

Sometimes these echoes reverberate in both the English translations at hand; and one such happy instance is Canto 12, Stanza 57, where Tasso's

> Tre volte il cavalier la donna stringe
> con le robuste braccia; ed altrettante
> da que' nodi tenaci ella si scinge,
> nodi di fier nemico, e non d'amante

becomes in Fairfax:

> Thrice his strong arms he folds about her waist,
> And thrice was forced to let the virgin go,
> For she disdainéd to be so embraced,
> No lover would have strained his mistress so

and in Wiffen:

> Thrice in his boisterous arms the maid he pressed,
> And thrice was forced to loose his sinewy clasp;
> She had no fancy to be so caressed;
> Empassioned Love is not an angry asp.

The emphatic iteration of "thrice" to stress the elusiveness of the in-accessible girl to her unknowing embracer arouses in the knowing reader a chain-reaction of images: Dante the pilgrim vainly trying to embrace his friend Casella in *Purgatorio* 2, Aeneas vainly trying to clasp the apparition of his wife Creusa in *Aeneid* 2, and Odysseus vainly trying to hold the shade of his mother in his arms in *Odyssey* 11. The immediate reference for an Italian reader is to Dante, triggering the others in turn:

> Oh ombre vane, fuor che nell'aspetto!
> Tre volte dietro lei le braccia avvinsi,
> E tante mi tornai con esse al petto.

Tasso's *tre volte* in its emphatic position awakens this cumulative memory not as inert heritage, but as a reactivation with ironic effects in the tragic context—since the frustrated Tancred here might as well be holding a ghost, and, before long, that's what will be left of Clorinda. At the same time, a Petrarchan oxymoron has found here its dramatic embodiment. Clorinda is the materialized metaphor of Laura the "sweet warrior" and "fierce enemy" in Petrarch's *Canzoniere*. Petrarch's war of love becomes an actual clash in shining armor for Tasso's dueling lovers, and this—an unromantic situation—duly registers with both translators, aided by their respective cultural affinities.

197

Clorinda is also something like a Christian Brunhild and a solar goddess who becomes human in death; or rather, she is human innocence
itself marked by a special destiny, an Amazon becoming fully woman
in a death-and-transfiguration climax which takes the place of erotic
consummation. Hence the erotic overtones in Tasso's treatment of the
complex duel scene. These overtones are well heard by Wiffen, who
faithfully transcribes, in Stanza 65, Tasso's *la trafitta vergine* as "the
pierced Virgin," whereas Fairfax in his innocence completely overlooks
the pointed cue by rendering it as "the wounded damsel." Fairfax in
fact deliberately reduces the erotic languors of the text; for instance, in
the previous stanza (64), which shows Tasso at a peak of sensual
innuendo:

> Spinge egli il ferro nel bel sen di punta,
> che vi s'immerge, e il sangue avido beve;
> e la veste, che d'ôr vago trapunta
> le mammelle stringea tenera e leve,
> l'empie d'un caldo fiume. Ella già sente
> morirsi, e 'l piè le manca egro e languente.

Fairfax has

> His sword into the bosom deep he drives,
> And bathed in lukewarm blood his iron cold,
> Between her breasts the cruel weapon rives
> Her curious square, embossed with swelling gold,
> Her knees grow weak, the pains of death she feels,
> And like a falling cedar bends and reels.

Not so scholarly Wiffen, who actually elaborates, for metrical reasons,
on Tasso's depiction of Clorinda's death languor:

> the hapless maid
> Feels her end nigh; her knees their strength forego;
> And her enfeebled frame droops languishing and low.

It is worth noticing here a striking divergence of the two poetical
translators. Fairfax, who comes well before the days of romantic historicism, feels free to interpret his text with some semantic latitude, at
least in the case of Clorinda's character, which he keeps on the formid-

able level to the last by injecting the "falling cedar" simile in the very teeth of Tasso's stage direction; but Wiffen goes too far the other way at the end of Stanza 65 by making Clorinda a "fond repentant Magdalene." Nothing of the sort, of course, is to be found in Tasso, who merely says that God wants Clorinda to become His servant (*ancella*) in the act of death just because she had been a rebel (*rubella*) against His law through her life. Now Wiffen's simile (like all his metaphoric expansions of the text) is far from gratuitous; it springs from his close awareness of Tasso's sensual counterpoint as well as from his own familiarity with mannerist and baroque painting, in which the Heaven-seeking eyes of lachrymose Magdalenes were a visual topos. Wiffen is known to have cultivated the art of drawing and to have been something of an antiquarian. And Tasso himself invited this ad-libbing when he abruptly dictated to the dying warrioress (Stanza 65) an *ex machina* spirit of "charity, faith and hope." Counter-Reformation ideology did not always stand him in good stead; the master of modulations here failed to modulate. But when everything is said and done, the reference to Magdalene is totally incongruous with Clorinda's character, who has no erotic sins to repent even though her Christian *agon* and agony, theatrically developed in the dead of night until sunrise, brought forth erotic overtones from the rich palette of her original portrayer.

On the other hand, the painterly bent usually helps Wiffen; we don't mind his "Vesuvian fire" at Stanza 57 to describe the hot fury of combat or his "Aurora/ Unbars Elysium" at Stanza 58 or his Gothic personification of Night in Stanza 54:

> Worthy of royal lists, and the clear shine
> Of suns would be the battle, if descried;
> Dark Abbess! thou that in thy Gothic shrine
> The mouldering relics of their tale dost hide!
> Grant me to lift thy cowl, to waft aside
> The curtain, and in radiant numbers braid
> Their deeds, for endless ages to abide;
> So with their glory, glorious shall be made,
> In pages of high Romance, the memory of thy shade.

The personification is in Tasso, but Wiffen adds a fine touch of his own with that "Dark Abbess!" Not that Fairfax's antithetical downplaying of the cue sounds wrong—it is in keeping with his reductive tendencies. But Wiffen here clarifies his own basic attitude to the text, his taste for Gothic romance à la Walter Scott in Shelleyan vein. And this without violating the assumptions of Tasso, who theatrically intervenes in his authorial capacity to rescue his heroes from oblivion and in so doing stresses the antagonistic force of obliterating darkness. We remember that Clorinda is a solar figure and that she dons a prophetically black armor when leaving for the fatal night sortie (Stanza 18); her progress in this canto is from eclipse to apocalypse; the dawn will smile on her transfigured death to restore her sunny image on an ethereal level.

The theatrical attitude of the poet in this episode was not lost, we know, on Claudio Monteverdi. It was likewise not lost on Wiffen, who, for instance, understood better than Fairfax the dramatic implications of tense shifts by sticking consistently to Tasso's historical present in Stanza 55. Fairfax instead flits from present to past several times in that pivotal stanza, which clearly embodies in its verb form the presentness of the scene evoked by the poet. Let us not forget that it comes right after the stanza in which Tasso begged personified Night to release from her hold the figures and events of his story, and that thanks to this very sequence it enacts the granting of the prayer, successful evocation following invocation. This in turn reflects on Tancred's request to his still-unknown adversary to reveal his name; it is a pity, Tancred says, their "prowess thus to spend/ On deeds which silence and these shades conceal" (Stanza 60). At the beginning of the poem (Canto 1, Stanza 36) Tasso had invoked the powers of Mind (Memory, Mnemosyne) *de gli anni e de l'oblio nemica*, inimical to Time and to oblivion, to tell him of the captains and armies of the Christian host, whose fame has been "silenced and overcast with darkness by long years." Thus the theatrical dimension in *Gerusalemme liberata* 12 springs from a hyperbole of the poet's concern with his story and his creatures—he is their necromantic summoner, and he will invoke and propitiate first the powers of light (Mind, Memory) and then—as here in Canto 12— the contrary powers of darkness, Night, oblivion, his Anti-Muse, to provide a Caravaggesque stage-setting for his two favorite characters in their supreme ordeal. Wiffen knows that he is performing a similar operation for Tasso's poem. And by the same token, Wiffen is alert to the reverberations of this theatrical light-and-darkness effect on the level of capillary imagery and dialogue: at Stanza 61, unlike Fairfax, he reproduces Tasso's quick sequence of images connecting by direct propagation the fire of war (Clorinda's burning of the Crusaders' siege tower) with the fire of anger (in a disappointed Tancred who had hoped, by an act of courtesy, to obtain self-revelation from her):

> . . . "Thou seest before thee one . . .
> Who gave your towering structure *to the flame.*"
> *Fired* at her answer, Tancred made exclaim . . .

The two English poets who made an English poet of Tasso necessarily adopted different solutions in their respective contexts. Even if Fairfax's cavalier naïveté toward the Italian text and Wiffen's scholarly metaphrase in neo-Gothic taste could at best only refract, in divergent ways, a part of the original image, English literature would be the poorer without them.

University of Connecticut

NOTE

1. I find it strange that an erudite and sensitive commentator like Piero Nardi (*La Gerusalemme liberata,* ed. Piero Nardi, Milan, 1961) should scoff at those critics who emphasized the Petrarchan reminiscence (p. 148) as if it detracted from genuine poetical inspiration. As my remarks on the *tre volte* passage from Canto 12 try to show, Tasso himself is involved in incorporating and transforming for his purposes the whole of the epic tradition—indeed more than that, if it includes Petrarch. A literary resonance is part of the effect, and this does not mean that the poetry should be considered bookish. Internal resonance in the *Jerusalem Delivered* is likewise carefully effected by thematic and stylistic recurrences, as a reading of the Armida episodes can show.

RALPH FREEDMAN

Eyesight and Vision: Forms of the Imagination in Coleridge and Novalis

For the poet as for the painter, for the novelist as for the sculptor, the vision that defines artistic experience begins with the *eye*. Sight, external and internal, of tree, of urn, of autumnal leaves, of the receding deluge caught in the spider's web, becomes the starting point of poetic imagery, the mirror of the world. The eye was for the Platonists what it remained for Stendhal—both receptacle and reflector of those objects and forms which fashion imagery and visions alike.

If the eye is the starting point for every poet's vision, its significance varies considerably in different ages and in different countries, within various literary and intellectual traditions. Eyes may reflect outer pageantry or inner dream, pastoral objects of nature or of artifice, diadems or factories, figures of fantasy or myth. But these differences are also differences in function. They may arise, more fully even, from various ways of seeing, of bestowing importance on this or that. Indeed, the poet's *manner* of seeing has often determined shifts in critical attitude and variations in poetic style.

Coleridge and Novalis may represent two different ways of seeing as "forms of the imagination," juxtaposing, in the spirit of René Wellek's *Confrontations,* a German and an English sensibility during the Romantic Age. Poets both, and both living at the same time under the lengthening shadow of Kant, these two highly sensitized spirits may also yield some insight into the crucial role played by poetic experience at the threshold of modernity. Both were intensely involved in the task of heightening sensible experience into art; both explored the relationship between personal and transpersonal experience which marked a fresh phase in the development of that "atmosphere in the mind" which has defined our age since the eighteenth century. In this context, verifiable historical connections are less important than the intellectual climate they shared. For each poet in his own way exemplified that point in intellectual history at which he stood at the opening of the nineteenth century: at the confluence of two currents simultaneously involving an intense preoccupation with palpable experience, with the observation of nature, and perhaps the last explosion of a valid mysticism that was to cast its light throughout that sober century of progress. A mysticism turned inward, a metaphysic devoutly rational, a belief in existence beyond experience yet paradoxically embedded in a firm empirical tradition—these are the contradictory qualities of that atmosphere, which has determined much of our own intellectual consciousness as well.

The English and the German poet, then, in their very divergent ways, exemplify that tradition, that circumstance. The years from 1795–1805 —the time of Coleridge's *Ancient Mariner* and *Dejection* ode, of Novalis' *Hymns to the Night* and *Heinrich von Ofterdingen*—were propitious for thoughts about private experience and its metaphysical projections. On the one hand, Kant's work had begun to settle, and his commentators, his interpreters, his followers, and his critics had started to explore and expand his system, his findings soon to be recognized as symptomatic of their age. On the other hand, similar pursuits developed also independently of Kant, as, for example, in Coleridge's early views compounding Neo-Platonic and empiricist traditions. His notion of imagination as a heightening of psychological experience had just been developed at this time through his conversations with Wordsworth and through their work together on a theory to explain the *Lyrical Ballads*. Coleridge was to buttress these views with his Kantian notions later on, but the outlines of his thought are clearly and concretely present in *The Rime of the Ancient Mariner*. Novalis, by contrast, was already deeply aware of the Kantian and even post-Kantian mystique when he composed his *Hymns to the Night*.

Directly or indirectly, then, both poets partook of an analogous intellectual atmosphere as they sought poetic means with which to dramatize the leap from the self's passive reception of experience to the reconstruction of forms of consciousness by the probing mind. Yet their differences are as important to us as their similarities. As we shall see, Coleridge shed his early engagement in empiricist thought and psychology as little as the mature Gide shed his symbolist past. Novalis, by contrast, seemed to be more centrally concerned with nature caught and transmuted through internal allegory—the transcendental symbolism of the spirit. How, then, precisely is experience reconstructed metaphysically by these two poets, how does it enter the language and drama of their poetry? To determine these differences, as particular manners of "sighting," of using the *eye*, we shall glance at a few sections of the *Ancient Mariner* and the first of Novalis' *Hymns to the Night*.

The *Mariner* and the *Hymns*, despite their obvious differences in form and in content, share sufficiently numerous points of resemblance to make a comparison fruitful. The artful ballad and the artful hymn follow a similar progression from nature or sightedness to the darkness and isolation of the soul and to the possibility of its final redemption. Eyesight for Coleridge and the all-pervasive light for Novalis turn objects with "magic fingers" until, after becoming part of the poet's consciousness, they assume a metaphysical life of their own. The Mariner enacts this procedure dramatically by performing, without apparent motive, the unforgivable act that separates him from nature. But precisely because throughout his ordeal he remains a knowing consciousness, the objects he perceives, however grotesque and unreal, remain somehow grounded in a world of fact. Novalis' hymns (particularly the first two poems) describe a similar cycle, but they are dramatic only in a removed, allegorical sense. A transformation of life into symbolic dream occurs, which proceeds through designs (and progressions) of imagery. Objects are briefly animated, and figures emerge suggesting way-stations in their progress towards an *internal* kind of infinity. Naturally, a large part of the difference can be accounted for by the differences in genre and subject matter chosen for the two poems. But a good part of it is also due to a different conception of reality, of the relationship between nature and spirit, between sightedness and dream.

The Rime of the Ancient Mariner, for all its apparent unity, is a mixture of modes and forms. Basically, of course, it is a ballad. The manner in which events are made to occur with unexpected suddenness, the imagery, diction, the narrative tone—all suggest the ballad. At the same time, the structure also suggests forms other than the ballad. The relationship between the wandering Mariner and the stationary guest (the almost Proustian duality of the containing memory and the narrative action) also points towards a different form, closer to romanticism, not only because of the implied Gothic and supernatural elements, but also because of the use of the passive wanderer, the moving percipient. Seen in this way, the poem's structure can be related to that of the romantic picaresque, as it occurred especially in Germany during the decades of the *fin de siècle* and beyond. Beginning with Schiller's *Geisterseher* (1787), culminating, variously, in Novalis' *Ofterdingen,* Eichendorff's *Taugenichts,* or even Kleist's *Michael Kohlhaas,* the structure we view is that of the protagonist who wanders through space and time, remolding the objects and encounters within the compass of his eye into objects of a higher moral, spiritual, or aesthetic significance. Seen in this way, *The Rime of the Ancient Mariner* stands out as an English parallel in verse to German romantic prose: the symbolic journey *par excellence.*

Coleridge's poem, however, also obtains its significance in a different way: as a companion to Wordsworth's "Tintern Abbey" and as a precursor, in its way, of his *Prelude.* The famous lines from Chapter 14 of *Biographia Literaria,* in which "it was agreed that [Coleridge's] endeavors should be directed towards persons and characters supernatural" while Wordsworth "was to propose to himself as his object . . . to excite a feeling analogous to the supernatural" by "directing it to the loveliness and wonders of the world before us," cannot be taken lightly. The division of labor seemed clear—a divergence of interest and concern yet stemming from the same root. We recall that Coleridge had joined William and Dorothy Wordsworth at Alfoxden in 1797–1798, at a time when they were all engaged in an intense observation of nature, for which, on their walks, Dorothy lent them "eye and ear." And indeed when we think of "Tintern Abbey," also of 1798, we can discern some of the motifs which appear in different guise in Coleridge's poem. The roving wanderer, or percipient, is of course a Wordsworthian theme and suggests a root both poems share: Wordsworth's observer developing the sense of glory, or halo, from the perception itself, Coleridge's Mariner (trained on the ship's lookout, to be sure) transforming images of sight directly into symbolic encounters. Clearly this root is suggested, for example, by the famous lines of "Tintern Abbey" which state that, in retrospect, "forms of beauty" had not been to the poet "as is a landscape to a blind man's eye." Indeed, the mutual stimulation of remembered and present perceptions, which informs Wordsworth's poem, is caught, in a characteristically different way, in Coleridge's alternation between the present confrontation with the wedding guest and the content of the vision—the Mariner's quest. Many more parallels can be cited: Wordsworth's narrowing of the focus of sight to the isolated hermit and, in a later stanza, Wordsworth's recollection of Dorothy's "wild eyes," in which he recaptured his sense of the isolation of the poet (as percipient) and his function as a perceiving and transforming agent. If, as Geoffrey Hartman has pointed out, *The Ancient Mariner* shows many features of Wordsworth's *Borderers,* it also imports into the realm of the "supernatural" many of the features of Wordsworth's poet as an observer of nature who discerns the imaginative glory beneath and behind the world of empirically observed reality. Indeed, it is Wordsworth who conceives of the poet as an observing wanderer (the empiricist and romantic equivalent of the epic hero), and it is perhaps Coleridge who, in his decisive pendant to the Wordsworthian quest, supplied the image of the *tragic* wanderer, the isolated figure transforming experienced reality precisely with the same eye with which he views it. *The Prelude* as a *Bildungsroman* of the mind, in which the poet develops as a seeing wanderer in time as well as in space, might suggest this ultimate parallel to Coleridge's irrational quest.

The Ancient Mariner, then, is a poem about eyes—eyes which transform the objects of their sight *immediately* upon sighting. Dorothy's "wild eyes" become for Coleridge mirrors, not of the world, but immediately of that irrational universe which lies behind their physical retinae. The wandering percipient of the German romantic tale, the hero of the ballad turned from actor to passive percipient, becomes a lonely tragic and in his way heroic figure who turns nature into spirit. He is the typical poet. Even the passive inwardness of "Tintern Abbey"—that famous "recollection in tranquility"—is suggested by the Mariner's confrontation with the Wedding Guest, who becomes the receptacle of the former's memory and its compulsive recitation. Coleridge's imagination is more dramatic than Wordsworth's. As in his abstract formulation of the act of imagination, so in its concrete enactment, the relationships between self, world, and poem are intensely and movingly dramatized. For in the passive percipient's eye, the world is turned into its metaphysical double as, with the Wedding Guest struck dumb, we watch the spectacular performance.

The empirical act of perception involves isolation and passivity. The Cartesian *ego*, a source of *active* reconstruction, becomes a *tabula rasa* on which experience is written. In this way, the Mariner is isolated as he confronts both the wedding party in the realm of reality and the increasingly supernatural world of his metaphysical nightmare. He begins by existing because he perceives, and perceives with accuracy because he *is* perceived. This is the substance that gives life to the form of his spiritual *Wanderschaft*: from the stare with which he holds the Wedding Guest's eye in the beginning to the Pilot's boy's rolling eyes with which he, in turn, beheld the Mariner's apparition in the end. In describing the *eyes* in the poem, we must therefore begin with their hypnotic or mesmerizing quality. But taking this much-explored dimension of the subject for granted, let us see what other functions the eye may perform. The famous lines introducing the eye may point toward this further dimension.

> He holds him with his glittering eye—
> The Wedding Guest stood still
> And listens like a three year child
> The Mariner hath his will.

What interests us here is the particular meaning of *to hold* (in "he *holds* him with his glittering eye"). In a previous stanza, the Mariner had actually held the Wedding Guest with his "skinny hand," suggesting that the Mariner's subsequent use of his eyes for a similar hold represents a further intensification and abstraction of that meeting. Each participant partakes of the world of the other: the Wedding Guest, the self of nature, mirrors in some sense sympathetically the Mariner's alienated self; the Mariner, having broken with nature, also reflects the Wedding Guest's world. The two are both projectors and receptacles, active and passive selves. Indeed, the very notion of the eye, in its most ancient Platonic tradition, bears within it both these functions: it is simultaneously the mirror and the reflective organ of the soul. It performs the function of Dorothy Wordsworth's wild eyes, which William recalls in "Tintern Abbey." The movement of the poem's first two parts, from this point forward, emphasizes this duality of function. The Mariner is active only as he focusses upon and mirrors the Wedding Guest, whom he fixes with the force of his weighted memories. He is passive in his tale—as passively exposed to the natural and soon thereafter supernatural forces of nature as Wordsworth, the passive observer, had been to the impact of its images and forms. In Coleridge's poem, then, the relationship between the world within nature and the world beyond nature is expressed through the function of viewing and being viewed. Indeed, the world emerges in its natural forms, which are at once transformed by such a viewing intelligence. The isolation of the polar sea, the appearance of the albatross (all seen by the Mariner), followed by the single transforming act, are the means whereby this change is accomplished.

Before we continue with Coleridge's poem, let us turn to Novalis' very different work. It is truly hymnal in tone; its free, elevated, yet proselike rhythms do not detract from its significance as a secular celebration of a religious quest. From a distant perspective it deals with man and world and their ultimate spiritual transformation in the world of Night. Yet especially in its earlier sections, the poem functions through progressions with which the relationship of these different worlds is explored. Nature, in the first hymn, is heralded as the world of light, the mystery of matter to which all sensible beings respond. As the opening lines entone:

> Welcher Lebendige, Sinnbegabte, liebt nicht vor allen
> Wundererscheinungen des verbreiteten Raumes
> um ihn, has all-erfreuliche Licht.

(What creature alive, and endowed with the gift of the senses does not, above all the wondrous appearances of expansive space, love the universally gladdening light.)

Instead of a confrontation of eyes, or mutual viewing, we focus on the light, the means and object of vision. In place of the Mariner's quest upon the endless ocean, we are surrounded by the world of concrete nature, rendered with as much empirical accuracy (however embellished

208

by poetic language) as had been the Mariner's sights. The confrontation
we have observed in Coleridge as essentially epistemological is here concretely rendered in terms of existences. The realm of day and the realm
of dream, like Rilke's analogous empires of life and death, become almost
geographically distinct worlds so that when the poet turns away from
the light he can actually descend to night in a Dantean quest:

> Abwärts wend ich mich zu der heiligen, unaussprechlichen,
> geheimnisvollen Nacht. Fernab liegt die Welt—in eine
> tiefe Gruft versenkt—wüst und einsam ist ihre Stelle.

(Downward I turn to the sacred, unspeakable, secret night. Far away lies the world—
sunk into a deep abyss—desolate and lonely in its place.)

If Coleridge sought his metaphysical reality through changing modes of
perception, Novalis developed his through contrasts of analogous modes
of being. Following from this preoccupation, Novalis' method is as thoroughly allegorical as his vision is deeply mystical. As we shall see, even
the references to concrete fact tend to be allegorized, whether we recall
the mineshafts of *Heinrich von Ofterdingen* or the images from geology
and astronomy we encounter in the *Hymns to the Night*.

At this point, we might do well to return to Coleridge, for the relationship between eye and vision which we are exploring assumes such
very different meanings for both poets. For Novalis it was the pervasive
light which ultimately focusses on man, the poet, as the splendid perceiving stranger. In *The Ancient Mariner* it is portrayed through confrontations of percipients. With an imagination trained in minute observation, the Mariner catches, holds, and instantaneously converts the
forms of nature he confronts. As Part III of the poem opens, the protagonist, the participants, their ship, all stand still, while the phantom
ship approaches on this Coleridgean equivalent of the Sargasso Sea.
What activity remains on the part of the participants is confined to
their eyes:

> How glazed each weary eye
> When looking westward I behold
> A something in the sky.

These words are appropriate to the language of any seaman scanning a
lonely ocean sky: *eye, looking, behold*. Yet while this encounter remains

epistemological, its object turns supernatural even before the percipients have realized it:

> A speck, a mist, a shape, I wist!
> And still it neared and neared.

Then, with "water sprite" as a cue, we witness the turnabout:

> As if it dodged a water sprite
> It plunged and tacked and veered.

A moment's uncertainty before the ship is seen driving between the mariners and the sun, becoming symbolic of disaster.

The sun takes on at this point the Mariner's or individual self's private perceptual power. For ship and sun repeat the relationship on a universal scale that we previously observed between Mariner and Wedding Guest. They confront one another visually, the sun taking on color as well as lending it to the objects beneath.

> And straight the sun was flecked with bars
> .   .   .   .
> As if through a dungeon gate he peered
> With broad and burning face.

In response, the phantom ship mirrors these glances with its lights and colors. It should be noted here, as again in the water-snake passage of Part IV, that all images of transformation are rendered through light; they are visual images. The Nightmare Life-in-Death is described through bright golden locks, through a white leprosy skin. Her *looks* were free; deliberately the world is drawn through the glazed eyes of men visually crazed, their eyes having turned from being instruments of sight to organs of mysterious envisioning.

The progression of this passage, then, is marked by sequences of sight in various forms. The phantom ship's approach and its gradual revelation to the passive percipients, its shift from beneath the umbrella of individual to that of universal perception—all of these suggest an empirical procedure in which observed forms are transformed at the moment of sight into symbols of a transcendental reality. They are observed, internalized, and endowed with a moral or spiritual value which lends them their heraldic significance. Moreover, it can be no coincidence that the deaths of the remaining members of the crew are also portrayed through images of eyes. The Mariner observes their souls flitting by; he views their dispirited bodies. Each dying man, in turn, cursed the Mariner with his eye leaving its mark upon him—the "glitter" of the dead men's eyes lending "glitter," the hypnotic quality, to the Mariner's eyes as well. Here we note once more the double use of "eye" and "seeing," turning from sight to a further "metaphysical" quality.

In *Hymns to the Night,* the sequence from empirical nature to interior experience, thence to the mystique of the spirit, proceeds in a similar way. It is the conception of reality that is so different. The imagery of light in the first paragraph of the hymn abounds with metaphoric statements of scientific facts. For example, Novalis' description of the daytime world moves easily from the macrocosm of the firmament to the mineral, vegetable, and animal worlds, finally to man, "that splendid stranger with the meaningful eyes." The image describing the stars may suffice:

> Wie des Lebens innerste Seele atmet es der rastlosen Gestirne
> Riesenwelt, und schwimmet tanzend in seiner blauen Flut.

(Like life's innermost soul, breathes the restless stars' gigantic world, and swims, dancing, in its blue sea.)

This is the world of nature, viewed objectively, before the poet introduces himself as descending into the realm of night. The description of the function of light towards the end of this section is even more revealing:

> Wie ein König der irdischen Natur ruft es jede Kraft zu zahl-
> losen Verwandlungen, knüpft und löst unendliche Bündnisse, hängt
> sein himmlisches Bild jedem irdischen Wesen um.

(Like a king of earthly nature, it (the light) calls up every power admonishing it to assume its numberless transformations; it binds and loosens an infinite number of alliances and hangs its heavenly image around each living thing.)

Experience is seen from the outside, the world suffused by light. It describes, with scientific detachment, the way light lends perceptibility to things.

211

In *The Ancient Mariner* the move towards redemption is shown through a psychological drama in which eyes and sight play a decisive role. Part IV, which is the pivotal section, begins with the suffering eye. Alone, isolated, the watery waste mirroring moral desolation:

> I looked upon the rotting sea
> And drew my eyes away.

Prior to the beginning of the redemption, heralded by the blessing of the water snakes, Coleridge dramatizes the hero's predicament in terms of sight and perception. The Mariner not only sees through his eyes, but he feels them and their relationship to the world with almost grotesque, feverish intensity:

> I closed my lids and kept them close
> And the balls like pulses beat.

Clearly, whatever these lines signify and whatever relation they may bear to the mystique of the voyage, this moment of highly dramatic insight portrays the core of the empiricist conversion. What, then, do these famous lines suggest? They portray, first of all, a keen sense of despair, of being alone on the ocean. They indicate Coleridge's awareness of his hero's *psychological* despair. But the poet also dramatizes, by turning it in on itself, the very drama of the act of knowledge. The dual relationship in which nature's eye is held through the very gaze of the percipient (the Mariner and the Wedding Guest, the sun and the ship) is given symbolic weight. The passive viewer experiences the world as an extension of himself, while the world acts upon him. A relationship, seen quite properly in epistemological terms, is now drawn materially, dramatically as well:

> For the sky and the sea and the sea and the sky
> Lay like a load on my weary eye
> And the dead were at my feet.

This is from the point of view of philosophically directed imagery the crucial passage of the poem, its announcement of conversion. Here Coleridge comes closer than he did anywhere else in translating the intellectual procedure of that mental process he was to define as imagination

212

into dramatically realized terms. Subject and object are actually joined, interacting with incredible pain. The redeeming, indeed happy, vision which subsequently emerges from this palpable demonstration of eyesight is again shown in terms of light and color. Prior to blessing the water snakes, he observes the transformed objects in the sea:

> Beyond the shadow of the ship
> I watched the water snakes.

And again:

> Within the shadow of the ship
> I watched their rich attire.

And the bright colors and luminosity of these beings is described in almost joyful detail. The Mariner blesses them unaware (transformation is an unconscious act), yet he becomes aware of their physical beauty. We must infer, then, that it is his joy that confers the blessing, that makes the metamorphosis possible.

We confront three distinct phases in Parts 3 and 4 of *The Ancient Mariner*: the phase of the passive viewer overwhelmed by the phantom ship; the phase of the suffering eye redolent with the curse of the dead man's eye, upon which rests, physically, the entire weight of the perceived world; the phase of awakening to miraculous forms which ushers in the final blessing. But what is most significant about these phases is the manner in which the reader is drawn from the Mariner's minute observations, his eyesight trained upon the ocean, to their transformation into symbolic or supernatural forms. Basically, this transformation takes place within the act of knowledge itself, as perceptions are weighted with the moral theme of the poem.

The conclusion of Part 4, then, actually suggests the closing of a cycle—from eyesight to suffering and redemption, or from "eye" to "vision"—which is elaborated and rendered precise in the remaining sections of the poem. For throughout the poem, the hero's passive activity of knowing through sight, of using sight and sightedness to penetrate to higher visions, is constantly portrayed. It is suggested through the intrusion of words like *eye* or *looked* or *watched* or *wist*. Within the ballad form, these activities are shown through the form of the romantic picaresque and *Bildungsroman*—the wandering hero's consciousness, growing through his perception of worlds which he incorporates into his vision. Here, on this endless voyage of confrontations, the eye also suggests a kind of drama revolving for Coleridge constantly around the posture of the act of knowledge and of its active and passive stance, of viewer and viewed. Towards the end, the harbor *appears to* the passive Mariner's gaze; conversely, the ship disappears in its ghostly way as the hermit and his companions look on. Even the Pilot's boy's horror, which makes him go crazy, is focussed on eyes, both constitutive (his eyes rolling to and fro, not unlike the eyeballs in Part 4) and functional:

> "Ha! Ha;" quoth he, "full plain I *see*
> The devil knows how to row.

Novalis' hymn suggests a similar process, which is begun with the celebration of the light. Instead of moral recognition narratively presented, we deal with such elements as sensation, memory, and dream. Psychology turned mystical metaphysic clearly compels the dialectical procedures of the poem. The confrontation of Coleridge's Mariner with the weight of his world is matched by the search of Novalis' poet within himself and by his recognition of the eternal night as the image of the universal as well as personal mother. The redemption, the blessing of the water snakes, finds its analogue in Novalis' concluding section: the eternal *unio mystica* of spiritual consummation with the bride sent by Mother Night.

The process of development from sight to vision in Novalis, then, is similar to Coleridge's. But for Novalis appearances are not palpably seen; they are usually symbolically presented without the intercession of vividly observing eyesight. Thus, even when Novalis describes experience physically, as in the opening third section of the first hymn, he eschews the possibility of sensation:

> Was quillet auf einmal so ahndungsvoll unter dem Herzen und verschluckt der Wehmut weiche Luft? Hast du Gefallen an uns, dunkle Nacht?

(What surges up from beneath the heart so full of foreboding and swallows the gentle air of sadness? Do we please you, dark night?)

In true mystical fashion, the poet introduces the religious experience of night through more and more explicit sexual imagery. But the feeling engendered by these images evaporates. Veiled objects, not sensations, are made into spiritual symbols. "Precious balsam," the poet writes about Night, "pours slowly from your [Night's] hand, from the bundle of poppies." If, just as in Coleridge's poem, we move farther and farther from a quotidian reality, we nevertheless do so in terms of images that describe changing states allegorically rather than in terms of images developed from the sensing mind and its palpable impressions. This is nowhere as apparent as in the very elaborate, indeed, contrived comparison between light's external firmament of the stars and the deeper, more infinite, internal world of night:

> Also nur darum, weil die Nacht dir abwendig macht die
> Dienenden, säetest du in des Raumes Weiten die leuchtenden
> Kugeln, zu verkünden deine Allmacht, deine Wiederkehr, in den
> Zeiten deiner Entfernung. Himmlischer, als jene blitzenden
> Sterne, dünken uns die unendlichen Augen, die die Nacht in uns
> geöffnet.

(Only because Night turns the servants away from you, did you sow the glowing globes in the expanses of space, to announce your power, your return, in the times of your absence. More heavenly than those sparkling stars appear to us the infinite eyes which the night has opened within us.)

The comparison of stars to eyes, the use of external and internal eyes, remains primarily allegorical. It serves a description of two states of being, two distinct realms of exterior and interior life. Even the final lines, which we compared to the Mariner's blessing of the water snakes as a preliminary act of conversion, do not suggest the confrontation of feeling or the moral torment of Coleridge's conversion. The beloved is the "gracious sun of the night." Awakening, the poet realizes, she has "prophesied night as life." She has made him human. . . . *Zehre,* he ends, *mit Geisterglut meinen Leib, dass ich luftiger mit dir inniger mich mische und dann ewig die Brautnacht währt.* "Devour my body with your ghostly fire, so that, more airily, I may yet mix more intimately with you and that bridal night may last eternally." Feeling, yes, to some extent we are made to *feel* the allegorical connection between mystical conversion and sexual consummation. But, being feeling entoned, it does not spring from powers of perception. Rather, the images state *analogies* to human feeling and form.

215

The critic who works comparatively could find no more fascinating insights than by thus turning from one ideologically related author to another. For while the sense of moral and spiritual sightedness is similar in *The Ancient Mariner* and *Hymns to the Night,* stepping from one to the other is like moving into a different world. It would be a gross error to assign this difference entirely to national or linguistic traditions. Analogues for Novalis' elevated hymns exist in English, not only in Young's *Night Thoughts,* but especially in the Ossianic mode. The grounds for their divergence lie elsewhere.

The search for transcendence, pursued by both poets, proceeds, it seems, on different levels of dialectic. Coleridge's approach is most probably connected with modes of poetic perception and their relationship to a universal moral sense. *The Ancient Mariner* is mentioned briefly in a note following the famous description of the imagination in Chapter 13 of the *Biographia*; the poem, Coleridge hints, may show what his exposition neglected to amplify. Moreover, the imagination, which Coleridge was to link up with the Kantian *Vernunft,* is a term by no means central to German transcendentalism (where the key literary term is irony). It arises from speculations about the nature of experience and its relationship to poetry. The ordering act of the imagination, to be connected with Kant in a belated *déjà vu,* thus emerges from Coleridge's analysis of the self's encounter with the empirical world and its moral meaning.

Novalis, by contrast, was far more traditionally mystical. The world beyond the world of sense had to be envisioned as a separate realm of existence. If Coleridge's key term was imagination, Novalis' was significantly his own brand of irony, the awareness, as he puts it, of life transcended by the true presence of the spirit. Aesthetic and spiritual freedom is obtained by the dissolution of the world of objects into a world of magic as the self turns towards a search for the ultimate realm of the spirit.

This difference may reflect two separate, not wholly reconciled aspects of the Kantian world view. Both suggest an ultimate intersubjective consciousness. But Coleridge's view, both prior to and after his reading of Kant, reflects the first critique, the critique of experience. Consciousness becomes symptomatic as the internalization of space and of time and of the conversion of perceived objects into schemata or forms of

216

the Understanding. Although later Coleridge went beyond this point, basically his description of experience suggests a concrete analysis of knowing which he poetically portrayed and dramatized—both before and after his actual acquaintance with Kant. The conversion of sight into vision follows its predestined course from the internalization of experience to the moral (or "higher") projection of nature's world. Novalis' irony, on the other hand, envisioned concretely the relationship to one another of the separate universe contained in the Kantian structure as a whole, particularly the empirical as opposed to the noumenal order. Novalis knew Kant thoroughly, yet with his mystical intensity he centered more fully on the teleological implications of life and spirit than on the *functioning* of the human understanding and its relevance to metaphysical knowledge.

Confidence in man's ability to perceive the transcendental is common to all mysticism. It is Coleridge's contribution to the dialectic of the imagination that he pursued the analysis of consciousness from an empirical base. Yet the conversion of sight into vision, the simultaneous rendering and symbolic distortion of experience, is shared by Coleridge and Novalis alike, as is the post-Kantian assumption of the basically mental structure of the world. Eye and vision, conscious and unconscious experience, sensation and symbol—all of these are now common terms in our critical vocabulary. But though they seem to derive from a narrowly "romantic" transformation of nature into spirit, they actually describe the perennial conditions of art.

Princeton University

PAUL FUSSELL, JR.

Writing as Imitation: Observations on the Literary Process

In this essay I want to put forward—although perhaps "revive" would be a better term—a theory of the way literature gets made. My main example of the writer will be Samuel Johnson, whom I choose for two reasons. First, I think his writing deserves to be better known, and known with more sophistication than has sometimes been brought to it. My second reason is that the sheer variety of his output offers an opportunity to test the theory I want to resuscitate in a number of compositional situations. During a very long lifetime of writing Johnson came to grips with more different kinds of compositional problems than most other writers we could name, for he worked in more "kinds"—sermon, prayer, letter, advertisement, dedication, petition, essay, Oriental tale, law lecture, dictionary, tragedy, poetic satire, domestic elegy. To understand what he was doing we must begin by establishing the theory of composition that presided over his performance as a writer.

Anyone who writes anything well imitates something. Every piece of writing which strikes readers as successful is the realization of a paradigm. When we say that a piece of writing is bad, one of the things we are implying is that it has imitated unsuccessfully the archetype which we perceive it is trying to resemble. Another way of putting it is to say that every new work—it will be well to abandon at the outset the term *original*—is a virtual translation into local terms of a pre-

218

existing model. In this sense the old orthodox critical word *imitation* retains its usefulness if we take it to suggest not an *imitatio naturae*—such an uncoded imitation is, on E. H. Gombrich's demonstration in *Art and Illusion,* impossible—but an *imitatio literarum,* an imitation of that which is written.

The best way to test the validity of these assertions is through empirical self-scrutiny and confession. Most of those reading this essay have written scholarly and critical works and know that it is a convention of such works that they come equipped with a preface. Every good preface is like every other good preface in containing the same materials and in presenting these materials in the same order. The conventional order is bipartite: (1) a statement of the intent and limits of the inquiry; (2) acknowledgments to persons, living or dead, together with acknowledgments of reprint permissions. It is an inviolable convention of the preface as a literary form that the second element, the acknowledgments, not appear first. If it does appear first, we justly tax the writer with amateurism or incompetence. He has done something that is "not done."

Now everyone who has written a preface to his own book knows—if he peers into his heart of hearts—that at some point he has carefully and very privately consulted other people's prefaces to see how it is done. Our own experiences of going about such literary actions, our own awareness of how we, as writers, imitate perforce, seem to me more trustworthy guides to a general theory of literary making than any amount of metaphysical or psychological speculation, no matter how rich and suggestive. We are all writers, and there seems no reason to suppose that we operate very differently from other people, once we set aside the undeniably colorful dramaturgy of pretension and illusion which a lively life of literature enjoins on her devotees.

Like a preface, a personal letter is a conventional literary performance. The reason children's letters are generally droll is that their writers haven't yet learned how conventional a letter is supposed to be and don't know that the reader will be either amused or disturbed by departures from convention. One convention of the letter is that the early part of it will make some allusion to the occasion that has prompted it, usually the receipt of a letter from the addressee. We are jolted, thus, when we encounter a letter like this one, written from summer camp by an eleven-year-old girl; and what jolts us is that it begins *in medias res:*

Dear Family,
   Please send me a Care package. If you don't know what it is, it is a big chock full box of candy and cookies. If you send it up make sure you get no black licorice and get red licorice instead. I like camp a lot. It's fun. Well, I can't think of anything else to say, but I will think of something.

In its own way the last sentence here seems to illustrate Gombrich's finding that "The code generates the message": if the code—read *conventions*—is not apparent to writer and reader alike, nothing can get said. It is no wonder that this child "can't think of anything else to say": what she means is that, being innocent of the conventional practice of the letter as a literary form, she can't think of anything else to say that conventionally belongs in a letter. It is doubtful that her friends at camp found her speechless: it is the literary form alone that is imposing speechlessness upon her. Because, as Northrop Frye perceives in *The Well-Tempered Critic,* the style of the personal letter is likely to imitate the style of "associative monologue," convention is even more important in it than in other forms. As he observes, "Convention has had to devise a great number of ways for getting a letter stopped. We must close now and do something else; we are in good health and hope you are the same; and we finally reach yours sincerely like a liner being towed into port." Although the object of this child's letter is something other than to make us smile, we do smile, and thus we can say that the letter is a rhetorical abortion. As a conveyor of information it did succeed—I did remit the red licorice—but as writing, that is, as conventional rhetoric, it was less successful.

To turn from a child's letters to Samuel Johnson's is of course not to play entirely fair, but to consider Johnson's letters in a context like this is to see immediately that his are rhetorically so happy because he has firmly in mind the paradigm of each of the kinds of letters he writes. Johnson instinctively denies that conception of the letter which would hold that it constitutes an opportunity for natural self-expression. Indeed, he goes so far as to perceive that "no transaction offers stronger temptations to fallacy and sophistication than epistolary intercourse." After his death an acquaintance recalled that "He spoke contemptuously of . . . professing to *pour out one's soul* upon paper."

For the Johnsonian theory of the letter, we turn to *Rambler* 152. The emphasis throughout is on art and artifice, and Johnson insists that as the substance of the letter is less weighty, the element of art must be more conspicuous. Although in his theory of the letter he is not entirely serious—he seldom is *entirely* serious when delivering literary views— we can perceive in it the analogy he makes between the personal letter and other fixed literary forms, forms whose fixity arises from the universality and uniformity of the rhetorical occasions in which they take place. He writes: "Letters that have no other end than the entertainment of the correspondents are more properly regulated by critical precepts [than letters with a more serious rhetorical purpose], because the matter and style are equally arbitrary, and rules are more necessary as there is a larger power of choice."

We should pause here to notice how remarkably Johnson's rhetorical theory of art anticipates Gombrich's in *Art and Illusion*. Johnson says: "Rules are more necessary as there is a larger power of choice." Gombrich says: "Where [in a work] everything is possible and nothing unexpected, communication must break down." We should not allow Johnson's word *rules* to mislead us into patronizing him as a merely prescriptive theorist: by *rules* he means publicly accepted conventions; he does not mean the prescriptions of critics which have no demonstrated, empirical basis in uniform human reactions to works of art. He goes on in *Rambler* 152:

> In letters of this kind [he is thinking of the trivial letter as a distinct literary genre], some conceive art graceful; and others think negligence amiable; some model them by the sonnet, and will allow them no means of delighting but the soft lapse of calm mellifluence; others adjust them by the epigram, and expect pointed sentences and forcible periods.

Although the party of the sonnet-analogy and the party of the epigram-analogy are both lightly satirized here, Johnson is rather smiling at the pedantic precision and exclusivism of the two prescriptions than ridiculing the analogies themselves. It strikes him as quite natural to find analogies for the trivial letter in well-known formal genres, in one

221

of which, the sonnet, the form is rigorously fixed, and in the other of which, the epigram, substance and tone are as rigorously predetermined. Focussing always on the reader and on his all-important reactions, Johnson concludes *Rambler* 152 thus:

> When the subject has no intrinsic dignity, it must owe its attractions to artificial embellishments, and may catch at all the advantages which the art of writing can supply. . . .

> The purpose for which letters are written when no intelligence is communicated, or business transacted, is to preserve in the minds of the absent either love or esteem: to excite love we must impart pleasure, and to raise esteem we must discover abilities. Pleasure will generally be given, as abilities are displayed, by scenes of imagery, points of conceit, unexpected sallies, and artful compliments. Trifles always require exuberance of ornament; the building which has no strength can be valued only for the grace of its decorations. The pebble must be polished with care which hopes to be valued as a diamond. . . .

Of all the "kinds" of letters that Johnson practices, from letters of condolence and of moral advice to artfully trivial letters to children, of no kind is he more a master than of the severe letter, or the letter of abuse. Indeed, his two best-known letters, to James ("Ossian") Macpherson and to Lord Chesterfield, are both of this kind. Both are full of art, but the art is very different to accord with their very different occasions and recipients.

Johnson's quarrel with Macpherson achieved full publicity when, in *A Journey to the Western Islands of Scotland* (1775), he commented thus on Macpherson's refusal to produce the Ossianic manuscripts: "The editor, or author, could never shew the original; nor can it be shewn by any other; to revenge reasonable incredulity by refusing evidence is a degree of insolence with which the world is not yet acquainted; and stubborn audacity is the last refuge of guilt." Reading this passage, Macpherson came alight and, as Arthur Murphy reports, "sent a threatening letter to the author; . . . Johnson answered him in the rough phrase of stern defiance." But we observe that even the rough phrase of stern defiance must find a pre-existing form to couch itself in. Johnson finds that form by remembering Richard Savage's distinguished performance in an abusive letter almost fifty years earlier. Johnson's model, I believe, is this splendid effort sent by Savage to Lord Tyrconnel, who, in Savage's view, had gravely wronged him:

Right Honorable Brute and Booby,

I find you want (as Mr. ——— is pleased to hint) to swear away my life, that is, the life of your creditor, because he asks you for a debt.—The public shall soon be acquainted with this, to judge whether you are not fitter to be an Irish evidence than to be an Irish peer.—I defy and despise you.

I am,

Your determined adversary,

R.S.

Johnson's version of Savage's letter goes as follows, and we will notice that even "stern defiance" must, for the sake of rhetorical clarity, condescend to observe the convention that the early part of the letter allude to the prompting occasion:

Mr. James Macpherson—I received your foolish and impudent note. Whatever insult is offered me I will do my best to repel, and what I cannot do for myself the law will do for me. I will not desist from detecting what I think a cheat, from any fear of the menaces of a ruffian.

You want me to retract. What shall I retract? I thought your book an imposture from the beginning; I think it upon yet surer reasons an imposture still. For this opinion I give the public my reasons, which I here dare you to refute.

But however I may despise you, I reverence truth, and if you can prove the genuineness of the work I will confess it. Your rage I defy, your abilities since your Homer are not so formidable, and what I have heard of your morals disposes me to pay regard not to what you shall say, but to what you can prove.

And then the last twist of the knife:

You may print this if you will.

Sam: Johnson

It seems suggestive of the whole context of literature as admitted rhetoric in which this letter was written and received that the recipient did not—as we should expect—destroy it in a fury but treasured it up for a lifetime; indeed, the modern text printed by R. W. Chapman in his edition derives from the original manuscript carefully saved by Macpherson. Macpherson's interesting behavior is like Lord Chesterfield's, who, upon receiving Johnson's other famous abusive letter, kept it on his library table to show people. Robert Dodsley says: "He read it to me; said, 'this man has great powers,' pointed out the severest passages, and observed how well they were expressed."

While the severe letter to Macpherson adopts a roughness of style appropriate to the imputed bucolic boorishness of the Scottish addressee, the severe letter to Chesterfield proceeds with an equally appropriate suavity. If the model of the letter to Macpherson is Savage's letter to Tyrconnel, the paradigms of the letter to Chesterfield are the general Ciceronian oration with the irony subtilized and the Horatian satire conceived as occurring in the mode of the Horatian epistle. Indeed, as Niall Rudd has suggested, Johnson's sentence beginning "Seven years, My Lord, have now passed since I waited in your outward rooms . . ." glances at Horace's sixth satire of the second book (*"Septimus octavo proprior jam fugerit annus"*) and thus brings Chesterfield as a patron into disadvantageous comparison with Horace's Maecenas. In the fictive character of the addressee which the letter establishes, we can find traces also of Pope's Atticus and even Pope's Sporus.

What needs emphasis now is Johnson's conviction that in the genre of the abusive letter the writer is no more "upon oath" than he is, as Johnson insisted, when writing an epitaph. The object of the abusive letter is to insult the recipient appropriately and plausibly. As genre, it is the dedication turned inside out.

A remark made by Johnson to his friend Bennet Langton testifies abundantly to his sense of the precedence of genre even in the abusive letter. Langton reports:

Dr. Johnson, when he gave me this copy of his letter [to Chesterfield], desired that I would annex to it his information to me, that whereas it is said in the letter that "no assistance has been received" [Johnson actually wrote "without one act of assistance, one word of encouragement, or one smile of favor"], he did once receive from Lord Chesterfield the sum of ten pounds, but as that was so inconsiderable a sum he thought the mention of it could not properly find place in a letter of the kind that this was.

Actually, ten pounds was quite a lot of money: it approaches the fifteen guineas Johnson earned by works like the *Life of Savage* or *The Vanity of Human Wishes*. Pope got only fifteen pounds for the five-canto version of *The Rape of the Lock,* and only seven for the two-canto version. But the paradigm Johnson is engaged in realizing in the letter to Chesterfield can admit mention of *no* act of assistance. Two words in Langton's comment particularly invite scrutiny: *properly* and *kind.* Prop-

erly asserts the precedence of the genre over mere occasional fact or mere idiosyncratic personal circumstance. And *kind* means something much more specific than we might imagine: Johnson defines *kind* in the *Dictionary* as "generical class"; and whenever he speaks of a literary work of a certain *kind,* he does not mean anything so loose as a work of a certain *sort*. In critical contexts he uses *kind* very exactly to mean a received public genre with well-known conventional differentia.

I want to turn now to some of Johnson's poems and inquire, as I have of his letters, what they are and what they are made of. What pre-existing models are they translating into local terms? With *The Vanity of Human Wishes,* the answer is provided in the subtitle: "The Tenth Satire of Juvenal Imitated." Equally obvious is the model in Proverbs 6:6 for "The Ant," which begins,

> Turn on the prudent ant thy heedful eyes,
> Observe her labors, sluggard, and be wise.

Somewhat less obvious is the provenance of the materials out of which his other poems are made. I use *materials* consciously to suggest the inert pre-existence of the quasi-architectural stuff of poems, stuff which must have achieved the status of public property before it can be disposed successfully as an element of poems.

Johnson's great art is the art of redeeming the received and even the commonplace. It is entirely typical of his literary procedure for him to take up a commonplace literary (or frequently sub-literary) kind, put into it exactly the sort of materials that belong there by rhetorical right, and so redeem the ordinary by sheer rhetorical acuteness. This is what he does not merely with the letter but with the dedication, the petition, the political advertisement, and the publisher's prospectus.

By Johnson's time hardly any genre had more of the commonplace about it than the theatrical prologue. Like the dedication and the petition, the theatrical prologue is dramatic writing in the sense that the author speaks not in his own person but in the role of the speaker assigned to deliver his words. In Johnson's *Drury Lane Prologue* of 1747 the speaker is not Johnson but David Garrick, and further, David Garrick not in his off-stage role of an amiable if vain companion but in his official role as actor-manager of a playhouse. Consequently, the

225

vignette history of the English drama which Johnson writes for Garrick to utter is appropriately couched in a raised, flamboyant style of the sort an actor-manager would conventionally affect. The images Johnson uses are slightly too bold, the antitheses are slightly too melodramatic, the issues overschematized and oversimplified both to lend verisimilitude to the speaker and to flatter the audience into imagining that it constitutes an appropriate tribunal of literary criticism. We can understand what Johnson's task is here if we imagine ourselves assigned the job of writing a brief comparison between the poetry of William Carlos Williams and Wallace Stevens that will sound entirely natural when spoken by David Susskind.

Johnson hated to write so much that he generally wrote as fast as possible to get it over with. In composing poems his usual method was to do the whole thing in his head before recording any of it on paper. In this way he could himself wield the stick from which the carrot before him depended. Of *The Vanity of Human Wishes* he says: "I wrote . . . the first seventy lines . . . in the course of one morning. . . . The whole number was composed before I threw a single couplet on paper." Notice the language here: *composed,* not created; *threw,* as if the couplets are inert, almost material objects. Johnson's comment on *throw* in the *Dictionary* seems to imply a very accurate image of his own compositional practices: "[The word *throw*] always comprises the idea of haste, force, or negligence." Of the *Drury Lane Prologue* he says: "The same method [as in writing *The Vanity of Human Wishes*] I pursued in regard to the Prologue on opening Drury-Lane Theatre. I did not afterwards change more than a word of it, and that was done at the remonstrance of Garrick. I did not think his criticism just, but it was necessary he should be satisfied with what he was to utter." (Actually, it turned out that Garrick didn't utter the lines at all: he was sick on the crucial evening. The play, by the way, was *The Merchant of Venice.*)

We can appreciate Johnson's ventriloquial powers if we compare the way Johnson-Garrick goes about praising Shakespeare with the way Johnson-as-"critic" praises him in the *Preface* to his formal edition of Shakespeare. Johnson-Garrick's emphasis is all on Shakespeare's powers of fancy, his capacities for exhausting known worlds and then imagining new ones, and for disdaining the boundaries of real existence:

226

> When Learning's triumph o'er her barb'rous foes
> First reared the stage, immortal Shakespeare rose;
> Each change of many-colored life he drew,
> Exhausted worlds, and then imagined new:
> Existence saw him spurn her bounded reign,
> And panting Time toiled after him in vain.

But in the *Preface,* Johnson in his role as critic praises Shakespeare for quite contrary qualities, namely, his fidelity to the natural—that is, the expected and familiar—in human character. Actually, what Johnson-Garrick delivers as a Shakespearean virtue Johnson-as-critic singles out as a defect: "He had no regard to distinction of time or place," we are told in the *Preface;* and this readiness to spurn the bounded kingdom of real existence leads Shakespeare into anachronism and confusion. Mrs. Thrale is one who would have been capable of perceiving the distinction between Johnson-Garrick and Johnson-as-critic. She notes "his extreme distance from those notions which the world has agreed . . . to call romantic," and she continues: "It is indeed observable in his Preface to Shakespeare that while other critics expatiate on the creative powers and vivid imagination of that matchless poet, Dr. Johnson commends him for giving so just a representation of human manners. . . ."

With the second verse-paragraph of the *Drury Lane Prologue* we begin to see what publicly available materials Johnson is inviting into the poem:

> Then Jonson came, instructed from the school,
> To please in method, and invent by rule;
> His studious patience and laborious art
> By regular approach essayed the heart;
> Cold approbation gave the ling'ring bays,
> For those who durst not censure scarce could praise.

The Shakespeare-Jonson antithesis had been a standard piece of literary goods ever since Dryden's *Essay of Dramatic Poesy* of 1668, where Jonson is taxed with elegant frigidity: "You seldom find him . . . endeavoring to move the passions," says Dryden. His antitype is Shakespeare, whose passion, as Johnson-Garrick is pleased to conceive of it, storms and immediately conquers the breast of the apprehender.

For the model for the next two paragraphs, which trace the history

227

of Restoration comedy through its career of bawdiness and of post-Restoration tragedy through its career of declamation and dullness, we need search no further than Pope's imitation of the first epistle of the second book of Horace, the *Epistle to Augustus,* and the versified literary history embedded there. And the sinister transformations of the next verse-paragraph, where theater is metamorphosed into raree show, will remind us of the similar transformations already enacted in the *Dunciad.*

Up to this point in the poem, we have heard, as it were, two voices speaking as one, Johnson's and Garrick's conducting a sort of recitative duet. But as the last two verse-paragraphs begin at line 47, each speaker seems to remain silent for a moment to allow the other an unmodified development of his own position in his own verbal way. Thus the speaker in the penultimate paragraph is Garrick taking over:

> Hard is his lot [the actor's], that here [on the
> front of the stage] by Fortune placed
> Must watch the wild vicissitudes of taste.

But in the last paragraph Garrick stands silent while Johnson takes over, which is to say that theatrical values yield, finally, to moral ones. The final injunction to the audience assumes an intimate connection between the artistic virtues of plays and the moral virtues of those who witness them. The redemption of the drama is to be accomplished only by a more important redemption of the audience:

> Then prompt no more the follies you decry.

This sober, moralistic call to the audience to change its ways is unexampled in Dryden's prologues, which are unremittingly frivolous: he can't even address the King and Queen without striking out conceits and descending to gags. The model for Johnson's solemn address to the audience is instead Pope's Prologue to Addison's *Cato* (1713). Pope's speaker shares the assumption of Johnson's that the office of writing is to do something to the audience, and at the outset of the Prologue to *Cato* we are lodged firmly in the same world in which Johnson-Garrick easily images Shakespeare's passion storming the breast:

> To wake the soul by tender strokes of art,
> To raise the genius, and to mend the heart;
> To make mankind in conscious virtue bold,
> Live o'er each scene, and be what they behold:
> For this the Tragic Muse first trod the stage.

Irresistible as Shakespeare's passion, the power of the tragic drama is to be withstood by neither the tyrannical nor the vicious:

> Tyrants no more their savage nature kept,
> And foes to virtue wondered how they wept.

After twenty-four lines devoted to the argument that the theme of *Cato*—patriot virtue—is nobler as material for tragedy than the common themes of heroic grandeur or love, Pope "turns" in the last ten lines, just as Johnson does in his last eight, exhorting the audience to moral improvement specifically as a means of theatrical redemption:

> Britons, attend: be worth like this approved,
> And show you have the virtue to be moved.
> With honest scorn the first famed Cato viewed
> Rome learning arts from Greece, whom she subdued;
> Our scene precariously subsists too long
> On French translation and Italian song.
> Dare to have sense yourselves; assert the stage,
> Be justly warmed with your own native rage.
> Such plays alone should please a British ear
> As Cato's self had not disdained to hear.

Johnson knew this poem by heart: he knew even its textual variants. As he writes in the *Life of Addison*:

When Pope brought [Addison] the Prologue . . . there were these words, "Britons, *arise!* . . ." meaning nothing more than, Britons, erect and exalt yourselves to the approbation of public virtue. Addison was frighted lest he should be thought a promoter of insurrection, and the line was liquidated to "Britons, attend."

It is notable that Johnson seems to know most about precisely that part of Pope's Prologue which has had the strongest impact on his own, that is, the final "turn" to direct moral-artistic exhortation. Arthur Murphy was striking very near the truth when he said of Johnson's

Drury Lane Prologue that it "may at least be placed on a level with Pope's to the tragedy of Cato."

Even Johnson's apparently most direct, natural, and "sincere" poem, the domestic elegy "On the Death of Dr. Robert Levet," cannot take place without the mechanism of imitation. Its essential paradigm is the Anglican hymn in long measure. Its images of "Hope's delusive mine" and "Misery's darkest caverns" seem to remember both Toplady's cleft Rock of Ages and the "unfathomable mines" of Cowper's "Light Shining out of Darkness." Johnson's curious final image,

> Death broke at once the vital chain
> And freed his soul the nearest way,

seems to recall Toplady's equally curious

> When my eye-strings break in death,

not to mention Isaac Watts'

> Dear Sovereign, break these vital strings,
> That bind me to my clay.

And so on. To attend to Johnson's work closely is to perceive its pervasive reliance on the pre-existent. And the important point is this: the compositional process of imitation which I have been examining is in no way unique to Johnson, or even to the "eighteenth century," or even to a vanished world in which writers are presumed to be learned and bookish. William Blake, for all his dramaturgy of inspiration and uniqueness of vision, requires Thomas Chatterton very much the way Johnson requires Pope, Toplady, and Watts, as we are reminded when we perceive a familiar something in this impressive image from the most inventive of Blake's early works, *The Marriage of Heaven and Hell*:

> How do you know but every bird that cuts the airy way
> Is an immense world of delight, closed to your senses five?

What generates a shock of recognition here is our memory of Charles Bawdin's speech in Chatterton's *Bristowe Tragedie*:

230

Howe dydd I knowe thatt ev'ry darte
  Thatt cutte the airie waie
Myghte nott fynde passage toe my harte
  And close myne eyes for aie?

And Blake goes further. He imitates not only Chatterton, who is easily conceived as an appropriate soul mate. Unlikely as it might seem, he even imitates Matthew Prior—wit, diplomatist, and Augustan, representative of exactly that Lockean skepticism and social sophistication which Blake's literary identity obliges him to appear to repudiate. In 1718 Prior committed this witty, patronizing epigram in the mode of the smoking-room story:

A True Maid

"No, no! for my virginity,
  When I lose that," says Rose, "I'll die."
"Behind the elms last night," cried Dick,
  "Rose, were you not extremely sick?"

Seventy-six years later Blake recovers this by resuming the voice of Dick and addressing Rose—transmuted now into "the Rose"—for very different ends:

The Sick Rose

O Rose, thou art sick!
The invisible worm
That flies in the night
In the howling storm,

Has found out thy bed
Of crimson joy,
And his dark secret love
Does thy life destroy.

Blake drains the wit out of Rose's sickness and redirects it towards the portentous and the wonderful. And the love-in-darkness of Prior's epigram, where it is an expression of mere social and sexual play, Blake manages to attach to the principle of dissolution. He has taken Prior's song of experience and made it one of his own. But we must emphasize that he has had to begin with a literary artifact to transmute.

231

Sometimes imitations are so subtle that our perception of them is fainter. But they are always there nevertheless. Consider, for example, the syntax and pattern of vowel sounds in the line from Yeats's "Sailing to Byzantium" where the speaker apostrophizes the sages to come

> And be the singing-masters of my soul.

The imitation here is of the last line of Keats's sonnet "To Sleep":

> And seal the hushèd casket of my soul.

The vowel sound of Keats's *seal* gives birth to Yeats's *be;* and Keats's *casket* creates, by its invitation to a near-rhyme, Yeats's *masters.*

If we proceed in this direction, a suspicion capable of troubling our sleep will now and then steal upon us: that given sufficient time, sufficient perceptiveness, sufficient analytic patience, and sufficient literary memory, we could ultimately track every written thing to all its imitations and end with no distinguishable separate works at all but only with one great *Ur*-source. "In the Beginning was the Word." Which is to say that the major condition of being a writer is being a reader. William Bowles remembered of Johnson that "He had . . . projected . . . a work to show how small a quantity of real fiction there is in the world; and that the same images, with very little variation, have served all the authors who have ever written."

One would imagine that the act of prayer would be one of the least literary and artificial of things. If a man can't be "natural" in privately addressing his Maker, when *can* he be? But Johnson's practice in his prayers suggests that even if one is going to pray, one must perforce imitate something. What Johnson imitates, even in his most open, anguished, "lyric" moments, is The Book of Common Prayer.

In praying as in any other kind of utterance, one has to adopt a style. Christian prayers are conventionally spoken in an archaic style less because of the dignity of the occasion than because of the archaism of the literary models available. Because of his chosen model for prayers, the style Johnson has to adopt is, as Stella Brook has designated it in *The Language of the Book of Common Prayer*, "a sixteenth-century liturgical vernacular with a seventeenth-century overlay." What makes the prayers so startling in something like *Are You Running with Me, Jesus?* by the Rev. Malcolm Boyd is less their substantive endorsement of fornication than their embrace of an unprecedented stylistic model for prayers, the nonchalant Hip or "mixed-up" vernacular.

The version of the Prayer Book used by Johnson was the revision of 1662, the first to include the Psalms and to employ for the Gospels and Epistles the text of the Authorized Version rather than that of the Great Bible. In Johnson's time the Book of Common Prayer, for all the conspicuous archaism of its usages, could be regarded as almost a work of contemporary literature. Its chronological relation to Johnson was roughly that of Shaw's *Widowers' Houses* to us. The Prayer Book imitated by Johnson appeared in the same year as Part I of Butler's *Hudibras* and only six years before Dryden's *Essay of Dramatic Poesy*. For the style of the Book of Common Prayer Johnson felt the sort of enthusiasm which he reserved for rare (and disturbing) masterpieces like *Paradise Lost*. One reason he hated to go to church was the painful literary contrast he witnessed there between the all but illiterate idiom of the sermon and the sublime rhetoric of the liturgy:

I am convinced [he once said] that I ought to be present at divine service more frequently than I am; but the provocations given by ignorant and affected preachers too often disturb the mental calm which otherwise would succeed to prayer. I am apt to whisper to myself on such occasions—How can this illiterate fellow dream of fixing attention after we have been listening to the sublimest truths, conveyed in the most chaste and exalted language, throughout a liturgy which must be regarded as the genuine offspring of piety impregnated by wisdom?

Johnson's literary way with the prayer as genre is like his way with the other kinds: it is the method of redeeming the received, of fusing the individual and local with the public and external, of advertising by practice the all-important balance between individual and species. A function of the method is to locate reality by mediating precisely between the unknowable inside and the cliché outside, of bringing into harmony the new and the known. A typical performance is the first prayer of any length Johnson recorded, the prayer on his twenty-ninth birthday, set down in 1738. This composition transmits an effect of naked sincerity, but paradoxically it does so only because we recognize in it Johnson's mastery of the elements of the genre "Anglican prayer."

The effect of sincerity is a function of the imitation of prayers already firmly in the public domain.

Johnson begins this prayer by adapting the salutation of the Prayer Book's "Prayer for All Conditions of Men": "O God, the Creator and Preserver of all Mankind." He then skips to the ascription element of the next prayer in the Book, "A General Thanksgiving," and imitates it very closely:

Father of all Mercies, I thine unworthy servant do give thee most humble thanks [the model reads 'most humble and hearty thanks'] for all thy goodness and loving-kindness to me. I bless thee for my creation, preservation, and redemption, for the knowledge of thy son Jesus Christ, for the means of Grace, and the hope of Glory.

Launched now with the indispensable aid of imitation and adaptation, Johnson is free to turn the paradigm to his own individual purposes. As he continues composing he brings himself to his obsessive theme of investing his talents and thus redeeming the time. And the stylistic device which animates him to this end is the same syntactical parallelism —taking the form primarily of triplets—he has begun by imitating:

In the days of childhood and youth, in the midst of weakness, blindness, and danger, Thou hast protected me; amidst afflictions of mind, body, and estate, Thou hast supported me; and amidst vanity and wickedness Thou hast spared me. . . . Create in me a contrite heart, that I may worthily lament my sins, acknowledge my wickedness, and obtain remission and forgiveness through the Satisfaction of Jesus Christ. And O Lord enable me by Thy grace to use all diligence in redeeming the time which I have spent in sloth, vanity, and wickedness; to make use of Thy gifts to the honor of Thy name; to lead a new life in Thy Faith, fear, and love. . . .

Even in writing like this we must be careful to assign to the writer what belongs to the writer and to literature what belongs to literature. As R. W. Chapman has observed in *Johnsonian and Other Essays and Reviews*, "Not even the *Prayers and Meditations* comprehend their author. Johnson, an accomplished writer of dedications, said that 'the known style of dedication is flattery.' He would have said that the proper topic of a Christian's and a sinner's meditations is self-examination and self-abasement. The *Prayers and Meditations* are true; but they are not autobiography."

"The point," says E. D. Hirsch in *Validity in Interpretation,* "is not that the author cannot communicate a totally unfamiliar type of meaning, but the less obvious one that he cannot even *formulate* [my emphasis] such a type. Pre-existing type conceptions are apparently as necessary to the imagination as they are to the exigencies of communication." The process of literary invention is thus a function of the process of recollection. Hobbes puts it accurately: "Imagination and memory are but one thing, which for divers considerations hath divers names." That Johnson, honest as always about literary process, is sensitive to the difficulty of distinguishing these two things is clear in his *Preface to Shakespeare,* where he observes about what he may unconsciously owe to earlier Shakespearean commentators,

Whatever I have taken from [earlier commentators], it was my intention to refer to its original author, and it is certain that what I have not given to another I believe when I wrote it to be my own . . . . If I am ever found to encroach upon the remarks of any other commentator, I am willing that the honor, be it more or less, should be transferred to the first claimant, for his right, and his alone, stands above dispute; the second can prove his pretensions only to himself, nor can himself always distinguish invention, with sufficient certainty, from recollection.

Johnson would have relished a passage in Harold Nicolson's recent *Diaries and Letters*: Nicolson sends Vita Sackville-West the remark of the poet Edward Shanks that one sign of increasing age is his not knowing "Whether a line is one of his own lines or something which he has read years ago." She replies:

As to remembering whether a line is by me or by someone else, you know very well that I never could. The first shock of this realization came when I very laboriously hammered out a line, choosing every word most carefully, and arrived at:

Men are but children of a larger growth.
[Dryden, *All for Love*, IV, i, 43]

Since then I have been cautious.

The theory of literary process I have been recommending does seem odd in a modern world dominated by images of "free enterprise" and sustained by laws about copyright and plagiarism. In *Anatomy of Criticism* Northrop Frye is as acute as usual on these matters:

235

All art is equally conventionalized, but we do not ordinarily notice this fact unless we are unaccustomed to the convention. In our day the conventional element in literature is elaborately disguised by a law of copyright pretending that every work of art is an invention distinctive enough to be patented.

(It would be interesting, by the way, to scrutinize the critical assumptions which generated the nineteenth-century laws of patent and to locate their precise origin in the romantic theory of creation.) Frye goes on:

Hence the conventionalizing forces of modern literature . . . often go unrecognized. Demonstrating the debt of A to B is merely scholarship if A is dead, but a proof of moral delinquency if A is alive. This state of things makes it difficult to appraise a literature which includes Chaucer, much of whose poetry is translated or paraphrased from others; Shakespeare, whose plays sometimes follow their sources almost verbatim; and Milton, who asked for nothing better than to steal as much as possible out of the Bible. It is not only the inexperienced reader who looks for a *residual* originality in such works. Most of us tend to think of a poet's real achievement as distinct from, or contrasted with, the achievement present in what he stole, and we are thus apt to concentrate on peripheral rather than on central critical facts.

The real state of literary affairs, Frye concludes, "was much clearer before the assimilation of literature to private enterprise concealed so many of the facts of criticism."

In emphasizing the imitative mechanism in writing I have of course started some embarrassing critical questions, among them: where do literary genres come from? are they generated *ex nihilo?* how do new ones come into being? In Johnson's time these questions were more easily answered. Assuming a static image of human character, most eighteenth-century critics found little difficulty in associating the main genres and even the main modes in writing with universal, unchanging elements in the more or less uniform human personality. Thus an older theorist of genres could reason somewhat as follows: each element of the unalterable and perpetually re-created human mind naturally has a literary form which accords with its expectations; since human nature is historically uniform and since, thus, the same very few essential human actions are played over and over again *ad infinitum,* the genres devised (or better, "discovered") by the Ancients may serve for eternity.

Thus the part of the mind which gratifies itself with gentle melancholy leans towards and sanctions elegy. The part that relishes enthusiasm or devotion sanctions the ode. The part delighting in ideas of justice is gratified by tragedy, comedy, or satire. The part that delights in fantasies of dissipation and irresponsibility has song or pastoral devised for its gratification. The part that hankers after an ideal of heroism sanctions the epic. And so on. Relying always on the Lockean image of the mind as a repository of all but uniform experience, the critics of Johnson's day, if they could ignore new things like the novel—and most of them did—embraced an account of the origin of genres which made them coterminous with the origin of the human mind itself.

In thinking about the matter we will find ourselves in a much more difficult position, although, like earlier theorists, we will necessarily begin with our habitual way of reasoning about genetics and trying to account for origins. Our own bent when we do this is probably towards the Hegelian and the sexual. We thus may find ourselves speculating as follows.

All distinct literary genres are the result of a "dialectical" synthesis between two earlier genres. The Gothic Novel, for example, is the result of a synthesis between the picaresque romance and the spooky eighteenth-century discursive poem like Young's *Night Thoughts,* a genre which, in its turn, constitutes a domesticated synthesis of elements of revenge play (*Hamlet*) with elements of Christian epic (*Paradise Lost*). The epistolary novel, as practiced by Richardson or Smollett, can be seen to be a synthesis of Renaissance prose romance, on the one hand, and the early eighteenth-century manual of letter-writing, on the other. And we can perform the same operation in trying to account for the appearance of modern genres like, say, the Absurd Play, which would seem to derive from a fusion of nineteenth-century domestic melodrama with nineteenth-century nonsense-fiction of the tradition handed by Sterne to Peacock, and passed by Peacock to Lewis Carroll.

The indispensable (if paradoxical) principle underlying this theory of genres is that nothing can come of nothing; for to be accepted as a genre by readers, that is, to be recognized as a coded context in which "literature" can occur, a literary form must carry with it something of the familiar, something that reminds the reader, however dimly, of an earlier form with which he is familiar and which he habitually regards

237

as a form, as an arena in which apparent literary purpose and value can show themselves. As Hirsch puts it: "In every new genre [a] process of assimilation is at work. No one would ever invent or understand a new type of meaning unless he were capable of perceiving analogies and making novel subsumptions under previously known types." And he continues: "Every new verbal type is a . . . metaphor that required an imaginative leap. The growth of new genres is founded on this quantum principle that governs all learning and thinking; by an imaginative leap the unknown is assimilated to the known, and something . . . new is realized."

Instructive here is the theatrical producer E. Martin Browne's experience with T. S. Eliot when the two of them had undertaken to compose and present a church pageant, the work which ultimately became *The Rock*. The trouble was that these two devisers had no form available in which to cast their material, "pageant" meaning to a lettered audience less a literary form than a vague mode of circus or nonverbal processional. As Browne reports:

We used to meet for lunch, about once a month . . . to search for a form in which to cast the show. . . . We talked round and round the problem each month, seeing no light until at last, the day before the deadline for a scenario, some broke upon me. We could model it upon the type of [stage] revue, bound together by a thin thread of plot, currently presented by C. B. Cochran [the British equivalent of Florenz Ziegfeld]. It would allow both for spectacular scenes acted to music and for a chorus, who instead of displaying their physical charms could use their speaking voices in delivering verse.

Thus the girlie-show was selected as the form with which the audience was already familiar—that is, prepared to regard as "a form"—and Eliot and Browne could now proceed to transmute it to their own uses.

It is important to see, as this example reminds us, that audiences are really more consequential in determining genres than writers are. As Frye says, "The basis of generic criticism . . . is rhetorical, in the sense that the genre is determined by the condition established between the poet and his public." We can appreciate how little a writer by himself can contrive a new genre by recalling things like the curtal sonnets of Gerard Manley Hopkins, which, for all their technical interest, reveal themselves to be one-shot performances *because* their readers perceive in them no profound new reason for such an abbreviation of sonnet form and consequently decline to call for more.

In the way I have been suggesting, then, literary elements and forms imitate organic history, reaching back irrecoverably into the abysm of time but, within our own limited view, procreating and occasionally mutating like the creatures depicted for us by the science of biology. It is ironic that the theory of the production of new genres which I have been suggesting accords exactly with the scandalous vision of the Goddess of Dullness in the *Dunciad*; peering down into the murky chasm of Grub Street, she perceives

> How Tragedy and Comedy embrace,
> How farce and epic get a jumbled race.

From Johnson to Blake, Yeats, Sackville-West, and Eliot would seem a long distance, but it may seem long because a later generation has chosen to surround the act of writing with a novel—and essentially propagandistic—"creative" terminology which implies that the nature of the literary process changed during the nineteenth century. Those who will inspect what writers do rather than what they say they are doing may want to conclude otherwise.

Rutgers University

ERICH KAHLER

Bilingualism and the Problems of Translation

Dear Francis:
Allow me to celebrate your life's achievements not by some contribution
to the study of Dante, Shakespeare, or the drama, which would remain
hopelessly inferior to your erudition and insight, but by the expression
of a very personal concern, deriving from my destiny and experience,
that seems to me not unworthy of wider attention.

Among the experiences I owe to Mr. Hitler there is one that revealed
itself as beneficial. He forced me to turn away from my native language,
German, or rather, to substitute for it a foreign language as my principal
medium of expression. Without wanting to give up my mother tongue,
I was compelled to write, to teach, to lecture in English, and thus to
embark on an overwhelming, mentally revolutionizing enterprise, a real
adventure of the mind, which has ever since influenced my manner of
thinking, of seeing and imagining things; it has indeed deeply affected
my whole mode of perception and sentiment. It has moreover succeeded
in putting me at a distance from myself, from my spontaneous idiom,
which up to then had been for me the only naturally, unconsciously
valid one. I discovered in the flesh as it were—and this constraint was
the only possibility of such a discovery—the insurmountable confines
of every language, those limits that make the communication and the
understanding among nations so extremely difficult.

The study of the sometimes very subtle differences of meaning, which

240

occur in the lexical attempt at synonymity, has helped me to attain an undefinable position beyond the given limitations of the languages; it has taught me much about the nature of language as such, and has opened for me a new, transcendentally simultaneous vista of the very things to be expressed. The specific word and its substratum are indissolubly linked with each other, they indeed keep creating each other; and all poetic or intellectual innovation derives from this creative reciprocity.

I thus came to realize that it is impossible to achieve a true synthesis of semantically different versions or to combine fundamentally distinct expressions of seemingly the same meaning. Any language possesses and develops words, figures of speech, conceptions, which are strictly untranslatable; and it is in the folds and depths of such ultimately inexplicable terms that the mystery of whole ethnic attitudes, even physical ones, is concealed. Nevertheless, through a kind of radiation as it were, which is rendered possible by an intrinsic acquaintance with two languages, certain complementary relations, or correspondences, between distinct phrasings may establish themselves for him who makes an effort to cultivate two languages, and in this manner they may, each in its own way, be widened and enriched. A simultaneous vision, resulting from such comparisons and substitutions, allows him to express an amplified thought in either language. It is this sphere, in between and above, fluctuating and unfixable—and still very real—which seems to me to produce a true, creative bilingualism.

Such experiences touch upon the problems of translation and the possibility of its artistic execution. True bilingualism has proved to be an indispensable prerequisite of a translation approximating an identity of meaning and thus capable of contributing to a rapprochement among nations. It is useful to consider the problems of translation specifically in the realm of poetry, since here they appear in their acutest form. For poetry is the most concise, the most intense mode of expression; it moves on the borderlines of the unspeakable, and its composition, in all its dimensions, has to be taken most seriously.

Prose, being essentially narration or interpretation, permits a certain largesse of paraphrasing, which in poetry is apt to violate the whole character of the work. In poetry not only the "wording" is important, indeed irreplaceable, but irrational, extrarational elements, the imagery and the tone, the *tonus*, of the whole are equally important; the union of all of it creates the atmosphere of the poem; it constitutes the very meaning of it. Thus, simply relating the palpable theme, the literal text, cannot be called rendering a poem; the lyrical substance, which is its source, the sonic and rhythmic qualities, have as much to say as the linguistic and semantic message; indeed the tone takes over much that the wording, be it ever so precise, is unable to tell. A "translation" of Gerard Manley Hopkins's poems, for instance, that omits the alliterations, the interior rhymes, the sprung rhythm, does not even impart the literal significance of the poem. It is reduced to sheer text, "information."

This unalterable nature of poetry, its being fundamentally lyrical and incapable of disowning its origination in song, implies that there are certain characteristics and rules to be observed.

(1) Poetry speaks in verse, but it is not to be confounded with versification. Poetry is language of a different quality. It is the *tone* that creates the genuine verse. Therefore, and only therefore, poetry translations in prose are invalid.

(2) Not all poems are translatable. Apart from generally linguistic impediments, a personal disposition is sometimes of decisive importance. A creative bilingualism, spirited by kinship of experience and emotion, may be able to overcome the linguistic obstacles.

(3) All translation involves certain sacrifices, imposed by the different character of languages. These sacrifices must be made with extreme caution, at such places where they hurt least. The German language, for instance, is by nature a protractive, outstretched language, as compared with the concretely contracted English. So a lengthening of German verse would seem appropriate, provided that the proportions within the whole are observed. There are poems where the rhyme may be abandoned without affecting the quality of the poem; there are others in which the rhyme is absolutely indispensable.

(4) It follows that a translation must be undertaken from the view of the *whole* poem, from its imaginary center, not peripherally, step by step.

(5) The pitfalls that have to be guarded against in translating are twofold; a pedantic literality and dryness that reduce the substance of a poem to sheer textual information, and its opposite, the temptation to

which Rilke often succumbed, to transgress the limits of faithfulness and, unawares, to escape into poetry of one's own.

It should not be necessary—but evidently it is—to emphasize that translation of poetry is a form of art. It demands, for all its precise closeness and delicate artistic balance, a free, unstrained flow of diction; which means that the verse must maintain the naturalness of personal speech. It goes without saying that the translator must have cultivated a special sensibility for the two languages between which the translation has to take place. A translation using a linguistic mediator, as in the case of Ezra Pound's Chinese or Auden's Russian, is as such of necessity untrustworthy. A valid artistic translation is possible only when it originates in the sphere of bilingualism.

Princeton, New Jersey

STEPHEN MILLER

The Poetry of Zbigniew Herbert

"Everything suffers by translation except a bishop," the Earl of Chester-field once said. All translations in some way betray the original, yet many writers and critics have distinguished between translations of novels and translations of poetry: the former are allowed, the latter are not. "A translation in verse," Victor Hugo said, "seems to me something absurd, impossible." The distinction, I think, is inaccurate; a novel such as *Ulysses*, in which the author imitates and burlesques the prose tradition of his language, may be more difficult to translate effectively than some poems. And certain novelists—Italo Svevo for example—whose style is a rather unimportant aspect of their work are not betrayed at all in translation. Likewise, some poets suffer the sea change of translation worse than others. In his introduction to *The Penguin Book of Modern Verse Translation,* George Steiner admits that he found himself "discarding translations of Pindar, Hölderlin and Leopardi. These three poets seem to mark the limits of possible restatement. Translations do not throw light on them but a penumbra." These poets do not metamorphose very well because their poetic effect rests predominantly on the way they exploit both the sound of their language and its distinctive syntactical possibilities. The music of poetry is untranslatable, but other aspects of poetry suffer only minor distortions in translation—metaphor and imagery for example. And if a poet tends to be aphoristic, the grit of his mind will rarely turn into sand in translation. Those who say, then, that poetry is untranslatable are only thinking of a particular kind of poetry.

244

Zbigniew Herbert, the contemporary Polish poet, is a case in point. Herbert's poetry moves into English without suffering much damage because, as Tymon Terlecki, a Polish critic, said: "[Herbert is] prone to treating poetry as a specific kind of intellectual prose." Reading Herbert in the translation by Czeslaw Milosz and Peter Dale Scott, we cannot of course judge the way Herbert uses the forms of Polish poetry, but we can judge the quality of his "intellectual prose." The complexity of his mind is apparent even in translation. Moreover, he draws his metaphors not from particular Polish poets or from the particular events of Polish history, but either from everyday objects—stools and pebbles—or from a common body of European culture: the Bible, Greek mythology, Thucydides, Tacitus, and Shakespeare. Herbert's originality lies in the way his mind works upon this common body of knowledge. Although the English reader cannot tell what Herbert's position may be among Polish poets, by virtue of this translation he can tell that Herbert in English is a good poet.

Herbert is a political poet, but the word political may be misleading for it brings to mind the bad verse of the thirties, verse damaged by causes: some of Auden's, some of Spender's, and many poems by a host of minor Marxist poets. The political poet who deals directly with the events of contemporary history usually plays a losing game. His moral outrage will probably overwhelm his poetry, making it self-righteous, predictable, and shrill. Reading a recent volume of poetry entitled *Where Is Vietnam? American Poets Respond*, we hear for the most part only public speech: the poet quarrels with others, not with himself. And, as Yeats said, quarreling with others results in rhetoric, not in poetry. Although Herbert's poetry is preoccupied with the nightmares of recent history (the lies, pretensions, and horrors of totalitarianism), it is not public speech. Herbert never advocates this or that cause and he never moralistically "cries" about contemporary experience. He approaches his subject obliquely; wandering among the ruins caused by such destructive forces, Herbert looks for objects that remind us of our stubborn desire to survive and remain sane. Subdued and casual, his poems shun both hysteria and apocalyptic intensity. To answer chaos with chaos, Herbert implies, is to succumb to the very forces we should resist.

Herbert's obliqueness and restraint derive in part from his use of biblical and Greek mythology. The lens of myth reduces the glare of contemporary experience, placing it in a perspective that enables him to look at it without losing his sanity and sense of humor. In several of Herbert's poems the language of religion becomes a metaphor for the language of the totalitarian state. Angels are flunkeys of the highest power and Paradise is the Utopia that supposedly exists. In "Report from Paradise," for example, Herbert satirizes the pretensions of such an ideology:

> At first it was to have been different
> luminous circles choirs and degrees of abstraction
> but they were not able to separate exactly
> the soul from the flesh and so it would come here
> with a drop of fat a thread of muscle . . .
>
> not many behold God
> he is only for those of 100 per cent pneuma
> the rest listen to communiqués about miracles and floods . . .

And in "The Seventh Angel" Herbert satirizes the rigidities of totalitarian aesthetics. Shemkel, an angelic misfit who cannot function very well in the totalitarian hierarchy,

> is black and nervous
> and has been fined many times
> for illegal import of sinners . . .

The "Byzantine artists" of the state, however, cannot admit that such an imperfect angel exists. He must be painted "just like all the rest,"

> because they suppose
> they might lapse into heresy
> if they were to portray him
> just as he is
> black nervous
> in his old threadbare nimbus.

The artists of the state must keep their art free from the contaminations of heresy; they must not paint anything just as it is.

Herbert's use of myth liberates him from the confines of particular historical events. The satire is not directed at one totalitarian regime, but at all such regimes. At the same time the use of myth fleshes out the thin bones of the satire, making it sly and elegant, not obvious and heavy-handed. Furthermore, Herbert's satirical humor is a way of resisting the dehumanizing and impersonal language of the state—the so-called higher truth of its ideology. Keeping a sense of humor means keeping a private language and avoiding the total politicization of the self. After all, "they"—the solemn angels of the state—never laugh.

Of course such humorless angels can be frighteningly effective. They can compel belief or they can compel guilt. A chilling poem, "Preliminary Investigation of an Angel," brings to mind the forced confessions of Stalin's purge trials, when even the most loyal members of the Communist Party were forced to confess their guilt. An angel—one who is a faithful member of the heavenly hierarchy—naturally thinks that he is spiritual and "innocent." The state, however, judges him as material and guilty, and so he slowly metamorphoses before our eyes. At first,

> When he stands before them
> in the shadow of a suspicion
> he is still all
> composed of light . . .

Soon, however, after "the blood is helped on/with instruments and interrogations,"

> the job is finished
> the leather throat of the angel
> is full of gluey agreement
>
> how beautiful is the moment
> when he falls on his knees
> incarnate into guilt
> saturated with contents . . .

No one can resist the inquisition of the state, not even such a faithful member of its hierarchy.

Yet after the "gluey agreement," when the torturers have gone away, something concrete remains that suggests a limit to the power and the effectiveness of the state. "Preliminary Investigation of an Angel" ends with the following lines:

247

his tongue hesitates
between knocked-out teeth
and confession

they hang him head downwards

from the hair of the angel
drops of wax run down
and shape on the floor
a simple prophecy.

It is only after the angel has been broken by the state that he becomes
real, and his reality undermines the unreal "spiritual" perfection of the
totalitarian order. Because of its ruthlessness and suspicion, the system
creates its own opposition, creates such a "simple prophecy." Icons of a
"faith" different from that of the state, the drops of wax deny the
"gluey agreement."

A similar parable is adumbrated in a poem that makes use of Greek
myth, "Apollo and Marsyas." Apollo, with his "absolute ear," pipes the
song of the state on his flute and therefore cannot lose the contest he
has with Marsyas. The latter, who dared to challenge Apollo, is flayed
alive, yet

only seemingly
is the voice of Marsyas
monotonous
and composed of a single vowel
Aaa . . .

In reality, the howling of Marsyas provokes a shudder of disgust in
Apollo, who is "cleaning his instrument," and the victorious god begins
to walk away from the flayed satyr, wondering

whether out of Marsyas' howling
there will not some day arise
a new kind
of art—let us say—concrete

suddenly
at his feet
falls a petrified nightingale

he looks back
and sees
that the hair of the tree to which Marsyas was fastened
is white
completely . . .

Like the drops of wax, the petrified nightingale and the white "hair" of the tree are a new kind of concrete art that grows out of the inquisition of the state. The latter two are deformations of nature that testify through their grotesque metamorphosis to the terror of the state. Marsyas' howl—the howl of contemporary experience—does not end in silence and nothingness; it ends in simple concrete prophecies whose existence denies the state its total victory.

Herbert's obliqueness and restraint, then, derive not only from the use he makes of myth, but also from the attention he pays to concrete things. In "At the Gate of the Valley," a poem in which the Last Judgment is seen as a parable of mass extermination, Herbert says:

those who as it seems
have obeyed the orders without pain
go lowering their heads as a sign of consent
but in their clenched fists they hide
fragments of letters ribbons clippings of hair
and photographs
which they naïvely think
won't be taken from them . . .

The objects that these people clutch make them individuals and not the statistics of a holocaust. Although threatened by a final solution, the victims refuse to give up their possessions. The disaster may be enormous but the responses to it are personal; the final solution happens to particular individuals at particular places and times.

This particularity is important. "Our fear," Herbert says in a poem of that name,

is a scrap of paper
found in a pocket
"warn Wójcik
the place on Dluga Street is hot"

> our fear
> does not rise on the wings of the tempest
> does not sit on a church tower
> it is down-to-earth
>
> it has the shape
> of a bundle made in haste
> with warm clothing
> provisions
> and arms . . .

Herbert rejects the fashionable idea that the horrors of recent history require a literature of apocalyptic intensity. He does not trust such a dark vision, for it obscures the human realities of fear and terror. Such a rhetoric, he implies, has its own kind of impersonality and inhumanity.

Herbert's particularity is also an attempt to clear the atmosphere of verbal smoke and fog—the smoke of literary hysteria and the fog of totalitarian lies. The poet wants to learn how to use words carefully again, and therefore he focusses on objects. The pebble, he says,

> is a perfect creature
>
> equal to itself
> mindful of its limits
>
> filled exactly
> with a pebbly meaning . . .
>
> > —Pebbles cannot be tamed
> > to the end they will look at us
> > with a calm and very clear eye.

And in another poem Herbert addresses a stool:

> you come always to the call of the eye
> with great immobility explaining by dumb-signs
> to a sorry intellect: we are genuine—
> At last the fidelity of things opens our eyes.

Such things have nothing to do with the confusions of hysteria or the lies of ideology. The mind disciplines itself by meditating on concrete objects and the sorry intellect is renewed. Mindful of its limits, the pebble is an island of clarity in a sea of chaos.

The pebble and the stool also work as analogies, implying both a basic human stubbornness ("Pebbles cannot be tamed") and an attitude toward life and art that might be called classical. Herbert's translators, Czeslaw Milosz and Peter Dale Scott, say that "critics in Poland have called him the most classical among his peers, though like most of them he has come to rely little on traditional metres or rhymes." Herbert's poetry, like the pebble, is "filled exactly/ with a pebbly meaning," and Herbert's poetry, like the pebble, looks at us "with a calm and very clear eye." Clarity and emotional restraint: these are classical virtues. Herbert's classicism, however, does not mean that he has removed himself from the present and that he looks at it in a sadly disillusioned manner from the ivory tower of the past. His classicism is a prescription for survival and sanity in the present—a method for swimming in the destructive element and not going under.

Herbert's clearest statement of his classicism is found in the poem "Why the Classics." Here he contrasts Thucydides, who honorably accepted the responsibility for his unsuccessful expedition to Amphipolis, with "generals of the most recent wars" who

> if a similar affair happens to them
> whine on their knees before posterity
> praise their heroism and innocence
>
> they accuse their subordinates
> envious colleagues
> unfavourable winds
>
> Thucydides says only
> that he had seven ships
> it was winter
> and he sailed quickly . . .

Unlike Thucydides, generals of the most recent wars evade the responsibility for their actions. Wallowing in self-pity, they break down and call everything a mess, say that everyone (and therefore no one) is responsible for the failure. They cannot make distinctions. Thucydides offers no excuses; he failed, and

for this he paid his native city
with lifelong exile

exiles of all times
know what price that is.

Thucydides, then, looks at his actions with the discipline and clarity of a calm and very clear eye. The classics, Herbert implies, teach us to spurn the anarchy of self-pity—not only in life but also in art. The poem ends with the following stanzas:

if art for its subject
will have a broken jar
a small broken soul
with a great self-pity

what will remain after us
will be like lovers' weeping
in a small dirty hotel
when wall-paper dawns.

An art full of self-pity is a broken and incoherent art, one that cannot make distinctions. It is an art of "lovers' weeping"—each one lost in the private world of his or her tears.

Self-pity for Herbert resides in our inner voice. In a poem called "Inner Voice" he says:

he is of no use to me
I could forget about him

I have no hope
a little regret
when he lies there
covered with pity
breathes heavily
opens his mouth
and tries to lift up
his inert head.

The inner voice, full of "syllables/stripped of all meaning," tempts us to lie down and cry. Herbert tries to ignore this siren song, but he does so with "a little regret." Crying is the easiest thing to do, yielding to what Hannah Arendt in *The Origins of Totalitarianism* called "the mere process of disintegration . . . because it has assumed the spurious grandeur of 'historical necessity' . . . [and] because everything outside it has begun to appear lifeless, bloodless, meaningless, and unreal." The classics show us how to resist such a temptation. Listening to Marsyas' howl, Herbert does not respond with a whine. Instead he disciplines himself by looking at objects—calm things of "great immobility" that "reprove us constantly for our instability." Such objects survive disaster; the classics help us to do the same thing.

As a classicist Herbert does not heed his incoherent inner voice; and as a classicist he makes very few claims for poetry. In "A Knocker," his art is "nothing special," and his imagination is a

> piece of board
> my sole instrument
> is a wooden stick . . .
>
> I thump on the board
> and it prompts me
> with the moralist's dry poem
> yes—yes
> no—no.

The symbol for his imaginative powers is not, as it was for the romantics, a fountain; it is a wooden stick. And myth for Herbert is not, as it was for Blake, a sign of the gods within the mind, an example of the inexhaustible fertility of the human imagination. Myth for Herbert is an order that we can turn to in order to get away from the anarchy of the self. It provides us with a way of placing contemporary experience in a larger perspective. Finally, unlike the romantics, Herbert writes the "moralist's dry poem"; he is neither a prophet nor an unacknowledged legislator.

Another aspect of Herbert's classical frame of mind is his skepticism about language itself. Throughout his poetry there rumbles an *ostinato* of linguistic despair. The poet can only thump his board, aware that words themselves are inadequate to convey the horrors of contemporary experience. "Episode" ends with the following lines:

what should I say on the shore
of a small dead sea

slowly the water fills
the shapes of feet which have vanished.

And in "Elegy of Fortinbras," Fortinbras says of Hamlet:

It is not for us to greet each other or bid farewell
we live on archipelagos
and that water these words what can they do what
can they do prince.

Looking at that water—the chaos of contemporary history—what can the poet say? Herbert's poetry is mindful of its limits because the poet is aware of the limitations of language itself.

But of course we must say something, and such a chaotic situation requires the voice of a Fortinbras, not a Hamlet. Hamlet's language is full of tragic intensity, but it is an intensity that arises from his despair and self-pity. Fortinbras, the man who arrives after the disaster and tries to make some sense of the ruins, is Herbert's hero, even though his task is a prosaic one, and what he does will never be worth a tragedy. In "Elegy of Fortinbras" the soldier says of the prince:

The rest is not silence but belongs to me
you chose the easier part an elegant thrust
but what is heroic death compared with eternal watching
with a cold apple in one's hand on a narrow chair
with a view of the ant-hill and the clock's dial

Adieu prince I have tasks a sewer project
and a decree on prostitutes and beggars . . .
I go to my affairs This night is born
a star named Hamlet We shall never meet
what I shall leave will not be worth a tragedy . . .

Fortinbras speaks with a good deal of regret, for he knows that Hamlet's "heroic death" is the "easier part," and as such it is tempting. By dying Hamlet avoided the mediocre tasks of survival; by dying Hamlet did not have to compromise himself. As Fortinbras says of him: "you believed in crystal notions not in human clay." By dying Hamlet kept his crystal notions intact.

Like death, exile is also the "easier part," for it keeps us away from the contaminations of mediocrity. The proconsul of "The Return of the Proconsul" does not want to choose the easier part; he does not want to accept the death-in-life of exile. He wants to return to the emperor's court although he knows that there he must compromise himself. At the beginning of the poem, he confidently announces his decision to return and "see if it's possible to live there." He knows that he could stay here in "this remote province," but, as he says:

> I cannot live among vineyards nothing here is mine
> trees have no roots houses no foundations the rain is
> glassy flowers smell of wax
> a dry cloud rattles against the empty sky
> so I shall return tomorrow or the day after in any case I
> shall return . . .

The stronger his desire to return, however, the more his mind fastens on what he must do if he does return:

> I must come to terms with my face again
> with my lower lip so it knows how to curb its scorn
> with my eyes so they remain ideally empty
> and with that miserable chin the hare of my face
> which trembles when the chief of guards walks in . . .

So powerful is his desire to avoid the sterility of exile that he tries to convince himself that the emperor will do him no harm:

> to a certain extent to a certain reasonable extent
> he is after all a man like everyone else
> and already tired by all those tricks with poison . . .

The proconsul's dilemma is agonizing: he cannot accept the "death" of exile nor can he bring himself to return to the emperor's court, where he would—at the least—become a mere flunkey. His decision to return, repeated several times in the poem, is only an *ignis fatuus* of his mind. He desperately wants to be convinced, yet he remains unconvinced: he continually postpones his return. Although at the end of the poem he says that "I've decided to return to the emperor's court/yes I hope that things will work out somehow," we believe that he will never return. His pathetic delusion, however, compels our admiration, for he cannot accept exile—the easier part. He never stops hoping that things will work out better somehow and then he will be able to return. Herbert's poem must not be read as a comment on real exiles, but as a parable about the man who always faces towards life, although he has more than enough reasons for turning towards death.

Will things work out better somehow? Such is the proconsul's hope, not the poet's. In the prose poem "When the World Stands Still," Herbert does say that "after a while the world moves on. The ocean swallows and regurgitates, valleys send off steam and . . . there is also heard the resounding clash of air against air." Yet, as in "The Longobards," the possibility always exists that a new barbarian force will over-run the cultivated valley:

> An immense coldness from the Longobards
> Their shadow sears the grass when they flock
> in to the valley
> Shouting their protracted nothing nothing nothing.

Hearing those apocalyptic and inhuman shouts, we can either choose the easier part or try to survive. Herbert, with his resolute and unsolemn stoicism, prescribes in a prose poem some "Practical Recommendations in the Event of a Catastrophe": "Place yourself as far as possible from the centre . . . before the whirling motion as it gets stronger from minute to minute begins to pour in towards the middle . . . Keep your head down. Have your two hands constantly free. Take good care of the muscles of your legs."

Like Fortinbras, Herbert does not choose the easier part; he does not yield to the mere process of disintegration. Instead, like Fortinbras, he tries to bring order to a situation that seems beyond ordering. "Such a sight as this," as Fortinbras says in *Hamlet*, requires a disciplined and measured voice, one mindful of its limits and filled exactly with a pebbly meaning. Paul Valery has said that "it takes no more energy to write *fortissimo* than to write *piano*, or *universo* than *garden*." Herbert's poetry is definitely *piano,* and he would rather use the word garden than universe. Considering the "sight" which he writes about, his restraint is a considerable act of moral and intellectual energy. The poet, struggling in the whirlpool of modern history, manages to stay above the surface. He takes good care of the muscles of his legs.

Beaver College

ROBERT PINSKY

"That Sweet Man, John Clare"

The idea of the peasant-poet has a record of great sentimental appeal, an appeal from which John Clare suffered along with other consequences of that horrible double fate. He was poor and as poorly educated as a writer of excellent poems could possibly be. His poverty and the sicknesses and deaths that went with it helped drive him insane and so too did the patronizing and fickle admirers who gave him his vogue. So he has the further appeal of being a mad poet.

Like the earlier mad poet Christopher Smart, Clare is frequently rediscovered. However, unlike Smart, Clare presents no violent or unrestrained way of writing that can seem "modern." Clare's stylistic means are conservative—strikingly so.

Yet of the two it is Clare who undertakes to tell about madness, while Smart's weirdly playful religious ecstasies are interesting in quite another way.

In this essay I want to show how Clare uses a kind of stylistic modesty and a shrewd fidelity to natural images in order to manage dark, aberrant materials. In particular, I want to show what is special and excellent in one group of Clare's poems.[1] They are his best poems; at the least, they provide a fine entry to his fairly large and diverse *oeuvre*. In most of them, the basic fiction is violent but small: various forms of animal life struggle for a precarious, often treacherous, shelter. The contest of sympathy and detachment in the poet's voice makes the poem.

As to the nature of the madness: Dr. Thomas Tennant, in *The Journal of Medical Science* (XCIX, 414), describes John Clare as a manic depressive, while Ernst Kris, in *Psychoanalytic Explorations in Art,* mentions Clare briefly as a schizophrenic. The value of such terms for literary study is widely and no doubt properly suspect. The critical uses of a word like "paranoia" (my own diagnosis) are rightly limited to the lightweight, yielding sense which a given term carries in the speech of the laity.

And yet the consistent, conscious self-portrait in Clare's most remarkable poems appears to demand some kind of generalization. It is nearly as though the poet set out to create a psychological category. The poems suggest that if we have no word or convenient myth for this particular state of perception, then there is a coinage lacking. Something in Clare's tone and material is, in short, archetypal. Such grand and general significance can inhere only, I propose, in a "sane" work of art. Otherwise the significance is the reader's creation, the art a symptom; sanity in writing is the tonal adjustment that changes confession into character-making. Clear even if impossible to paraphrase, the writer's knowing and accurate tone—his preternaturally *sane* tone—makes "normal" life seem confused by comparison. Authentic clarity is the style's proof that the fiction is true: not a patient's tortured, oblique version of a dream, but the authoritative dream itself, naked and magisterial.

So, since style has a sanity of its own, a mad poet, by virtue of such habits as meter and form, may write sane poetry. He is like the dancer whose guard asked her to dance on the threshold of the gas chamber; her art dispelled the insanity of defeat, so as she danced she took his rifle and shot him. Clare's strange accomplishment is to show with all but cold precision what was otherwise too painful for him to face. I think that the odd, consequent mood of obsession and objectivity explains the continuing attraction of his poems.

That mood rises above the defects of "Badger," the best-known of a related group of poems which precede or coincide with the poet's emotional breakdown:

> When midnight comes a host of dogs and men
> Go out and track the badger to his den,
> And put a sack within the hole, and lie
> Till the old grunting badger passes by.
> He comes and hears—they let the strongest loose.   5
> The old fox hears the noise and drops the goose.

The poacher shoots and hurries from the cry,
And the old hare half wounded buzzes by.
They get a forked stick to bear him down
And clap the dogs and take him to the town, 10
And bait him all the day with many dogs,
And laugh and shout and fright the scampering hogs.
He runs along and bites at all he meets:
They shout and hollo down the noisy streets.

He turns about to face the loud uproar 15
And drives the rebels to their very door.
The frequent stone is hurled where'er they go;
When badgers fight, then every one's a foe.
The dogs are clapt and urged to join the fray;
The badger turns and drives them all away. 20
Though scarcely half as big, demure and small,
He fights with dogs for hours and beats them all.
The heavy mastiff, savage in the fray,
Lies down and licks his feet and turns away.
The bulldog knows his match and waxes cold, 25
The badger grins and never leaves his hold.
He drives the crowd and follows at their heels
And bites them through—the drunkard swears and reels.

The frightened women take the boys away,
The blackguard laughs and hurries on the fray. 30
He tries to reach the woods, an awkward race,
But sticks and cudgels quickly stop the chase.
He turns agen and drives the noisy crowd
And beats the many dogs in noises loud.
He drives away and beats them every one, 35
And then they loose them all and set them on.
He falls as dead and kicked by boys and men,
Then starts and grins and drives the crowd agen;
Till kicked and torn and beaten out he lies
And leaves his hold and cackles, groans, and dies.[2] 40

The poem's faults are characteristic and fairly obvious, although it survives these flaws. They are weaknesses in areas where the poem does not attempt much or where Clare compensates with other energies. The process of compensation, buying an effect of painful reticence by sacrificing fluidity, may even have been conscious, since earlier poems are often more fluent and less interesting.

The often unimaginative, cramped, and monotonous sentence-structure of "The Badger" might be blamed on the shabby education of a peasant-poet. On the other hand, with more formal schooling he might have been content with still more of the Augustan literary formula which mars lines seventeen, eighteen, and twenty-five. In a similar way, plain stylistic elements like the repetition of the "noise" root in lines thirty-three and thirty-four might have been avoided by a writer of more orthodox sophistication; but that repetition, flat from one point of view, in fact contributes vitally to the tone of strict, unrhetorical truth. His "roughness" is genuinely unsentimental, yet emotionally wider than mere reportage. Word-choice on the whole is quite unmannered, and as is often the case Clare's grammatical dullness serves to create a corresponding sense of enormous pent energy. Apart from participial forms like "grunting," the first six lines contain eleven active verbs. This high incidence of inflected verbs, resulting in a slow, distinctly accented line, characterizes Clare's many brilliant descriptive passages. "Badger" at times averages three verb-forms to a line; the poem crackles with action. The terse sentences contain and control the violence of the subject within the stubborn, almost reportorial calm of their rhythms. Though the style seems stationary, the scene breathes and moves.

Beyond attractions and limitations of technique, the poem presents less apparent problems of aspiration and conception. I think that it represents a rather special and interesting approach to the use of natural detail. John Keats, through a letter to Clare from their mutual friend and publisher John Taylor, provides a suggestive criticism of Clare's verse:

If he recovers his strength he will write to you. I think he wishes to say to you that your Images from Nature are too much introduced without being called for by a particular Sentiment—To meddle with this subject is bad policy when I am in haste, but perhaps you conceive what he means.[3]

If Taylor's paraphrase is at all accurate, then Keats is in this instance on the side of explicit statement, or at least of paraphrasable, reasonably explicit "Sentiment." The passage is another reminder that in such matters Keats was not nearly so romantic as many postromantic theorists of the "Image."

Tibble is content, as I think Keats would not be, to accept literally Clare's statement that he "found the poems in the fields"; to be accurate, we have to add that Clare's statement is a way of saying that he found the poems while in the fields—and that the poems needed the sense-experiences that he found in the fields.[4] My justification for such finicky definition is the ever-recurring distortion and confusion that surround poems with "Images from Nature." This distortion seems to spread and settle as the traditions of "modern" poetry grow older and more established, rendering poems like "Badger" too easily taken for granted.

A technique enormously elaborated by modernist poetry is to convey the illusion that an object is eloquent—in other words, that the poem exists outside of the author's or reader's consciousness, "in the fields." Clare uses this rhetoric, and Keats, sensitive to its dangers, looks on its valid use as a matter of degree. But Clare's editor is content to explain Clare's procedure by quoting a classic misapprehension of "imagism" (or post-symbolism, or whatever one calls it) as an artistic *procedure:*

An object or incident in life arouses an overwhelming emotion in him, and a desire to express the emotion. The crystallization is, as it were, automatically accomplished; for the only way he can communicate his emotion is by describing the objects which aroused it. If his emotion was a true one, the vividness and particularity of his description will carry it over to us . . . Thus, quite simply, the cause of the emotion becomes the symbol. The miracle is accomplished.[5]

According to this view, Clare could best have communicated the emotional content of "Badger" by inviting me to attend a particular or representative badger-baiting. I dwell on a mistaken version of Clare's procedure in order to emphasize that he is the sort of poet likely to suggest such an explanation: his use of physical detail is acute and highly implicit, as in many modern poems, yet he is neither a modern poet nor a mere superseded primitive.

Thus, Clare's poem is liable to the serious criticism which is a reversed image of Tibble's remarks, a criticism suggested by Keats's reported statement about "pure" or unmotivated description. That is, ingenious theories of poetry can abolish the pathetic fallacy, but the objection of a literalist retains its force: we have an intensely-written poem, nearly twice as long as Jonson's "To Heaven," about very little. Tone, one aspect of which is length, is so much in excess of the apparent stimulus in "Badger" that the poem must be defended, if not from the charge of madness, then from that of sentimentality. I think, in fact, that the tone of intense suffering becomes stronger with successive rereadings—an effect of understatement and simplicity of organization. If these forty lines are "just descriptive" or if their "sentiment" is that of a Humane Society pamphlet, then Tibble's diametric opponent will agree that the best of the poem is inherent in the natural object: in this case, a pejorative judgment.

By taking such a straw man seriously, we can discover how artful Clare's poem is, in its way; the artfulness is evident in the air of authenticity, a sense of no fallacy in the scene or between the scene and the tone. To show what I mean, I will quote a poem late in the modernist tradition. This poem seems to me apt to strike contemporary readers as more plausible than "Badger," and more clearly a good poem. Yet I suspect that the modern poem, despite its apparent polish, is less persuasive and even less shrewd than Clare's.

Orchids

They lean over the path,
Adder-mouthed,
Swaying close to the face,
Coming out, soft and deceptive,
Limp and damp, delicate as a young bird's tongue;
Their fluttery fledgling lips
Move slowly,
Drawing in the warm air.

And at night,
The faint moon falling through whitewashed glass,
The heat going down
So their musky smell comes even stronger,
Drifting down from their mossy cradles:
So many devouring infants!
Soft luminescent fingers,
Lips neither dead nor alive,
Loose ghastly mouths
Breathing.[6]

Roethke's free verse is end-stopped and slow, and like Clare's poem this one moves in rather small grammatical units; but the predominance of active verbs that characterizes "Badger" is reversed in "Orchids." The last five lines are largely a list of substantives, for example, and lines two through four a list of modifiers. This suspended, almost unpredicated syntax could be referred to static or passive aspects of the object, but it works primarily to help voice the speaker's feeling: he is obsessed, nearly overwhelmed, and more caught up by the object and its aspects than by statements he could predicate about them. And the same emotional direction is suggested by the poem's other notable stylistic parts: the present tense, for example, which works oddly with the two-part structure of time of day so as to suggest revery while maintaining the natural object's dominance over the mental process. Similarly, the rhythm moves in slow, short, equal spasms, well defined by pronounced pauses and assonances ("soft and deceptive,/limp and damp") that suggest absorbed helplessness. A sort of enervated panic aroused by the unconscious life of the natural object becomes, by the poem's isolated last word, so emphatically suggested that we might call it explicit.

"Badger" and "Orchids" have in common the general technique of description and also an experience, the experience of fascination with a physical scene—its cruelty and its persistent unconsciousness. And of course that is the (perhaps obvious) answer for the literalist: the experience in "Badger" is not the baiting, but the speaker's experience of figuratively being the badger. The obsession with the hunted animal is more vital even than the narrative itself. The poet both engages and implicitly examines his fierce, perhaps helpless, identification with nature.

Both poems, then, render the experience of being dominated by a metaphor—and by the unsuitable, unlike parts of it: orchids are like human life; but, not conscious, they have an eery persistence that is both repellently and hypnotically nonhuman. And the badger's agony is like human suffering; here, however, the distinction from human life is the pervasive force of the whole utterance while the affinity with human life builds invisibly and by implication. It builds through the workmanlike exposition as if it were a ringing in the ears.

I have pointed out several ways in which Roethke's poem—in its syntax, its rhythm, the arrangement of the parts—elaborates and perhaps insists upon its principal emotion and that emotion's close connection with the natural object. Clare's more indirect and cumulative method is probably most apparent in the matter of diction. The striking choices in "Orchids" tend to be affective and anthropomorphic: "deceptive," "delicate," "devouring," "ghostly." In "Badger," too, the most notable moments in the diction suggest human life, but more quietly and subtly—and with a purely descriptive aspect. This descriptive aptness can be attributed only to the rather pedestrian "delicate" of the word-choices from "Orchids" quoted above. In "Badger," the word or phrase with human or emotional overtones also subdues those overtones by its purely descriptive justice: "grunting" (line 4), "demure" (line 21), "grins" (line 26), "awkward" (line 31), "starts" (line 38), "cackles" (line 40). The diction is fine yet unobtrusive.

Clare, in other words, causes the natural object to take on both its physical life and its human force gradually, depending upon a deceptively quiet surface of reportage. Like his diction, the other aspects of his style work with modesty. The organization is sequential, divided into a roughly equal beginning, middle, and end. The rhythm is a tight, minimally varied kind of pentameter surprisingly well-suited to the careful presentation of a natural scene—as is the case, in fact, in some of Roethke's early, descriptive poems. Roethke's "Heron" ends:

> He jerks a frog across his bony lip,
> Then points his heavy bill above the wood.
> The wide wings flap but once to lift him up.
> A single ripple starts from where he stood.[7]

The stiff texture that creates fluid life recalls Clare, but Clare uses the same stolid manner to suggest moral as well as visual fascination. That fascination, for the modern poet, requires another style.

To summarize, the poem "Orchids" takes the fusion of emotion with the natural object as an accepted starting point. There is no gesture towards defining a literal, personal motivation for the emotion; neither does the poet try to suggest that the emotion is irresistibly part of the orchids—this is frankly a special sensibility or mood, and the poem consists of rhetorical elaboration of the emotion by means of the natural object. Questions of motivation or connection between natural object and emotion are not part of the poet's business here; they are disposed of by his convention, his accepted starting point.

The poem "Badger," in contrast, takes the fusion of emotion with the natural object as an eventual goal. And though the poet does not offer literal, personal motivations, his poem is a sustained effort to establish a powerful sense of irresistible, necessary connection between scene and feeling—exactly that sense of connection which the modern convention takes almost for granted, as something which the writer can claim at once. The elaboration of the orchids is explicit and rhetorical; they are an example of a mood and a sense of life; but the agony of the badger is presented as an actual and self-sufficiently awful fate. The elaboration of the modern poem and its "image" is a valid procedure in a convention that we know well, but to dismiss the less familiar method and basis of "Badger" is to make a judgment conventional in the bad sense.

Clare's subject, like his natural scene, is considerably more complex than the subject of the other poem. "Badger's" theme can be said to include the theme of "Orchids," which I take to be the powerful aspect of natural life that is quite alien to consciousness. The implied spectator of the badger-baiting is aware of this aspect of the physical world: it is what compels his reticent attention. But the modern poem in effect insists upon the object's predominance in a manner (or convention) that emphasizes its own voice; Clare, keeping the object actually predominant, uses it to propound a deep human difficulty. By means of its tone, his poem treats that difficulty or fate with balance and sensitivity. This fate—call it the unjust failure of an uncommon man—is the larger experience of "Badger" and was in fact Clare's fate.

What Clare's use of descriptive detail does, which abstract exposition could not do, is to reproduce something of the color and aura of contingency. The experience (that there is no satisfactory term for it is the point) includes the victim's bewildered sense of a swarm of events distracting but not deflecting his fate: as though even in the assurance of grim defeat there was a tormenting sense of accident, a coincidental doom. The evidence and metaphor for treacherous, multiple possibility as an element of experience is the world of things. Unconscious life is, as Roethke says, "devouring." Some aspects of moral pain can be best evoked by a sense of the physical universe.

I hope that the reader will have come at least part of the way towards accepting my favorable comparison of "Badger" with a poem that I assume to be more immediately appealing. It will be enough if the comparison has suggested the merits of "Badger" and its peculiar subject.

The shorter, related poems emphasize the points of method and subject raised so far. Each of these poems gains power and clarity from the whole group, bound together by theme, method, and period of composition.

First, it is worth establishing that the stolid, conservative relation between syntax and pentameter line constitutes a chosen manner; Clare could write other ways. The evidence is in many lyric poems with a short line or a rapid longer one, and syntactical units that cross the line, as in the first stanza of "The Pale Sun":

> Pale sunbeams gleam
> That nurture a few flowers,
> Pilewort and daisy and a sprig of green
> On whitethorn bushes
> In the leafless hedge.

This movement can be described as unrhymed iambics, and with a little forcing the lines above could be scanned as three lines of blank verse; but later passages vary still more from the iambic under-rhythm:

> 'Tis chill but pleasant;
> In the hedge-bottom lined
> With brown sear leaves the last
> Year littered there and left,
> Mopes the hedge-sparrow,
>
> With trembling wings, and cheeps
> Its welcome to pale sunbeams
> Creeping through . . .

In fact, the rhythm can be called free verse, rather similar to the free verse of Wallace Stevens when it is light and quick in movement.

Further evidence that the grammatical and metrical restraints of "Badger" are a carefully established part of that poem's tone is provided by the other poems which share "Badger's" manner. In "The Hedgehog," precisely observed animal life again objectifies human feelings of defeat and privation. The human, personal quality of the feeling in "The Hedgehog" rests upon the controlled judgment implied by the last line: the poet's judgment of the animal's meat is presented as plain fact, the gypsies' as wrong. The poet is separating himself from the gypsies in the least sentimental of ways, and so persuades the reader of good faith; at the same time the grammatical shape of his last line and the whole force of the poem view the animal with a sympathy that is all but anthropomorphic. The poet is not "identified" with the hedge-hog, but his way of seeing it speaks of a human isolation that is painful and victimized:

> The hedgehog hides beneath the rotten hedge
> And makes a great round nest of grass and sedge,
> Or in a bush or in a hollow tree;
> And many often stop and say they see
> Him roll and fill his prickles full of crabs 5
> And creep away; and where the magpie dabs
> His wing at muddy dike, in aged root
> He makes a nest and fills it full of fruit,
> On the hedge bottom hunts for crabs and sloes
> And whistles like a cricket as he goes. 10
> It rolls up like a ball or shapeless hog
> When gipsies hunt it with their noisy dog;
> I've seen it in their camps—they call it sweet,
> Though black and bitter and unsavoury meat.

The style is somewhat more fluid than in "Badger." For instance, the long sentence-unit beginning with "and where the magpie dabs" is both complex and clear; the omitted conjunction between lines succeeds because the line-ending there helps clarify the grammar, which is balanced by line ten. The rhymes work in a way that is neither Popean wit nor Marlovian sensual discovery; their quality is rather one of conviction.

On the other hand, the poem has its defects, the most egregious of which is only apparent. The last word in the line

> It rolls up like a ball or shapeless hog

looks like a failure of imagination that sends Clare's stolidity into the ludicrous; but "hog" here is pretty certainly the localism "hog, a heap of potatoes or turnips covered with straw and soil" (*N.E.D, English Dialect Dictionary*). The omitted articles in line seven have no such justification and may annoy some readers. At first, the change of pronoun from "he" in line ten to "it" in eleven may seem a similar small blemish, but that change is entirely consistent with the sudden change in what the animal does and with the simultaneous, abrupt increase in apparent distance from the subject. The nearly startling "it" is the first shock to the nature-poem intimacy of the preceding description; the second increase of distance—significantly in the voice of the poet, not the predatory gypsies—comes with the final word, "meat."

That hard, clipped rhyme-word is the extremity of the part of the poem which begins with the fulcrum of the word "it" in line eleven. The poem's success depends upon a balance between the small, exquisitely gathering shock of these four lines and the gentle, rapt description of the first ten lines. Clare's power to pack serious feeling into an apparently neutral tone in lines like the last four grows out of the biological minuteness of observation in lines like the first ten. Neither Frost nor any other poet in English is more of a nature-poet in keeping the eye carefully on the object. The revelation of this detailed knowledge makes the animal an acceptable vehicle for the poem's submerged human feeling. As Wordsworth celebrates expansive freedom of spirit with broad, smokily suggestive landscapes, Clare often associates entrapment of emotion with harshly clear, finely-focussed biological discovery.

As a motivation for romantic wonder, I find these sharply authentic discoveries appealing and perhaps more persuasive than most of the moors and vistas in literature. In the following poem, Clare's subject is explicitly wonder: his fascination with the quality of completeness or authenticity yielded by the sensory discovery of nature. The mood, characteristically threatening and violent in the "Badger"-group, is subdued here. This poem instead presents the state of mind, the kind of wonder, which furnishes the detailed life of "Badger," "Birds in Alarm," "The Hedgehog," or "Wild Duck's Nest"; this is what Clare finds in the fields:

The Squirrel's Nest

One day, when all the woods were bare and blea,
I wandered out to take a pleasant walk
And saw a strange-formed nest on stoven tree
Where startled pigeon buzzed from bouncing hawk.

I wondered strangely what the nest could be   5
And thought besure it was some foreign bird,
So up I scrambled in the highest glee,
And my heart jumped at every thing that stirred.
'Twas oval shaped; strange wonder filled my breast;
I hoped to catch the old one on her nest   10
When something bolted out—I turned to see—
And a brown squirrel pattered up the tree.
'Twas lined with moss and leaves, compact and strong;
I sluthered down and wondering went along.

("Blea" and "sluther" are Northamptonshire Fen-region words for "bleak" and "slide.") Because the subject of wonder is so explicit and the experience so truly rendered, the "strange wonder" itself is convincing. The poem successfully defines the sort of activity behind Clare's way of imbedding his themes in natural details; at the same time, it gains from the context of the group because the other poems bar the application of the phrase "nature poet" here in any patronizing way.

Characteristically, the verbs—here, those whose subject is the speaker—exemplify the progress of the poem and the definition of wonder. From the receptive, pleasant wandering of the second line, feeling develops into the still ignorant, but specifically aroused "wondered strangely" of line five; this point embodies a feeling which for a different writer might seem the most satisfyingly poetic stage of the experience. But Clare's stake in nature as a source for impressions of reality, and as a symbolic battleground of the emotional life, sends him further in his definition of the object. The anticipation of this definition (lines 8–9, "strange wonder") leads to the imaginative possession of the final couplet. This mature, or satisfied, wonder is introduced by the effectively abrupt transition of attention back to the nest—the modest thing itself—at the beginning of the thirteenth line.

Mature wonder in "The Vixen," as in "The Badger" and "The Hedgehog," reveals animal distress as a fitting emblem of human feeling. Again, the intensity of tone is balanced by the virtually scientific authenticity of the details:

Among the taller wood with ivy hung,
The old fox plays and dances round her young.
She snuffs and barks if any passes by
And swings her tail and turns prepared to fly.

The horseman hurries by, she bolts to see,   5
And turns again, from danger never free.
If any stands she runs among the poles
And barks and snaps and drives them in the holes.
The shepherd sees them and the boy goes by
And gets a stick and progs the hole to try.   10
They get all still and lie in safety sure,
And out again when everything's secure,
And start and snap at blackbirds bouncing by
To fight and catch the great white butterfly.

This poem, together with the poems I have quoted previously, should make clear the way in which the group of poems add to one another. The concluding image in "The Vixen" is fine in itself, but like "safety sure" and "from danger never free" it works as part of a larger poetic whole. The poems present a consistent, large view of Clare's "woods," a land of singular preoccupations.

In the main, the poems realize life that is trapped or menaced or defeated, yet remains vigorously active. Typical moments are the badger's final grin and charge, or the wild geese in "The Fowler": "The wounded whirl and whirl and fall again." What could fall into indulgent, monotonous violence in Clare's use of such images is balanced in the group as a whole by a mingling in each poem of the ominous with the innocent. The quietness of wonder, which tends to be content with the subject as reported, prevents melodrama with a plainness resembling humor, a quiet devotion to the way things really happen in the fields. Thus, the "loaded" details blend indistinguishably with the reportage. It is as though Roethke combined the disturbed sensibility of "Orchids" with the taciturn wonder of his "Heron," the descriptive poem from which I quoted earlier and which could—and may—have been written in conscious imitation of Clare.

Only by considering more than one poem can we see how far beyond description, how dominated by personality and obsession the verse is: then, certain motifs stand out to demonstrate that Clare's poems are neither slight curiosities nor overwrought natural descriptions. For instance, there is the recurrence of nests, places of desperate, innocent, often futile retreat: in jargon, womb-images. Compare the eleventh line of "The Vixen" above with the closing lines of the longer poem, "Marten":

> And gipsies often, and bird-nesting boys
> Look in the hole and hear a hissing noise . . .
> The gray owl comes and drives them all away,
> And leaves the marten twisting round his den,
> Left free from boys and dogs and noisy men.

And the mother mouse in "Mouse's Nest" looks "grotesque" as she bolts "With all her young ones hanging from her teats," but ends in security again.

The mingling of this potentially sentimental ideal of nonhuman quiet with brutal violence is best shown in two poems which represent the violent and gentle extremes of Clare's imagery: "The Fox" and "Young Rabbits." In the former, the shepherd and the plowman hear a barking dog, and the plowman

> found a weary fox and beat him out.
> The ploughman laughed and would have plowed him in,
> But the old shepherd took him for the skin.
> He lay upon the furrow stretched for dead,
> The old dog lay and licked the wounds that bled,
> The ploughman beat him till his ribs would crack,
> And then the shepherd slung him at his back . . .

But the fox "started from his dead disguise" to escape into a badger hole after sixteen further lines of chase. In "Young Rabbits" boys go to the rabbits' breeding places, and then to where the "moulds" are fresh:

> And clap the dog to scrat the moulds away;
> He scrats and looks and barks and snuffs to find
> The sleepy young ones lapt in down and blind.
> They put them in again and look for more
> And lap them up again as quiet as before.

In both selections the apparent stiffness of the lines is overcome by a pronounced excitement, yet the potential melodrama of the plot is suppressed. If we find such writing attractive poem by poem, then these developing themes of hostility and retreat, entrapment and escape, give a concentrated fascination to the group of poems. These preoccupations are not unconscious symptoms, but deliberate choices of subject; artistically, they resist psychiatric categories inasmuch as there is very little that anyone could tell Clare on the subject that he did not know—while writing these poems—in the highest way.

Any view of Clare is inevitably colored by his biography. It is clear that Clare found his characteristic poetic voice in ways full of pathos and his overwhelming troubles in the same sources. There is considerable evidence that he was driven to insanity and away from life by poverty, the cruelty of which was intensified by his talent and ambitions. His public was condescending and fickle, and as he came in and out of vogue he was subjected to handouts of small change and to lessons in spelling. This obtuse and selfish reception by his contemporaries bedevils his reputation today: the constant "discovery," as distinct from the reading, of his work. This recurring critical attitude may result from the distracting but irresistible interest of Clare as a figure. I have tried in this essay to move a small step beyond that attitude toward actual criticism of the poems. I close with a brief example of the kind of problem Clare's life brought to him and that his biography presents to us.

In the serious mental decay of his middle and old age, Clare believed that he had married a childhood playmate for whom, incredibly enough, he preserved a lifetime's unspoken passion. Mary Joyce's father was a relatively prosperous farmer, Clare's a laborer. The stereotyped relationship is stripped of all the superficial varieties of dignity by the squalor and disorder of Clare's actual life. Pat, yet authentic, the situation invites at a remove of time questions resembling those that surround a fictional character, say Fitzgerald's Gatsby: certainly the painfully confined feeling was real—but for Clare's romantic imagination did the girl become a symbol for peace, escape, money, or did his other frustrations simply become more unbearable because he lost her?

In short, we are tempted to say that Clare's poetry is in a way a less "sentimental" version of his misery than the version presented by the facts of his life. The persecution was no delusion. That the poet found a way to preserve the experience of such pain within the requirements of his art provides a body of work that is, though narrow, unique and commanding. The effect of those neutral requirements upon his rage is to create a haunting, paradoxical sense of gentleness: the risk and sweetness of a nest.

Heard in a Violent Ward

In heaven, too,
You'd be institutionalized.
But that's all right,—
If they let you eat and swear
With the likes of Blake,
And Christopher Smart,
And that sweet man, John Clare.

Theodore Roethke,
The Far Field [8]

Wellesley College

NOTES

1. A tentative list: "Badger," "The Fox," "Hedgehog," "The Vixen," "Marten," "The Squirrel's Nest," "The Swallow's Nest," "Young Rabbits," "Birds in Alarm," "Dyke Side," "Quail's Nest," "The Nuthatch," "The Firetail's Nest," "Wild Duck's Nest," "The Fowler," "Blackbird's Nest," "The Groundlark," "Mouse's Nest." (After finishing this essay, I discovered Paul Schwaber's 1966 unpublished Columbia University doctoral thesis, "Stays against Confusion: The Poems of John Clare," one section of which praises some of these same poems, for what I think are similar reasons, arrived at by a rather different line of thought.)

2. All texts of Clare's poems quoted in this essay are based upon *The Poems of John Clare*, ed. J. W. Tibble (London, 1935).

3. John and Anne Tibble, *John Clare: His Life And Poetry* (London, 1956), p. 77.

4. J. W. Tibble, *Poems*, pp. viii–ix.

5. Ibid., p. ix.

6. Theodore Roethke, *The Collected Poems of Theodore Roethke* (New York, 1966), p. 39.

7. Ibid., p. 15.

8. Ibid., p. 228.

JOHN CIARDI

Paradiso

Canto XXXIII

St. Bernard
Prayer to the Virgin
The Vision of God

St. Bernard offers a lofty Prayer to the Virgin, asking her to intercede in Dante's behalf, and in answer Dante feels his soul swell with new power and grow calm in rapture as his eyes are permitted the Direct Vision of God.

There can be no measure of how long the vision endures. It passes, and Dante is once more mortal and fallible. Raised by God's presence, he had looked into the Mystery and had begun to understand its power and majesty. Returned to himself, there is no power in him capable of speaking the truth of what he saw. Yet the impress of the truth is stamped upon his soul, which he now knows will return to be one with God's Love.

> "Virgin Mother, daughter of thy son;
>   humble beyond all creatures and more exalted;
>   predestined turning point of God's intention;   3
> thy merit so ennobled human nature
>   that its divine Creator did not scorn
>   to make Himself the creature of His creature.   6
> The Love that was rekindled in thy womb
>   sends forth the warmth of the eternal peace
>   within whose ray this flower has come to bloom.   9

275

Here, to us, thou art the noon and scope
    of Love revealed; and among mortal men,
    the living fountain of eternal hope.   12
Lady, thou art so near God's reckonings
    that who seeks grace and does not first seek thee
    would have his wish fly upward without wings.   15
Not only does thy sweet benignity
    flow out to all who beg, but oftentimes
    thy charity arrives before the plea.   18
In thee is pity, in thee munificence,
    in thee the tenderest heart, in thee unites
    all that creation knows of excellence!   21
Now comes this man who from the final pit
    of the universe up to this height has seen,
    one by one, the three lives of the spirit.   24
He prays to thee in fervent supplication
    for grace and strength, that he may raise his eyes
    to the all-healing final revelation.   27
And I, who never more desired to see
    the vision myself than I do that he may see It,
    add my own prayer, and pray that it may be   30
enough to move you to dispel the trace
    of every mortal shadow by thy prayers
    and let him see revealed the Sum of Grace.   33
I pray thee further, all-persuading Queen,
    keep whole the natural bent of his affections
    and of his powers after his eyes have seen.   36
Protect him from the stirrings of man's clay;
    see how Beatrice and the blessed host
    clasp reverent hands to join me as I pray."   39
The eyes that God reveres and loves the best
    glowed on the speaker, making clear the joy
    with which true prayer is heard by the most blest.   42
Those eyes turned then to the Eternal Ray,
    through which, we must indeed believe, the eyes
    of others do not find such ready way.   45
I, who neared the goal of all my nature,
    felt my soul, at the climax of its yearning,
    suddenly, as it ought, grow calm with rapture.   48
Bernard then, smiling sweetly, gestured to me
    to look up, but I had already become
    within myself all he would have me be.   51

Little by little as my vision grew
    it penetrated further through the aura
    of that high lamp which in Itself is true.   54
What then I saw is more than tongue can say.
    Our human speech is dark before the vision.
    The ravished memory swoons and falls away.   57
As one who sees in dreams and wakes to find
    the emotional impression of his vision
    still powerful while its parts fade from his mind—   60
just such am I, having lost nearly all
    the vision itself, while in my heart I feel
    the sweetness of it yet distill and fall.   63
So, in the sun, the footprints fade from snow.
    On the wild wind that bore the tumbling leaves
    the Sybil's oracles were scattered so.   66
O Light Supreme who doth Thyself withdraw
    so far above man's mortal understanding,
    lend me again some glimpse of what I saw;   69
make Thou my tongue so eloquent it may
    of all Thy glory speak a single clue
    to those who follow me in the world's day;   72
for by returning to my memory
    somewhat, and somewhat sounding in these verses,
    Thou shalt show man more of Thy victory.   75
So dazzling was the splendor of that Ray,
    that I must certainly have lost my senses
    had I, but for an instant, turned away.   78
And so it was, as I recall, I could
    the better bear to look, until at last
    my vision made one with the Eternal Good.   81
Oh grace abounding that had made me fit
    to fix my eyes on the Eternal Light
    until my vision was consumed in It!   84
I saw within Its depth how It conceives
    all things in a single volume bound by Love,
    of which the universe is the scattered leaves;   87
substance, accident, and their relation
    so fused that all I say could do no more
    than yield a glimpse of that bright revelation.   90
I think I saw the universal form
    that binds these things, for as I speak these words
    I feel my joy swell and my spirits warm.   93

Twenty-five centuries since Neptune saw
    the Argo's keel have not moved all mankind,
    recalling that adventure, to such awe   96
as I felt in an instant. My tranced being
    stared fixed and motionless upon that vision,
    ever more fervent to see in the act of seeing.   99
Experiencing that Radiance, the spirit
    is so indrawn it is impossible
    even to think of ever turning from It.   102
For the good which is the will's ultimate object
    is all subsumed in It; and, being removed,
    all is defective which in It is perfect.   105
Now in my recollection of the rest
    I have less power to speak than any infant
    wetting its tongue yet at its mother's breast;   108
and not because that Living Radiance bore
    more than one semblance, for It is unchanging
    and is forever as It was before;   111
but because, as I grew worthier to see,
    the more I looked, the more unchanging semblance
    seemed to change with every change in me.   114
Within the depthless deep and clear existence
    of that abyss of light three circles shone—
    three in color, one in circumference: 117
the second from the first, rainbow from rainbow;
    the third, an exhalation of pure fire
    equally breathed forth by the other two.   120
But oh how much my words miss my conception,
    which is itself so far from what I saw
    that to call it feeble would be rank deception!   123
O Light Eternal fixed in Itself alone,
    by Itself alone understood, which from Itself
    loves and glows, self-knowing and self-known;   126
that second aureole which shone forth in Thee,
    conceived as a reflection of the first—
    or which appeared so to my scrutiny—   129
seemed in Itself of Its own coloration
    to be painted with man's image. I fixed my eyes
    on that alone in rapturous contemplation.   132
Like a geometer wholly dedicated
    to squaring the circle, but who cannot find,
    think as he may, the principle indicated—   135
so did I study the supernal face.

I yearned to know just how our image merges
    into that circle, and how it there finds place;   138
but mine were not the wings for such a flight.
    Yet as I wished, the truth I wished for came
    cleaving my mind in a great flash of light.   141
Here my powers rest from their high fantasy,
    but already I could feel my being turned—
    instinct and intellect balanced equally   144
as in a wheel whose motion nothing mars—
by the Love that moves the Sun and the other stars.

                              Metuchen, New Jersey

THE HUMAN IMAGE

ROBERT FITZGERALD

---

*The Place of Forms**

> *Mind is in a sense potentially whatever is thinkable, though actually it is*
> *nothing until it has thought . . . [and mind so understood] is what it is*
> *by virtue of becoming all things, while there is another which is what it is by*
> *virtue of making all things: this is a sort of positive state like light . . .*
> *Actual knowledge is identical with its object: in the individual, potential*
> *knowledge is in time prior to actual knowledge, but in the universe as a*
> *whole it is not prior even in time.*
>
> Aristotle, *De anima*, tr. R. D. Hicks

We must admire Aristotle's power of paying close attention. The text
of the *De anima* is ragged in spots, like an unrevised draft, but where
it is smooth the reader follows a meticulous course of thought. As a
result of the thinker's close attention, the subject takes on scale. From
the simplest organism, capable only of self-nutrition and growth, to
man and beyond man seems an immense gamut when you see it all
under the heading *anima,* or soul. We are commonly a little vague about
the soul, considered as a rather embarrassing attachment bobbing around
each of us like a toy balloon, to float away when the individual turns

* The great program of discussion at Princeton that became known as the Gauss Seminars
was conceived by Francis Fergusson and Richard Blackmur in the third and fourth years
after the Second World War. It began with seminars conducted by Erich Auerbach in September
1949. I went to Princeton in September 1950 to be Blackmur's assistant in the Creative
Writing program and to conduct a series of five seminars in midwinter, chiefly on Aristotle
and Sophocles. Without the encouragement and interest of Francis Fergusson, Director of
what were then called the Princeton Seminars in Literary Criticism, and chairman of each
meeting, I would never have attempted the papers that I offered for discussion. I have chosen
and slightly revised parts of two of these for the pages that I here contribute in his honor.

cold. We have heard, too, about the "dignity of the individual," and this, if we think of dignity as something dignified, would be embarrassing if we constantly applied it to our often undignified selves. What is more, neither this dignity nor the vague soul itself seems to have much to do with the universe, where in the scientific view neither dignity nor soul exist. In the *De anima* Aristotle was putting these pieces together—for of course they *are* together—to see the human soul as an intelligible entity in an intelligible world and to see that without having to be dignified in the least it has quite remarkable dignity.

The degree of abstraction in the premises of the *De anima* is that of what Aristotle considered the theoretical sciences as distinguished from the practical sciences. In Book 2 he starts with definitions so general that they apply to everything. The term substance, for example, means only a "determinate [i.e., definable] kind of what is" and matter, or potentiality, is only one kind of substance; the other two substances are form or "whatness" or formulable essence (these are all terms for the same thing) by which the potential becomes actualized as a "this," and the composite "this," the actual thing itself. Whatever is belongs to one of the three kinds of substance; "reality" therefore is of these three kinds, and no one substance is any more "real" than the other. Thus potentiality is real, and "whatnesses" are real; they are made for each other; their marriage as actuality always comes about through the agency of a prior, match-making actuality; but in some cases they may never marry: there may be no resultant "actual" thing.

By defining the soul as the form or whatness of a living body, Aristotle places it within nature, relates each soul uniquely to its particular body, and at once concedes the whole battle over whether or not the human soul is similar to the soul of animals; not only is it similar, it is just the same in certain of its properties. Having conceded this, however, Aristotle in the third chapter of Book 2 goes on to the rest of the truth, which is that there is a power of soul possessed by no animal but only by "another order of animate beings, i.e. man and possibly another order like man or superior to him, the power of thinking."

He does not at once proceed to consider what this means. Instead, in the fourth chapter of Book 2 of the *De anima*, the definition of soul is amplified in a remarkable way. Here it is called the cause or source of the living body in three senses. first, as the efficient cause, since it is what animates the body and makes it move; second, as the formal cause, since it is what makes the body be *this* body; and third, as the final cause, since it is "the being in whose interest," *tò hoû héneka*, the body exists. We become aware of a distinct difference between Aristotle's understanding and our own modern uncertainty over which comes first —our usual assumption being that the body comes first and the soul, if there is one, is a cloud of thoughts thrown up unaccountably out of a physicochemical system. Aristotle's account of the matter may be improvable but at least it covers the whole problem. And if we see the soul as the cause of the body in Aristotle's three senses of cause, "the dignity of the individual" gains a good deal of meaning. As follows:

When Aristotle puts his mind on the matter of "perception," he notices that each one of our senses "has the power of receiving into itself the sensible forms of things without the matter"—which is putting something obvious in an arresting way. It is still more arresting but perfectly consistent to say, as the next step, that "when that which can hear is actively hearing and that which can sound is sounding, then the actual hearing and the actual sound are one." So it is, though we may not have thought of it in this way before. Then there is no sounding apart from hearing? There is no actual sounding, but there is potential sounding, and such sounding is real, too. Therefore, "the earlier students of nature," he says, "were mistaken in their view that without sight there was no white and black, without taste no savour." Without sight and taste these things are real but unactualized. It follows that, in all cases in order that such things should become actual, what is necessary is sense perception. And what is necessary to sense perception is not just a sense organ but a soul capable of perceiving by means of a sense organ —since the soul is "that for the sake of which" in this specific instance the bodily organ exists.

Now, the "sensitive" soul—that is, the soul considered as a being that has sensation—would seem to be endowed by the foregoing with quite a lot of dignity, since if there were no sensitive soul the sensible forms of things in the universe would remain unactualized forever. There would be, for example, no actual starlight, no actual light at all. There would be a real universe, but it would lack this admirable feature, which it now includes because it includes us and because light is a product of our interaction with other real things. But what of the mind? Well, between sense perception understood in these terms and the part played by the intellectual or uniquely human power of the soul, there is an analogy. Aristotle says that mind is related to what is thinkable as sense is to what is sensible; that actual knowledge is identical with its object just as the act of hearing is identical with sound. And what are the objects of knowledge as distinguished from those of sense or imagination? "What actual sensation apprehends is particulars, what knowledge apprehends is universals, and these are in a sense within the soul."

Here as elsewhere I am subject to correction and speak simply from my best understanding of this matter as Aristotle and St. Thomas, a close student of Aristotle, treated it. Universal concepts are begotten in us by the essences or intelligible forms of real things with which we are directly in contact. Strictly speaking, it is the essences or forms that may be said to have independent existence, not the universals. The universals are hard to distinguish from the real forms, but the distinction must be clearly made and kept, for universals exist only in our minds and only after abstraction from things, of whose forms or essences they constitute weak but faithful knowledge. We do not know essences except through universals, but we do know them.

For example: the soul, Aristotle says in an effort at closer definition, is "the formulable essence of the body"—that is, the essence which may be apprehended in a formula composed of universals. This is its intelligibility. And here is a formula apprehending it: "The soul is the first grade of actuality of a natural body having life potentially within it." Every word in this sentence signifies a universal—"first," "grade," "of," —all of them; and each of the universals or concepts signified corresponds to some structural or formal element in reality.

Take, instead of Aristotle's improved formula for the definition of soul, Einstein's formula for the definition of energy: E equals mc^2, where "m" is the symbol for mass and "c" the symbol for the constant velocity of light. The symbols here stand for universals, just as in Aristotle's definition "first," "grade" and so on stand for universals. I am not certain, but I would suppose that, if necessary, any mathematical statement can be put into words, and what the symbols, or words, represent are universal concepts. These concepts are the products of an interaction between the mind of the scientist and the world outside his mind; *they* are not in the world outside his mind or ours, but some things certainly are, and the scientist is able to think of these things by means of the universals: "energy," "mass," "velocity," "light," and "squared." Still, he doesn't fully know the essences these concepts represent.

As to how the scientist comes to know what he knows, Aristotle thought that it all begins with sense perception. Einstein had been aware of a movement in himself or elsewhere; his sense memory kept the image or feeling of it; and his mind, in its aspect as a receptacle or memory, the place of forms, kept the notion, abstracted from the occasion. But that is not the end of the matter, for the mind also—this time in its aspect as a "positive state like light"—the attentive mind, or *noûs poetikós*, sees that, just as an idea is abstracted from an actual perceptible occasion, it may enter into any number of actual and perceptible occasions. It is therefore a "universal," and the mind—the "active intellect" as the scholastics called it, tags it with a word or symbol, such as "energy," in order to identify it when the next occasion arises.

Nihil in intellectu nisi prius in sensu—that is the Aristotelian and Thomist statement of the matter in brief. Étienne Gilson quotes Leibniz as improving on it by saying, "There is nothing in the intellect that was not first in the senses—except the intellect itself." And it seems that though physiology and neurology can explain a good deal, they cannot account for the presence in the universe of the faculty by which the human being understands his environment. Certainly this understanding is reached by means of the body, and therefore the removal of a small part of the brain will greatly inhibit it. So will decapitation, for that matter. But taken in itself the activity of the intellect is nonmaterial as its concepts are and inexplicable in material terms. As a power of the soul, however, of the soul considered as the formal and final cause of the body—that for the sake of which the body exists—it is at least dimly comprehensible in its full reach. I take it that Aristotle understood it thus; he understood that the mind is without magnitude though registering all magnitudes, without time though registering time; and so he rather thought it was imperishable, though in what sense we have difficulty in grasping.

To understand more fully what Aristotle meant by calling the mind the place of forms it might be well to read that passage in St. Augustine's *Confessions*, Book 10, in which he speaks of the magnitudes that are within the soul's range in the act of memory, or rather of reminis-

287

cence. Aristotle distinguished between memory and reminiscence, and the distinction should be borne in mind, for it is in the power of reminiscence or deliberate recollection that our memory of sensible things differs from the memory of animals. And to understand, not fully, but better, what Aristotle meant in his conjecture that the mind was eternal, outside time, we can do nothing more useful perhaps than study the fervent and successful effort of sheer attention by which St. Augustine, in Book XI of the *Confessions,* demonstrated himself to be extratemporal.

But one more note to complete this little outline. The Arabian student of Aristotle, Averroës of Córdoba, argued that since the universals were the same for all minds there could be but one active intellect; that is, he probably interpreted the "positive state like light" alluded to by Aristotle as belonging to God alone. St. Thomas's reply was in effect to ask, "Why, if so, do you speak of minds in the plural?" And the position taken by St. Thomas—a sufficiently striking one in view of the things I've been discussing—was that each human soul was *par excellence* an active intellect because that alone could be sufficient cause, formal and final, of the whole range of psychic activity.

I have not yet completed my comments upon the first sentence in my epigraph. For my immediate purpose it is the most important of all. For if the first sentence is true—and it is scarcely possible to read it without recognizing that it is—then the kind of confidence we may take in the mind and its work is at once subject to an enormous qualification. The intellect that we have seen endowed with imperishability of a kind difficult to grasp is here acknowledged to be momentary in a sense not at all difficult to grasp. "Actually it is nothing until it has thought." I am aware that this can be called tautological, since by "actually" what Aristotle meant was "in act" as the scholastics put it, so you might think he is only saying that the mind is not in act except when it is in act. But actuality is very important for Aristotle, more so, notoriously, than it was for Plato. If it were not, he would not have put the matter so strongly as to use the word "nothing."

Here are some numbered propositions, for brevity's sake:

1. Between the being known to any one of us and created being as a whole there is a difference of scale.

2. Between real being and what we may call intellectual being—the abstract being of thought—there is a difference expressible as difference of scale.

3. Between actual real being and nonactual, i.e. potential or possible real being, there is a difference likewise expressible as difference of scale.

4. The differences of scale I have mentioned are incalculable and entail for the individual being or thinking an incalculable humility.

5. Intellectual being—the being of thought—is derivative from real being and refers to it; we have some knowledge of real being.

We distinguish between being as real and being as intellectual, between the real entity and the intellectual or intelligible entity, the abstraction. When I say that the difference between these is "expressible as" a difference of scale, I mean to take account of the fact that strictly speaking thought is without magnitude, which belongs exclusively to certain real objects of thought. The two are in truth incommensurable, but we may use the notion of scale to suggest what that means. And we may say that between any real thing and any abstraction from it in thought the difference is no less but in fact greater than the difference or proportion established, for example, between my being and being as a whole. I can illustrate this easily. A telescope may be pointed all night at a star in the night sky, a star that is in reality the great nebula in the constellation Andromeda, a galaxy millions of light years away and so on; during the hours the telescope is pointed an impression is being gathered on a photosensitive plate. The difference between this impression, this blur, and the real galaxy is very great; but it is less than the difference between our thought, our abstraction answering to the term "nebula in Andromeda," and the real galaxy. It is less, for that matter, than the difference between our abstraction answering to the term "photosensitive plate" and the plate itself.

There are further things to be said about this difference. The abstraction answering to the term "nebula in Andromeda" is only one of an indefinite number of abstractions that can be drawn from the real thing in question. We have extracted from a real thing much too big to handle —and too hot—a characteristic of class, "nebula," and a point of apparent location, "in Andromeda": that leaves the real thing still there, rich literally beyond conception, powerful in its being, and multiple in the aspects of being to which we may turn our minds if we care to. The example is a little showy, but the statements hold true likewise of the photosensitive plate.

Now, one consequence of this is that every abstraction has about it something of the temporary, being one in a possible series. Moreover, this series is endless. The analysis of any given real entity by means of our abstractions cannot be exhaustive.

In the third proposition our expressive purpose may make use in fact of two differences and two scales. When we think on the scale of the actual, all the rest of the real is minuscule:

> Ah, que le monde est grand à la clarté des lampes!
> Aux yeux du souvenir, que le monde est petit!

But actual real being as we know it is a selection moment by moment from a great range of potential being and a still greater range of possible being. The actual real is likened by Gerard Manley Hopkins to a slice made by a knife, the possible real to the melon in which the slice is made—if you turn the image about and think of the cleft as "substantial" and visible, the melon as "insubstantial" and invisible.

We term a certain kind of thought or abstraction a concept because it is something conceived when a mind has been impregnated by—has become one in act with—formal reality outside the mind. The concept witnesses to its parentage as the blur on the plate witnesses to the nebula in Andromeda. It is a trace of the reality, a sign. But it is not real in the same sense as the blur on the plate is: its being is in its reference, it is open and transparent toward the real, which is the first object of thought. This is not to be forgotten when in reflection thought takes thought for object, when abstraction is made from abstraction, when we achieve the concept "concept" and the further "conceptual"—the reference in these cases being to entities in thought. All begins with the real and the bare mind.

Now let me offer you a second series of propositions:

1. Just as the abstraction made by thought is a trace and a sign of the reality from which it is abstracted, the word spoken is a trace and a sign of the abstraction.

2. Just as the word spoken, the vocal thing, is a trace and a sign of

THE PLACE OF FORMS

the abstraction or notion, the word written, a visual thing, is a trace and a sign of the word spoken.

3. Between the word written and the real therefore there are three stages or removes of signification: the written word signifies the spoken, the spoken word signifies the abstract notion, the notion signifies the real.

4. Just as the abstract notion has about it something of the temporary and provisional, as I have said, being one in a possible series, drawn from and signifying the real object of thought, so the word spoken has about it something provisional and imperfect. The choice of the word for the notion will be made from available words by a kind of matching process, a search for that one which signifies a notion most nearly approximate to the notion present in the mind. This is true even when a selected word is arbitrarily given a defined significance in all cases where the word and its previous significances cannot be parted. Take "nebula," for example. With respect to the galactic system in Andromeda, the word "nebula" signifies the notion "multitude of stars," but the previous meaning of the word—"mist or cloud" remains and relates it in fact as much to the blur on the photosensitive plate as to the real entity signified. On the other hand, the arbitrary invention of a new word with a defined signification is possible. "Nylon" is perhaps such a word.

The distinctions I have been making have the effect of showing, as it were, "open spaces," distances, between the things distinguished. It seems to me that rashness and error in thought and idolatry among thinkers often begins when these spaces, distances, which really exist, are ignored. Words are treated as if they were notions, notions of one kind as if they were notions of another, and as if they were things. The faint and provisional character of all abstractions is overlooked; so is their character as signs, their original transparency toward the real from which they were abstracted.

It will be evident, it seems to me, that there are many apparent conflicts and indeed agonies of thought from which we may be delivered by remembering these things; and to remember them is perhaps a requisite for practicing that mode of thought known to Plato and Aristotle as dialectic. The best definition for this that I can think of at the moment is "the criticism of abstractions through the contemplation of reality and the exchange of corrections made necessary thereby."

The critic Marcel Raymond says that Paul Valéry declined the title of poet-philosopher with the remark that "philosophy is defined by its apparatus and not by its object" (from *Baudelaire to Surrealism*, New York, 1950). Raymond adds that if it is true that modern philosophy tends to define itself by its apparatus, it is permissible to think that this should not be a source of pride. He goes on to say that although Valéry does not treat or raise "problems" that are strictly speaking metaphysical in the modern sense, nevertheless a very profound experience bearing upon the relations between soul and body leads him to create "the psychological and vital movement that compels the formulation of these problems and makes their solution urgent and infinitely remote." As to the "relations between soul and body," do we not have in Aristotle's *De anima* an account of them in which, at least, we find a recognizable contemplation, or in the Greek, *theoría,* of the full reality as given? There is at least a refreshing scope in his definition of the soul as the cause of the body in three senses of cause—efficient, as the animating principle; formal, as the essence or quiddity, and final, in the sense of *tò hoû héneka*, that in whose interest the body exists. We are no less relieved, I think, by the likeness acknowledged between ourselves and the animals than we are by the recognition of what distinguishes us from them—the intelligence concerning which Aristotle speaks in the passage I have quoted as epigraph. And the thing we have to realize about the mind, urgent and infinitely remote, is that its order of being is *sui generis;* that although without location, magnitude, or quality it may apprehend all magnitude, location, and quality. This Aristotle reinforces for us by calmly noting that until it thinks it is nothing, it is no actual thing; just as, when it does think, it becomes merely that which it thinks about. Meanwhile it is a potency, a place of forms. Valéry stated that the man of intellect "must knowingly reduce himself to an unlimited refusal to be anything whatsoever." By Aristotle's account, this is a refusal that the intellect, in fact, as distinguished from the man of intellect, scarcely needs to make since the intellect is nothing actual whatsoever and this indeed is a condition of its being. At death no doubt everything goes but this: we reach, as Eliot put it in "Little Gidding," "a condition of complete simplicity, costing not less than everything." Hamlet seems to have spoken out of a perception of this when he asked, "Since no man has aught of what he leaves, what is't to leave betimes?"

I should like to quote three excerpts from the Commentary written by St. Thomas Aquinas on Aristotle's *De anima*. They are selected from the seventh, tenth, and thirteenth *lectiones* on Book 3 of *De anima*.

I. "Every thing which is in potency to something and receptive of it, lacks that to which it is in potency and of which it is receptive. Thus the pupil of the eye, which is in potency to colors and is receptive of them, lacks all color. Now our intellect knows intelligible things because it is in potency to them and susceptive of them, just as sense is of sensible things: therefore it lacks all those things which it was born to know. Since our intellect was born to know all things sensible and corporal, it must needs lack any corporal nature, just as the visual sense lacks all color for the reason that it is cognoscitive of color. If it had any color, that color would keep it from seeing other colors . . . In the same way, if the intellect had any determined nature, that nature native to it would keep it from the cognition of other natures . . . He [Aristotle] concludes that the intellect . . . has this nature only, that it is in potency with respect to all. . . . Further, that what is called the soul's intellect, before it knows, is not any actual thing."

II. "Aristotle says it [i.e., the active intellect] is a positive state like light, because light in a certain way makes colors existing in potency be colors in actuality . . . But light does this, makes a color be actual, only insofar as it makes an actual transparency which may be affected by the color and thus the color may be seen. The active intellect makes intelligible things, which were in potency before, become actual by virtue of the fact that it draws them out, or abstracts them, from the material; for it is thus that they become actually intelligible . . ."

III. "It must be admitted that the intelligible things of our intellect have their being in sense impressions, and this is true just as much of what are called abstractions, like those of mathematics, as it is of the states and feelings of sensitivity. And because of this fact no man can learn anything in the way of newly acquired knowledge, or know anything in the sense of using knowledge already acquired, without the sense [impressions]. No; when a man is actually thinking speculatively, he must at the same time form for himself some phantasma or sensible image . . . It is plain that Avicenna was wrong in laying it down that the intellect has no need of sense after acquiring knowledge . . ."

The second of these quotations suggests to me that the poet Coleridge drew his doctrine of the primary imagination from an insight very profound and ancient which he slightly misunderstood. The active intellect—a postulate of Aristotle's at the root of intellectual life—is said to "make all things" and to be "a positive state like light" in a sense that we here see St. Thomas delimiting and qualifying. The world of intelligibles is actualized by the mind but the mind does not create them; no, it only seizes them out of potency; and there is but one Creator of all things and all minds alike. As to the imagination proper, the domain of *phantásmata*, the third quotation suggests how intimately it is bound in with purest thought itself.

Take the table, that perennial object of popular epistemology. My eyes tell me that there is a *this* here. What do they see? A shape, color, and texture at a certain distance and angle. Any more? No, that is all I see. But I speak of *this table* and my eyes do not supply me with the words. There is, then, something else at work or at play in the little cognitive event. Is it my phonetic apparatus—tongue, teeth, lips, and breath? No, because I thought the words as I spoke them, or more likely before. Let us call whatever gave me the words my mind. What was my mind doing while my eyes were seeing *this*? The answer I have outlined is that my mind was apprehending this, taking it in, and that the apprehension in the mind, drawn from this, was an abstraction, which according to the Latin version of the word is something drawn from another thing. But more precisely what was drawn by the mind from this? A shape? A color? A texture? No, the eyes got those. So the mind's apprehension was something else again, to be distinguished from the visual. We may call it a notion. It did not itself have shape, color, or texture; it was a notion *of* something that had these. Its being, the being of the abstract notion, was in its reference. It was transparent toward the object, as I have put it. But while it referred to this, it referred to it after the mind's mode or manner of referring to anything. That is, it referred to what Aristotle called the *ousía* or *tì tò ên*—the essence, form, quiddity or whatness, which is what the mind as a "positive state like light," the *noûs poetikós*, "makes of" the object almost in our colloquial sense. On the one hand we have the object as it exists in itself, on the other the concept of its essence, and finally the two words, "this" and "table," to express the concept.

Now what I have been trying to say, after Aristotle and St. Thomas as I understand them, was that just as these two words are far from expressing all the possible abstractions from the object, the possible abstractions are far from having, all together, any such reality as the object has. The object is particular, it is a *particula,* a little part, of reality. It is unique. But each of our abstractions from it is a universal in the sense that it is repeatable, discoverable in other objects: "wood," "smooth," "varnished," "massive," "four-legged"—so the analysis of the object by means of abstract notions can proceed indefinitely. The further it proceeds the more we know about the object, and we can indeed know a great deal about it. It can be elaborately described. It can be subjected, also, to laboratory analysis, from which we'll get first a microscopic-slide report on certain formations of ligneous fibers and ultimately a page of mathematics indicating certain configurations of energy in a limited field. This is all interesting; our knowledge grows. But no matter how far it grows, the terms of our knowledge are what we possess. They are what is in our mind, and they are universal, as Aristotle said; their being is of another order. We do not possess the object, the real thing, no man has aught of what he leaves, and one of the easiest and worst of our delusions is to think that we do.

This being the case, we may be amenable to another kind of thinking that might go, very briefly, like this:

The change began when two men with a two-handed saw came up the lane in the early morning. The hoar frost was so thick they left footprints on the grass. The saw made the usual noise, regular, like a branchful of cicadas, but dry and dull. I didn't feel anything until I began to crack, and then it all happened very surprisingly: I had never felt *heavy* before.

On the way down I smashed a couple of pine saplings and a birch. I felt a little faint lying there while they went on with it. One wore a stocking cap and his ears were red. The truck came when it was getting dark, and they used some tackle to hoist me on in sections. At the mill next day I had to marvel at the speed of the blade; nothing could stop it. The man who put me through had a kind of knob on his right hand where the first finger usually is.

Perhaps only because I had grown used to it, I liked the bark and hated to see it go. I felt naked as well as cut before they were through with me there. That winter and the next I stayed in a pile under canvas; sometimes in summer a poor man would come and crawl under late at night.

At the factory the carpenter handled me with respect; he spoke well of my grain. At least he was making something other than pieces out of me. The varnishing gave me an astringent feeling, everything tightened and closed. I didn't stay in the warehouse long. They sent me here in a truck with my corners bound up in excelsior and brown paper.

I scarcely know what it's like, now, to stand up outside with leaves on, and I miss the bathing and drinking and blowing around in storms. But there is something to be said for being structural and serviceable.

Here, then, is a little story, a micromyth, and what does it remind us of? We are reminded, I think, of the fact that full contemplation of reality will be contemplation of something happening, some action, or *prâxis*—the Greek word—in actuality. We are also reminded of a fact that our previous and narrow look at the table had tended to obscure: that the full being of anything will not be comprehended except in terms of what has happened and what is possibly still to happen: the being is the full tale of the becoming.

Aristotle's statement of this, in his own particular set of abstractions from the real, is that reality—everything that is—may be found as form (*eîdos* or *morphé*), potentiality (*dýnamis* or *hýle*), and the actual, in which continually the two are joined. The larger the lens of intelligence, the more it will take in of all three. This is why, in the *Poetics*, Aristotle said poetry was more like *philosophía*, weightier and more significant than history. It is because "the poet's function is not to tell what has happened but the kind of thing that might happen and is potentially capable of happening." Aristotle doesn't refer to the kind of thing that might have happened, but that is implied in the discussion. He does say in Chapter 9 *tà dè genómena phanerón hóti dynatá*—what has happened is manifestly possible or potential—and he also says in Chapter 25 that among the subjects of *mímesis* are *hoîa ên è éstin*—such things as were or are. The potentiality of the piece of wood includes being a heap of charcoal as well as a part of a tree.

The statement might lead us to still another point of which my little myth may remind us. Each existing thing, though it be real and substantial, existing in itself, cannot be understood apart from the context of the real to which it is related. "No one thing remains alone," Valéry

THE PLACE OF FORMS

said, "for I associate it with another in my heart . . . It follows that the principle task of the metaphor is to bear witness to the totality of the world." There should be more to say about this in relation to tragedy and tragic poetry. But we may say now that any happening, or becoming, necessarily involves not only the acting or *práxis* but the being acted upon, or *páthos;* the movement self-initiated and the movement compelled. In the human case, it implies contact at every moment with the large world outside, of which sense and mind take cognizance, by which indeed the singular being is filled with—made pregnant of—multiple being; the memory stores its phantasmata; and mind, the place of forms, fulfills itself in apprehending the forms, the *intelligibilia,* drawn from things.

Now, if this account—rough as it is—squares with the facts about the life of the intelligent soul, let us ask what, in consequence, is the status of pure thought as it is called and what the status of poetry or the myth composed in phantasmata. In our context as established the answers should come fairly readily. The humble nature of abstractions requires that we esteem any discourse like the present one as a necessary convenience, but only faintly representative of the process by which it is achieved or the reality to which it refers. The process itself, even in the case of original mathematical thought—and I have verified this with a great physicist of our day—is rich in phantasmata, the gifts or deliverances of the senses and of memory. Insofar as these are present in the myth or poem, the myth or poem may represent more fully the work of the intelligent soul and the world in which it finds itself. In any case, it will add, or rather restore, to the *intelligibilia* of the mind a taste of the material penumbra out of which they have been seized.

There is here no necessary conflict nor ground for anything but courtesy between the workman who limits himself to abstraction and the workman whose bent is for *mímesis* in phantasmal material. Neither may think the other *per se* disrespectful of the reality both should love; each may recognize in the other, as I think Aristotle recognized in both, an aspect of *philosophía.*

We will have noticed in the *Poetics* that Aristotle thinks of *mímesis* as a kind of representation from which people learn something, and since to learn something is a delight, he accounts in this way for the popularity of Homer and dramatic poetry. It is well to bear this in mind

297

when he praises Homer for having taught other poets "how to tell lies properly"—*pseúde légein hòs deî*. The great myths of Homer no less than the micromyth I made up about the table have qualities that Plato stigmatized as lying—the qualities of being arbitrary, conventional, and at a distance from the real. But Aristotle understood more clearly than Plato did that precisely the same can be said of ideas. We may learn something, but not everything, from the truth-telling discourse in the order of truth. We may learn something, but not everything, from the fiction properly constructed in the order of art. And we are unfortunate if we cannot see these orders as mutually complementary—for example, in one of the great dialogues of Plato.

One further point may be made here, as to the meaning of *prâxis*, or action, that which Aristotle considered the subject of *mímesis* in tragedy. In the micromyth about the table we might think that the narrator had not acted at all, but had only been acted upon. Aristotle would not, 1 think, say this. By *prâxis*, as his editor, S. H. Butcher, has remarked, he meant not merely the outward locomotory movement, as of an obvious kind of efficient cause, but the inward apprehension, the judging and willing movement of the the soul, *enérgeia psychês* or activity of soul, as he calls it in the *Ethics*. In poetry this may well be apparent as nothing but style; and I should say it was the style, in my little story, with which the piece of wood speaks.

Finally, I should point out that Aristotle's account of the intelligence *per se* is not such as could be affected by the modern science of the soul. *Noûs* is that which discovers and names the id, ego, and superego, for example, for whatever these categories may be worth: *noûs* is prior to them and could not, if it would, make them prior to itself. Again, it can be seen that the facts are better recognized in Aristotle's account of them than in Coleridge's account of the Primary Imagination, which is the *noûs poetikós* obfuscated by philosophic idealism and thus exalted as creative of reality, whereas to Aristotle it is creative of thought *out of* reality. Here certainly we have touched on a specifically "literary" notion that has had great influence, whether the notion was Coleridge's originally or Kant's, no matter whose. The *noûs poetikós*, however, is a postulate beyond consciousness though consciousness demands it; it is not the same thing as that specific excellence of the mind that makes poems or works of art. It is not, like a *téchne*, necessarily deliberative.

But, as the Greek root word *poieîn* attests, there is an analogy between the two.

Actuality, the actual, in this world is forever what we have and where we are—actuality, to which it seems to me Aristotle's close attention may direct ours, alerted and finely trained, freed from two contrary sorts of enchantment. One is the comfortable sort that supposes things including ourselves to be the things of convention—commonsense objects made of this stuff or that stuff, the material as the only actuality, changing, yes, but so slowly—a comfortable view but one that is perpetually being upset. The other is of more recent fashion, and Humean, I suppose, though Plato has had some credit for starting it; it sees everything as "appearance" and doubts reality or discerns none—a very uncomfortable view, though held by some fairly cozy individuals. No: the concrete actual thing, the "fact of experience" as we say, is real and has eminent metaphysical status. The empiricist and materialist are so far right. But reality only begins there; and actuality is inherently precarious, a changing union of form with potentiality. Prime matter to Aristotle is pure potentiality, which seems to be what our physicists make of it. The mind barely escapes being nothing actual and so does everything else. If we take to this near nonentity as ducks to water, that is because *we* can only exist in *it;* but we are not ducks and can realize this much about it; we can know also that, vanishing though any actual thing may be, it is still enormously real and beyond our power wholly to grasp.

We need not on this account lose confidence in intelligence but we ought rather to keep a different kind of confidence, aware of what I have called the distances, the open spaces, between degrees of abstraction and between them and the reality from which they are drawn. This, it seems to me, should liberate the individual making poems, say, as it liberates the individual in action: you go ahead and form the poem or you go ahead and act in the circumstances, knowing equally well that what you make or do cannot have been but roughly planned or formed or predicted in the mind aforetime, and that while being made or done and after being made or done, the work can be understood in the mind and in the mind alone. When we think, we conceptualize; actuality overbrims our concepts, they but faintly embody it; but we may think how faintly, we may think how they are overbrimmed. One respect in which they are inadequate is in their grasp of those important constituents of any actual thing or person, the potential or possible forms— those that have been, those that are to be fulfilled, and those that neither have been nor are to be.

I tried to show in a sufficiently slight instance of my own how the fictional or poetic art—the subject of Aristotle's *Poetics*—may supply us with at least a *homoíoma,* a likeness of such potential or possible forms, and so bring home to us their presence in the given actual thing. Thus I thought to locate within the context of Aristotle's general thinking his well-known estimate of poetry as more like *philosophía* and more meaningful—that is, wider and finer in its reference to reality— than the chronicle of actualized particulars or facts which he understood as history. And thus a ground appears for seeing that the representational arts give *knowledge,* not through "instruction"—not *didaktikós*—as the pedantic understanding of later theory would have it, but by being what they are; one reason we delight in them, as Aristotle says, is that we delight in learning things.

Harvard University

JOSEPH FRANK

Dostoevsky and Russian Populism

Dostoevsky's return to Russia in July 1871 marked the end of his four-year sojourn abroad and the beginning of a new epoch in his life and work. Once before, eleven years earlier, he had returned to Russia from exile in Siberia—a half-forgotten figure of the 1840s whose literary career had been snapped in two by Tsarist repression. This time he returned as the famous author of *Crime and Punishment, The Idiot,* and a new novel, *The Devils,* which was creating a sensation by appearing in installments exactly at the moment when the followers of Nechaev were being publicly tried and sentenced. There was no question about Dostoevsky's right to rank with the very greatest names in contemporary Russian literature, though he was a disputed and controversial figure who stood very much alone and could not be easily placed in any of the current Russian socioliterary tendencies. Evidence of his new status may be inferred from the request made to Dostoevsky in March 1872 by the rich art-fancier, P. M. Tretyakov, who asked Dostoevsky to allow his portrait to be painted by the well-known artist V. G. Perov. Tretyakov was assembling a gallery of portraits of famous Russian personalities, and Dostoevsky was naturally to be included in their midst.

For all his new prestige, however, Dostoevsky's financial situation had not improved in the slightest during the four harried years of his second exile. He had planned to recoup his fortunes during this period and return to Russia after repaying the ever-vigilant creditors of *Epoch;* but he was still living in the same hand-to-mouth fashion as when he had left, and the threat of debtor's prison still loomed as a possibility after his return. Mrs. Dostoevsky, though, decided to take the matter of creditors into her own capable hands, and she soon persuaded them that, if they wished to be repaid at all, it was wiser to leave Dostoevsky in freedom and able to continue his literary career. Moreover, she also determined to put into practice Dostoevsky's long-cherished idea of publishing his own works; and early in 1873 an edition of *The Devils* appeared issued by the Dostoevskys themselves. This successful venture established the foundation of Dostoevsky's relative affluence during the last ten years of his life, when he lived modestly but comfortably, relieved at last from the frantic economic pressure under which he had labored ever since the collapse of *Epoch*.

After having completed *The Devils* in the final months of 1872, Dostoevsky accepted a remunerative editorial post as editor-in-chief of a new weekly magazine called *The Citizen*. This publication had been founded and was financed by a minor novelist, dramatist, and journalist named Prince V. M. Meshchersky, who had achieved some reputation with satirical novels about high-society life. Meshchersky was well-connected in the highest circles of the Russian court and also acquainted with Dostoevsky's oldest and closest friend Apollon Maikov as well as with the ubiquitous N. N. Strakhov. It was probably through Maikov that Dostoevsky met Meshchersky, who was the center of a literary circle that included the novelist Nikolai Leskov, the great poet F. M. Tyutchev, the tutor to the Crown Prince Alexander, K. D. Pobedonostsev, and other writers and publicists of a predominantly Slavophil and antiliberal cast. *The Citizen* was thus definitely a conservative organ, though it had not been blatantly reactionary under its first editor, the liberal K. D. Gradovsky; nor did it become any more reactionary under Dostoevsky's guidance. Dostoevsky's connection with this magazine, however, coupled with the vehemence of his antiradicalism in *The Devils*, definitely alienated the younger readers who had till then regarded him sympathetically. "This was the period just after the noise of the Nechaev case, and of the publication of *The Devils* in *The Russian Messenger*, had died down" writes V. V. Timofeeva, a bright young woman and aspiring writer, who worked as a proofreader on *The Citizen* but who was also closely connected with left-wing literary and intellectual circles. "We, the youth, had read the speeches of the famous lawyers for the defense in *The Voice* and the *St. Petersburg Gazette*, and Dostoevsky's new novel seemed to us then a monstrous caricature, a nightmare of mystical ecstasies and psychopathology. And that the author of *The Devils* took up the editorship of *The Citizen* caused many of his earlier admirers and friends to break with him once and for all." [1]

This move appeared to have aligned Dostoevsky irrevocably with the camp of reaction; but once again he proved much too volatile to be conveniently categorized under any simple label. The break had hardly occurred before it was healed again in a remarkable and unexpected fashion. Dostoevsky's next novel, *A Raw Youth,* began to appear in 1875—and it was serialized, not in *The Russian Messenger* or any other of the conservative and right-wing organs, but in that citadel of left-wing opposition in the 1870s, the *Notes of the Fatherland!* It is true that Dostoevsky first offered this novel to Katkov (who refused it because he had already bought *Anna Karenina* for that year), and that *Notes of the Fatherland* agreed to pay Dostoevsky more than he had ever gotten before in space-rates. But the fact that the leading left-wing journal should even have thought it possible to publish the next novel of the author of *The Devils* and that Dostoevsky should have himself first intimated his desire for such an arrangement through V. V. Timofeeva indicates to what an extent the whole Russian sociocultural climate had changed between 1869 and 1874–1875. For the 1870s had ushered in a new left-wing ideology called Populism (*narodnichestvo*), which differed markedly from the nihilism that Dostoevsky had fought so unceasingly all through the 1860s. And to understand Dostoevsky's work in this last period of his life, it is necessary briefly to fill in the background of this transformation.

Dostoevsky had seen in the Nechaev affair the materialization of all his worst fears about the moral-political consequences of the Russian nihilism that he had campaigned against so vigorously all through the 1860s. So it was indeed; but he had no way of knowing that a feeling of revulsion against nihilism had already begun to set in among the left-wing intelligentsia even before Nechaev and that the revelations of this affair were to give nihilism its *coup de grâce*. Out of this revulsion came the new Populist ideology of the 1870s, which, though still dedicated to establishing a more just and equitable social order in Russia, took up this task under the influence of attitudes and beliefs significantly different from those of the 1860s. These new ideas began to come to the fore just as Dostoevsky returned to Petersburg from his second exile and were most effectively expressed in the journal of the new movement, *Notes of the Fatherland*. This magazine had been taken over by Nekrasov and Saltykov-Schedrin after the closing of *The Contemporary* in 1866; and in the next few years they gradually acquired a group of fresh young contributors who gave left-wing sentiment a new orientation. The most important of these new figures in the magazine was N. K. Mikhailovsky. The older P. M. Lavrov, whom Chernyshevsky had dismissed as an eclectic in the early 1860s, also became a significant and independent Populist influence with the publication of his *Historical Letters* in 1869–1870.

If we look at Russian Populism through the prism of Dostoevsky's opposition to Russian nihilism, it is not difficult to see why his attitude toward the radicals in the 1870s should have undergone a notable mutation. No one had attacked the materialistic determinism of Chernyshevsky as bitingly and caustically as the author of *Notes from Underground*. And the Populists too, while still paying homage to Chernyshevsky, the political martyr and defender of the peasant commune, nonetheless broke as decisively as Dostoevsky had done with his metaphysics. They replaced his monistic materialism with a Kantian dualism, which left ample room for the free exercise of the will and of moral initiative. "It is unquestionable," wrote Mikhailovsky in 1872, "that society obeys certain laws in its development; but no less unquestionable is man's *inherent consciousness of a free choice of action*. At the moment of action I am aware that I freely give myself a goal, completely independent of the influence of historical conditions. Perhaps this is an illusion, but it is what makes history move." [2] Human consciousness, with its ineluctable need for freedom and moral responsibility, is thus no longer trapped in the dilemmas dramatized in the first part of *Notes from Underground*. And for the Populist, indeed, all history was to be judged in the light of its reference to a moral ideal. "Consciously or unconsciously," Lavrov writes, "man applies to the whole history of mankind the degree of moral development that he has reached himself." [3]

Along with the determinism of Chernyshevsky, which attempted to subordinate man to the workings of some "scientific" law of nature, the

Populists also discarded his utilitarian ethics of "rational egoism" based on supposed calculations of self-interest. By the end of the 1860s, under the influence of Pisarev, nihilist "egoism" had become less and less "rational" and more and more individual and self-gratifying; and the creator of Raskolnikov could hardly refuse his sympathy to the Populist restorers of a morality of obligation and self-sacrifice. The generation of the 1860s, Mikhailovsky wrote in 1870, had discovered during the Crimean War "that the talk about sacrifice was quite compatible with saving one's skin at any price, with delivering to the army shoes without soles, rotten flour, etc." As a result, this generation began to investigate "the real base of a whole series of phenomena linked with the ideas of sacrifice and self-denial. The real base turned out to be very simple: man is an egoist. Every step he takes, even seemingly the most noble and self-denying, is entirely for his own profit and enjoyment; self-denial is only a special case of self-preservation; sacrifice is a fiction, something not really existing—sheer nonsense. Clinging to this [Chernyshevsky's] formula, we lost sight of the fact that, in the first place, the extension of our personal ego to the point of self-sacrifice, to the possibility of identification with an alien life—is just as real as the crudest egoism. And that, in the second place, the formula that sacrifice is sheer nonsense does not at all cover our own psychic situation, for more than ever before are we ready to endure the most extreme sacrifices."

It is scarcely surprising, after such a passage, to learn that Mikhailovsky had read *Crime and Punishment* with great admiration. And this revival among the Populists of an ethics of self-sacrifice, with all its explicitly Christian overtones, went hand-in-hand with a renewed respect for Christianity itself. Mikhailovsky cited with approval in 1873 the following passage of an article published in the 1840s by K. D. Kavelin, a liberal historian who had been tutored by Belinsky. "The ancient world did not have any idea of personality," wrote Kavelin, paraphrasing a key historical concept of German idealism. "Antiquity did not understand man except as a particular caste, class, or nationality; man himself, we might say, was completely unknown. . . . Christianity gave a completely new impulse to history. It gave birth to the idea of the unconditional value of man and the human personality outside all the narrow determinisms set by nature." [4]

No idea about Christianity could have corresponded more to Dostoevsky's taste; and to have such an idea quoted affirmatively by a leading radical spokesman was sufficent to indicate the shift of feeling from the militant atheism of the 1860s noted by all students of the period. Distinguishing the generation of the 1870s from its nihilist predecessor Ovsyaniko-Kulikovski, the best historian of the Russian intelligentsia, writes: "The indifferentism and skepticism in religion, which so sharply marked out the 'Pisarevist' tendency, notably declined. Unconcerned with dogmatic religion, with official religion, the new generation displayed unmistakable interest in the Gospels, in Christian ethics, and in Christ the man." [5] "Russian Populism," writes James Billington succinctly, "was in truth . . . a 'new Christianity,' in which the Jesus of the New Testament provided the hope of glory for men who no longer looked to Him for means of grace." [6] The Populists exhibited a lively interest in the religious doctrines of the Russian raskol and admired the sectarians for the application of the Christian principles of love and brotherhood to their daily lives and to the social organization of their communities. The utopian socialist traditions of the early 1840s also flourished vigorously once again among the Populists, and the influence of Proudhon—who had once called the modern working class the Divine Paraclete, come to fulfill the predictions of Christ—was particularly strong. Socialism once again was seen as the practical realization of Christ's message on earth, and the Populists specifically appealed to the example of the Christ of the Gospels both in their propaganda and in their self-defense when placed on trial.

These general features of the Populism of the 1870s could hardly have helped appealing to Dostoevsky; and they noticeably lessened the distance between the radical intelligentsia and the principles and values he had long upheld. Even more, the specifically sociopolitical attitudes of Russian Populism also came quite close to the theses of Dostoevsky's then-defunct but still privately cherished doctrine of pochvennichestvo.[7] This ideology had preached the necessity for the intelligentsia to return to the people and accept their basic beliefs, while at the same time helping them to attain the benefits of European enlightenment; and it had glorified the Russian people as the source of an all-reconciling force destined to regenerate the world. The democratic radicalism of Herzen and

Chernyshevsky, to be sure, had also idealized and glorified the Russian people; but they had looked upon the people largely as a potentially revolutionary force which would provide the dynamism for the transition to a future socialist order. The existing institutions of the people, such as the commune and the *artel* (a wage-pooling worker's co-operative), were for them only an embryo that would have to be carefully nurtured and developed in a consciously socialist direction. Like Dostoevsky and the Slavophils, however, the Populists were much more prone to regard the existing economic institutions of the peasantry as uniquely valuable and precious *in themselves and in their present form;* and they saw as their primary task, in face of the growing industrialization of Russia, the *preservation* of these institutions rather than their revolutionary transformation. "The working question in Europe is a revolutionary question," Mikhailovsky wrote unequivocally in 1872; "there it demands the *transfer* of the tools of labor into the hands of the worker, the expropriation of the present proprietors. The working question in Russia is a conservative question; here only the *preservation* of the means of labor in the hands of the workers is required, a guarantee to the present proprietors [the peasants] of their property." This is the classic Slavophil argument, which had also been used by Dostoevsky in the early 1860s, that social revolution on the European model was an absurdity under Russian economic conditions.

The Populists did not idealize the peasant in the same moral-religious terms as Dostoevsky; but they worked out their own "philosophical" and "sociological" variant of this pervasive ideological pattern. Mikhailovsky's most important systematic work (he was primarily a journalist) was an attack on Herbert Spencer in 1867 called *What Is Progress?;* and it amounted to a Slavophil-tinged critique of the West in up-to-date terminology. The only criterion of progress, Mikhailovsky argued, was the happiness of the concrete individual, the development of the most harmonious and well-rounded personality. From this point of view, the Russian peasant represented a higher "type" of progress than the industrial worker of Europe, though European society as a whole had reached a higher "stage" of social development. The industrial worker, more and more splintered by the division of labor, had been finally reduced to being a dehumanized cog; while the Russian peasant, whose diversified tasks stimulated him to employ all his physical and spiritual capacities, had a much more fully developed and harmonious personality. Just as with *pochvennichestvo*, the aim of Populism was to guard the unique values of this higher "type" of life embodied in the Russian peasantry, and eventually to fuse it—without destroying its irreplaceable virtues— with the higher "stage" of social development already attained by Europe.

Even though the ideological content of Populism differed somewhat from that of *pochvennichestvo*, the similarity in overall perspective is very striking. And the inherent, quasi-Slavophil bias against Europe evident in Mikhailovsky's ideas was strengthened after 1870 by a wide-spread Populist disillusionment with the West caused by the bloody suppression of the Paris Commune. As a result, Mikhailovsky manifested a general suspicion of European civilization that became typical of the Populists, who saw Europe exclusively as a soulless and heartless nightmare of capitalist exploitation. "Reason and moral feeling," Mikhailovsky wrote in 1872, attacking the advocates of Russian capitalist expansion, "did not influence the economic development of Europe." "We must admit," Lavrov had written a few years earlier, "that the benefits of modern civilization are paid for not only by unavoidable evil, but by a monstrous accumulation of totally unnecessary evil." [8] This was a far cry from Pisarev's indiscriminate embrace of capitalist industrial expansion in the mid-1860s and comes much closer to Dostoevsky's depiction of European industrialism in *Winter Notes* as the triumph of the flesh-god Baal. To exorcise this monstrous image of evil, Dostoevsky had appealed to the moral values still alive at the roots of Russian life; and the Populists, horrified by Europe, exhibited exactly the same reflex. Reviewing Marx's *Das Kapital* in 1872, a book which he found impressive but irrelevant for Russia, Mikhailovsky asserted: "We not only do not scorn Russia, but we see in its past, and still in its present, much on which we can rely to ward off the falsities of European civilization." This Messianic juxtaposition of Russia and Europe—the one poor but humane and morally sensitive, the other wealthy, proud, and corrupt— corresponded completely to Dostoevsky's most passionately-held beliefs; and it provided still another link in the chain of sympathy that began to be forged between the erstwhile author of *The Devils* and the new cadres of the radical intelligentsia.

Whenever Dostoevsky had tried to express concretely his own alternative to radical ideas of a revolutionary sociopolitical change, he had always done so by images of individual devotion to the welfare of the less fortunate stemming from a sense of moral obligation. Mockingly giving some good advice to the "superfluous men" of the 1840s, Dostoevsky had urged them in 1861 to abandon their disdainful decision to do nothing because they could not walk with "seven-league boots" [i.e., revolution]. Why could they not apply the remarkable abilities they complained of being unable to use to a simple but highly desirable task? "You always said that there was nothing you could do. But just try—can't you find something even now? Teach just one child the alphabet—there's your activity! . . . Sacrifice yourself, oh giants!, for the general good. . . . Lower yourself, limit yourself to this one child." [9] All through Dostoevsky's work, universal and grandiose abstractions blind his negative heroes to the elementary obligations of an individual and personal concern with individual human beings. And Shatov advises the most glamorous of these negative heroes, Stavrogin, where to find the source of that moral sense of good and evil whose loss is leading him to perdition. Go, he says, "to find God through work. . . . Peasant's work. Go, give up your riches."

With all this as background, the concrete form of the sociopolitical activity of the Russian Populists in the early 1870s probably seemed to Dostoevsky a spontaneous response to everything he had been advocating in his works. The classic description of this activity, which reached its peak in the spring of 1874, is contained in the memoirs of the later anarchist Prince Kropotkin, who was a member of a key Populist group in St. Petersburg at this time. The primary concern of all these groups, he says, was to find the answer to one great question: "In what way could they be useful to the masses? Gradually, they came to the idea that the only way was to settle amongst the people and to live the people's life. Young men went to the villages as doctors, doctor's helpers, village scribes, even as agricultural laborers, blacksmiths, woodcutters, and so on, and tried to live there in close contact with the peasants. Girls passed teacher's examinations, learned midwifery, or nursing, and went by the hundreds to the villages, devoting themselves to the poorest part of the population. These people went without any ideal of social reconstruction in their minds or any thought of revolution. They simply wanted to teach the mass of the peasants to read, to instruct them in other things, to give them medical help, and in any way to aid in raising them from their darkness and misery, and to learn at the same time what were *their* popular ideals of a better social life." [10]

This picture as it stands is certainly a little too idyllic to be entirely accurate. The Populists who "went to the people" incontestably did so with a burning desire to help the peasants in every possible practical way; but they also distributed books and pamphlets designed to stir up discontent and to propagandize the ideas of socialism. The mood of this movement, nonetheless, did involve assimilating oneself to the people, living their lives, and attempting to learn from them; it thus came much closer to Dostoevsky's own sociopolitical ideal of a *fusion* between the people and the intelligentsia than anything he had ever encountered in the left-wing ideologies of the 1860s. Moreover, the self-sacrificing ardor of these apostles to the people, many of whom came from wealthy and highly placed families, also served to confirm Dostoevsky's long-held and constantly reiterated opinion that the left-wing intelligentsia as a whole, misguided though their aims might be, were yet inspired by a pure-hearted moral idealism. From a letter to Dostoevsky by a minor writer named Dimitri Kishenskii, one of the contributors to *The Citizen*, we can see that Dostoevsky continued to remain true to this conviction. "You recognize in them *a thirst for renewal*," wrote Kishenskii (July 29, 1873), who objected to changes Dostoevsky had made in his antinihilist play. "I recognize in them ignorance and a thirst for chatter."

It is difficult to judge just how familiar Dostoevsky was with this shift of left-wing opinion in the years during which it gradually crystallized. Dostoevsky, as we know, unfailingly kept an eye on Russian literary and cultural developments, and we can hardly believe that he had not cast an occasional glance at the pages of *Notes of the Fatherland* (in which most of the material quoted above originally appeared). It is likely, however, that such straws in the wind made little impression on the isolated and embittered exile, nourishing his frustrated love for his homeland on an increasingly intolerant hatred of his European surroundings and regarding all of Russian radicalism root and branch as a noxious European weed flourishing on Russian soil. Only when he returned to Russia did it become emotionally possible for Dostoevsky to begin to distinguish between the various nuances of radical doctrine. And in his role as editor of *The Citizen* as well as intermittent contributor of a widely-read column called the *Diary of a Writer,* he naturally began to pay close attention once again to the existing spectrum of opinion on the Russian scene. If Dostoevsky was only dimly aware of the changed character of left-wing attitudes before 1873, however, he was quickly brought up to date in the early months of that year by two articles by Mikhailovsky. One was a general survey of recent writing which contained some remarks about Dostoevsky's *Diary of a Writer.* The second, entirely devoted to Dostoevsky and *The Devils,* contained the most important and noteworthy declaration of the ideological faith of the left-wing Populists of the early 1870s.

One of Dostoevsky's first entries in his *Diary of a Writer* contained some reminiscences of Belinsky, whom he depicted as the original be-getter of the atheistic socialism that had plagued Russia ever since. Be-linsky, he wrote, "knew that the revolution must necessarily begin with atheism. He had to dethrone that religion whence the moral foundations of the society rejected by him had sprung up. Family, property, per-sonal moral responsibility—these he denied radically." Mikhailovsky commented on this article that while "revolutionary in Europe, social-ism in Russia is conservative"; and he added that, as an economic doc-trine, socialism was not necessarily atheistic. In other words, Mikhailov-sky indicated to Dostoevsky that Populist socialism was primarily con-cerned with defending the Russian commune, and not with finding any new, non-Christian moral foundations for society. Also, by denying that socialism was necessarily atheistic, Mikhailovsky was endeavoring to dissociate it from the damaging context of the 1860s and to leave the way open for the Populists to accept, if not the Christian faith, then at least the moral and ethical tenets of Christianity which were so integral a part of Russian peasant life. That this was Mikhailovsky's intention becomes quite clear in his brilliant reflections on *The Devils.*

The publication of Dostoevsky's novel had, of course, been greeted with considerable hostility by the liberal and radical organs of the Rus-sian press. A particularly venomous and abusive review had been printed in *The Cause,* a journal that carried on the traditions and ideas of the "immoderate nihilism" of *The Russian Word.*[11] The author of this arti-cle, writing under a pseudonym, was the same P. N. Tkachev who had collaborated with Nechaev in 1869 and who perhaps recognized some allusions to his own ideas about "equality" in the system of Shigalev. In

311

any event, the article by Mikhailovsky sharply contrasted in tone with that of all the others emanating from sources sympathetic to the radical intelligentsia. Here Dostoevsky was called "one of the most talented of our contemporary writers"; and he was also complimented indirectly by Mikhailovsky's remarks on Dostoevsky's having taken over the editorship of *The Citizen*. If this publication were really harmful and objectionable, Mikhailovsky says, we might regret that so clever and gifted an editor was now in charge; but since *The Citizen* "had never advocated any clearly delineated absurdities and incongruities" (this indicates the relatively anodyne character of the magazine's conservatism), all we could feel was pity for Dostoevsky at becoming involved with so colorless and characterless a publication. The best thing about the magazine, he adds, are the *feuilletons* of *The Diary of a Writer*, "which without question one reads with great interest."

Mikhailovsky's opinion about *The Devils* as a work of art, whatever the personal respectfulness of his attitude toward its author, did not differ essentially from that of other hostile critics of the book. Referring to Dostoevsky's "brilliant psychiatric talent" (once again an echo of Belinsky's animadversions on *The Double* in 1847), Mikhailovsky wonders, with ironic innocence, why Dostoevsky does not write novels about European life between the fourteenth and sixteenth centuries. "All those flagellants, demoniacs, lycanthropes, all those *danses macabres*, feasts in time of plague and so forth, all that startling intermixture of egoism with a sense of sin and a thirst for expiation—what a fruitful theme that would be for Mr. Dostoevsky!" This is the prelude to Mikhailovsky's assertion that Dostoevsky has loaded down his characters with his own wealth of "eccentric ideas"—though he exempts the von Lembkes, Stephan Trofimovich, and Karmazinov from these strictures—and, as a result, has undermined the value of his book. Does Dostoevsky, he asks, "have any basis . . . for grouping around the Nechaev affair people soaked through with mysticism? I think not, and even less does he have the right to present them as types of contemporary Russian youth in general." The characters in the book represent only the obsessions and concerns of their author, not the prototypes on which the book is presumably based.

Indeed, in Mikhailovsky's view, even to have chosen the Nechaev affair as the subject for a novel was a mistake. For if Dostoevsky's vision were not so self-enclosed, "he would become convinced . . . that the Nechaev affair is a monster to such a degree and in so many ways that it cannot serve as a theme for a novel with a more or less broad range. It could serve as the material for a criminal novel, narrow and limited, and perhaps it might take a place in a picture of contemporary life, but not otherwise than as a third-rate episode." Mikhailovsky, incidentally, minced no words in his condemnation of the Nechaev affair, which he called "a painful, mistaken and criminal exception"; and two years earlier, covering the trial of Nechaev's followers for *Notes of the Fatherland*, he had expressed his approval of the conviction of twenty-seven of the defendants and praised the manner in which the trial had been conducted.

Beginning as a criticism of Dostoevsky's *The Devils*—whose characters, Mikhailovsky says, are not so much crushed by ideas of their own as by those arbitrarily invented for them by their author—the article broadens out into the most penetrating analysis of Dostoevsky's literary-ideological position yet to have appeared in Russian criticism. Using both the novel and several of Dostoevsky's early articles in *The Diary of a Writer*, Mikhailovsky focusses on Dostoevsky's conception of Russian radicalism as the final product of the disintegrating European influence on Russian culture. The Russian educated class, Dostoevsky believed, became detached from their people and from their people's religious faith and lost all capacity to distinguish between good and evil; hence they are inevitably doomed to the destruction that is shown to be their lot in *The Devils*. What Mikhailovsky argues—though he was forced, because of the censorship, to do so largely by implication—is that it is not necessary to share the people's religious faith in order to accept their moral values. Dostoevsky, he points out, like everyone else sometimes uses the word "God" in *The Devils* to mean a Supreme Being and sometimes he uses it as a synonym for "national particularities" and national customs; and in this way he identifies attachment to his people with religious faith. This theory, says Mikhailovsky, is "simply impossible," and in explicitly refusing to discuss it any further he clearly indicates his desire to disengage the question of religious faith from that of the relation between the intelligentsia and the people.

This relation is much more complicated, Mikhailovsky argues, than Dostoevsky is willing to admit. For him there is only, on the one hand,

313

the unequivocal condemnation of the intelligentsia from Stavrogin to Shatov pronounced in *The Devils*; or on the other, the equally unequivocal and uncritical glorification of the people in some of the pieces in *The Diary of a Writer*. "He [Dostoevsky] is a happy man," writes Mikhailovsky sharply. "He knows that whatever happens with the people, in the end it will save itself and us." All those who do not share this total acceptance of the people, with all its customs and beliefs, are called *citoyens* by Dostoevsky, who gives them this French label to stress their total alienation from their country. But whatever may have been the case in the past, Mikhailovsky asserts, Dostoevsky is making a serious mistake in overlooking the new group of *citoyens* who do not fit his classifications. For this new group, while fully sharing his own reverence for "the Russian people's truth," nonetheless finds the traditions of this "truth" contradictory and confusing, and it accepts only that part of it which coincides with the general principles of "humanity" acquired from other sources (the ideals of political liberty, social justice, and economic equality embodied in socialism). Indeed, as Mikhailovsky tellingly remarks, Dostoevsky does the very same thing himself in many instances, though he refuses to admit that he is arbitrarily identifying his own humane values with "the Russian people's truth."

What characterizes this new group of *citoyens*, in any case, is precisely their devotion to the Russian people and their feeling of guilt toward and indebtedness to those at whose expense their own advantages have been acquired. "We have come to the conclusion that we are the debtors of the people," Mikhailovsky writes, in a passage that instantly became famous. "Perhaps this paragraph is not in the people's truth, surely it is not, but we place it at the center of our life and activity, though perhaps not always fully consciously." As a result, the radicals for whom Mikhailovsky undertakes to speak are willing to forgo agitation for legal and political rights, which would benefit only themselves, and they devote their energies to working for social changes of immediate benefit to the people. "Giving the preference to social reforms over political ones," Mikhailovsky explains, "we are only renouncing the strengthening of our rights and the development of our freedom as instruments for the oppression of the people and even further sin." The situation of the *citoyens* is thus deeply tragic precisely because the very "progress" they wish to bring to the people is itself tainted with the age-old injustice they are repenting. "The expiation of an involuntary sin with the aid of means attained by sin—that is the task of the *citoyens*, though I am not of course speaking of all."

All this, written in Dostoevsky's own Christian vocabulary, aims at showing him that his conception of the radical intelligentsia is woefully mistaken. "If you would stop playing with the word 'God,' " Mikhailovsky says directly, "and became acquainted somewhat more closely with your shameful socialism, you would be convinced that it coincides with at least some of the elements of the Russian people's truth." And Mikhailovsky concludes by enumerating all the new "devils" which have recently emerged to plague Russia, but which Dostoevsky has neglected to include in his book. "Russia, that frenzied invalid that you have depicted, is being girded with railroads, besprinkled with factories and banks—and in your novel there is not a single indication of this world! You focus your attention on an insignificant handful of madmen and scoundrels! There is no devil of national wealth [industrial expansion] in your novel, the most widespread devil of all and less than all the others knowing the boundaries of good and evil . . . The devil of service to the people—even if it is a devil, driven out of the ailing body of Russia—thirsts for expiation in one or another form, and this is its entire substance. Better avoid it entirely if you can see only its pathological forms."

This article made a considerable impression on Dostoevsky, and he hastened to acknowledge its impact in the *Diary of a Writer*. The next issue of *The Citizen* (February 19, 1873) contained the following words: "I have read the articles by Messers. Skabichevsky and N. M. in the *Notes of the Fatherland*. Both these articles were in some sense for me a new revelation." [12] Several months later he drops Skabichevsky, the Populist literary critic, and returns specifically to speak of N. M. alone and of the "revelation" of his article. "I cannot forget N. M. of the *Notes of the Fatherland* and of my 'debts' to him" Dostoevsky writes, adroitly using the Populists' own terminology. "I have not the honor of knowing him personally, and likewise have never had the pleasure of hearing anything about him as a private individual. But I am convinced with all my heart that he is one of the most sincere publicists to be found in Petersburg." [13] This tribute to Mikhailovsky shows

315

that Dostoevsky was only too eager to enter into the dialogue with the radical intelligentsia that this new cultural situation made possible—and to which, he could justly feel, he had been invited by Mikhailovsky.

At the same time, Dostoevsky had no illusions—nor did Mikhailovsky's article allow him to have any—about the major point on which he and the radicals would continue to differ. "Mr. N. M. attracted my attention for the first time by his opinions about my opinions of Belinsky, socialism, and atheism, and then about my novel *The Devils*," he writes. ". . . The main thing is that I cannot at all understand what Mr. N. M. wishes to say by assuring me that socialism in Russia will unquestionably be conservative. Did he not think somehow to console me in this way, assuming that I was a diehard conservative? I venture to assure Mr. N. M. that 'this earthly realm' also displeases me very much. But to write and assert that socialism is not atheistic, that socialism is not at all the formula for atheism, and that atheism is not at all its central, fundamental essence—that surprises me extremely in a writer who, apparently, has been so much taken up with this subject."

Dostoevsky thus continues to insist on identifying socialism with atheism, as he had done all through the 1860s; but this does not mean, as might appear at first sight, that nothing has been fundamentally changed in his position. Certainly he did not alter his bedrock convictions in the slightest; but there is a noticeable shift of accent and emphasis during the 1870s in the way these convictions are opposed to those of the radical intelligentsia. Since "atheism" no longer meant a negation of Christian morality *as such*, there is a new mildness of tone toward the radicals in this last period of his career. Moreover, the focus of attention is no longer on figures like the underground man (who denies, in Part I, the possibility of any kind of morality because of a theory of moral determinism), or like Raskolnikov and Stavrogin (who replace Christian conscience by a utilitarian calculus, or by a theory of total amoral indifferentism). The Populists, however, while accepting the moral-ethical tenets of "the Russian people's truth," refused to accept their people's traditional Christian beliefs: they denied the supernatural divinity of Christ and all the miraculous consequences that flow from this divinity, which for Dostoevsky was the only firm anchorage for Christian values. Hence we find such figures as Versilov in *A Raw Youth* and Ivan Karamazov, who fully and consciously accept Christian moral-ethical values but cannot ground them in the assurance of a firmly held faith. Sketches of such a character type had, of course, appeared earlier in Ippolit Terentyev and Kirillov; but this character type does not occupy the center of the stage in Dostoevsky's novels until the 1870s. It represents his anticipation of an ideological mutation which occurred at this time and which allowed him to adapt his artistic resources to the new phase of left-wing ideology.

Among the factors contributing to Dostoevsky's awareness of this new mood of the intelligentsia, we must certainly include his friendly and semipaternal working relations with V. V. Timofeeva, who was at the same time a member of the inner circle of young Populist contributors to *Notes of the Fatherland*. And two anecdotes about Dostoevsky in 1873–1874, culled from her extremely valuable memoir about him, take on their full significance only when seen in relation to this general shift of attitudes. Once she told him that she had just read *Notes from Underground*, and that it had kept her up all night. " 'I couldn't rid myself of the impression . . . How horrible—the soul of man! But what a frightening truth!' . . . Feodor Mikhailovich smiled with a clear, open smile. 'Kraevsky told me then [he responded], that it was my *chef d'oeuvre*, and that I should always write in that manner. But I don't agree with him. It's too gloomy. *Es ist schon ein überwundener Standpunkt.* Now I am able to write more brightly, in a more conciliatory way!' " [14] Dostoevsky's use of the German phrase here, with its semiparodistic evocation of a ponderous philosophical tome, appears to indicate that he is not talking primarily about the standpoint of his personal feelings (as has often been conjectured) but about the published doctrines to which *Notes from Underground* was a response and which had necessitated the underground man's frenzied protest.

In an even more revelatory exchange between the two on the subject of religion, the central theme of Dostoevsky's dialogue with the Populists is expressed with superbly plastic simplicity. Challenged to define her "ideal" by Dostoevsky, the spirited young woman replies that it is contained in the Gospels.

"As a child [she says] I was very religious, and read them constantly."
"But since then, of course, you have grown up, become wiser, and, having received an education from science and art . . ." On the corners of his [Dostoevsky's] lips appeared the "crooked" smile so well-known to me.

317

"Then," I continued in the same tone, "under the influence of science, this religiosity began to take another form, but I have always thought, and still think, that we have nothing better and finer than the Gospels."

"But how do you understand the Gospels? They are interpreted in different ways. In your opinion, what is their essential substance?"

The question he posed to me made me think about the matter for the first time. But immediately—like some far-off voice from the depths of my memory—the answer came: "The realization of the teachings of Christ on earth, in our life, in our conscience . . ."

"And that's all?"—he said slowly, in a tone of disillusionment.

This seemed very little indeed even to me. "No, there's still . . . Not everything finishes here, on earth. All this life on earth is only a step . . . to another existence."

"To other worlds!" he exclaimed triumphantly, throwing up his arm to the wide-open window, through which could be seen then a beautiful, bright, and luminous June sky.[15]

Not all the Populists by any means shared Miss Timofeeva's sense that life on earth was a transition to other worlds; but the hope of bringing them to this realization and recognition, on the basis of their own reverence for the teachings of Christ, is what inspired Dostoevsky's works in the 1870s.

Princeton University

NOTES

1. V. V. Timofeeva, in *F. M. Dostoevskii v Vospominanyakh Sovremennikov*, ed. A. S. Dolinin (Moscow, 1964), 2. 127.

2. All quotations (unless otherwise indicated in the article) by N. K. Mikhailovsky come from articles in *Notes of the Fatherland* for the years indicated.

3. P. M. Lavrov, cited in *Istoria Russkoi Literaturi XIX v.*, ed. D. N. Ovsyaniko-Kulikovskii (Moscow, 1910), 4. 22.

4. K. D. Kavelin, cited in *Sochinenia N. K. Mikhailovskogo* (St. Petersburg, 1896–1897), 1. 641.

5. D. N. Ovsyaniko-Kulikovskii, *Istoria Russkoi Intelligentsii* (St. Petersburg, 1909), 2. 197.

6. James H. Billington, *Mikhailovsky and Russian Populism* (London, 1958), p. 120.

7. The magazines edited by Dostoevsky and his elder brother Mikhail in the early 1860s preached this ideology (pochvennichestvo, from *pochva*—soil). This doctrine also stressed the importance for the Russian intelligentsia of deriving inspiration from the beliefs—and particularly from the moral and religious values—of the Russian peo-

ple. Other prominent representatives of this ideology and contributors to the journals of the Dostoevsky brothers were N. N. Strakhov and Apollon Grigoriev.

8. Peter Lavrov, *Historical Letters,* tr. James P. Scanlan (Berkeley–Los Angeles, 1967), p. 138.

9. *Dostoevsky's Occasional Writings,* translated by David Magarschack (New York, 1963), p. 82.

10. Peter Kropotkin, *Memoirs of a Revolutionist,* ed. James Allen Rogers (New York, 1962), pp. 198–199.

11. *Delo (The Cause),* 1873, No. 3, pp. 151–179; No. 4, pp. 359–381.

12. F. M. Dostoevsky, *The Diary of a Writer,* tr. Boris Brasol (New York, 1954), p. 57.

13. A. S. Dolinin, *Poslednie romani Dostoevskogo* (Moscow–Leningrad, 1963), p. 11.

14. Timofeeva, *F. M. Dostoevskii,* p. 176.

15. Ibid., p. 150.

JOHN O. MC CORMICK

Emerson, Vico, and History

Whoever has read both Vico and Emerson has been nagged by the similarity of the two men's minds and by the similarity of the questions they raise, yet a precise image of that similarity will not readily yield itself; it is rather a mirror-image seen in the dusk. I propose here to dissipate the dusk somewhat by indicating how Emerson might have known Vico, by examining points of contiguity in their works, and by so doing, to invite from some future scholar the full scrutiny that the subject deserves.

The subject is attractive in two major, overlapping, respects. First as an example of genuine influence extending from eighteenth-century Naples to nineteenth-century Concord. One writes "genuine influence" defensively, since in literary circles of late, if not in historical or philosophical circles, the value of influence studies has been questioned. The value of determining how Emerson's mind took shape does not need abstract defense here. Secondly, both Vico and Emerson are major points of reference for our understanding of romanticism in Europe and America, while at the same time their relationship is richly informing to us of the still mysterious manner in which ideas moved between Europe and America in the nineteenth century.

Let us first dispose of the mechanical matter of Emerson's acquaintance, direct or indirect, with Vico. Although we know a good deal about Emerson's reading, we lack evidence that Emerson ever had a volume of Vico's in his hands.[1] From our considerable, although still incomplete, knowledge of the diffusion of Vico's work and thought throughout

320

Europe and North America before and during the years of Emerson's intellectual apprenticeship (Emerson was born in 1803 and died in 1882), we may with high certainty speculate upon the sources of Emerson's secondary, if not primary, acquaintanceship with the great Neapolitan. While Emerson continued to shift and evolve his philosophical position from the time of his graduation from Harvard in 1821 to approximately 1870, he took up his basic attitudes in the years between 1821 and the publication of *Nature* in 1836. The outer biographical landmarks of that period were his appointment as pastor of the Second Church of Boston in 1829; the death of his first wife in 1831; his resignation from his pastorate in September 1832, followed by his departure for Europe in December. He remained in Europe for nine months, returning in October 1833. He remarried in 1835, and wrote *Nature,* the essay which contains in essence or in full statement the ideas that were to occupy him for the rest of his life. Emerson travelled again to Europe, to England and to France, in 1847–1848, and once again in 1872, although by that date his career was effectively over. The old-fashioned, debunking view of Emerson as a provincial, village-Pollyanna pseudophilosopher, writing cheery essays for framed quotation in the town bank is of course unworthy. He was, rather, cosmopolitan, sophisticated, humble in the best sense, and both brave and energetic in his lifelong quest for philosophical enlightenment. That he was eclectic, disorganized, by turns brilliant and repetitious, has made him difficult for us to see in hard outline. Given those qualities and that career, it was probable if not inevitable that he should have met Vico in one guise or another, and possibly on Vico's home ground.

Emerson, aged twenty-nine, landed at Syracuse from Malta on 23 February 1833 and arrived at Naples on 12 March. He remained in Naples until 25 March, then until mid-June he toured on to Rome, Florence, and other Italian cities.[2] Emerson knew Italian, although indifferently; he does not report having met the kind of Italian intellectual who would have directed his attention to Vico, nor does Vico's name appear in the voluminous journals. After Italy, Emerson travelled to Switzerland, France, and England, where among others he met Carlyle and Wordsworth. Although Emerson was already deeply immersed in romanticism, his meeting with Carlyle served to sharpen his focus upon the German romantics, whom Carlyle so fully admired, and to give authority to insights, both literary and historical, that we can see flitting across Emerson's mind in the early journals, sermons, and letters.

Here the question of Emerson's acquaintance with the Germans arises, together with the possibility of his having met Vico by way of German translation and German derivation from Vico. Emerson's German was better than his Italian, although he seems always to have read German works in English translation when a translation was available. Weber's translation into German of *The New Science* appeared in 1822; it is possible that Emerson encountered the volume in his travels. It is certain that his intellectual travels took him to a large number of German writers who we know were familiar with Vico and in varying degrees influenced by him.[3] Emerson's foremost German connection with Vico was Churchill's translation of Herder, *Outlines of a Philosophy of History of Man* (London, 1800), which Emerson took out of the Harvard College Library in 1829.[4] Emerson's friend and associate, Ripley, popularized Herder among the New England transcendentalists. Second only to Herder was of course Goethe, whom Emerson knew well, early and late; not only is Goethe "The Writer" in *Representative Men*, but the journals and letters also abound in references to and discussions of him. *Representative Men* (Boston, 1850) tantalizingly anticipates portions of Baron von Bunsen's *Egypt's Place in Universal History* (1852), which Cameron lists in a five-volume edition (London, 1848–1867). Cameron also lists works of Friedrich Jacobi, Barthold Niebuhr, Hegel, and Friedrich von Schlegel, all of whom we know to be likely sources of Vichian influence.[5]

Among British writers, the pattern of influence upon Emerson remains obscure; much research remains to be done. In the case of Carlyle, for example, no one has yet convincingly demonstrated a link to Vico, yet one suspects it is there. Emerson revered Carlyle above all others, to the degree that he served as Carlyle's unpaid American literary agent. Emerson studied Hume's *History of England* while still a student at Harvard. A devoted although critical reader of Coleridge, Emerson might have encountered Vico in the *Theory of Life* or in other utterances by Coleridge; here, again, the exact dimensions of Coleridge's connections with Vico need further investigation than they have received.[6] If, as Fisch suggests, "the Vichian ideas scattered through the writings" of, among others, Hume, Lowth, Burke, Warburton, and Wollaston are indeed Vico's,[7] so then they may well have been Emerson's sources, for their works appear in Cameron's lists of Emerson's reading.

In France, the pattern of influence is clearer than it is in Britain. Nor is it merely a matter of Emerson's coming to Vico by way of Michelet and Cousin; Emerson himself exerted a certain influence upon a circle at the Collège de France consisting of Adam Mickiéwicz, Edgar Quinet, Michelet, and possibly Cousin himself.[8] The Polish poet and professor of Slavonic, Mickiéwicz, read some of Emerson's essays in 1838 and promptly infected Quinet with his enthusiasm. Quinet, a professor of European literature, generated considerable excitement over Emerson, presenting him to his students in company with Vico, Condorcet, Herder, and Hegel. Michelet, too, admired Emerson.[9] But the center of Vichian influence in France was Victor Cousin. Cousin knew Vico through the Neapolitan Pietro de Angelis, and it was Cousin who urged Michelet to translate *The New Science*. Michelet's abridgement, *Principes de la philosophie de l'histoire*, appeared in 1827. Emerson may or may not have read the *Principes*; he did read Michelet's vast *Histoire de France*,[10] which of course is fundamentally Vichian. Ironically, Emerson was in Paris on 15 May 1848, the day of the abortive uprising. He had not a clue to the revolution that he in part witnessed, but he wrote to his wife that he "heard Michelet on Indian Philosophy" that day.[11]

Victor Cousin's Sorbonne lectures of 1828–1830, in which he presented his eclectic philosophy and his philosophy of history, had an impact both in France and abroad similar to the impact of Sartre's work after World War II. Those lectures were published in three volumes entitled *Cours de philosophie* (Paris, 1829), and Emerson bought them soon after publication.[12] He also doubtless knew the translations in America of Cousin's work by a Boston Swedenborgian, Henning Gotfried Linberg, *Introduction to the History of Philosophy* (Boston, 1832); and that of O. W. Wright, *Course of the History of Modern Philosophy*, in two volumes (New York, 1857). Cousin's Lecture XI, "Historians of Humanity," is most relevant, for he cited there Bossuet, Vico's *New Science*, Herder's *Ideen*, and more briefly, Voltaire, Adam Ferguson, Turgot, and Condorcet.

Cousin's work, like Emerson's, reinforces our conception of nineteenth-century interest in philosophical history, an interest that insured the dissemination of Vico's ideas. I want now to indicate the nature of Emerson's idea of history and to show that often the movement of his mind parallels Vico's, if it does not frankly derive, at least in part, from Vico's system. At the outset it must be emphasized that reading Emerson is like walking through a rich archaeological site; you turn up potsherds with your toe, then you dig for the fragments of the whole. Not all readers turn up the same potsherds. Emerson has been accused, for example, of resisting history and of conceiving reality itself as "ultimately ahistorical. That this course of thought involves the reduction of history to an illusion and experience to a pin-point present, and finally to the obliteration of the distinction between contingent and absolute Being, Emerson is well aware." [13] Such a view, based upon an interpretation of Emerson's theological leanings, is partial and indeed wrong. As a good romantic, Emerson was concerned not to separate nature from history, but rather to incorporate history into nature. In the process, Emerson met Vico in at least four central points: in his view of language; in his lifelong obsession with the relationship between the individual and social institutions; in his awareness of the difficulty of reconciling Christianity with history; and in his apprehension of what history in fact is.

Early in *The New Science,* Vico emphasizes the importance of etymologies for our understanding of institutions, "beginning with . . . original and proper meanings and pursuing the natural progress of their metaphors according to the order of ideas, on which the history of languages must proceed." [14] Vico further asserts his proof that human social institutions share the same "mental vocabulary," are substantially the same in all nations, "but are diversely expressed in language according to their diverse modifications . . ." (par. 355). Vico's tracing of the etymology of *"persona,"* for example, emphasizes his eye for precision, his distaste for abstraction, his bravery in conjecture, and his confidence in his method (par. 1034). Vico's theory of language, which is allied to his grasp of the importance of archaeology, constituted a revolution in the European idea of historical cognition; it opened doors upon entire areas of historical reality. Its simplicity was illusory, and such philosophical historians as we have are still working out the implications of Vico's ideas.

Emerson's theory of language is similar in outline to Vico's, although, predictably, Emerson's impulse is to encompass language and history within his theory of nature. Part 4 of *Nature* (1836) begins:

Language is a third use [after "Commodity" and "Beauty"] which Nature subserves to man. Nature is the vehicle of thought, and in a simple, double, and threefold degree.
1. Words are signs of natural facts.
2. Particular natural facts are symbols of particular spiritual facts.
3. Nature is the symbol of spirit.

1. Words are signs of natural facts. The use of natural history is to give us aid in supernatural history; the use of the outer creation, to give us language for the beings and changes of the inward creation. Every word which is used to express a moral or intellectual fact, if traced to its root, is found to be borrowed from some material appearance. *Right* means *straight; wrong* means *twisted; Spirit* primarily means *wind; transgression,* the crossing of a *line; supercilious,* the raising of an *eyebrow.*[15]

Having established a spiritual footing, Emerson moves on. He repeats, possibly after Herder, the romantic theory of the origin of poetry in the origins of language itself, associating the primitive with the poetic. "As we go back in history, language becomes more picturesque, until its infancy, when it is all poetry; or all spiritual facts are represented by natural symbols." [16] Herder perhaps, but just as likely Vico's *New Science* (pars. 374–377), where poetry is associated with the language of the "first men," with the origins of religion, and where Vico, like Emerson, proposes an ethical purpose for great poetry: "to teach the vulgar to act virtuously, as the poets have taught themselves . . ." (par. 376). Great poetry for Vico, to be sure, is not the language of his first, brutal men, but of a later age. Emerson, in the tradition of Herder and Rousseau, associates natural, untainted man with poetic vision. "A man's power to connect his thought with its proper symbol, and so to utter it, depends on the simplicity of his character. . . . The corruption of man is followed by the corruption of language." Country life, then, is superior to "the artificial and curtailed life of cities," for the language of the country derives directly from things in nature, and therefore it is close to ultimate truth. "A fact is the end or last issue of spirit." [17] Nature for Emerson is what the development of institutions is for Vico, but, in his theory of language, each has a vision of unity and an impulse to associate poetry with divinity. And each constructs a theory of language in historical terms, although with contrasting points of emphasis that are more clearly seen in other contexts.

The lectures which Emerson published under the title *Representative Men* might seem to negate utterly Vico's attention to institutions in *The New Science*. Individual men figure almost not at all in Vico's work, while Emerson was capable of saying that "there is properly no history, only biography." [18] Like Cousin, Emerson developed the romantic theory that institutions are the products of great men, of genius in fact, rather than the reverse. Yet in developing his theory, Emerson is vulnerable to doubt, and his language displays an awareness of history that can only be called Vichian; we become aware that his easy formula of history as biography does not do justice to the actual complexity of his idea of history. Emerson would like to account for genius in the biographies of great men and to suppress evidence obvious to him from observation of human institutions. Embedded in *Representative Men* is a vision very like Vico's wonderfully compact "Men first feel necessity, then look for utility, next attend to comfort, still later amuse themselves with pleasure, thence grow dissolute in luxury, and finally go mad and waste their substance" (par. 241). In "Uses of Great Men," Emerson meditates upon the social context in which great men arise, then writes "But enormous populations, if they be beggars, are disgusting, like moving cheese, like hills of ants, or of fleas—the more, the worse." [19] Here we may hear an echo of Vico's idea of men as serfs: "The nature of peoples is first crude . . ." (par. 242). Emerson says immediately that "The gods of fable are the shining moments of great men," and again we may sense Vico's second kind of "nature," the heroic (par. 917).

Emerson's mind ranges through history for *exempla*. He moves back and forth in a restless attempt to discover transcendental unity: "The student of history is like a man going into a warehouse to buy cloths or carpets. He fancies he has a new article. If he go to the factory, he shall find that his new stuff still repeats the scrolls and rosettes which are found on the interior walls of the pyramids of Thebes. Man can paint, or make, or think nothing but man. He believes that the great material elements had their origin from his thought. And our philosophy finds one essence collected or distributed." [20] In place of Vico's excessively logical system and its triads within triads, Emerson forces all experience into "polarities"—he constructs a dialectic where no dialectic may in fact exist. Of the virtues of great men against their vices he writes, "The centripetence augments the contrifugence. We balance one man with his opposite, and the health of the state depends on the see-saw." [21] Plato is one of Emerson's representative men, and like Vico, Plato identifies the "nature" of a thing with its "origin," believing that "all nations must pass through the same course of development, according to one universal law." [22] For Emerson, Plato is "the Bible of the learned for twenty-two hundred years, every brisk young man, who says in succession fine things to each reluctant generation—Boethius, Rabelais, Erasmus, Bruno, Locke, Rousseau, Alfieri, Coleridge—is some reader of Plato, translating into the vernacular, wittily, his good things. . . . Calvinism is in his Phaedo: Christianity is in it. Mahometanism draws all its philosophy, in its handbook of morals, the Akhlak-y-Jalaly, from him. Mysticism finds in Plato all its texts." [23] As is so often the case with Emerson, this sort of thing resists analysis; we may only look at it and sense the play of the mind. Other portions of the essay on Plato are more amenable to analysis. Emerson says that the exterior biography of Plato is unimportant, but that what matters is Plato's "supreme elevation . . . in the intellectual history of our race. . . ." Emerson then quietly gives us a startlingly Vico-like statement: "The first period of a nation, as of an individual, is the period of unconscious strength. . . . The progress is to accuracy, to skill, to truth, from blind force." He continues, "There is a moment, in the history of every nation, when, proceeding out of this brute youth, the perceptive powers reach their ripeness, and have not yet become microscopic . . . That is the moment of adult health, the culmination of power." [24] Thus, Emerson writes, the history of Europe is unfolded. The obvious parallels to Vico, however, must be seen in the perspective of Emerson's awareness of evolutionary theory, particularly that of Laplace.

At this point the whole question of Emerson's ambiguous relationship to the nineteenth-century idea of progress must be briefly examined. Through his readings of natural history and his apparent acceptance of the American dominantly optimistic view of human and social potentiality, Emerson would seem not only to belong to, but to lead the party of the future, the troops of perfection. Such is not the fact. Emerson's Calvinism, which produced his meditation in *Nature* on human and historical degeneration,[25] together with numerous entries in the journals, unite to deny any simple view of the optimistic Emerson. Emerson undeniably wanted to share wholeheartedly in the American ethos, but events such as the slavery controversy, the Mexican War, and the Civil War combined to deny his impulse.[26] Throughout *Representative Men* a significant tension exists between the romantic view of the glory and genius of great men and a quite unromantic determinism that suggests Vico. Emerson, for example, moves from his idea of the vegetable theory of genius (in "Swedenborg; or, The Mystic") to an odd sort of determinism in the essays on "Napoleon" and "Goethe." After establishing Bonaparte as the prototypical representative man, Emerson writes of the European cry in 1814, "*Assez de Bonaparte*": "It was not Bonaparte's fault. He did all that in him lay, to live and thrive without moral principle. It was the nature of things, the eternal law of man and of the world, which baulked and ruined him; and the result, in a million experiments, will be the same." [27] The example of Goethe leads Emerson to a meditation on the superiority of contemplation to action. "Act, if you like—but you do it at your peril. Men's actions are too strong for them. Show me a man who has acted, and who has not been the victim and slave of his action. What they have done commits and enforces them to do the same again. The first act, which was to be an experiment, becomes a sacrament. The fiery reformer embodies his aspiration in some rite or covenant, and he and his friends cleave to the form, and lose the aspiration. The Quaker has established Quakerism, and the Shaker has established his monastery and his dance; and, although each prates of spirit, there is no spirit, but repetition, which is anti-spiritual." [28] The statement seems to fall back upon itself like egg whites in a cake. Emerson says both more and less than he sets out to say. He reverts to the idea of "repetition," and repetition is not only in his term "anti-spiritual" but also pessimistic and reminiscent of Vico. Our final impression of *Representative Men* is that of a man groping for a philosophy which will at once affirm his temperamental outlook and accommodate his not-fully-realized intellectual convictions. History itself both stands in the way and offers an ambiguous resolution. We must therefore turn to Emerson's confrontation with history before we may summarize Emerson's points of reference to Vico.

One source of difficulty is that, in Auerbach's phrase, Emerson is an "aesthetic historicist." History for Emerson is both poetry and process. He shares with Vico an attempt to find Christian unity in history; we are continually reminded in reading Emerson of Vico's phrase, "Thus all ancient Rome was a serious poem . . . and ancient jurisprudence was a severe poetry" (par. 343), words that Emerson himself might have written. Where Vico uncovers unity in the *ricorsi*, Emerson discovers unity through a process of reducing historical events to aspects of individual experience. Although Vico's theory of history violates the traditional Christian idea of continuum, he asserts unity under a basically Christian view. Emerson fought a lifelong skirmish with Christianity, yet whenever he meditated upon history, he emerged with a guilt-laden assertion of Christian unity. "This life of ours," he wrote in the essay "History," "is stuck round with Egypt, Greece, Gaul, England, War, Colonization, Church, Court and Commerce, as with so many flowers and wild ornaments grave and gay. I will not make more account of them. I believe in Eternity. I can find Greece, Asia, Italy, Spain and the Islands—the genius and creative principle of each and of all eras, in my own mind." [29] Out of context, such a statement may sound fatuous, but Emerson is getting at what he calls the intrinsic identity of history. "There is, at the surface, infinite variety of things; at the centre there is simplicity of cause." [30] His mind reverts continually to the Greeks: "Every man passes personally through a Grecian period." And again of Greek tragedy, "Our admiration of the antique is not admiration of the old, but of the natural." [31] The Greek myths for Emerson contain universal verities, while Prometheus is a prototype of Jesus Christ. Emerson's historical chronology is very like Vico's, "To determine the times and places for such a history . . . and thus to give it certainty by means of its own . . . metaphysical chronology and geography, our Science applies a likewise metaphysical art of criticism with regard to the founders of these same nations . . ." (par. 348). Emerson's is indeed a "metaphysical chronology," if not geography and criticism. Emerson writes of Belzoni's excavation at Thebes, "They live again to the mind, or are *now*." [32] All historical experience is individual as a result of what Emerson calls "correspondency." In the conclusion to "History" he writes, "Thus in all ways does the soul concentrate and reproduce its treasures for each pupil. He too shall pass through the whole cycle of experience." [33] This is followed by an almost despairing outcry at man's inability to comprehend history: "I hold our actual knowledge very cheap. Hear the rats in the wall, see the lizard on the fence, the fungus under foot, the lichen on the log. What do I know sympathetically, morally, of either of these worlds of life? . . . what does history yet record of the metaphysical annals of man? What light does it shed on those mysteries which we hide under the names Death and Immortality? Yet every history should be written in a wisdom which divined the range of our affinities and looked at facts as symbols. I am ashamed to see what a shallow village tale our so-called History is. How many times we must say Rome, and Paris, and Constantinople! What does Rome know of rat and lizard? What are Olympiads and Consulates to these neighboring systems of being? Nay, what food or experience or succor have they for the Esquimaux seal-hunter, for the Kanáka in his canoe, for the fisherman, the stevedore, the porter?" [34] In such a statement with its anti-intellectual overtones, we see the distance that the romantics had travelled from Vico, but more significantly we see the dimensions of their debt to Vico.

The number of correspondences between Emerson's thought and *The New Science* are too great to be charged to coincidence. Although Emerson is in no sense as original a writer as Vico, his historical thought is a valuable chapter in the intellectual history of romanticism. Emerson's frequent use of words such as "repetition," "correspondencies," "rotation," his many metaphors of movement and change, indicate a lively affinity for Vico's system. What Emerson seems to do, finally, is to flatten out the *ricorsi* in an apparently unhistorical manner. He cannot escape from history, however, nor does he really want to. History for him becomes both a spiral and a simultaneity. Where Vico is rational and logical, Emerson to the modern ear is annoyingly vatic. Both men were teasing into being a system, beginning from opposite points and arriving at a place which, if it is not exactly the same, is interestingly similar.

Rutgers University

NOTES

1. Thanks to K. W. Cameron, *Ralph Waldo Emerson's Reading* (Raleigh, N.C., 1941) and *Emerson the Essayist*, 2 vols. (Raleigh, N.C., 1945). In the nature of things, however, Cameron's lists are not and cannot be complete.

2. *The Journals and Miscellaneous Notebooks of R. W. Emerson,* ed. Alfred R. Ferguson, 5 vols. (Cambridge, Mass., 1964), 4. 122–123.

3. As Max H. Fisch has shown in brilliant outline in his "Introduction" to *The Autobiography of Giambattista Vico,* tr. M. H. Fisch and T. G. Bergin (Ithaca, N.Y., 1963, 1st printing 1944), pp. 67–72.

4. Cameron, *Emerson's Reading,* p. 47.

5. See also René Wellek, "Emerson and German Philosophy," *New England Quarterly,* XVI (1943), 41–62.

6. Fisch, "Introduction," *The Autobiography of Giambattista Vico,* pp. 83–84.

7. Ibid., p. 82.

8. And here is another inviting subject for research: the French Emerson. One suspects that the French Emerson, like the French Poë and the French Whitman, may differ substantially from their American prototypes. The existing studies in French, always intelligent but oddly oblique, of Marie Dugard, Régis Michaud, and Maurice Gonnaud offer a way into the subject.

9. Ralph L. Rusk, *The Life of Ralph Waldo Emerson* (New York, 1949), p. 327.

10. Cameron, *Emerson's Reading,* p. 91.

11. Ralph L. Rusk, ed., *The Letters of Ralph Waldo Emerson,* 6 vols. (New York, 1939), 4. 72–73. Emerson also mentions Michelet in a letter to Hedge concerning *The Dial. Letters,* 3. 84.

12. Cameron, *Emerson the Essayist,* 1. 304.

13. A. Robert Caponigri, "Brownson and Emerson: Nature and History," *New England Quarterly,* XVIII (1945), 371.

14. *The New Science of Giambattista Vico,* tr. T. G. Bergin and M. H. Fisch (New York, 1961), par. 354.

15. *The Complete Essays; and Other Writings of Ralph Waldo Emerson,* ed., Brooks Atkinson (New York, 1950), p. 14.

16. *Complete Essays,* p. 16.

17. Ibid., pp. 17–19.

18. In "History," *Complete Essays,* p. 127.

19. R. W. Emerson, *Representative Men* (Boston, 1865; 1st ed. 1850), p. 10.

20. Ibid., p. 11.

21. Ibid., p. 32.

22. K. R. Popper, *The Open Society and Its Enemies,* 2 vols. (London, 1957), 1. 221, note 4.

23. *Representative Men,* pp. 43–44.

24. Ibid., pp. 48–50.

25. *Complete Essays,* p. 36.

26. C. Mildred Silver, "Emerson and the Idea of Progress," *American Literature,* XII (1940), 1–19. Miss Silver's excellent article does not seem to me to do justice to Emerson's dark side.

27. *Representative Men,* p. 252.

28. Ibid., pp. 262–263.

29. *Complete Essays,* p. 126.
30. Ibid., p. 129.
31. Ibid., pp. 134–135.
32. Ibid., p. 127.
33. Ibid., p. 142.
34. Ibid., p. 143.

HOWARD NEMEROV

On the Resemblances between Science and Religion

This is a poetic exercise. I begin by assuming that the evident, large, and significant differences between science and religion, scientist and priest, have been amply acknowledged and endlessly elaborated, so that the characteristic relation between science and religion has been either enmity, that is, polar opposition, or no relation at all (the claim that they occupy mutually exclusive realms of discourse). It will be obvious at once that polar opposites must necessarily have much in common; and as to the other claim, that they divide the world between them, maintaining separate spheres of influence, that is a common interim and compromise solution for polar opposites and may be no more satisfactory or enduring here than it is seen to be in politics.

When two things are said to be opposites, it becomes a duty of the intelligence to look for their similarities.

When two things are said to have nothing in common, it becomes a pleasure of the intelligence to find out what they have in common.

The essential procedure of physical science is the experiment, a compound of hypothesis and observation which will produce the same results for anyone, anywhere, at any time, so long as the conditions and steps of the original are scrupulously and rigorously adhered to. If the same results are not obtained, either the hypothesis is incorrect or the person repeating the experiment repeated it inexactly in some way. In prin-

ciple, the first alternative is always possible, for even the most adequately supported and long-established hypotheses are not supposed,
quite, to become doctrine or dogma; but in practice, when the physics
teacher sets up his apparatus before the class and the predicted result
fails to occur he does not commonly announce a revolution in physics
but apologizes for his error.

The essential procedure of religion is the ritual, a compound of explanation and observation which will produce the same results that have
made the assertions of the original *quod semper, quod ubique, quod ab
omnibus,* but only if the conditions and steps of the original are scrupulously and rigorously followed in the repetition. If the same results
(prosperity at the harvest, victory in war, protection from calamity)
are not produced the fault in principle is always thought to be an incorrect following of the procedures either technically or spiritually (in
much the same way as prolonged investigation of almost every major
air disaster finds the cause in "pilot error"), but in practice, over long
periods, gods do disappear, rituals decay, become modified or transformed, are applied to allegedly different purposes.

The assertion that religious ritual is the product of observation may
seem strange these days. But priesthood and its procedures were from
the beginning connected with astronomy, as among the Chaldeans;
Lord Raglan tells us that what priests observably do (whatever they
claim to be doing) is keep a sacred calendar; and, as Christopher Caudwell said of savages, they dance the rain dance at the approach of the
rainy season, not in the dry.

Ideally, the scientific experiment can be performed by any sane person who goes about it in the right spirit, that is, a spirit of obedience
to instructions. In practice, however, this is rarely possible, and then
only with the simplest procedures. I can verify for myself, perhaps, the
existence of interference patterns in light. But I do not own or have
access to a particle accelerator and would not know what to do with
it if I had. So it turns out that experiments are typically carried out
by a separate class of persons trained from their youth in experimental
procedures; in theory, any young person may belong to this class, but
in practice it is standard for applicants to be screened by aptitude tests
and by a long, arduous novitiate, during which they learn the esoteric
language of their vocation.

334

In certain sects of an allegedly ecumenical religion, especially those sects which refer their beliefs, correctly or not, to a return to primitive practices, anyone who feels moved by the spirit may say the rituals; in the Old Testament, for example, the establishment of one tribe, the Levites, as priest-specialists is relatively late; it occurs simultaneously with the rigorous codifying of doctrine and the forming of a nation. But after and apart from the primitive, the rituals of world religions are typically carried out by a separate class of persons trained from youth in the procedures of ritual; in theory, any young person may belong to this class, but in practice it is standard for applicants to be screened for signs of a vocation and, if they show such signs, by a long, arduous novitiate, in which they learn the esoteric language in which alone the rituals can be efficacious.

The language of science, mathematics, is esoteric and abstruse but international for its initiates; it refers to a supramundane or purely mental reality; it is in its purest form a language about itself, like music, refined of every worldly consideration and yet immensely powerful when applied to the world. The Fratres Arvali in Rome are said to have done their rites in a Latin so dead that they themselves did not know what its formulae meant (it is also said they winked at one another when they met in the street), and Bertrand Russell tells us plainly that "Mathematics is a science in which we never know what we are talking about nor whether what we say is true" (quoted in Lucienne Felix, *The Modern Aspect of Mathematics*, p. 53), though the printed page will not record a wink.

Even when rituals are recited in the living language of the communicants, that language is highly specialized by archaic forms, lofty and traditional phrasing, and so on. But in our best example for the purpose of comparison, the Latin of the Catholic Church is esoteric and yet international for its initiates, refers to a supramundane or purely mental reality, is in its purest form a language about itself (note the linguistic problems involved in speaking of three persons as both one and three, or of bread and wine as becoming body and blood), ritually associated with music, and yet immensely powerful when applied to the world (as the same linguistic difficulties, when applied to the world, produced numerous bodies and a great deal of blood).

335

Scholium. We might pause here to look at music as the model language for both science and religion. Music is like that machine built a few years back by someone in California; it had thousands of moving parts and no identifiable function. The first digital computer (and pedal computer too, for that matter) was the cathedral organ, programmed by J. S. Bach, among others, to exhaust all the possible combinational resources of the total language as then understood. The musical language is in one respect observably unique, however: nobody died young and poor of Mozart, except Mozart.

Religion and science both have at least three ways of being understood (or not understood). These ways might be listed (for both) as aristocratic, bourgeois, and proletarian, or (also for both) as esoteric, exoteric, and superstitious. They might be diagrammatically set forth as follows:

1. Mysticism, vision, theology	Pure, or creative, science; philosophy of science
2. Morals, the good life, order	Technology, progress, order
3. The devil	The mad scientist

I should emphasize that my first description of the three possibilities as aristocratic, bourgeois, and proletarian does not assert these as fixed limitations of class; nothing in his own nature will prevent the child of a laborer from becoming a theologian or a theoretical physicist, but either will be a very aristocratic thing for him to become. Nor, obviously, is a member of the middle class condemned to be a bourgeois in religion or in science. Salvation to all that will is nigh, we might say, and so is damnation. Now to specify somewhat more elaborately the description of my three categories:

1. Here is the true source of what is generally and laughably called— with a straight face—the practical world: in the dreams and visions of gentle and profound and imaginative men whose word is peace. These men deal purely and in a humble spirit with the most immense and fundamental forces imaginable, with the simple and ineluctable mystery of The Word, The Logos, The Divine Name, Energy, Mass, Light, Number, and so on. They characteristically give utterance to brief, cryptic, word-transforming statements such as Know Thyself, I am the Light of the World, $E = mc^2$, or .000 000 000 000 000 000 000 000 006 6 . . . . . x frequency = quantum of energy. It seems rarely

to occur to them that such announcements could ever become bloody instructions, and indeed the idea does look improbable. And they have their faithful followers, too, men generally regarded as either insane or disloyal by the establishment.

2. These great spirits have their equally faithful followers in the second realm, too. This is the so-called practical world referred to above, where the Logos descended into matter and crucified there becomes the weapon and the cause. This is the world where the great intuition that number is the nature of all things is translated to say that money is the number which is the nature of all things. It is the world of banners inscribed *Gott mit uns, Dieu et mon droit,* of coinage that reads on one side "In God we trust" and on the other "Five cents."

This is not to say that we, who are largely the inhabitants of this second realm, are personally villainous; it is far more likely that we view ourselves, not incorrectly with respect to our situation in society, as driven by necessities beyond our control or understanding, impersonal necessities, compulsions to realize and exhaust all possibility, compulsions to incarnate in corruptible form everything divined for us by the dreamers of the realm above. Here, in our realm, even in metaphysical respects the middle class, live the great administrators of the Word: St. Paul, Innocent III, Ignatius Loyola, Luther, Calvin . . . I refrain from naming the scientific opposite numbers, who are still alive. But this is the realm in which the power of order is more important than anything else, where love another as thyself necessarily becomes the Albigensian Crusade and $E = mc^2$ is necessarily realized as a nuclear weapon.

But it is also and at the same time another realm, this second one, or it can be more benignly regarded: it is the world of that extremely active god from whom all blessings flow. In science these blessings are technological, and extend from the rather humble electric toaster through the remarkable or even miraculous invention of television and so on to splendors untold. In religion these blessings are a little more metaphorical but at least as real in their effects: our invisible identification with the Father above takes the visible form of our affiliation with the brothers below, and the regular iteration of forms of words that at least assure us we are talking about the same world has the effect of giving society a certain appearance of stability and meaningfulness surely as important to the good life as airplanes that run on time.

This is the exoteric realm, where both science and religion are taught as doctrines, or habits, concerning which no doubts exist that will not be cleared up sooner or later, somehow, by someone. It is the realm pre-eminently where human purpose is assumed to exist and where the nature of that purpose is assumed to be known, so that no metaphysical nonsense is tolerated unless it is clearly understood to be exterior decoration.

3. The third realm is, at the simplest, where both religion and science are credited with immediate and magical powers, where their instrumentalities are hypostatized as "beings"—the realm of overt and unsophisticated demonisms, dynamisms, projections, and introjections. As Bruno Bettelheim says, when electrical machines became familiar and important in daily life, "influencing machines" became important in schizophrenia (see *The Informed Heart*, pp. 52–61, for a discussion of the general theme). Here we have the more and less complicated idolatries, parodies of the ones in the second realm, dealing with mad scientists, death rays, machines turning on their makers—all these now within the practical realm, by the way—or, on the religious side, with getting in touch with the dead, with cosmic forces, lucky amulets, astrology, fortune-telling, and so forth. There is perhaps nothing more insane here than its equivalent in the second realm, but here it tends to affect individuals, not whole societies.

To the three ways of being (or not being) understood there correspond, in both science and religion, three teachings: 1. Science for scientists, religion for the religious. 2. Science, or religion, for "the intelligent layman." 3. Science, or religion, for children.

1. Where the arcana are opened, much is in doubt; even the most fundamental things are open to dispute.

2. That is largely left implicit, however, where the mysteries are explained "in simple nontechnical language."

3. "The Wonderful Story of Religion." "The Wonders of Science." Color pictures, enthusiasm.

Two final points of comparison may be briefly stated. 1. Scientist and priest are both in the habit, though they regard it not as a habit but as a duty, of using their professional mystery to confer authority on their private opinions in matters concerning the common good. Religion and science both profess peace (and the sincerity of the professors is not being doubted), but each always turns out to have a dominant part in any war that is going or contemplated. 2. Both religion and science cost a great deal of money, much of which is spent on projects, realizable and not realizable, such as space ships and the Tower of Babel, of which the intelligence is not always or easily perceptible to people in other professions.

Washington University, St. Louis

JAY WRIGHT

Myth and Discovery

We know little about myth. We know little enough about history. These deficiencies feed each other. Artists who try to use myth or history in their work tend to cut away the complexity of mythical and historical thinking. But myth and history can be "used" intelligently and creatively. Mythological, historical, and artistic thinking have common grounds. They are imaginative, critical, conceptual, and abstractive ways of thinking. They are formal modes. Each of them tries to present its forms as objectively as possible. And in each there is the possibility of and necessity for individual and collective discovery.

These last ideas are not, of course, entirely my own. I have read and use primarily the work of Cassirer, Langer, and Collingwood. Without any pretense of giving an exhaustive account of the literature on myth, my primary task is to suggest some other ways of approaching mythological and historical thinking and an artistic manner in which they can be used.

The first problem is the difficulty of defining myth satisfactorily. I am prepared to define it as an historical body of beliefs held and practiced by an homogeneous group of people. I must, of course, go further than that. Collingwood has said that myth is antihistorical.[1] But men do practice it in time. In this sense, it is historical. It is historical too in that the body of beliefs presented in ritual practice have their bases in the cultural values and cosmological view of a particular people. Myth is theological. I mean by this that all myth is theocentric. Myth is philosophical in that, to use Collingwood's definition of philosophy, we learn from it more about a subject matter of which we already have some knowledge.[2]

In trying to define myth further, we almost find ourselves reduced to saying what it is not, as a simpler course. We say that myth can never be separated from its social context, and yet it has nothing to do with social solidarity.[3] It is seldom used to "draw people together." It might be better to say that it is used to express the historical fact that the members of a group of people *are* together and hold a common set of values. Langer observes that rites are not practical but expressive. "Ritual," she says, "like art, is essentially the active termination of a symbolic transformation of experience." [4] Mythical thinking, just as historical and artistic thinking, is abstraction from experience. What is presented is carefully chosen. We have been led to believe that, in ritual participation, the participants allow themselves to act out and release their deepest, private feelings indiscriminately. This is not what happens. Langer has written,

Ritual "expresses feelings" in the logical rather than the physiological sense. It may have what Aristotle called "cathartic" value, but that is not its characteristic; it is primarily an *articulation* of feeling. The ultimate product of such articulation is not a simple emotion, but a complex, permanent *attitude* . . . a rite regularly performed is the constant reiteration of sentiments toward "first and last things"; it is not a free expression of emotion, but a disciplined rehearsal of "right attitudes." [5]

We can approach this last idea in another way. It is still a fairly common practice to speak of catharsis in ritual, sometimes even of recognition. The writers who do this push the Aristotelian idea of traumatic recognition to its extreme. But, if the ritual participant suffers this recognition, it is not that he sees only what he knows himself to be, but that he also sees what he does not know himself to be. I cannot help thinking that this is true, even in Greek drama, where we hear much of catharsis and recognition. "A true work of art," Langer writes, "—certainly any great work—is often above sympathy, and the role of empathy in our understanding of it is trivial. Art is an image of human experience, which means an objective presentation." [6] Myth (the ritual) and history, too, are finally beyond empathy. They require a detachment and formulative ability on the part of the participant precisely because they are objectively presented. We should not allow the fervor of the participant to keep us from seeing this. It should be obvious that in ritual, as an example, the conditions for its practice and fulfillment are carefully chosen and controlled; there is a high degree of selectivity in what is presented. Through this selectivity, the participant is asked to focus his attention upon certain emotions and certain events. He is, in fact, asked to re-create a set of historical gestures and is being limited to them, disciplined in his act of re-creation. He knows, certainly, that he is doing what he does because of the authority underlying the gestures. He knows, also, that he is re-creating them, and he does not and cannot stand in the same relationship to the ritual as those who gave it to him. It is not possible for him to become his ancestors. All that he wants is to affirm the values inherent in the ritual, along with the historical value and necessity of it. This is not empathy; it is the ultimate in abstraction.

In distinguishing between empathy and abstraction, we have gone a little beyond Wörringer. In *Abstraction and Empathy*, he writes, "Whereas the pre-condition for the urge to empathy is a happy pantheistic relationship of confidence between man and the phenomena of the external world, the urge to abstraction is the outcome of a great inner unrest inspired in man by the phenomena of the outside world." [7] The will to abstraction in art, for Wörringer, is peculiar to "primitive" and certain Oriental peoples. Abstraction is also the primary urge of every art, and remains for some peoples, even at a high level of culture, the dominant tendency. With the Greeks and other Occidental peoples this urge recedes, and empathy becomes the dominant tendency. Obviously, Wörringer thinks that this move from abstraction to empathy in art is necessary and salutary, though he can admit to a causal connection between "primitive" culture and the highest, purest art forms. [8] I think he is right about this, and I think he is right in seeing that the most powerful urge of these peoples is "to wrest the object . . . out of its natural context . . . [and] to purify it of all dependence on life . . . [and] to approximate it to its *absolute* value." [9] But on two further points, I think Wörringer is wrong. He has, in his chapter on "Naturalism and Style," so polarized his concepts that only what is natural appears organic and what is abstract purely ornamental or dead. This is not a felicitous distinction. As he convincingly suggests, tribal and certain Oriental peoples tend to oppose the rationalistic tendency of

Occidental peoples and in their construction of abstract forms may find a point of tranquility, a refuge from appearances.[10] But I do not think they find themselves as thoroughly alienated from natural phenomena as Wörringer suggests. They do, after all, though perhaps not now nearly so much as before, live in a more vital relationship with their environment than we. They cannot stand in absolute awe of the world; they must manipulate it in order to live. Tribal man abstracts from his experience to participate in his mythic world. The distinction between the abstractive and empathic sensibilities is not all that neat. Wörringer's difficulty is that he has equated rationalism with realism. Occidental peoples, who are at home with the world and capable of explaining its processes, tend to stick close to the appearance of natural phenomena in art. This, as we can see, has not always been, nor is it now, true of Western art. Behind Wörringer's analysis lies the assumption that "primitive" and Oriental peoples do not have, or at least have not demonstrated, an ability to explain natural processes. They may not explain them or talk about them in the ways that Wörringer, as a product of Western culture, might, but their "spiritual dread" of natural phenomena is not ignorance of them. What is important, as Wörringer knows, is the will toward abstraction. Empathy in myth is trivial. For myth, at least on the abstractive level, forces the participant into thinking about the presented forms.

The abstractive vision, the conceptualizing processes in myth are similar to those in art.

That process which symbolic projection brings with it is the objectification of feeling, which continues into the building up of a whole objective world of perceptible things and verifiable facts. But as soon as it begins to build "the world"—and that is probably very soon, almost *ab initio*—it also presents abstractable forms, such as the external world provides us with, and the process of objectification engenders its counterpart, the symbolic use of natural forms to envisage feeling, i.e., the endowment of such forms with emotional import, mystical and mythical and moral. That is the subjectification of nature. The dialectic of the two functions is, I think, the process of human experience. Its image is "the poetic," more generally "the artistic," and it can appear in art from either pole of the dialectical tension.[11]

We tend to think that art proceeds in a manner other than this, and that, both in art and ritual participation, what is dominant and desirable is the absolutely free discharge of emotion. The more immediately discernible this discharge is, the more dynamic and true, the more in tune it seems to be with the world as it appears to us. This is a limitation imposed upon myth partially by scholars who could not divest themselves of the idea of myth as fantasy. Even Cassirer, though he disagrees with Sir Edward Burnett Tylor's assertion that myth is a confusion between conscious and unconscious experience, contends that mythical thought "lacks any fixed dividing line between mere 'representation' and 'real' perception, between wish and fulfillment, between image and thing." It hovers, he says, between the two.[12] Mythical thinking is not scientific; neither is it logical in the logician's sense of the word. It is not true, however, that differentiation, logical subordination, abstraction, and determination are alien to myth.[13] The recent work of anthropologists easily refutes this assertion. Tribal cosmological systems exhibit the very attributes that Cassirer will not allow them to have.[14] It is hard to say, too, to what extent Frazer's idea of the magical in ritual has influenced subsequent thinking about myth. It is, I think, a primary mistake to see the mythical world view as essentially magical. Even Cassirer is trapped in this. The mythical world view is not, for him, the equal of the truly religious one.[15] Myth simply substitutes one form of materiality for another.[16] The implication is that the mythical spirit, mythical thought, is totally subordinated to the things that it uses. But we must understand, as Lévi-Strauss has said, that natural phenomena are not "what myths seek to explain [but] . . . rather the *medium through which* myths try to explain facts which are themselves not of a natural but a logical order." [17] Neither mythic nor artistic vision, nor, as I shall argue later, the historical view, is ever limited to a given. The most important acts of myth and art are structural. And this structuring is essentially abstractive.

I think that abstraction is ruled out of myth because it is difficult to think of a ritual participant as one who is at once participating in and criticizing the ritual. A Nuer tribesman, for example, knows, to a great extent, the language and form of his rituals. He does not have to re-create them entirely, again and again. But, to some extent, he does re-create the language and form over again. In order to participate, he has to know what he is in and that he is present in it. He has to be conscious to some degree of the function and ground, the historical and temporal processes of the rituals. He has, in fact, to exercise a critical intelligence. I do not believe we are aware of this. This is, I suspect, the reason why Collingwood could not respect mythical thinking as he respected historical thinking. Thought, he asserts, has to be reflective to be subject matter for history; [18] all history is the history of thought; the history of thought is a re-enactment of the past in the historian's mind.[19] The important requisites are the historian's critical and formulative abilities and his ability to conceptualize. He is at once working with his own conceptual view of the world and trying to enter into another. This, I submit, is what is happening to one who is involved in mythical thinking; everything given in myth is not necessarily his. In another way, this, too, is happening to the artist as he creates. He has not only his vision but a history of artistic vision. The forms that result in myth, history, and art are the forms abstractable from the experience of the individual and the history of the forms abstracted from experience prior to him. Through selection and imagination he structures, as Langer would put it, an image of human experience.

I have been insisting on the importance of abstraction in myth and art. This can be carried too far; they can come up bloodless and unreal. The ultimate end of myth, after all, "is not wishful distortion of the world, but serious envisagement of its fundamental truths; moral orientation, not escape." It presents a world view, a general insight into life, not a personal, imaginary biography.[20] No artist takes abstract form as an ideal. Abstracted forms act as symbols and become expressive of human feeling.[21] Expression is important. But what is expressed?

Cassirer has written that Plato, in spite of his opposition to myth, was most characteristic in his thinking about it as a conceptual language in which the world of becoming was expressed.[22] Plato was a tragic figure who, if he did not like politics, at least was fascinated by it and in some despair over the kind of politics he could see being played about him. The world moved about too much for him; nothing remained settled. The solution was to create a cosmology so that the world of becoming could be *expressed*, held. The forms try to express a world in flux.

Myth, too, comes into being in an attempt to express what is, finally, almost inexpressible—historical and ideational continuity. Myth, history, and art are related in this tragedy of not being able to say, "at least this stands still, is real and knowable." The necessity in each of them is to make the attempt to express not only the historical and intellectual

345

continuity of a people but the participant's relationship to these three things. Cassirer has argued that mythical consciousness does not try to arrive at fundamental constants which would explain variation and change, that it articulates space and time by introducing the opposition of the sacred and profane into spatial and temporal reality.[23] Symbolic form has no limit between the I and established reality but creates this limit with each fundamental form.[24] Myth sets up a relation of kinship and tension between the individual and the community.[25] More than that, it sets up a tension between the individual and any given, as a result of its expression. And, in doing so, it forces the individual into a critical attitude. Myth, far from being closed, is open, and open to the extent that the participant, given fundamental conditions, establishes the limits of the I and the mythic world and the "real" world. The establishment of these limits can only come about through the *expression* of the myth.

Collingwood calls the characteristic mark of expression its lucidity or intelligibility; anyone who expresses something becomes conscious of what is it that he is expressing, and enables others to become conscious of what he expresses.[26] Langer, in discussing Émile Durkheim's analysis of images, has stated that his "whole analysis of totemism bears out the contention that it is, like all sacraments, a form of *ideation,* an expression of concepts in purely presentational metaphor." [27] What art expresses, she suggests, is not actual feeling, but ideas of feeling; [28] through thought and imagination we have not only feelings but a life of feelings.[29] There is a similar detachment of the mythic consciousness.[30] Cassirer says that the concrete mythic world arises, like art and cognition, in a process of separation from immediate reality.[31] What we confront in reading history is individual consciousness detaching itself from the evidence presented. We cannot say that the historian's art is total abstraction, but we can say, I think, that, through the process of selection, through choosing what to express, the historian tends toward abstraction and conceptualization. He reports, as Collingwood argues, what goes on in his mind as he confronts his material. This process is the dialectic, too, of myth and art. The material is there for a mind. The form is symbolic of a process of thought. We finally know both form and thought through, and only through, its expression.

This expression is never intended to deceive the senses. "The function of artistic illusion is not 'make-believe' . . . but the very opposite, disengagement from belief. . . . The knowledge that what is before us has no practical significance in the world is what enables us to give attention to its appearance as such." [32] Myth calls its world to our attention in the same way. An historian asks us to attend to what is important in a chaos of events and motives. We may choose not to pay attention to what is presented, but that is the only alternative. What we have in any coherent structure in any of these modes of thought I choose to call, borrowing from Langer, abstracted form. But, as we have said, that is not the end of it. Each of these modes expresses human feeling. The drive is to articulate this feeling as clearly as possible.

We can now approach this in another way. In Langer's words,

Feeling is *like* the dynamic and rhythmic structures created by artists; artistic form is always the form of felt life, whether of impression, emotion, overt action, thought, dream or even obscure organic process rising to a high level and going into psychical phase, perhaps acutely, perhaps barely and vaguely. It is the way acts and impacts feel that makes them important in art . . . it serves artistic purposes only in so far as it helps the expressive function.[33]

The frame of all feeling is vital organization. Feeling only exists in living organisms. The logic of all symbols that can express feeling is the logic of organic processes.[34] Langer has tried to relate artistic form to vital form, seeing rhythm as the principle attribute in both vital and artistic form.[35] "Rhythmic concatenation," she says,

is what really holds an organism together from moment to moment; it is a dynamic pattern, i.e., a pattern of events, into which acts and act-like phenomena very readily fall; a sequence wherein the subsiding phase, or cadence, of one act (or similar element) is the up-take of its successor. It occurs in nonvital as well as vital processes, but in the latter it is paramount, and reaches degrees of differentiation and intensity unrivaled by anything in the inanimate realm.[36]

Rhythm is tension building up to a crisis, the decrease in that tension, and a gradual rise in intensity to the next crisis.[37] Rhythm does not mean exact repetition of a pattern.[38] Every act, every vital impulse, arises from a situation. This situation is composed of acts in progress, which have arisen from previous situations punctuated by previous impacts.[39]

347

Langer has said that, in fact, an organism is made up of its acts.[40] It takes a series of smaller acts to establish a larger act, and some acts are never wholly articulated, never reach a psychical phase.[41] Nevertheless, the process of tension-building and release goes on, though the impact may never be consciously felt.[42] I think that it is justifiable to conceive of the work of art as an organism; it becomes organic through its expressiveness. And what it expresses is "the nature of feelings conceived, imaginatively realized, and rendered by a labor of formulation and abstractive vision." [43] From Langer we learn that feeling is like the dynamic and rhythmic structures created by artists. I should add that feeling is like the structures created in mythical and historical thinking. The idea of feeling has here, thanks to Langer, been broadened to include conceptual and expressive power. The organic myth, the historical piece, and the work of art arise like feeling from a situation. This situation is made up of what is historical, cultural, and individual. The resultant acts, in the process of expression, are both articulated and non-articulated. The importance of acts that are not articulated but which are contributory to those that are cannot be overlooked.

It is a commonplace among us that a work of art, for example, must be coherent and complete. Poets of any range often find their work rejected because it does not keep to its "tone." Though we may come into being with a limited genetic potential, life itself simply violates our idea of "tone." There are, to repeat, within any organism, any number of acts which are never fully realized, and yet they are participants in the larger acts that reach what Langer calls a psychical phase. Within any given context, an organism has choices it can make. "Life is the progressive realization of potential acts; and as every act changes the pattern and range of what is possible, the living body is an ever-new constellation of possibilities." [44] Certainly, art is not, in its strictest sense, like life. But, if it is true that "art . . . is the making of virtual forms, symbolic of the elusive forms of feeling," [45] then it is conceivably possible that there could be a work of art in which some, even most, of the elements are not, or only slightly, articulated. The coherence and completeness of such a work would lie in the interdependence of its elements, in the dialectical pattern of their relations; [46] in a word, in the tensions produced by the visual or verbal realization of acts and the existence of unrealized yet contributory acts that underlie those that come to consciousness. We should approach the dynamic elements of a work of art in a dynamic manner. The conventional manner of moving a plot or narrative line, for example, leads us to believe that we always have all of the information that we need. If we follow this movement, we think we have points in space and time to grasp. But we do not. There is always something inarticulate in a work of art. When there is not, we have an arrested movement, a dead organism. A vital organism offers us its movement. We know it, of course, through what reaches a psychical phase, through what is expressed. We know it through its impact. "Artistic import requires no interpretation; it requires a full and clear perception of the presented form, and the form sometimes needs to be construed before one can appreciate it . . . the vital import of a work of art need not and cannot be derived by any exegesis." [47] But, though it cannot be derived by any exegesis, we need not fall back into the trap of empathy. We must keep in mind that the work of art is a presented form, that it records the conceived and imaginatively realized feelings of an individual, whose physiological and psychical rhythms, for all their similarities to ours, are not ours. No matter what the emotional impact of a work of art upon us, we can never fully grasp the work through emotion alone. Any work of value always impresses us as having an intellectual underpinning and as open-ended. It renews itself. This is its vital relationship to our lives. It mirrors our lives in that it is filled with potential acts, with possibility. It is like myth and history, again, in that it is a way of bringing our feelings, by discipline, into a life of feelings, and our life of feelings into a realm of consciousness where we are enabled to place ourselves historically. Through this placement, we become conscious of the values we hold and of whatever coherence and continuity our lives have. Nothing of this, however, is ever complete. The tension is always there.

When we introduce ourselves as participants in myth, history, and art, we radically change their processes, and, in doing so, change our relationship to them. The presence and subjectivity of the individual make the exact repetition of any process, or construct, in them impossible. Though it may now appear heresy, it is impossible ever to get back to "first things" in myth; we cannot reconstruct any work of art or its process in the way the artist has structured it. We are, in a sense, forever outside. But total immersion in a mythic ritual, historical event, or work of art would be disastrous. We must hold some part of ourselves apart to see what is happening to us, so that we may discover whatever is discoverable in the ritual, event, or work of art. And because there is this possibility of discovery, we are, far from being totally reinforced by myth, history, and art, led into a realm of uncertainty. Certainly, the presented forms are there before us, objectively presented. But we can never, organisms being what they are, approach them in the same way each time we come to them. We and what we have before us and in us turn and present new tensions, new questions, new solutions. Our glory, as well as the glory of myth, history, and art, is that nothing can bring the process of growth and change to an end.

Growth and change and the tensions produced by them are frightening even to those who proclaim and declare themselves totally committed to them. In periods of crisis, when the swiftest, most effective, and most traumatic changes are taking place, man seems almost always to turn toward myth, history, and art as havens or as targets—the objectification of all that has gone wrong with his world. This is not to say that politics is forgotten. But the burdens of a tangled political life seem, somehow, to get shifted onto these other modes. We feel betrayed by them because they do not and cannot offer any stability. We seem not to understand that the vitality of these modes of thought is that they mirror our lives in their dynamism. They are useful in that they force us to confront this dynamism in them and in us. The complexity in myth and history, as in art, is precisely the complexity in us. They are capable of growth because we are. But they will never give easy answers or do away with the anguish of discovering our place in the world.

We are, as I have said, not now close to mythical or historical thinking, but they are not lost to us. The myths, the history, that we tend to appropriate present the humane gestures of men as they confront their own lives and deaths. We cannot understand these if we simply give in to them. We can only understand them through an imaginative and critical restructuring of myth and history. And so with art. If we understand them also as formal, conceptual, and abstractive ways of thinking, we release ourselves into a larger world of feeling. We can

never be alone with them, and we can never be with them until we are
—each of us—alone, taking their uncertainties as a point of departure
into the moral certainties that we may discover.

Princeton University

NOTES

1. R. G. Collingwood, *The Idea of History* (New York, 1956), p. 15. Collingwood
says more precisely that myth is not human. For him, to be nonhuman is to be
antihistorical.

2. R. G. Collingwood, *Essay on Philosophical Method* (Oxford, 1933), pp. 97, 98.

3. Susanne K. Langer, *Philosophy in a New Key* (New York, 2nd ed., 1951), p. 51.

4. Ibid., p. 49.

5. Ibid., p. 134.

6. Susanne K. Langer, *Mind: An Essay on Human Feeling* (Baltimore, 1967), 1. 164.

7. Wilhelm Wörringer, *Abstraction and Empathy*, tr. Michael Bullock (Cleveland
and New York, 1967; 1st German ed., 1908), p. 15.

8. Ibid., p. 17.

9. Ibid.

10. Ibid., p. 16.

11. Langer, *Mind*, p. 241.

12. Ernst Cassirer, *The Philosophy of Symbolic Forms*, vol. 2: *Mythical Thought*,
tr. Ralph Manheim (New Haven, 1955), p. 36.

13. Cassirer, *Mythical Thought*, p. 69.

14. Cf. for example, *African Worlds*, ed. Daryll Forde, published for the International African Institute by Oxford University Press (New York, 1954).

15. Cassirer, *Mythical Thought*, p. 25.

16. Ibid., p. 24.

17. Claude Lévi-Strauss, *The Savage Mind* (Chicago, 1966, no translator given),
p. 95. See also the essays in *Myth and Cosmos*, ed. John Middleton (Garden City,
N.Y., 1967).

18. Collingwood, *The Idea of History*, p. 308.

19. Ibid., p. 215.

20. Langer, *Philosophy in a New Key*, p. 153.

21. Susanne K. Langer, *Feeling and Form* (New York, 1953), p. 51.

22. Cassirer, *Mythical Thought*, p. 2.

23. Ibid., p. 81.

24. Ibid., p. 156.

25. Ibid., p. 177.

26. R. G. Collingwood, *The Principles of Art* (New York, 1958), p. 122.

27. Langer, *Philosophy in a New Key*, p. 144.

28. Langer, *Feeling and Form*, p. 59.

351

29. Ibid., p. 372.

30. Cassirer, *Mythical Thought*, p. 15.

31. Ibid., p. 24. Cf. Herbert Read, *A Concise History of Sculpture* (New York, 1964), p. 54, where he writes that art is best when it is abstracted both from the immediacy of our feelings and from the objective world.

32. Langer, *Feeling and Form*, p. 49.

33. Langer, *Mind*, p. 64.

34. Langer, *Feeling and Form*, p. 126.

35. Langer, *Mind*, p. 211. I am also indebted to Dr. Arthur Bacon of Talladega College for aid in interpreting much of the biological information.

36. Ibid., p. 323.

37. Ibid., p. 324.

38. Ibid., p. 205.

39. Ibid., p. 281.

40. Ibid., p. 204.

41. Ibid., p. 55.

42. Ibid., pp. 55, 323.

43. Ibid., p. 90. Langer acknowledges the influence on some of her thinking here of Ivy Campbell-Fisher's essay, "Aesthetics and the Logic of Sense," *Journal of General Psychology*, XLIV (1951), 3–24.

44. Langer, *Mind*, p. 206.

45. Ibid., p. xix.

46. Ibid., p. 205.

47. Ibid., p. 88.

RAY ELLENWOOD

A List of the Writings of
Francis Fergusson

Mr. Fergusson was born in Albuquerque, New Mexico, in 1904. He had his early schooling in Albuquerque, Washington, D.C., and New York; his university studies at Harvard and Queen's College, Oxford, where he was a Rhodes Scholar in the Honor School of Philosophy, Politics and Economics.

He was early involved with the theater as Associate Director of the American Laboratory Theater in New York (1926–1930), Drama Critic for *The Bookman* (1930–1933), Director of the College Theater at Bennington College, and as author of *The King and the Duke* and a modern adaptation of Sophocles' *Electra*. He is also a Dante scholar and has been Lecturer or Professor of Literature at the New School of Social Research (1932–1934), Bennington College (1934–1947), The Institute for Advanced Study in Princeton (1948–1949), Princeton University (1949–1952), Indiana University (1952–1953) and Rutgers University (1953–1969).

His varied interests are harmonized by his conviction that the concepts of action and imitation of action as Aristotle used them can give a radical perspective for the creation and the study of art. So Mr. Fergusson's poems and plays, his writings on dance, the practical theater, Dante and Shakespeare, literature and aesthetics in general—all have an uncommon unity and consistency.

Mr. Fergusson received the Annual Award for Literature from the National Institute of Arts and Letters in 1953, and was elected a member in 1962. He received the Christian Gauss Award of the Phi Beta Kappa Society (for Dante's *Drama of the Mind*) in 1954, and was elected an honorary Phi Beta Kappa by the Rutgers Chapter in 1966. The University of New Mexico awarded him an Honorary D. Litt. in 1955. In 1969, he was elected a member of the American Academy of Arts and Sciences. He is a senior Fellow of the School of Letters of Indiana University, and a member of the editorial board of *Sewanee Review*.

Entries in this list are arranged in chronological order under the headings "Books," "Editing and Introductions," "Articles," "Book Reviews," "Theater and Film Reviews," "Poems," and "Plays." Many of Mr. Fergusson's articles, as well as sections from his books, have been reprinted in periodicals and anthologies. No attempt has been made to notice all of them.

BOOKS

The Idea of a Theater: A Study of Ten Plays, The Art of Drama in Changing Perspective (Princeton, Princeton University Press, 1949). [Reprinted in paperback by Anchor Books, 1953, and by Princeton University Press, 1968. Translations of this book have been made, or are to be made, into Japanese, Spanish, Portuguese, Italian, Serbo-Croatian, German, Arabic, Persian, Urdu, Bengali, Indonesian. Excerpts from it have been printed in such editions as the Prentice Hall collection of critical essays on Chekhov, Ibsen, and *Oedipus Rex; Moderns on Tragedy*, ed. Lionel Abel; *Pirandello*, ed. Glauco Cambon; *Essays in Modern Literary Criticism*, ed. R. B. West, Jr.]

Dante's Drama of the Mind: A Modern Reading of the Purgatorio (Princeton, Princeton University Press, 1953). [Reprinted in paperback, 1968.]

The Human Image in Dramatic Literature: Essays (New York, Doubleday and Company, 1957). [Excerpts from this book have been printed in such editions as *Modern Drama, Essays in Criticism*, ed. Travis Bogard and William I. Oliver; *Myth and Literature, Contemporary Theory and Practice*, ed. John B. Vickery; *The Modern American Theater*, ed. Alvin B. Kernan; *Explication as Criticism, Selected*

Papers from The English Institute, 1941–1952, ed. W. K. Wimsatt.]
Poems 1929–1961 (New Brunswick, Rutgers University Press, 1962).
Dante (New York, Macmillan, 1966). [Published simultaneously in
London by Weidenfeld and Nicolson.]
Shakespeare, The Pattern in His Carpet (New York, Delacorte Press,
1970). [This is a collection of the introductions from *The Laurel
Shakespeare*—see under "Editing and Introductions," plus five origi-
nal essays on Shakespeare's development and cosmology.]

EDITING AND INTRODUCTIONS

"A Reading of *Exiles,*" introduction to the play by James Joyce (Nor-
folk, Conn., New Directions, 1945).
"Introduction," *Plays of Molière* (New York, Modern Library, 1950).
Editor of *Dante Alighieri: A Symposium of Modern Critics* (*Kenyon
Review,* XIV [Spring 1952], 177–323).
"Introduction," *Paul Valéry, Plays* (tr. David Paul and Robert Fitzgerald, Bolingen Series, XLV, 3, Pantheon Books, 1960).
"Introduction," *Aristotle's Poetics* (tr. S. H. Butcher, New York, Hill
and Wang, 1961).
General Editor of *The Laurel Shakespeare* (37 volumes, New York,
1958–1968). Mr. Fergusson contributed an introduction to the play
and an essay, "Shakespeare and His Theatre," for each volume in the
series that is devoted to drama.

ARTICLES

"T. S. Eliot and His Impersonal Theory of Art," *The American Caravan,* I (1927), 446–453.
"Eugene O'Neill," *Hound and Horn,* III (January–March 1930), 145–
160.
"*Exiles* and Ibsen's Work," *Hound and Horn,* VI (April–June 1932),
345–353.
"D. H. Lawrence's Sensibility," *Hound and Horn,* VI (April–June
1933), 447–463.

"The Drama in *The Golden Bowl*," *Hound and Horn*, VII (April–May 1934), 407–413.

"James' Idea of Dramatic Form," *Kenyon Review*, V (1943), 495–507.

"Action as Passion: *Tristan* and *Murder in the Cathedral*," *Kenyon Review*, IX (Spring 1947), 201–221. [Reprinted in *The Idea of a Theater*.]

"*Oedipus Rex*: The Tragic Rhythm of Action," *Accent*, VIII (Spring 1948), 145–168. [Reprinted in *The Idea of a Theater*.]

"Action as Rational: Racine's *Bérénice*," *The Hudson Review*, I (Summer 1948), 188–203. [Reprinted in *The Idea of a Theater*.]

"Sartre as Playwright," *Partisan Review*, XVI (April 1949), 407–449.

"The Theatricality of Shaw and Pirandello," *Partisan Review*, XVI (June 1949), 589–603. [Reprinted in *The Idea of a Theater*.]

"*Hamlet*: The Analogy of Action," *Hudson Review*, II (Summer 1949), 165–210. [Reprinted in *The Idea of a Theater*.]

"Poetry in the Theater and Poetry of the Theater: Cocteau's *Infernal Machine*," *English Institute Essays, 1949*, ed. Alan S. Downer (New York, Columbia University Press, 1950), pp. 55–72.

"Two Acts of Dante's Drama of the Mind," *Thought*, XXVII (1951), 47–56. [Reprinted in *Dante's Drama of the Mind*.]

"*Macbeth* as the Imitation of an Action," *English Institute Essays, 1951* (New York, Columbia University Press, 1952), pp. 31–45. [Reprinted in *The Human Image*.]

"*Purgatory, Canto XVIII*: The Fruit of Philosophy," *Kenyon Review*, XIV (Spring 1952), 243–255. [Reprinted in *Dante's Drama of the Mind*.]

"The Pilgrim on the Threshold of Purgation," *The Hudson Review*, IV (Winter 1952), 552–561. [Reprinted in *Dante's Drama of the Mind*.]

"Philosophy and Theater in *Measure for Measure*," *Kenyon Review*, XIV (Winter 1952), 103–120. [Reprinted in *The Human Image*.]

"Drama and the Industrial Manager," *Saturday Review*, 21 November 1953, pp. 44–46.

"*The Comedy of Errors* and *Much Ado about Nothing*," *Sewanee Review*, LXII (January 1954), 24–37. [Reprinted in *The Human Image*.]

"Theater and the Academy," *Partisan Review*, XXI (September 1954), 510 517. [Reprinted in *The Human Image*.]

"Beyond the Close Embrace: Speculations on the American Stage," *The Anchor Review* (New York, Doubleday, 1955), pp. 189–203.

"Don Perlimplín: Lorca's Theater Poetry," *Kenyon Review,* XVII (Summer 1955), 337–348. [Reprinted in *The Human Image.*]

"The Search for New Standards in the Theater," *Kenyon Review,* XVII (Fall 1955), 581–596.

"*The Golden Bowl* Revisited," *Sewanee Review,* LXIII (Winter 1955), 13–28. [Reprinted in *The Human Image.*]

" 'Myth' and the Literary Scruple," *Sewanee Review,* LXIV (Spring 1956), 171–185. [Reprinted in *The Human Image.*]

"Three Allegorists: Brecht, Wilder, and Eliot," *Sewanee Review,* LXIV (Fall 1956), 544–73. [Reprinted in *The Human Image.*]

"Broadway's Musical Hullabaloo," *Saturday Review,* 15 September 1956, pp. 11–13 and 47–48.

"Language of the Theater," *Language: An Enquiry into Its Meaning and Function,* ed. R. N. Anshen (New York, Harper and Brothers, 1957), pp. 285–295.

"The Human Image," *Kenyon Review,* XIX (Winter 1957), 1–14. [Reprinted in *The Human Image.*]

"A Note on the Vitality of Allen Tate's Prose," *Sewanee Review,* LXVII (Fall 1959), 579–581.

"Poetic Intuition and Action in Maritain's *Creative Intuition in Art and Poetry,*" *Jacques Maritain, the Man and His Achievement,* ed. Joseph W. Evans (New York, Sheed and Ward, 1963), pp. 128–138.

"A Voice of One's Own: A Note on Mr. Ransom's Style," *Shenandoah,* XIV (Spring 1963), 13–14.

"After Paranoia, What Next," *Tulane Drama Review,* VII (Summer 1963), 22–26.

"The Notion of 'Action,' " *Tulane Drama Review,* IX (Fall 1964), 85–87.

"On Reading Dante in 1965: The *Divine Comedy* as a Bridge across Time," *Dante Alighieri, Three Lectures* (Washington, Library of Congress, 1965), pp. 23–34.

"The Lady from the Sea," *Contemporary Approaches to Ibsen. Proceedings of the First International Ibsen Seminar, Oslo, August 1965, Ibsen Yearbook* [IBSEN ÅRBOKEN], VIII, 1965–1966, ed. Daniel Haakonsen (Oslo, Universitets Forlaget, 1966), pp. 51–59.

"A Conversation with Digby R. Diehl," *Transatlantic Review*, XIX (Autumn 1965), 115–121.

"Trope and Allegory: Some Themes Common to Dante and Shakespeare, *Dante Studies*, LXXXVI (1968), 113–125.

Book Reviews

Some of these reviews are full critical essays inspired by books. The length of the review may give some indication of its importance.

The Second American Caravan, ed. Alfred Kreymborg, Paul Rosenfeld, Lewis Mumford, in *Hound and Horn*, II (January–March 1929), 174–177.

For Lancelot Andrewes, by T. S. Eliot, in *Hound and Horn*, II (April–June 1929), 297–299.

The Modern Temper, by Joseph Wood Krutch, in *Hound and Horn*, II (July–September 1929), 451–452.

Hawthorne, by Newton Arvin, in *Hound and Horn*, III (April–June 1930), 436–438.

Humanism and America, ed. Norman Foerster, and *The Critique of Humanism*, ed. C. Hartley Grattan, in *Hound and Horn*, III (July–September 1930), 609–614.

Willa Cather, by René Rapin, in *The Bookman*, LXX (December 1930), 437–438.

Upstage, John Mason Brown, in *The Bookman*, LXX (December 1930), 446–447.

God without Thunder: An Unorthodox Defense of Orthodoxy, by John Crowe Ransom, in *The Bookman*, LXXIII (March 1931), 100–101.

James Joyce's 'Ulysses,' A Study, by Stuart Gilbert, in *Hound and Horn*, V (October–December 1931), 135–137.

Dramatic Theory and the Rhymed Heroic Play, by Cecil V. Deane, in *The Bookman*, LXXIV (November 1931), 331–332.

The Theory of the Drama, by Allardyce Nicoll; *European Theories of Drama*, by Barrett H. Clark; *The Theater from Athens to Broadway*, by Thomas Wood Stevens; *Creative Theater*, by Roy Mitchell; *Our Changing Theater*, by R. Dana Skinner, in *The Bookman*, LXXV (August 1932), 388–390.

The Stage is Set, by Lee Simonson, in *The Bookman,* LXXV (November 1932), 723–725.

1919, by John Dos Passos, in *Hound and Horn,* VI (January–March 1933), 343–344.

Acting: The First Six Lessons, by Richard Boleslavsky, in *Hound and Horn,* VI (July–September 1933), 701–706. [Reprinted in *The Human Image.*]

The Autobiography of Alice B. Toklas, by Gertrude Stein; *Eimi,* by E. E. Cummings; *Intimate Memoirs: Volume I: Background,* by Mabel Dodge Luhan, in *Hound and Horn,* VII (October–December 1933), 148–152.

The Use of Poetry and the Use of Criticism, by T. S. Eliot, in *Hound and Horn,* VII (January–March 1934), 356–358.

Days without End, by Eugene O'Neill, in *The American Review,* II (February 1934), 491–495.

Dance, by Lincoln Kirstein, in *The Nation,* 12 February 1936, p. 200.

America Dancing, by John Martin, in *The Nation,* 6 February 1937, p. 163.

Christ's Comet, by Christopher Hassall, in *Southern Review,* V (1940), 559–567.

The American Drama Since 1918: An Informal History, by Joseph Wood Krutch, in *Kenyon Review,* II (Summer 1940), 376–379.

The Revolutionists, by Selden Rodman, in *Partisan Review,* X (March–April 1943), 202–204.

Mission of the University, by José Ortega y Gasset, tr. Howard Lee Nostrand; *Education at the Crossroads,* by Jacques Maritain; *The United States and Civilization,* by John U. Nef; *The Universities Look for Unity,* by John U. Nef; *Rebirth of Liberal Education,* by Fred B. Millett; *Teacher in America,* by Jacques Barzun, in *Sewanee Review,* LIII (July–September 1945), 466–476.

Seven Plays of Maxim Gorky, tr. Alexander Bakshy, in collaboration with Paul S. Nathan, in *Kenyon Review,* VII (Autumn 1945), 700–703.

A Grammar of Motives, by Kenneth Burke, in *Sewanee Review,* LIV (Spring 1946), 325–333. [Reprinted in *The Human Image.*]

The Use of the Drama, by Harley Granville-Barker, in *Kenyon Review,* VIII (Winter 1946), 171–173.

The Classical Moment, by Martin Turnell, in *Kenyon Review,* XI (Winter 1949), 148–152.

The Little Blue Light, by Edmund Wilson, in *The New York Times Book Review,* 25 June 1950, p. 14.

The Complete Plays of Henry James, ed. Leon Edel, in *Partisan Review,* XVII (July–August 1950), 623–626.

The Psychology of Art, by André Malraux, in *Poetry,* LXXVI (August 1950), 288–291.

Eimi, by E. E. Cummings, in *Kenyon Review,* XII (Autumn 1950), 701–705.

Poetry and Drama, by T. S. Eliot, in *The New York Times Book Review,* 10 June 1951, p. 14.

Drama and Society in the Age of Jonson, by L. C. Knights, in *The New York Times Book Review,* 8 July 1951, p. 4.

Poetry and Drama, by T. S. Eliot, in *Partisan Review,* XVIII (September–October 1951), 582–586. [Reprinted in *The Human Image.*]

Auden, by Richard Hoggart, in *Partisan Review,* XIX (July–August 1952), 483–487.

The Days Before, by Katherine Anne Porter, in *Sewanee Review,* LXI (1953), 340–342.

The Common Pursuit, by F. R. Leavis, in *Partisan Review,* XX (March–April 1953), 232–235.

All the King's Men, by Robert Penn Warren; *Guard of Honor,* by James Gould Cozzens; *The Middle of the Journey,* by Lionel Trilling, in *Perspectives U.S.A.,* VI (1954), 30–44.

European Literature and the Latin Middle Ages, by Ernst Robert Curtius; *Mimesis,* by Erich Auerbach, in *Hudson Review,* VII (Spring 1954), 118–122. [Reprinted in *The Human Image.*]

Five Plays, by Edmund Wilson, in *The New York Times Book Review,* 15 August 1954, p. 4.

How Not to Write a Play, by Walter Kerr, in *Saturday Review,* 9 July 1955, p. 17.

Dante Studies, Commedia: Elements of Structure, by Charles Singleton, in *Comparative Literature,* VII (Winter 1955), 79–80.

The Modern Theater, ed. Eric Bentley, in *Kenyon Review,* XVIII (Spring 1956), 310–311.

The Dramatic Imagination, by Robert Edmond Jones; *On the Art of the Theater*, by Gordon Craig, in *The Nation*, 24 November 1956, pp. 460–462.

La Poesía Mítica de Federico Garcia Lorca, by Gustavo Correa, in *Comparative Literature*, IX (Summer 1957,), 261–262.

Aristotle's Poetics: The Argument, by Gerald F. Else, in *Tulane Drama Review*, IV (May 1960), 23–32.

The Divine Comedy in English: A Critical Bibliography, 1782–1900, by Gilbert F. Cunningham; *Dante into English*, by William J. De Sua; *The Divine Comedy of Dante Alighieri*, tr. Geoffrey L. Bickersteth; *Dante, a Collection of Critical Essays*, ed. John Freccero; *Essays on Dante*, ed. Mark Musa; *The Mind of Dante*, ed. U. Limentani; *Dante Alighieri, His Life and Works*, by Paget Toynbee, ed. with an introduction by Charles S. Singleton; *Dante*, by Thomas G. Bergin; *A Concordance to the Divine Comedy*, ed. Ernest Hatch Wilkins and Thomas Goddard Bergin, in *The New York Review of Books*, 17 February 1966, pp. 17–19.

William Troy: Selected Essays, ed. Stanley Edgar Hyman, in *Commentary*, XLIV (July 1967) 79–80.

Prometheus Bound, by Robert Lowell, in *The New York Review of Books*, 3 August 1967, pp. 30–32.

Tragedy and Philosophy, by Walter Kaufmann; *The Identity of Oedipus the King*, by Alastair Cameron; *Reality and the Heroic Pattern*, by David Grene, in *The New York Review of Books*, 20 November 1969, pp. 22–25.

THEATER AND FILM REVIEWS

Titles for these reviews, for which Mr. Fergusson was not responsible, are only given when judged informative. Entries from *The Bookman* comprise a monthly series called first "The Theater" and then "A Month of the Theater."

Hound and Horn, III (April–June 1930), 414–416. [*The Little Show, Wake Up and Dream, Red Rust, At the Bottom, Cherry Orchard.*]

Hound and Horn, III (July–September 1930), 564–567. [*Green Pastures,* comments on the Chinese actor, Mei Lan-Fang.]

The Bookman, LXXII (November 1930), 295–299. [*Bad Girl, A Farewell to Arms, Stepdaughters of War, Mr. Gilhooley, Lysistrata, Twelfth Night.*]

The Bookman, LXXII (December 1930), 409–412. ["What Is the Revue?": *The Vanderbilt Review, Blackbirds, Brown Buddies, Fine and Dandy, Three's a Crowd, Once in a Lifetime.*]

The Bookman, LXXII (January 1931), 513–516. [Comments on Eva Le Gallienne, Ethel Barrymore, *This Is New York* and *Grand Hotel.*]

The Bookman, LXXII (February 1931), 627–630. ["The Theatre Versus Certain Artists of the Theater." Comments on the Theatre Guild and its productions of *Roar China* and *Elizabeth the Queen;* the one-woman theater of Anga Enters, Mary Wigman, La Argentina, and Ruth Draper.]

The Bookman, LXXIII (March 1931), 70–73. [*The Vinegar Tree, The Greeks Had a Word for It, Philip Goes Forth, The Inspector General, Anatol, Overture, Tomorrow and Tomorrow.*]

The Bookman, LXXIII (April 1931), 182–185. [Katherine Cornell, Marika Cotopouli, and Charlie Chaplin in *The Barretts of Wimpole Street, Electra,* and *City Lights* (movie), respectively.]

The Bookman, LXXIII (May 1931), 293–296. ["Lynn Riggs, Rachel Crothers and Others." *Green Grow the Lilacs, As Husbands Go, Green Pastures, Peter Ibbetson.*]

The Bookman, LXXIII (June 1931), 408–411. [*The Wonder Bar* (revue), *As You Desire Me, Miracle at Verdun, Getting Married.*]

The Bookman, LXXIII (July 1931), 522–524. [*Melo, Private Lives* (Noel Coward), *Old Man Murphy, A Modern Virgin.*]

The Bookman, LXXIII (August 1931), 632–634. [*The Alchemist, The Third Little Show* (a revue with Beatrice Lillie), *The Band Wagon* (revue), *Tabu* (movie), *Le Million* (movie by René Clair).]

The Bookman, LXXIV (September 1931), 71–73. ["The Season Reconsidered." Comments on the Pulitzer Prize, *Alison's House, The Ziegfeld Follies.*]

The Bookman, LXXIV (October 1931), 186–188. [*Shoot the Works, Vanities* (revue), *Cloudy with Showers, Three Times the Hour, After Tomorrow, Just to Remind You, The Horses Ate the Hat* (movie, René Clair).]

The Bookman, LXXIV (November 1931), 298–302. ["The New Group and Others." Comments on The New Group Theatre, *House of Connelly, He, Payment Deferred, The Good Companions, Singing the Blues, The Left Bank.*]

The Bookman, LXXIV (December 1931), 440–445. [Entirely devoted to O'Neill's *Mourning Becomes Electra.*]

The Bookman, LXXIV (January–February 1932), 561–566. ["Comedies, Satirical and Sweet." *Of Thee I Sing, The Animal Kingdom, Springtime for Henry, Retrospect, Reunion in Vienna, The Good Fairy* (with Helen Hayes); comments on Cornelia Otis Skinner.]

The Bookman, LXXIV (March 1932), 665–668. [*The Moon in the Yellow River, Blessed Event, Face the Music, There's Always Juliet, Whistling in the Dark.* Comments on Vincente Escudero, a Spanish Gypsy dancer.]

The Bookman, LXXV (April 1932), 75–77. [*Too True to Be Good, Riddle Me This, Hot-Cha* (Ziegfeld and Bert Lahr). Comments on Pauline Lord in *Distant Drums* and Laurette Taylor in *The Truth about Blayds.*]

The Bookman, LXXV (May 1932), 176–178. [*Another Language, A Thousand Summers.*]

The Bookman, LXXV (June–July 1932), 288–291. ["Recalling the High Lights." *Troilus and Cressida, Of Thee I Sing.* Comments on Shaw, The Group Theatre, O'Neill.]

Sewanee Review, LXII (July 1954), 474–485. ["On the Edge of Broadway." *John Murray Anderson's Almanac, The Confidential Clerk, American Gothic, Othello, Coriolanus;* comments on The City Center Ballet productions of "Four Temperaments," "The Afternoon of a Faun," "Firebird," "The Pied Piper," "The Nutcracker."]

Poems

"The Oxford Manner," *The Bookman*, LXXII (November 1930), 266.

"Ruth and Boaz," "Pioneer and His Children," *Hound and Horn*, V (July–September 1932), 620–621.

"Two Portraits: Westerner; Mr. Lyle Hereford," *Poetry*, XLIII (February 1934), 252–253.

"Five Poems: Song, after Dryden; 'Questi Non Furon Ribelli'; Mrs. White; The Blumenscheins, or Liebe, Amor, Love and Libido; Mannikin," *New Directions in Prose and Poetry* (Norfolk, Conn., New Directions, 1937).

"Five Poems: Under the Mist the Clear Grey Wave; Le Temps Retrouvé; The Charm; The Head of the Wife; Antique Tale," *New Directions in Prose and Poetry* (Norfolk, Conn., New Directions, 1938).

"Sunday Afternoon: Avenue A Considered as a Grave," *Partisan Review*, VI (Summer 1939), 22–23.

"Aesop in Hell: The Fox and the Crow," *Partisan Review*, XX (November–December 1953), 632–633.

"A Suite for Winter," *Sewanee Review*, LXIII (1955), 241–245.

"Wedding Day," *Sewanee Review*, LXV (Summer 1957), 434–438.

"The Bookstore: Evening," Rutgers University *Anthologist*, XXX (1959), 28. [The first printing of this poem, which was slightly changed to its final version in *Sewanee Review*.]

"The Bookstore: Evening," *Sewanee Review*, LXIX (Summer 1961), 399–401.

"The Big Branch: A Memorandum," *Poetry*, XCVIII (August 1961), 297.

PLAYS

Sophocles' Electra: A Version for the Modern Stage with Notes on Production and Critical Bibliography (New York, William R. Scott, 1938). [Reprinted in *Greek Plays in Modern Translations*, ed. Dudley Fitts, New York, The Dial Press, 1947; as a paperback in *The Laurel Classical Drama*, New York, 1965, and in Theatre Arts Books, New York, 1969.]

The King and the Duke (play with music, copyright 1939), in *From the Modern Repertoire, Series Two*, ed. Eric Bentley (Denver, University of Denver Press, 1952).

Rutgers University

Index

Cain and Abel story, Unamuno use of, 179–80

Calderón de la Barca, Pedro, *The Constant Prince of,* 123, 124–25, 129

Caligula (Camus), *xiii*

Calley, Lt. William L., 134*n*38

Calvin, John, 337

Calvinism, 327–28, 337

Cambon, Glauco, 191–201

Cameron, K. W., cited, 322, 323

Campbell-Fisher, Ivy, 352*n*43

Camus, Albert, *xiii–xiv*

Canzoniere (Petrarch), 197

capitalism, 37, 41, 42, 44, 144, 308; science and, 337; Shaw on, 16, 17

Captives (Plautus), 85

Capture of Miletus (Phrynichus), 36

Carlyle, Thomas, 191, 321–22

Carroll, Lewis, 237

Carthaginian (Menander), 88

Casella, in Dante's *Divine Comedy,* 167, 197

Cassirer, Ernst, 340; quoted, 105, 124–25, 344, 345, 346

catharsis, 5–6, 183; epic theater and, 45, 46; ritual and, 120, 341, 343–44

Cathay (Pound), 191

Cato, in Dante's *Divine Comedy,* 166, 167, 176

Cato (Addison), 228–29, 230

Catullus, 177, 192

Caucasian Chalk Circle, The (Brecht), 21, 22, 47, 48

Caudwell, Christopher, quoted, 334

causality, Aristotle on, 284–85, 287, 292

Cause, The (periodical), 311

censorship: in Ancient Greece, 36, 37; in England, 229; Herbert on, 246; in Russia, 313

Chaldeans, 334

Chapman, George, *Bussy d'Ambois* of, 34

Chapman, R. W., 223–24; quoted, 234

Charney, Maurice, 24–35

Chatterton, Thomas, 230–31

Chaucer, Geoffrey, 178*n*6, 236

Chekhov, Anton, 42, 46; quoted, 11

Chernyshevsky, Nicholas G., 304, 305, 307

Chesterfield, Philip Stanhope, Lord, 222, 223, 224, 244

Chettle, Henry, *Hoffman* of, 34

Chiaromonte, Nicola, 36–54

China, 142, 158

Chinese language, English translations, 191, 243

Choëphoroe (Aeschylus), 77, 92*n*10

chorus, the, 40, 141; Euripides' use of, 71–72, 73, 74, 75–76, 79, 83, 94*n*22

Christianity, 20, 335–39; Aristotle and, 287–88, 294; of Dante, 104, 161, 162–63, 164, 167, 168, 172, 176, 178*n*7, 275–79; of Dostoevsky, 305–306, 309, 311, 313, 315, 316–18; of Eliot, 10, 238; of Emerson, 321, 323, 324, 327–28, 329; the epic form and, 237; of Johnson, 230, 232–34; of Unamuno, 185

Churchill, T. O., 322

Ciardi, John, 275–79

Cieslak, Ryszard, 124, 125; quoted, 115–16, 123

Cinderella motif, *King Lear* and, 66

circus, 114

Citizen, The (periodical), 302–303, 310–11, 312, 315

Citizens of the World (Barr), 143

Civil War (American), 328

class attitudes, *see* society, class and

classicism, *xvi*, 24–25; of Emerson, 329; Elizabethan alternatives to, 24–35; of Herbert, 245, 246, 251–52, 253, 256–57; Ibsen and, 7–8, 9, 10; imitation and, 236–37, 238–39; Pope and, 228–29; Shaw and, 13; Unamuno and, 183–84

Cleon, 36–37, 39

Clorinda (in Tasso's *Gerusalemme liberata*), 193–201

Cochran, C. B., 238

Coleridge, Samuel Taylor: Aristotle and, 192, 294, 298; Emerson and, 322, 327; Novalis compared with, 202–17

Collège de France, 323

isms in, 268, 270; Herbert (Zbigniew) in, 244–45; Old English elegy form, 177; Tasso in, 191–201
environmental theater, 101, 129–30
epic tradition, 13, 237; Brecht and, 19, 44–45, 46, 47–48, 49–50; Indian, 140, 141–42; Tasso and, 201*n*1
epigrams, 221–22, 231
"Episode" (Herbert), 253–54
Epistle to Augustus (Horace), 228
Epistle Dedicatory to *Man and Superman* (Shaw), 11
Epoch (periodical), 301, 302
Epstein, Jason, *xiv*
Erasmus, Desiderius, 327
Essay of Dramatic Poesy (Dryden), 227, 233
essences, concept of, 286–87, 326; apprehension of, 292, 294–95, 296–98, 299–300
Ethics (Aristotle), 177, 298
Étourdi, L' (Molière), 86
Euanthius, quoted, 86, 95*n*31
Eumenides, The (Aeschylus), 8, 95*n*37
Euripides, 8, 36, 41, 45, 99; comedy and, 68–96
Europe, 50, 156, 159, 320–21; Emerson and, 320–21, 327, 328; Russian socialism and, 306, 307, 308, 310, 311, 313, 314; shamanism in, 133*n*7. *See also specific countries*
experience: animal, 266; art and, 97–135
eyesight, imagination and, 202–17

Fairfax, Edward, 191–201
Falstaff, of Shakespeare, 85, 88
Family Reunion (Eliot), 10
Far Field, The (Roethke), 274
fate, 40, 75, 100; freedom and, 17–18; Ibsen's view of, 8–9, 10–11, 14, 20
Faulkner, William, *xviii*
Faustus, of Marlowe, 32–33
Felix, Lucienne, cited, 335
Ferguson, Adam, 323
Fergusson, Francis, *ix–xviii*, 240, 283*n*; on Aristotle, 100, 192; list of works of, 353–64; on political theater, 37; on

the *Purgatorio, xi*, 166, 354; on romanticism, 186
Feuerbach, Ludwig, 4
Fiction and the Unconscious (Lesser), 16
Fielding, Henry: quoted, 89; *Tom Jones* of, 85, 86
Fiji, *nanda* ritual of, 125–28
Fisch, Max H., quoted, 322–23
Fitzgerald, 283–300; Homer translation by, 191
Fluids (Kaprow), 98–99, 116
Fortinbras, in Shakespeare's *Hamlet*, 254–55, 256
Fortune Theater, London, 27
Foscolo, Ugo, 193
"Fowler, The" (Clare), 271
"Fox, The" (Clare), 272
Fraenkel, E., cited, 92*n*10
France, 16, 49; Emerson in, 321, 323; Russia and, 308, 314
Frank, Joseph, 301–19
Frazer, James George, 344
Freedman, Ralph, 202–17
freedom, 17–18, 216, 304; the youth movements and, 101–102
free verse, Clare and, 267
free will, 304
French language, 323, 331*n*8
French Revolution of 15 May 1848, 323
Freud, Sigmund, 156
Frey, Leonard H., quoted, 177
Friedrich, Hugo, 195
Friedrich, Wolf H., quoted, 91*n*2, 94*n*29
Frogs, The (Aristophanes), 74–75, 79
Frost, Robert, 269
Frye, Northrop, quoted, 86, 178*n*1, 220, 235–36, 238
Fussell, Paul, Jr., 218–39
Futurism, 99

Galileo (Brecht), 44
Gandhi, Mohandas, mahatma, 143, 144, 145, 149, 153, 160
Garrick, David, 225–27, 228
Gay, John, Macheath of, 85
Gaya, India, 147–48
Geisterseher (Schiller), 205

The text of this book was set in Garamond Linotype and printed by offset on P & S Old Forge manufactured by P. H. Glatfelter Co., Spring Grove, Pa. Composed, printed and bound by Quinn & Boden Company, Inc., Rahway, N.J.